The
Kingdom
of Good

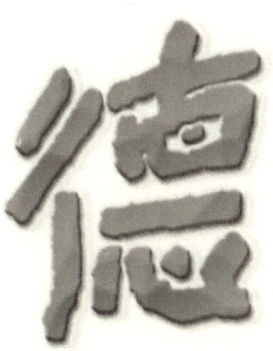

Revolution
of
Consciousness

Paul Wesley Norberg

...The Challenge of all Challenges...
Our Generation will Decide the Fate of Life on Earth!

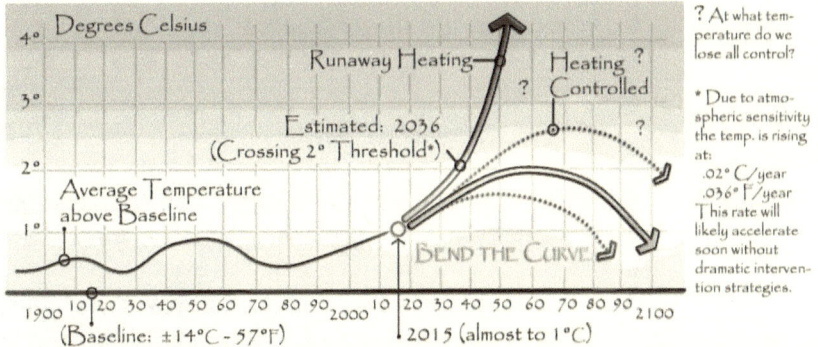

? At what temperature do we lose all control?

* Due to atmospheric sensitivity the temp. is rising at:
.02° C/year
.036° F/year
This rate will likely accelerate soon without dramatic intervention strategies.

This diagram probably more than any other represents the future for life on Earth.
Climate scientists warn us that runaway heating will lead to catastropic consequences.
To preserve a habitable climate we must BEND THE CURVE of temperature.

Dedication

This novel is dedicated to everyone who is committed to preserving the habitability of Earth.

Acknowledgements

There are certain people I want to acknowledge for their comments and affects on me that has led to the writing of this story.

First I want to thank my parents. I want to thank my wildlife biologist father for taking me on the trips to wilds of Alaska and Northern Idaho when I was very young and affording me the experience of the magic of Creation. I want to thank my mother for her strength through the many years; and for her success and courage confronting cancer twice, when I was eight and nine years old, from likely human induced poisons in our environment.

I want to thank my many good friends and family who graciously read the various iterations of this story and offered their opinions. Many were taken to heart and are a part of this final work.

A few individuals, among many, whose writings had an enormous impact on my thinking and created the background for this effort, are: Al Gore, E. O. Wilson, and Eckhart Tolle.

And very importantly, I want to thank Sir Paul McCartney for the statement made by him that I read a long time ago that got the entire effort going. His observation that he felt people, and religion, had personified the spirits of good and evil - creating God and the devil - starts me on this journey. My personal interpretation of his observation makes up a major premise of the story.

Table of Contents

Foreword...1

Book Introduction...5

Part One: Values

Chapter One..18
Chapter Two..56

Part Two: Hopes and Dreams

Chapter Three..72
Chapter Four...87
Chapter Five...101
Chapter Six..105
Chapter Seven...109
Chapter Eight..117
Chapter Nine..122
Chapter Ten..144
Chapter Eleven..161
Chapter Twelve..182
Chapter Thirteen..187
Chapter Fourteen...191
Chapter Fifteen..194

Part Three: Epiphany

Chapter Sixteen...199
Chapter Seventeen..211
Chapter Eighteen..233
Chapter Nineteen...245
Chapter Twenty...261
Chapter Twenty One..263
Chapter Twenty Two..266
Chapter Twenty Three..275
Chapter Twenty Four...297

Part Four: Joining the Revolution

Chapter Twenty Five...305
Chapter Twenty Six..321
Chapter Twenty Seven..325
Chapter Twenty Eight...329

Part Five: Unforeseen Consequences

Chapter Twenty Nine..337

Foreword

It must have been sometime in the summer of 1961 and I was six years old when my wildlife biologist/ecologist father took me with him to the *sticks*, as he would refer to the forest. It was green, I remember that, and the road was gravel and narrow. He pulled the pickup into some opening and told me we would walk down to the stream. We were living near Anchorage, Alaska and I suspect there had been a good rain the night before our visit. Maybe it was just the dew of the morning or earlier rains affect, I just remember that great musky smell of the forest.

It was a short walk to the stream. I could hear the sound of the water moving rapidly through the boulders that nature had distributed along its course. Dad said something about the silvers, I didn't really understand what he meant, but then I saw them. My eyes must have enlarged like those of a six year old on Christmas morning seeing all the new colorful packages under the tree. The stream was filled with them. It wasn't wide where we were standing, maybe twenty five feet or so, but the water was tumultuous among the boulders and steep grade it was passing. I suspect dad explained a little to me, but of that I can't remember. What I do remember is the *feeling* I had, experiencing the many jumping and darting silver salmon making their way home. They were following the primordial imprints upon their consciousness of the journey they had taken as juveniles only a few years earlier.

They were silver and pearly-white with ephemeral flashes of sky blue and fuzzy neon pink. Even now I remember how something in me wanted to grab one. The notion of calling an experience "beautiful" or "captivating" was beyond me then. There was only the visceral feeling. To this day I have not been privileged to that scene again. But the feeling of course has stayed with me. I suspect much of my own love for the natural world was born that day by that stirring I have no real words for.

I've heard that *magic* is the word for phenomenon's we do not understand. In conversation with a friend Albert Einstein is said to have posited the question/notion that at its core all of creation is either magic or it is not. They allegedly agreed it was all magic. For those who have ventured into attempting to fathom the edges of the quantum world physicists are telling us underlies the reality we experience, I would have to agree with Dr. Einstein; at least for now. The notion of anything being *solid* is false we are told. We and all of creation are waves of energy rattling and humming. What is energy? A sound we make for something we only vaguely understand.

Creation and nature are complex and at many levels staggeringly beyond our current understanding, and *possibly* beyond all mortal understanding; forever. But I don't know that beyond any doubt. Manipulating the natural systems of creation, though, by use of what we consider our technological advancements can be problematic. But saying that, I'm not anti-technology at all, it simply must be implemented wisely. It's entirely proper to keep poking and prodding to understand it; just don't f... mindlessly with systems that can kill us that you/we don't competently understand. Sorry, making a point.

The typical person is said to be made of between 100 and 200 trillion cells, depending on your size! Each of these cells is performing roughly on average on the order of 10,000 biochemical functions each second. This is complexity well beyond the limits of our minds to comprehend. And, how do all these quarks, atoms, molecules, organelles and on up the organizational ladder *know* what to do? How does this unfathomable complexity create our *feelings*? Magic is seemingly infinite and ubiquitous.

Years ago, in my early twenties, while struggling with one of my own hurtles of consciousness emerging, I was told by someone that my heart and my head where in conflict. I was taken back; I intuitively thought the observation correct, but did not really understand it. For whatever reason, at that time, this idea of there being a heart and a head to which my motivations were subject had not been explained and had not occurred to me. This was a small epiphany. And they were right, whiskey and thinking could not deduce the conflict for me.

My conflict had much in common with my experience with the silver salmon; my subconscious was motivating me. Scientists tell us that something on the order of over 80% of our decisions are actually the product of the subconscious mind at work. Why that color and texture of a rug over another? Why that face over another? Little wonder our motivational processing works that way, after all, for over 3 ¾ billion years our ancestors did not use complex language to reason or communicate.

This brings me back to the sense of *heart* and *magic*. The dire environmental crisis we are now facing is at its core a reflection of humanities shared insensitivity. The wonder and love for the magic that is all around us does not resonate at a high enough pitch in enough of us. If it did, the problems we currently face would have been avoided. Certainly there are many that within which it does, but still too few. The crisis is a reflection of our hearts and the lack of effective empathy for the magic. To confront the climate crisis competently we must persuade the effective few to feel the magic and respond.

The following are among the major premises the story is based upon.

- The most basic problem is the insufficient mental/spiritual consciousness level of an effective number of people to lead our civilization towards sustainability.
- Similar to monitoring our own bodies for underlying disease that is making us ill, temperature is the most important metric to pay close attention to. In this case, it is the Earth's average surface temperature.
- Polluting of our shared atmosphere with heat trapping gases (carbon dioxide, nitrous oxide, among others) is driving the deleterious temperature anomaly. The fossil fuels and synthetic chemical agriculture industries are among the most egregious societal behaviors fueling this pollution.
- Climate scientists warn of a potentially very near tipping point of atmospheric pollution and temperature rise where we would lose all ability to control runaway heating. Collapse of civilization and potentially extinction could follow.
- Humanity faces many problems, but none other matter if the habitability of Earth is lost.

Analogy with a Guest

Humanity is a guest on Earth. Just like any other species you get to stay as long as you are in balance with the overall ecosystem and fit a niche that supports you. Extinction of species is a normal part of maintaining the balance. Historically and normally about one species per month (10 -12 per year) went extinct. Currently Science tells us that *at least* 5,000 species go extinct each year, and some think the number is much higher. The industrious behavior of humanity is causing this. By any reasonable measure we are not a good guest.

If someone was to visit your home and bring their unruly children and a dog that loves to jump and dig it's probably a good bet their welcome would very quickly run out. What would be the tipping point for when they'd be directed to leave?

The Earth doesn't have a vocal cord and talk directly to us. We have to be observant enough to recognize the ills we are creating. With glaciers disappearing, sea levels rising, storms becoming much more intense, weird

3

unseasonable weather, drought and flooding beyond the norm; and many other ills, at some point a reasonable person must be able to connect the dots between cause and effect.

Our welcome on Earth is running short. We can be removed by a climate system that goes entirely off-the-rail. The wise and caring among us can only hope that the "effective few" will wake up in time to respond to our unsustainable behavior and set us on a course for salvation.

Book Introduction

Observation:

My motivation for writing this story begins with these observations. Climate scientists have been warning the rest of us for over twenty years that our polluting of the atmosphere with excessive carbon dioxide is causing unnatural heating of the planet. This subsequently leads to accelerated climate change and all the problems associated with that.

Human population has now grown so large that some scientists say we are over harvesting the bounty of the Earth and exceeding our carrying capacity by many fold. Ecosystems around the world are collapsing.

Our social structure is doing poorly as well, here in the United States and around the world. Many have left the labor force entirely and among those that are working, there compensation over the last thirty or forty years has stagnated or actually declined. To be sure there are those doing just fine. But there is an unnatural chasm in terms of wealth opening between the top 20% and the bottom 80%. There is already wide disgruntlement about this. But it, too, is poorly understood.

Considering this, it seems reasonable to ask: Why? What is the deep reason for this? And is there a cure? I move to try and answer that next.

How to Think about it and what can we do?

Our planet is reacting negatively to our presence. It is running a fever and telling us something is terribly wrong. Science tells us that the Earth's temperature should be maintaining if not falling, but it is unnaturally rising. And it is rising rapidly. There are credible predictions of a very dire catastrophe looming and that humanity is to blame. It's said that we are putting our very existence on the Earth at risk. The fabric of our civilization's social structure is fraying as well.

But how could such a clever species as humanity create such a situation for itself? Various pundits provide their answer. But one answer in particular resonates with me: a **crisis of consciousness**. Central to this crisis is that worldwide we lack and do not currently follow a sustainable guiding principle.

Ecology is the name science gives to the grand interplay of life on Earth. It is *the* foundation of all knowledge our species should direct its sustainable behavior by. But, unfortunately this is not the case. The functioning of all the life systems on the planet is extremely complex and requires deep study to understand. The tools to do so: advanced microscopes like electron microscopes, genetic sequencing, and just the ability to gather, study, and inventory the myriad of life forms and their interconnectedness has only recently emerged. And those tools and abilities are certainly still evolving.

5

But human desire to advance the tools of industry (like creating electricity by burning coal, or using synthetic chemicals as part of growing our food) advanced much faster than the science of understanding the ecology did. A great many of our problems can be traced to this. We sort of leaped before we looked. The principle of Ecological Wisdom has only modestly been heeded and much to our detriment. Centering our civilization on Ecological Wisdom is essential and must emerge soon.

If someone was to ask you by what guiding principle or moral ethos do you conduct your life? What would your answer be? Perhaps, 'do unto others as you'd have done to you.' Okay, we here that a lot. Does it matter if a person (or civilization) has a central principle or moral ethos to guide them through the maze of choices and decisions they make in a lifetime that will, at the end, represent their life? I believe strongly that of course it would matter.

Humanity is just one species that has emerged on Earth. Like all species (life forms) we are just visitors as individuals and as a species. As individuals we all eventually die. As a species we last for some period then either go extinct or evolve to a different species which is compatible with a changed environment. Humans, being the only species that is aware of this relationship it seems should ask: *What behavior is required for our species to live on this planet indefinitely?*

We know that the balance of the Earth's biosphere changes due to naturally occurring factors, such as the Milankovitch Cycles that define the various elements of the Earth's travel around the sun. Because of these and other factors we know, future generations would simply have to adapt to over time. Those factors would happen slowly and give future generations plenty of ability to adapt.

But scientists are telling us emphatically that we face an existential threat we have created that if not dealt with effectively can destroy our civilization. These same scientists would agree that it is our worldwide industrious behavior that exceeds acceptable limits for maintaining a stable climate and healthy environment, which is at fault.

So, getting back to what a guiding principle for a person's life might be. I've said that I believe it matters. So what would this principle be? Do our parents tell us what it is? Are we supposed to just know what it is? Can we just figure it out on our own? Did some philosopher tell us what it is? Ha! That may be it. That feels right.

Religions represent moral ethos, or codes of acceptable behavior within a group. These codes have certainly been with us for millions of years. They would evolve over time and match up with the evolving *politics* among groups of people.

6

Today, with over seven billion people on Earth, the number and belief systems of the varying religions is vast. The three Abrahamic monotheistic religions: Judaism, Christianity and Islam have the largest number of people associating with them.

Upon recognizing what I felt was the need for a central guiding principle that each of us and humanity as a whole might follow. I decided that if one exists it must come from the teachings of the philosophers (spiritual leaders) that these religions (or others) are based upon. I spent considerable time researching them. What I believe I found in common was a root connection with Buddhism. Buddhism is basically about the path a person must take to become enlightened. A Buddha is simply an enlightened person. And as The Buddha (born ~563 BCE) Siddhartha Gautama noted; there were certainly other Buddha's before him. He was unique though in that he established baseline concepts. I'll leave it to my readers to explore all that more.

Humanity is the *only* species among the millions on Earth today, and the tens of millions that have existed through the eons, to reach a level of consciousness capable of asking deep questions about reality and our own individual existence. We stand alone after about 3.8 billion years of biological evolution on this planet, in this realm of consciousness.

So, is it too great a leap of the imagination to think that a message from divinity *might* have been revealed to us? We represent an entirely new realm of consciousness that seeks to understand why it exists? These questions have been emanating from people's minds for millennia. Were they being heard by divinity? Or were those seekers discovering a secret passage (deep meditation or prayer) to enlightenment? I'll say I think it possible.

Okay, if I believe that, then to whom can I/we look to for this revelation? The Buddha, possibly. Or the monotheistic prophets of Islam: Adam, Abraham, Moses, Jesus, and Muhammad? There are others as well.

But as I considered all of the sources it simply seemed that only one, Jesus, established a bedrock moral principle. To the best of my knowledge he is the only major spiritual figure to have stated that he was divinity (God) in the form of a man. And as we are taught, he died and was resurrected. If that is true, then obviously he was different than any other person or life form that ever existed. *I do not claim to know one way of the other*. All of you will have your own speculations on that.

I'm a product of Christianity (within limits) so was familiar with the teachings associated with Jesus. There is substantial overlap in the teachings of The Buddha with that of Jesus and later with Muhammad that, at least to me, they certainly seem to emerge from a common source of enlightenment. Was Jesus a Buddha…an enlightened mortal person? Some speculate to this…how can we know?

Regardless, but again, it is from Jesus that I believe we can look to find the one simple principle or moral ethos to guide ourselves and humanity as a whole.

Most of us are raised with at least some knowledge of the 10 commandments that Moses is said to have received from God. Very interestingly, and likely by no coincidence, the 5 Precepts of behavior noted in Buddhism are all to be found in the 10 commandments. It is from these 10 concepts (commandments), though, that I believe the one single and elegant moral ethos might be garnered.

When asked by a scribe what were the most important commandments Jesus is reported to have said (approximately): "Love the Lord your God with all your heart and with all your soul and with all your mind. And love your neighbor as yourself." Since divinity's (God) most tangible expression to our senses is creation, which includes all of nature and us, it seems that lengthy statement could be condensed to 3 words: Love Creation Entirely.

Love is the quality of mind to hold something in extremely high esteem. The feelings are visceral.

Creation is everything we know of that makes up the reality we experience.

Entirely includes the vast spectrum of all things.

Could this be considered humanities simple, single, elegant and most basic '*moral ethos?*' Wouldn't an individual or species that accepts this ethos then insist that nurturing the life and habitability on/of this planet is *the* preeminent responsibility of humanity?

One of my central characters in the story, Dr. W. W. Sherman, who is singly spreading the importance of *The Kingdom of Good*, believes it is. The foundation of his premise is that humanity is untethered from a competent moral ethos and that is the true disease inflicting the planet. It is humanities '*crisis of consciousness*' at the root of all our unsustainable behaviors.

We humans, like all species and individual organisms within a species, have emerged through an evolutionary ascent of about 3.8 billion years. The first cell, referred to by science as LUCA (Last Universal Common Ancestor), appeared at the beginning of that ascent. The struggle for survival is ubiquitous throughout nature. Instinctual strategies were essential for any organism, and the species it was a part of, to be successful. Finding replacement energy, reproduction, and avoiding being prematurely killed, has always been the basis for survival. The organizing mental quality (drivers) of those 3 factors (I believe, though I do not find this explicitly defined in the reading I've done) taken together represents what we call the ego (self) today.

The ego is a mental quality and to varying degrees exists in all organisms from bacteria to blue whales. The degree to which an aware *self* directs the ego varies among the life forms and the complexity of their mind/brain/body (MBB) continuum. Species and individuals within a species operate in varying niches. The sophistication of the MBBs of varying species varies then as well. The emergence in the mind of a self is a quality of more complex and sophisticated organisms. Humans have the most highly evolved sense of self (at least we think so). What we believe to be true our, *mental model of reality,* emerges organically (back and forth) from the state of consciousness level of the ego.

Very interestingly, and again most likely not a coincidence, the 3 temptations of Jesus and The Buddha are quite similar. The 3 poisons of humanity described by The Buddha (greed, hatred, and stupidity) seem to follow a similar context with those associated with the temptations of Jesus.

Accepting that humanity is just one species of organism that has emerged in nature, it seems reasonable to associate the 3 organismal instinctual strategies (drives: greed/food; power/sex; avoiding disaster or death (opposite of stupidity)/mindfulness) which are ego-captured with the 3 poisons noted by The Buddha and seemingly representative in the temptations of Jesus. In this respect, then, the ego and the poisons are a duality.

Again, my character Dr. W. W. Sherman says to look there: to the duality of the ego and the poisons for the true root of humanities incompetent behavior.

Psychologists have noted 7 levels of human consciousness within the larger context of overall human awareness. They all emerge from general archaic consciousness or organismal consciousness associated with what we call the animals. Levels 1 – 4 all have to do with ego-captured mental qualities, which we all pass through as we mature, but they are still a part of the ego-captured realm. Even at level four a person has not advanced to a *spiritual* level of consciousness where the great philosophers say enlightenment begins/dwells. Many seemingly very successful individuals are *stuck* in this non-spiritual, but often very clever level.

Revolution of Consciousness: Level 5 represents the first step of spiritual and truly ego-awareness consciousness. At this threshold of transformation an individual becomes aware of the ego and its controlling quality. They understand that this controlling quality can lead to dysfunctional, anti-social, and unsustainable behaviors. True *wisdom (which considers the long term competently)* versus *cleverness (which can be very myopic, centered on the short term)* begins to emerge.

9

In levels 6 and 7 this awareness grows more and more. It is one of the main premises of this story that the revolution of consciousness from level 4 (the organismal and still ego-captured realm) to level/realm of #5 and above (the spiritual and beginning ego-aware realm) among an effective number of people, is what is critically needed in our civilization now. It is at this phase transition where a person becomes truly spiritually conscious as they escape the dysfunctional aspects of being ego-captured. There are beneficial aspects of the ego and I believe will always be a part of consciousness. Awareness of it and the ability to thwart dysfunctional behavior driven by it, is a part of wisdom emerging.

In the realm of the *Kingdom of Good* (#5 and above) an individual becomes more and more awakened which leads to greater desire for truth and knowledge. The awakened mind seeks *truth* wherever it leads. Science is the tool humans use to find truth. What science reveals is not always perfect and at times is rethought. But it is the only process we have to parse out the truth. Truth leads to a more competent understanding of Creation. It is at this point and in the larger context that true *Ecological Wisdom* in a person emerges.

This greater understanding coupled with the central moral ethos (Love Creation Entirely) leads then to competent behaviors for existing on Earth. An individual that truly directs their life by this ethos will, by definition, lead others and our civilization towards sustainable behavior.

Far too many of us are spiritually asleep; not awakened or enlightened to the *Kingdom of Good*. Their/our (I struggle of course with this too) ego captures their spirit to a degree where they cannot grasp the failings in their beliefs and subsequent behavior. This has led to behaviors that are destroying/killing the biosphere. Accepting that premise then, one could say: as a worldwide civilization humanity is at present collectively insane.

How else can a reasoned person account for the climate/environmental crisis we have created for ourselves, our descendants, and all the other creatures we share the Earth with?

Some think our time is short on this planet if we do not change. We desperately need the effective few, some say 4 -5% of all people, to transform to this new realm of spirituality and ego-aware consciousness.

I believe it is reasonable to call this level (realm) of consciousness *The Kingdom of Good* . Theologians now posit "The Kingdom of God" was Jesus' central message based upon how often he discussed it. Goodness (behaviors that benefit creation) and Evil (behaviors that do not benefit creation) and the vast spectrum in between are what make up our potential behaviors. How the naming of Goodness and God may have been confused for the will of divinity is discussed in the story. Jesus described it as a quality that was within and among us. It seems he must have been directing us to prayer (meditation) and the potential for goodness (divine guidance) of behavior to flow from it. Is it a part of the Akashic Field? I will leave it to my readers to seek that question for themselves.

By what path/effort does a person guide themselves to this new realm? Is it possible that people who rise mentally/emotionally into this realm have willed themselves to enlightenment through grace? Grace being subtle divine intervention.

The moral ethos of 'Love Creation Entirely' is then the foundation from which their beliefs and how they guide all of their behavior emerges. It is there, within and among those that ideas of goodness arise and manifest in the material world. I believe that it is from this realm of consciousness that humanity has its only route to sustainability.

This is one story of how that enlightenment may arise among an effective few; that then may lead our civilization along that road of sustainable behavior and to salvation.

About the: "Bend the Curve Graph"

This graph, more than any I can think of, depicts the potential future for life on Earth. It depicts where the control of heating is either lost or controlled. A very few scientists are already claiming we are captured in a runaway heating pathway. The majority of climate scientists, I believe, do not agree with that "yet." The red line shows the current proposed approximate runaway trajectory. The green line is the "hope" line. The effort to control heating and what the shape of that line ultimately looks like is what I'm calling the *Bend the Curve* effort! If we are successful, we save ourselves and a great deal of the rest of life on Earth.

There are many questions. Climate scientists are warning that rising above the 2 degree Celsius line is very problematic for initiating the runaway scenario. But none can say definitively what the exact temperature for that is. To me, this represents humanities Faustian Bargain. We currently are not willing, civilization-wide; to set aside our material drives to truly direct our behavior towards avoiding this potentially cataclysmic temperature danger zone. At what point will we pass the *Mephistopheles Moment* (a certain temperature amount and time) of no return when heating becomes runaway? I have shown points with question marks next to them to illustrate that idea. The truth is, we'll never know what it really is or was, we'll only know when we've gone past it and all of our efforts to stop the heating are failing. In contrast, if we actually *Bend the Curve* and start it down, we'll know we have avoided hitting that unknown threshold and our countless mitigating efforts have been successful.

To avoid catastrophe the climate scientists tell us we need to reduce the carbon dioxide and other green house gases from the atmosphere.

Strategies for that then must be to stop adding the excess carbon dioxide and to also draw down to safe levels (under 350 ppm) that is there. Some of the specific potential methods for doing this are presented in the story.

My question is this though: why would we push our luck as to discovering what that number is? I believe this is the most important concept to keep in your mind as you discover more of the dots being connected throughout the story.

About the story:
There are five sections to the story. I want to provide you a brief understanding of how they connect to each other.

Part One: Values. It is one of my main premises that the varying values we have as individuals is at the core of our unsustainable behavior on Earth. In Part One the lives of two brothers are examined. They have followed different paths into their adult lives. The consequences of those divergent lifestyles and value systems are explored.

Part Two: Hopes and Dreams. The consequences of climate change we are told will become greater and greater in the future. The young millennial-aged primary characters in my story are well aware of that fact. Their expectations for the future will be under assault. But they do have dreams and they want to be able to live them as well as possible. And that includes passing along a planet to their children where their great dreams can come true too.

Part Three: Epiphany. Again, a major premise of my story is that a certain group of people will need to have their "oh my God" moment and realize that their current model of reality just isn't correct. Nearly all of us can point to a moment when we suddenly realized that the way we had thought about something just didn't square with what we believe about the subject now. There are small steps as our consciousness expands and then at times there are life-changing epiphanies. One of my primary characters has the latter.

Part Four: Joining the Revolution. Millions of people around the world have for many years already been tirelessly working to bring the climate crisis to the awareness of the masses of people. The characters in my story learn of the bigger picture and are motivated to join the movement as they can.

Part Five: Unforeseen Consequences. As we are pushing the climate system into new energy levels, the consequences of that will transpire. We have statistical estimates of how drought, extreme heat, flooding, crop failures, high intensity storms, among others may occur. But the truth is things will play out in the way the physics direct them. And there will be all the unforeseen things that will happen. Our opinions, what we believe to be true, will begin to be tested even more than they already are. People will react in ways even they may currently believe they would not. As things get worse, holding onto the strings of our humanity will be tested first and in scenarios we'd never expect.

Major Characters: There are seven individuals that make up the core of the story.

Mathew (Matt) Lundquist: Born in Boise, Idaho in 1982. His father, a wildlife biologist, has died by the time of the story. He meets David Herrick at the University of Idaho where they become good friends. After college they travel together to Europe and meet more of the characters and listen to the lecture given by Dr. W. W. Sherman called *The Kingdom of Good.*

David Herrick: Born in Spokane, Washington in 1981. His mother died when he was in grade school. He and his brother are raised by his single dad. In response to his mother dying he focuses on schooling as a way to find some control in his life. He is a very talented student. Along with Matt he attends Dr. Sherman's lecture and becomes highly motivated to spread the message he learned. Matt's nickname for him in college was Poncho.

Maria Ladacci: Born in Bilbao, Spain in 1982. Her Spanish uncle, Sebastian, a very wealthy businessman, provides the impetus for her to pursue a life in the biological sciences. She meets Matt and Dave at the same lecture given by Dr. Sherman. A love relationship emerges between her and Matt. A friend's death adds to the bonding process.

Joan Lebeau: Born in Connecticut in 1980. She receives a large inheritance from her uncle who did not have children. During the 9/11 tragedy she loses the man she loved and anticipated marrying. About ten years later she meets Dave at a function in San Diego and a love interest emerges.

Stone Fischer: Born in Northern California in 1972. Stone is a molecular biologist and a rising star in the genetic engineering field related to industrial agriculture. He's a bit brash and a talented athlete. The knowledge he gains is a pivotal part of the entire story.

Uncle Danny Bonner: Born in Boise, Idaho in 1955. He is Matt's uncle, his mother's brother. Danny is a very talented musician and finish carpenter. He wears his hair long and has a penchant for displaying his 'Scots-Irish' curt temperament.

Tyler Contadino: Born in Tennessee in 1970. She manages an inn where she hopes some of her patron's hearts can be turned for the good. She's gifted with a very feminine physicality. She exposes Stone to ideas that assist in his potential transformation.

Some final thoughts:

This story is like so many, a different look at the struggle between good and evil. I believe that most people, well over 90%, actually want to do what is good and fair. There certainly are differences of opinion as to where the line for good and fair is at. But in general, I don't believe that the vast majority of people want to destroy the habitability of the Earth. Of course not! Most folks simply are not engaged enough on the issue to recognize that we are actually nearing the point of doing that. They just don't believe it's possible. It's their current mental model of reality.

None of our other political struggles will matter if we lose the habitability of the planet of course. So, logically it must be the single most important issue to deal with. The players and industries in our civilization that science tells us are causing the most harm are the ones I focus on.

Some agricultural ecologists and others, I believe, feel that industrial agriculture based on synthesized fertilizers, herbicides, pesticides and so on, as it is currently practiced, is the single most dangerous group behavior humanity has ever followed. It represents a fundamental and currently tragic misunderstanding of the ecological rules humanity must exist within to live sustainably on Earth. To my mind, synthetic chemical industrial agriculture and the associated fossil fuels industries represent the single most important societal behaviors to confront and address wisely/effectively if the worst consequences of the climate crisis are to be avoided. If we successfully accept and implement a paradigm shift and quickly move to an *ecological wise-tech* agrarian paradigm of food production and general existence *Agricultural Ecology*, all other major problems should follow suit.

I say this because it will mean that our collective base consciousness level will have shifted, risen, to accepting our responsibility for competently and sustainably living in balance with the greater ecology of Earth. The moral ethos of *Love Creation Entirely* would systematically then emerge. All other dysfunctional behaviors would theoretically fall in line and be avoided.

This will not just occur. There is an economical paradigm of food and energy production that has emerged over the last 150 years or so that has created a very powerful block of businesses and people. Being blinded by their ego and its power on their greater model of reality, they and many others will likely continue to deny this existing dysfunctional paradigm. *Breaking this log-jam will be the civilization-saving central effort of the effective few.*

That said, I don't believe that the vast majority of people who work in those industries are evil or even just bad, and certainly not stupid. Most of them are just trying to make a living. They are doing what work there is to support themselves and their families. The existing energy/agriculture paradigm is what most of us thought was perfectly fine as we were taught growing up, including me. But when enough people agree that what your company or industry is doing actually is detrimental to the common good, then something has to change. Currently the drum beat for change among an effective number of us is just not loud enough; yet!

These problem industries have great wealth, it is well within their ability to accept that they must change their business models and still retain reasonable wealth within the broader economy. Change does not have to be a conundrum. Acceptance and deep reason of course will be required.

This story and the genre in general, are likely in a category by themselves. The newly emergent genre of Cli-Fi (climate fiction) is likely its home. My intent is to connect a lot of dots so people can rather quickly get the big picture about what is going on. The action and story-telling is probably a tick or two off from real life. Perhaps a little 'zap bam.' Much, and I want to emphasize this, is metaphor.

For years I read the scientific books on the climate issue. As I did, more of the dots became connected in my own mind. But I did not find a book that connected them in a way that was compelling (hopefully interesting and fun) and very relevant for today. I'm not a scientist or journalist, but I've had this desire to tone in on the subject. The idea occurred to me that to my knowledge no one had as yet written an action fiction novel with characters involved in the unfolding crisis. So I chose to do so.

The information provided is as current and as accurate as I could find in my research. Everything is open to interpretation though, and I make no claim to anything being absolutely true. So I will leave it to my readers to search any of the topics to satisfy their own sense of truth. I believe all the subjects can be found in articles available on the Internet and the general media. I'm attempting to connect a lot of dots and create much food for thought. I certainly don't have all the answers. But I hope that some of what I'm saying helps to stir the *pot of thought* and encourage activism.

In the end, it is what we believe to be true (whether it is or not) that motivates our behavior. The hope I have with this book and its sequel, is that at least some of the readers will become motivated enough to join in the peaceful, but vigorous revolution to change the hearts and minds of an effective number of people so that the true political change we need, occurs. This story and the thoughts in it will be of little use unless a lot of people choose to take action.

The real heavy-lifting will be done by countless people who, with courage and resolve, take this message along with parts of their own to the many that are not listening. That father, uncle, aunt, brother, sister, friend, distant friend, even the stranger you know that might be open to listening whose heart and mind you could redirect.

To be successful the revolution will need numbers of people and more specifically voters. The change that will truly be needed will have to come from the American Federal Government. If the United States does not lead greater civilization then the revolution will fail. Our impact is just too great/enormous in the world to not be the leaders. Be aware that on the order of 30 to 40% in America of eligible voters often don't vote. This represents a large source of political muscle that can be tapped.

It is not inconceivable to me that either of the two major political parties in America, the Republicans or the Democrats, could actually transform and lead us. The problem is how captured they are by the money'd interests. Personally, I think it will require the rise of a third party, likely the Greens, to either take control of the government or push one or the other parties to this place of true Ecological Wisdom. Remember that Abraham Lincoln was a Republican and considered by many our most wise and affective leader. I don't believe that true conservatism is in and of itself anti-ecology. But selfish ego-driven power and greed controlling political power though often is, and is thereby our great enemy to confront.

Cover Symbol: I chose the Taoist symbol for wisdom to be centered on the book cover. Ultimately it is the wisdom of our collective consciousness that is on trial. I wonder how we'll do.

The Sequel:
This book *Revolution of Consciousness* is to be followed by *Endurance of Consciousness*. The first book introduces the problem to my cast of characters. The second book follows on how they respond. The existing paradigm of industrial-centered energy and agriculture is confronted by the emerging and countervailing paradigm of agrarian-centered energy and agriculture. A monumental conflict is certain to ensue as the status quo attempts to maintain its control. But the Earth's climate system cares nothing of human passions; physics rule. The ongoing effects of the overloading of the atmosphere will continue to play out. Tragedy and turmoil will grow, year by year, with even more dire effects on our civilization. Where is the tipping point of no return?

My characters will be hell-bent on bringing the recently emerging transcendent science of the *Earth's magnificent skin*: its soil, and the magical abilities of the microbial life that dwells there to sequester oceans of carbon, to the consciousness of the effective few. Here lies the true cost effective massive ecological mechanism we can employ to mitigate the dangerous carbon loading. Farm and rangeland, if managed with this ecological wisdom using agrarian practices to build and store soil carbon, would both draw the excess carbon out of the atmosphere, but also create dynamic spiritually-healthy soils that would provide similar food for us all. But can we change the human heart, inspired by the magic that is Creation, in time?

REVOLUTION OF CONSCIOUSNESS

Part One: Values

Chapter One

Now in his middle sixties Kurt had long ago parted ways with any outward guilt associated with his style of living. He was a self made multi-millionaire and if his track held true, he'd be in the billionaires club by the time he'd turn seventy in little over three years. Kurt got his toughness from the mean streets around Los Angeles, his cleverness and ambition were innate; to that he'd leveraged his good looks and charm, and in the process had become one of agribusinesses biggest players. To his way of thinking, he deserved every damned thing he owned and probably more.

Kurt's German immigrant grandfather, August, had started the family business in the thirties, finding good deals on land in the Los Angeles Basin during the depths of the Depression.

August had left Germany in 1911 while still in his late teens, and headed originally for the American heartland, the Great Plains, to seek a better life on land being promoted by American developers. Fortunately August missed being dragged into World War I by aristocrats throwing temper tantrums.

By the early 1920s August had purchased his own land near Norman, Oklahoma, where he met the woman he would marry. He was ambitious and worked hard using the newly-invented deep plowing implements of the emerging gasoline powered age. Little did he know the damage being done by thousands like him churning the vulnerable soils that rested on the sands of ancient ocean bottoms.

Learning of the Los Angeles Basin in rapidly developing Southern California, August, and his new wife Nona of some Cherokee lineage, and their two children Carl and Rosa, born in the early twenties, followed the migration there.

Through good fortune they sold the farm outside of Norman for a handsome profit, and missed by a few years the perils of the Dust Bowl caused by ignorant agricultural practices.

In good spirits and ready for a new life they arrived in Mission Viejo on Christmas Eve 1928. August and Nona purchased a small home just on the west side of the then very small town center and began the process of establishing themselves as tenant farmers in this new land.

By the time the Depression was in full sway and with land prices substantially depressed, August was able to put the needed money down on a parcel of land capable of supporting a tidy small family business. Using the rapidly evolving farming implement technology of tractors fueled by gasoline, August was able to produce good organic crops, feeding the soil with composted manure, practices he'd learned growing up in Germany.

Through the war years, when Germans were considered suspect, the family kept a low profile, but produced quality fruits and vegetables for trade which gained them a reputation of trustworthiness. Krastle Enterprises boomed after the war ended and by then Kurt's father Carl was running most of the business.

Carl was flamboyant and loved the night life that could be found throughout the valley. Dark-haired, glowing and approachable, Mary caught his eye one night. She fell for his broad shoulders and quick smile. Having grown up in a family that only spoke Spanish, Mary's English was spotty, but she was a quick study once she got around more English speaking people. They were a striking couple, bringing together desirable elements of both ethnicities. Kurt was born in 1947, his younger brother Louis followed two years later.

Shortly after the birth of both of her boys, Mary would study their little faces and bodies to get a glimpse of whom she thought they were inside. Hair color can be misleading at such young ages as it often will change from dark to blond or vice versa after just a few months. She studied their eyes; what little hint of personhood could she see? In both cases it took a little over a day to decide, but her oldest somehow suggested the name Kurt, and her youngest Louis; the north and the south, as she would think of them.

Carl was Lutheran and Mary was Catholic; one thing the couple agreed on was that no religion had a monopoly on truth. Carl drifted from religion, finding his business and wanderings more compelling; he'd leave that influence on his sons to Mary. They were both good boys wanting to please their mother and father, but Kurt in particular seemed very determined to always find more. There always seemed to be something just beyond his fingertips that he wanted. Not so much with Louis; he could often be seen wandering off into the orchards with his dog, just at bliss with the world. The two brothers would follow divergent lives.

Ever since he'd made his first million at 28 in 1975, Kurt had been in the fast lane. The money grew very quickly; he had the vision to invest in the right companies that were building the new post World War II economy. It was being driven by the emergent science of chemical agriculture, which had the promise to grow bountiful amounts of dependable food, which led to more and more people requiring more and more energy. More and more!

The gross world product had exploded from around $1.35 trillion in 1960 to over $70 trillion in 2012. Kurt had caught a hold of that growth in the 1970s and had ridden it like a wild bull ever since. With a net worth now of over $900 million, he'd been a major player in that game.

He was 33 when he married first. Kurt thought he understood what he was doing as he thought he had some deep connection with that beauty. But eight years and three kids later, it ended. After that there was one child he accepted responsibility for, but Kurt never married her mother.

The second and third Mrs. Kurt Krastle, to most of the world appeared pretty much to be trophy wives, though Kurt would roundly disagree. In his third try at 55 Kurt had married Yvette, twenty-five years his junior, she was bright and very pretty of course. Yvette had gone to Milan for several weeks to be a part of the fashion world's party life, and to drop a quarter of a million dollars on a wardrobe update. Their two young children Sasha and Ian, both less than ten years old, had gone with her. Kurt's other four grown children all had their place in his empire, but they didn't have to work very hard.

Having chosen an entirely different path in life, Louis had placed his inheritance of stock in Krastle Foods in a trust when his brother began running the company. By the 1980s seeing the industrial direction Kurt was taking the company, Louis sold his shares and used the money to follow a different way.

~~~~~

Mostly alone in his 18,500 square foot villa, except for the four household workers, Kurt studied the entry drive from his veranda for the limousine he was expecting. Upon seeing it, he returned to his very large bedroom. When Yvette was away Kurt was inclined to indulge himself in some of his erotic fantasies that had seemed to blossom more and more in his imagination as he had gotten older. He felt entitled to it; this was hurting no one he convinced himself!

On his large bed a black robe with his name engraved on the lower arm was laid out by those he paid very well to coordinate his adventures. A short distance away a white rose was sitting in some water as the sign that his young liaison was now ready and waiting for him in the steam room. As meticulously as he did everything, for the last ten years Kurt had taken his dose of testosterone supplement that helped him maintain the libido he'd known in his youth and which brought him the wild pleasure he very much still craved.

You could not see a streak of grey on the top of Kurt's head as that was taken care of. For the rest of his body, waxing did a great job of removing the signs of his true age. For him, there had always been the energy-rich and toxic-free food from his organic gardens and quality time for exercise; he definitely could pass for ten, perhaps even fifteen years younger than his true age. Kurt spent three hours twice a week in his gym driven by his personal fitness advisor. He was exceedingly fit for a sixty six year old man.

The harvest from his agribusiness and multitude of investments in the modern energy driven economy was anything but non toxic. But Kurt had found ways to justify virtually everything. Any self doubt in his conscience concerning any negative consequences of his enterprises was held deep behind a door in his mind. The key was nowhere to be found.

~~~~~

The steam room had cost more to construct than what most middle class Americans spend on an entire home; the sense of high technology glowed throughout. Ten foot tall glass doors that opened with the slightest help from the hand, deep blue tile of stone imported from Brazil finished many of the surfaces. It was warm but not overly so and a very faint steam floated in the room.

"Issabella?" The glass door slid quietly closed behind him.

"Yes," the voice of innocence replied. She lifted her head; some of her soft sandy-blond hair fell further down across her high forehead.

He reached out and touched the light-copper-flawless and smooth-velvety-skin of her right cheek. His fingers drifted over to her full and somewhat pouty lips. Kurt lingered for a moment and savored the feeling rising in his loins. He sat down next to her robed body and put his hand on the inside of her nearest long leg. He knew Issabella was in need of nothing as others saw to it that she was well prepared. There was no need for talking since there was nothing that a girl only in her late teens could tell him he wanted to hear, nor anything he wanted to tell her.

Issi had been prepared, knowing she'd be exceptionally well compensated for only responding when questioned and for offering many sounds of pleasure from her young, and in this case, nearly virgin body. Kurt didn't want that realism, but as close to it as possible.

She had been spotted on a beach in Caracas by a quite beautiful young woman who worked for the agency. The currency of such economic activity is trust, even if it emanates from the darker parts of the human spirit. Issi's preparation had required several months, but now it was her turn to earn $15,000 for what she was told most people think of as pure pleasure.

21

The agency made sure she was physically and, at least outwardly, mentally ready for her several hours with Kurt.

From the steam room they moved to the showers and then on to the bedroom. And as she was told, the man of great means would help her with everything that just comes naturally.

~~~~~

Kurt watched again from his veranda as the leaving limousine briskly passed through the gate of his villa and then off through his estate covered in olive trees and grape vines. He looked east, off to a new vista and could see his land across the rolling landscape about a mile distant to where another family's estate met with his. Kurt could look off to the west over the vast expanse of the southern end of the San Joaquin Valley and towards Bakersfield and see thousands of acres of agricultural cropland he owned. Below was the Kern River and in the distance almost due east was Breckenridge Mountain. He'd bought the land in the mid eighties before much of the nearby residential development got into full swing. His was a highly coveted piece of real estate.

Kurt discovered the Bakersfield area in the late sixties. Like his father he was a cat-about-town. He would venture from Mission Viejo and take in the Rock-a-Billy night life inspired by Merle Haggard and Buck Owens. In 1969 he was finishing his degree in agricultural economics from Cal Poly Pomona where he would graduate summa cum laude. He learned the new agriculture, the Green Revolution as it was sold; the way to feed a hungry world. He learned how man could bypass the age old ways of growing things and use the new tools of fumigation, synthetic fertilization, insecticides, herbicides, pesticides, among others. Kurt believed the proof of this superior approach was everywhere; just look at how much was being produced. Just look at how many people the Green Revolution provided food for, and how the world population had grown exponentially in the past fifty or so years since the Green Revolution had begun. Who could question the superiority of industrial agriculture to the quaint "organic" approach? Over forty years had passed since he'd made his move from the LA Basin, and he had prospered immensely. Kurt considered himself a great producer of wealth, just look at all those he employed.

However, Kurt was oblivious to much that transpired below in the valley where the people worked. Where he lived, perched above the valley, the winds and rains kept the air mostly free of the unnatural particulates that those living in the lower areas had to endure. There, where so much of the land was covered by pavement, concrete, and buildings, heat islands had been created which would hold heat and be ten or more degrees hotter than normal. Cars, trucks, and even dairies released particles that caused health issues. Some health officials knew that the problems being seen by the start of the first decade of the twenty first century were just harbingers for what was to come as Earth heats up due to callous disregard for atmospheric pollution. But for any of this Kurt would see none of it; he was like a cow gazing unconsciously at a passing vehicle.

Kurt had long ago decided that there was virtually nothing that could not be engineered, including the climate issue (if it was real) and it was being over blown anyway. The entire thing was just the government after his money. He actually believed that some days.

It was a beautiful late April afternoon, warm but not overly so; in fact there was a slight breeze. Wearing only his bathrobe and leather sandals, Kurt mixed himself a splash of whiskey on the rocks, and then opened the top of one of the boxes of his favorite cigars. COC was written on the top of the box, Cigars-of-Cuba…Edicion Limitados. He lifted one from the box, embossed in a yellow background was a picture of President Bolivar, it was a recent favorite. He sat down on a modern-looking boxy-type chair; his legs spread slightly, his drink in his left hand and his cigar in his right. 'All of this proved he was an expert in living,' Kurt thought to himself.

A light was flashing on his mobile phone. The flashing had a certain pattern to it and he knew who the call was from. Communications with this person were encoded to a degree they believed even the NSA could not track as they had tentacles there too. Still, they never discussed anything directly that could be used against them successfully. Kurt was a part of a powerful cartel which had secrets to keep from the world.

He played the recording, "Kurt," this voice was older, deep, and full of itself; long arms of the voice connected with those who coordinated the assassination of JFK back in 1963. "Got a little something I'm needin' to get together with you on, uh some of these kook enviros are startin' to get a little too much air time on our balancin' blue network. Yeah, we're needin' to put a fuckin' halt to it. Gonna need to have you make some phone calls to the right folks, get these pricks attention. Maybe we hook up out fishin' for some whoppers? I'll get my people hookin' up with yours, get it arranged. Okay cowboy see you out on the blue."

Kurt knew that the intention would be for a meeting of their two yachts somewhere out in the Pacific Ocean in the near future. He'd heard a little about this himself, someone had mentioned to him that the enviros were getting quite a bit of time on The World This Morning, the two-hour-long morning news and current affairs program. The show's two main personalities; Brooks Rose, a Democrat, and Ingrid Lutz, a Republican, were seemingly meant to give the program a sense of being balanced which would supposedly draw them a larger audience as those in the middle of the political spectrum would be more inclined to tune in.

Oddly, at times the panel would include climate scientists and others speaking of an environmental crisis being caused greatly by burning of fossil fuels. Then conversely would be followed by an advertisement from the coal, oil, or natural gas industry depicting the benefit to our economy these energy sources provide. It seems that the right wing shadow cabinet decided they didn't want much if any of that climate change stuff being discussed anymore. Just like the tobacco industry had been on smoking, they had been successful for the past few years creating doubt in the minds of enough people that there was a credible crisis. They had *their* "scientists" who could be counted on to let the public know that this stuff was just "theory" and nothing's proven. Kurt settled back, knowing they'd get the details on that figured out shortly, hopefully after landing a few Marlins or other large ocean fishes.

After just letting his mind settle and think about very little, Kurt's attention moved to the scuba dives magazine he'd wanted to look through. A decade earlier, Kurt had discovered the thrill of ocean diving and had ventured to many a remote place around the world in search of testosterone driving experiences. Only six months earlier, he'd dove with experts in waters of the Great Barrier Reef off of the north eastern Australian coast. At one time diving with those who understood the ecosystem, Kurt and others were lowered to the bottom, about twenty feet below the surface in a steel cage so they could be among the Great White Sharks that were gathered in the area. One estimated to be twenty-one feet long had come up and bumped the cage and Kurt had the film footage to prove it. Before the dive he'd been reminded that their numbers had been in decline, so finding a group of them as they did was a more and more rare thing.

Kurt was looking for someplace a little more nearby where he could get that big rush again by being in the water with these immense and very dangerous creatures. He wanted someplace to take the group of divers from his various companies and in particular the biotech company he'd purchased several years earlier. He'd made his millions leveraging the science of the Green Revolution. But now the second Green Revolution was beginning and this one had ever more clever tools in its arsenal. Genetic engineering was at the nexus and the new tool for the really big boys. Kurt intended to make sure he wasn't left behind.

He knew that the pests were starting to get a new hold on things across his vast agricultural empire. The herbicides, fungicides, and insecticides of the first Green Revolution were losing ground to the ever evolving world of weeds. The implicit goal was that genetic engineering of plants would put the growers far ahead of the pests. They'd then have many years of clear sailing in their harvests and particularly with their profits, before the pests caught up and then the cycle would just repeat. But there was a wisdom he and the others simply were missing:

The notion that nature was not mechanistic, like a bunch of little car parts you could mix and match as you want, but holistic "some say Holy" complex and integrated to levels far beyond our current understanding, and was possibly forever that way.

It was well known among the executive types in Kurt's empire that he very much liked to challenge them to compete with him in adventures. Every year for the past twelve he'd put a team together to enter in the Baja 1000. When he discovered diving, Kurt sought out those that were already a part of his inner circle. If you were great at your job and part of this elite group, your place in the companies and your bonuses were secure and large.

Kurt, with his very brown and just a touch of green eyes, focused on his computer screen and typed a message to his executive assistant. He had just studied his 2012 calendar for important dates he'd need to attend to business and Kurt had found a good break time. "Veronique, send a message to my aqua team that I intend to dive near Cabo on May 17, 18, and 19, Friday through Sunday. We go to Socorro Island first, then finish at Guadalupe Island and swim with the Great Whites. Please gets the ball rolling on all the details."

Veronique would need to contact the dive teams they had worked with in the past to make sure there would be the best professional divers available to take them into the water. Kurt had his own specialists too. He'd been to these waters before, years earlier when he first started diving. It was quite enjoyable and he wanted to return.

In the depths off of Socorro Island, two hundred and fifty miles due south of Cabo, he'd been able to swim within a meter of a giant manta ray, he was told the ray was probably 25 feet wide to the tips of its giant wings. Even for Kurt it was a heart pounding experience. In those waters, too, were the enormous whale sharks some as much as 35 feet long. Hammerhead sharks, orcas, hump back whales, dolphins, even sea lions could also be found. Great White sharks, sperm whales and other scary-big creatures certainly passed by, but they weren't predictable here. Kurt wanted to see the big Great Whites up close, again, but that would be their second stop off at Guadalupe Island which is farther north and about 150 miles west from Cabo.

His stomach was talking. Those two hours of sex with Issi had left him a bit drained, so he headed to his kitchen. Passing through his office with walls filled with trophies from hunts around the world, Kurt walked near where pictures of his many generations of family were displayed. He lingered for a moment looking at the image of his mother holding him after he'd fallen and cut the skin above his right eye. You could still see a small scar if you looked closely. He'd fallen while trying to get a model race car off of a shelf. He liked its deep red color. 'You're always trying to grab for things that are beyond your reach,' she had told her six-year-old. Years later, she would still be telling him he was reaching too far; and for what?

Kurt's mom knew of his method of growing food using chemicals men had made and it did not seem like a wise thing to do in her mind. His father did not raise food in such a way by going around nature's ways she thought. "Remember the temptations of our Lord Jesus," she would remind Kurt. "Are you trying to turn stones into bread?" Mary would ask. "Kurt, live like your brother does and grow the food the way our world was meant to. You are always wanting more and more my son. It is the sickness of our souls," she would say. "Our Lord was tempted to reach for great heights and to own the world. His temptation, Kurt, is yours, as it is everyone's to consider." He would hear her again, sometime much later in his life "the 'more' you seek is not truly more; find the more your brother has found as you will never be truly happy until you do."

"Silly woman," he would think to himself, "I'd be average like my brother too." There was nothing wrong with the way I grow my crops, he had convinced himself many years earlier, 'look at how much fruit and nuts we grow in California, and how much meat can be created feeding his corn and soy to cattle from his farms in Mexico.' But there was much more to that story.

He'd brought efficiency to his Mexican agribusiness and created a lot of jobs there too. The fact that many a small person lost their ancestral land and now lived in the sprawl of Mexico City after the cartel he was part of forced them off through violent means did not bother him. "Survival of the fittest, the strongest," was his mantra. Still, Kurt thought himself an ethical person, a good Christian. Well, for the most part. He did give a lot of money to the church.

(San Diego; April, 2013)

The 2013 white BMW briskly moved through the heavily landscaped parking lot heading to "his" designated stall. A high tech looking sign at the end of the stall read simply "Stone." It was a nickname the early forty something had acquired while in college and it stuck. Stone Fischer looked like he was meant to be a fighter pilot, his brown with a light sprinkle of gray hair was cut fairly short on the sides and slicked back with gunk, and the top was a little longer and very full. Above his forehead the hair was spiked up with a little more gunk. He tucked his Persol dark sunglasses in a case and stored them in his consul. It was a warm late April day even for San Diego. He liked living here better than in Davis where he'd spent a lot of time developing in the biotech industry. He had two more meetings with his team to crunch in before 6:00. After that Stone was scheduled for nine holes of golf with several friends. He was good and loved to bet on everything.

In 2010 after twelve years working for other start up Genetic Engineering companies Stone had joined New Genome Bio, NGB for short. He'd completed his Ph.D by the time he was twenty six. He never let much moss grow under his toes. Even though Stone didn't work for him he had a picture of Craig Venter on his office wall, Venter was the guy he most wanted to emulate. Maverick genius, that's how he wanted others to think of him. Stone!

Kurt wanted to find such a maverick, someone driven…Elon Musk like, if possible. Of course, brilliant, full of vision, energy, and courage. Then, give him - or her - the financial backing needed to launch into the biotech field and compete with the established companies like Monsanto, Syngenta, ADM, and Cargill. Kurt had been concerned for sometime about the power the agronomy and agrochemical companies that provided his seed, fertilizer, insecticide, herbicide, and fungicide had over him. He'd gotten in early though, became huge, and acquired enormous financial stability before the crunch of a mature industry began squeezing those on the margins out. He wanted to keep what he had and grow it even larger. That's where Stone fit in.

The strategy that had emerged in some portions of agribusiness was to genetically alter the seed of the money crops like wheat, corn, and soy so they could be sprayed with chemicals that would kill other plants that emerged along with them in the growing cycle, but not kill or damage the money plants. The strategy had worked exceedingly well for a number of years. But the bad guys, meaning the weeds, were evolving and becoming resilient to the spraying, so new genetics would be needed in the plants of the future. In this constant weapons race, Kurt wanted a game changer, some novel way of beating the weeds for the water and nutrients in the ground.

Word had got to Kurt of an avant-garde young researcher who was using an innovative new twist to the developed protocol directing agro bacterium tumefactions, a gram negative soil bacterium, to insert new genes into plants. This researcher, Stone, had been on teams using the biolistic method, otherwise called a particle gun, to blast the genes into place, but had found the new method much more effective. He and the teams he'd directed had been successful in creating some interesting new plants with very desirable traits using this relatively new and very secret technology.

Ever since Cleanse was introduced with its active ingredient of glyphosate that interferes with the biochemical shikimate pathway which causes a plant to be unable to construct amino acids, proteins, and so on, which eventually leads to death; competitors had looked for other ways that might be cheaper or more effective in pursuit of this goal. Kurt was among them. He held a Ph.D in biochemistry and was capable of reviewing exceedingly technical papers. The work that Stone was doing using p-Hydroxybenzoic acid to initiate agro bacterium to infect plant cells intrigued him. Kurt recognized it as a critical technical step that could lead to some revolutionary changes in plant physiology. Kurt understood it and he wanted this guy on his team.

Stone didn't accept the first offer. He wanted to as it was great but he just didn't want to let on to Kurt that he could get him on the first try. Stone knew the game, and was pretty certain Kurt would be back. He was.

After three years of intense research the teams Stone had assembled for Kurt were getting close to producing their own suite of "seeds and cides" the combination of altered seeds and chemicals to control the weeds and the microbes that competed with the money crops. The days of buying his seed and pest controls from others were nearing an end, Kurt envisioned. And Stone was the driving force behind that. If all went as to plan Stone would soon have a major part in his empire. "More" would flow to them both, and they both wanted more, but in different ways!

~~~~~

"Perfect," Gezana said after taking the first sip of wine. Stone settled into the beautiful, geometric and somewhat Arabic custom crafted hot tub next to her. Twelve people could have fit into it, but tonight it was just the two of them. A light blue light illuminated the water and all around succulent rather tropical looking plants provided a very comforting space.

If cashed out, his stock options would already put millions in the bank. But Stone didn't want it yet, and his contract would only let him withdraw just so much at a time anyway. He could afford a place in a ritzier part of town, but he was content here. Stone had bought the place at the right time and had just been fixing it up for the past ten years. The architect and landscape architect he'd been working with were sometimes referred to as the Frey and Henley of their craft around San Diego. Their work here was spectacular, so why would he want to live anywhere else?

Though he was driven in his business pursuits and wanted to achieve much, consuming numerous women didn't resonate with him as he was a one woman man. Quality not quantity did.

"Mother called today," Gezana began, "she wants to know if I can come to Santiago for a few weeks. I really want to see her and Bruna too." Bruna or BB was her younger sister.

Stone gave her a kiss and moved over next to the jet so it could massage his back. He was visualizing her mom, Mrs. Bardales, a very attractive woman in her own right, at sixty two. "When would that be?"

"I think Mom said the middle part of May. I'd need to look on a calendar."

He dunked his head for a moment and then took a sip of his wine. "I got a message from Kurt today that he wants to do some diving south of Cabo next month, down around Socorro Island, maybe up around Guadalupe Island too."

She shook her head, "I've never heard of them."

"They're out in the ocean a ways, a couple hundred miles south or west of Cabo."

During the previous year's summer Gezana had flown to New Zealand with Stone and was part of the group on Kurt's yacht. She didn't dive but enjoyed seeing the films they'd watch in the media room after each of the dives. There was very little danger associated with those excursions, just beautiful fish and interesting seascapes. She knew nothing of Kurt's growing interest in extreme adventures, especially sharing the water with Great White Sharks.

"We should see if we can put the two trips together," Stone suggested. "We could fly to Cabo and enjoy some time there before Kurt arrives in his yacht. You could fly on to Santiago, and when I'm done with the dive trip, I could meet you there. I'm excited to see your family too."

Gezana rose up from the water. Her long five foot seven frame shed the aqua along her smooth, light brown skin. Her dark brown hair was wet and parted in the middle and settled just above her shoulders. Her posture was so graceful, elegant, and certainly erotic. Stone smiled, seeing the beautiful arc of her frame, the same one that had captured his imagination several years earlier on a beach near Valparaiso, an ocean side town near Santiago.

He had gained his nick name for a reason; courage, the courage to not consume himself with the fear of failing. He was within that range of good looking. The idea of striking up a conversation with a beautiful and exotic woman on a beach far from where he was from was too alluring to resist. And now she was part of his life.

Often, after they had made love and Gezana had slipped off to sleep, Stone would get up and spend time on his computer, usually updating himself on all the information flowing from his various research and testing groups. But he had many other fields of interest too and would read about the latest in earthquake research, space exploration, alternative energy designs, and a little on climate change.

The last one bothered him some to read about, especially the part where agribusiness was starting to be blamed for part of it. He'd seen the charts where the human population just jacked like a hockey stick straight up, seven billion, eight billion, maybe ten billion by the end of this century.

Those were his customers, his industry needed to keep up with the new mouths to feed. There were other points of view of course on this: that there was actually plenty of food created each year but its distribution, especially to those who had so little to pay for it with, weren't getting their share and mostly now starved to death. However, Stone chose to not spend much time reflecting on them. He had a comfort zone in his head around the whole issue, and for now "conveniently" it had to do with feeding a growing world.

(Cabo San Lucas, May 17, 2013)

"I love you," Stone whispered in her ear after giving her a brief kiss. Her eyes told him she loved him too. In a moment, she was gone down the corridor leading to the plane she would travel on to Santiago. They'd had three days in Cabo together and now he'd meet Kurt and journey to Socorro Island on his yacht.

After checking in with his group and reviewing the data from some recent experiments, Stone decided to watch some videos on marlin fishing. He knew they'd be doing some of that on the trip as well. One video caught his eye as it had something to do with a marlin that was eaten by some squid. 'Hum, what's that all about?' The scene starts out during the day but the marlin was big and strong so the battle continues until it is twilight. With the marlin tired and near the boat the line suddenly becomes very jerky, eventually it just stops. They then discover what had been happening, the marlin had been found by a group of squid, they had plucked its central body clean, leaving the head and tail the only identifiable parts of the fish. It was gruesome. 'What an awful death for any creature.' The thought went through Stone's mind. There was that part of him that was empathetic.

He noticed another article in the search list, something about red devils. 'Hum, Humboldt squid, diablo rojo,' Spanish for red devils. "Mexican fishermen pulled from their boat and eaten by squid," the article was titled.

'Huh?' Two Mexican fishermen were pulled from their boat by the squid and were brutally killed. Their bodies were not even identifiable by their relatives. The squid ate them alive. "Is this crap, God, it looks real." He read on, "the Humboldt squid grows in a single year to about five feet long, weighs around 100 pounds, and has 40,000 teeth. It has one central parrot like mouth that can inflict great damage to a person. They're opportunistic carnivores often cannibalizing their own kind. They travel in shoals (groups) of up to 1,200 individuals. They usually are only aggressive towards humans when they are already in a feeding mode."

A retired navy diver told of one encounter with a large group of squid. They'd tugged on him to the point one shoulder was pulled out of socket and bit him nearly thirty times, mostly around his head. Intent on taking their prey with them, they had sucked onto him and were pulling him into the abyss, but miraculously he escaped.

Stone had been in the water with squid several times. He'd been coached that they are curious creatures but typically of no threat to humans. They could be excited by flashing light, but since they were diving during the day that wouldn't be a factor.

He'd heard that there was such a thing as a colossal squid, but they lived far to the south around Antarctica and typically at great depths far from where humans would be diving. 'What's this: sperm whale strangled by colossal squid?' He read on. In 1965 the crew of a Russian whaler ship watched a forty-ton sperm whale battle a colossal squid, it turned out that neither won as the whale was strangled to death but managed to chomp off the head of the squid.

'Bizarre,' Stone thought, "the colossal squid will feed on its smaller cousins the Humboldt squid or red devils … some scientists speculate that the colossal squid might move its range some distance north following the migrations of the Humboldt squid, though this is only speculation."

"We will be two thousand miles away from these things," Stone was reassuring himself.

(Aboard Kurt's Yacht, late, May 18, 2013)

The waiter lowered his drink to him. Stone smiled and thanked the young woman that was busy taking care of the guests on Kurt's yacht. "Shit, what a monster," Kurt was narrating and interpreting the encounter they'd videotaped last fall when his group had gone to the Great Barrier Reef of Australia. He'd already had four or five stout drinks and was feeling pretty testosterone. "I wanted to reach out of the cage and tap his ass as he swam by."

"What ass?" Andy Zeick asked, the comptroller of what was still his primary venture, Krastle Enterprises. I don't see two legs coming together and creating an ass on those things." Everyone had been drinking long enough that such a comment was pretty funny. Kurt actually knew that the shark skin was very much like sand paper, made up of millions of tiny scales which look something like teeth. You didn't want to get a rub from one of these giants.

"Look at him eyeing us," Kurt went on. The shark was circling about 20 feet away from their cage, another one joined it. Suddenly for no apparent reason the second great white attacked the metal cage they were drifting in. Audio had been recorded as you could hear the sound of their respirators, corresponding to the ongoing ejection of bubbles from their oxygen tanks. "Thud. Crank," the metal cage reverberated the collision, the divers moved back from the edge where the shark's mouth had penetrated shortly into the cage. The larger space between the steel allowed for easier photography, but it still seemed a bit odd for such a large opening. "What a fuckin' beast," Kurt said, mostly to himself, with certain awe in his voice. Film eventually gave way to some serious poker as this crew had gambling in their blood.

~~~~~

Stone was an early riser by nature. He liked that time of day and almost always felt very refreshed; ready for the day. The passage from Cabo to Socorro Island had been completed mostly during the night while Kurt and his guests played or slept. They were now anchored a few hundred yards from the island in a reasonably protected location.

Waking, Stone sensed that the boat was stationary as the steady buzz of the engines was no longer heard. There was some soft New Age music just barely discernible that created a little bit of background sound. He decided to take a walk up onto the deck and see what the ocean looked like in the early hours just before the sun came up over the Pacific Ocean. Stone made himself some coffee and headed on deck. The smell of the ocean was more intense and he was now standing in the open cradling his cup of coffee. There was just enough light that he could see the outline of Socorro Island. He could tell that they were fairly close to land.

The island covered about a hundred square miles and at its highest point is about 3,445 feet above the sea. The Mexican government had maintained a small naval base there since the mid 1950s, so there were several hundred year-round residents. Socorro is one of four islands in what is called the Revillagigedo Archipelago; San Benedicto, Roca Partida, and Clarion being the other three. They are volcanoes that have been largely still for over 3 million years. The rocky base of the volcanoes stretching for great distances under the water, provide habitat for many types of fishes, including many of the Earth's large marine predators including at least seven species of sharks. For many years, sports fishermen have been coming to these waters to hook into these various beasts. They have been successful, but this has also led to declines in the populations, even the sharks. This creates an imbalance, and where there is an imbalance nature will seek a new equilibrium.

Stone walked to the rear of the yacht where he could get a broader view of the island and the sea around it. Anchored several hundred yards away he saw another yacht, this one even bigger than Kurt's. In fact, it looked to be nearly twice as big as the one he was on. It was absolutely enormous and very high tech looking. 'Where did that come from? It's big enough to be a battle ship.' he thought to himself. 'There must be a connection or why else would they be anchored so close?'

Stone rested his upper body against the side of the boat and let his eyes settle on the deep blue-grey of the water. He was thinking about Gezana. When she got to her mom's place she had sent him a text message letting him know she was safe. 'How did he get so lucky to find her?' was going through his mind.

Then, something caught his attention. Some light seemed to have just pulsed in the sea only a few hundred yards out. There it went again. 'He wasn't imagining something was he?' Then there was another pulse; this one much more near to him, just thirty of forty feet from the yacht. 'What the hell,' the light was a pink to red color, and was wavy–varying in intensity. The pulsing light moved underneath the yacht. It suddenly occurred to him it must be a shoal of Humboldt squid. He'd learned in his reading how they sometimes pulse with their reddish body light. It was a communication they used when they were hunting. That thought caused his stomach to turn just a little. He walked to the other side of the boat and watched as several more pulses were emitted. The last one was several hundred yards from the boat and moving away. 'Kinda spooky,' he was thinking.

~~~~~

Stone looked over the breakfast menu and he knew that whatever he selected would be top notch in quality and taste. Kurt had two chefs who traveled with him all the time. They knew what he liked and kept him very well nourished. His guests would receive the same. Stone chose a hash of various potatoes, onions, and topped with two lightly scrambled eggs. The waiter suggested a drink that was a mixture of probiotics and freshly squeezed grapefruit juice. Stone agreed.

He was busy reading his iPad reviewing the lead stories from several news outlets he followed. Stone used the advice given by the web site News Trust to select the outlets he followed: The New York Times and Rolling Stone magazine. Waiting for his food to arrive, he noted the date on the article, Thursday, May 17, 2013. He'd found an article about Jamaica needing more mechanical engineers or else they faced a crumbling economy. There was some movement to his left; it was Kurt and several others coming towards where he was sitting. He closed his iPad and directed his attention to them.

"Been up for awhile?" Kurt asked, sitting down near him.

"An hour maybe, caught it just as the sun was coming up. I like that time of day."

"It looks like we have company." Stone said. The large yacht was hard to miss from their vantage point.

Kurt put on his squareish glasses and studied the breakfast menu, "Yes, well, they are people I know, you'll meet them later, we'll be going over to the yacht for a short meeting. They'll be doing a little fishing and diving with us."

"Who is it?" Stone asked.

Kurt looked towards the other yacht, "Doolin, he's Texan."

Stone knew right away who he was talking about, Black Jack Doolin, one of the wealthiest men in the oil business…and fossil fuels generally. 'Wow!' How was it that he was going to meet this guy? 'What's this all about?' moved rapidly through Stone's mind.

"You have any 'eco's' in your family or friends?" Kurt asked, quickly and pointedly.

"Eco's?" Stone responded.

Kurt moved the conversation quickly to a question he'd wanted answered, "The nuts who think we're destroying the Earth. Those tree hugger types. Any of those types hanging around you? You still as dedicated to our business model as you were when you started with me?"

In the interview process Kurt had had the talk with him about his philosophy on business, the nonsense interference the eco types wanted put on his enterprise, and the established business order as a whole. One of the first things Kurt had shared with the cartel more than a decade earlier when their business interests began to entangle, was his own brother. He had made it extremely clear that he and his brother were two different animals. Time had proved that to be true.

Stone had invested the last 22 years of his life becoming an agribusiness technologist. He was a genetic engineer and modifying the gene sequence of food crops represented his substantial investment in his own future. This was where the honey flowed from. Of course he was on board.

"I'm passionate about the second Green Revolution and don't accept that our approach to growing food crops is wrong. We're feeding millions and millions of people with our technology. Is that what you're asking me?" Stone let his boss know he was a stalwart warrior in the high technology of food production.

Kurt knew that Stone was about to meet one of the most notorious contrarians of the climate crisis and wanted to double-check his intuitions since when he'd hired the young dynamo several years earlier. Stone's background had been checked out quite substantially at that time and had nothing there to lead Kurt to think his allegiance otherwise. He wasn't even sure why he'd asked the question. "When we're with Black Jack let me do the talking, unless he asks you a direct question."

'Holly shit,' went through Stone's head. He was going to meet Black Jack Doolin; he and his brother, and their sister who rarely gets talked about, were among the richest people in the fossil fuels industry, the whole world for that matter. They were major backers of *The American Fund*, the lead organization to counter the eco's nonsense. It was a think tank and a media coordination organization, mostly the product of the multi trillion dollar fossil fuels industry with all its tentacles into the modern American and world's economic system.

"Black Jack's got something itching at him, I think the eco's are starting to nip where they hadn't better. The pit bulls are gonna be nippin' back; maybe a few momma griz too!" Kurt said in a breath filled with annoyance towards those that thought they could challenge his and their power. His voice was filled with indignation and distain.

~~~~~

Kurt's delegation: Stone, Andy, Bob Rose his director of communications, and three more vice presidents of Krastle Enterprises stepped from the transfer boat onto the deck of Black Jack's sleek vessel. A very attractive woman greeted them all and asked that they would follow her.

'What a piece of work, the ship and the woman. Don't look at her too much,' Stone warned himself. Something men and women often feel compelled to do, when their compass is getting distracted. But this was definitely an environment he'd not experienced before: materials and dimensions of space that were seductive.

Around were several men that looked like they might have recently been in Iraq or Afghanistan protecting someone. They followed the woman up a flight of steps to a deck level that commanded not only a view of the rest of the ship, but the seascape around. A man was standing with his hands on the rail looking towards the island. He turned around as they approached.

The breeze blew his dark hair that had streaks of grey growing through it. Black Jack was actually comfortable with aging. "Kurt," his deep voice cracked.

"Black Jack!" They shook hands, each man having their own reason for some level of admiration for the other.

Kurt quickly introduced the men who were along with him. Black Jack would have no problem remembering their names, it was a talent he had. They'd all be out fishing and diving soon, get this business stuff out of the way and then go have some fun.

Black Jack had a few of his people close, "Why don't you take our guests down to the media room and give them a tour of my memorabilia?" Black Jack had a conversation he wanted to have with Kurt and Stone, alone. Kurt had let him know Stone could be trusted. He was a rising star; very much an elite. It was time some younger blood began to understand the cartel and their place in it.

They were both given a drink of some sort to sip on while they talked. "You heard of this 'Risky Business' thing that Michael Bloomberg and Hank Paulson teamed up on with that hedge fund crank. Steyer?" They've got Robert Rubin and God damn it, George Schultz as part of some advisory group too."

"I got the email telling me to review their website." Kurt answered.

"What do you think?" Black Jack led them to a small table where they could sit alone.

"So they're going to divide the country up into what, eight zones, then give them risk analysis ratings for climate changing weather. More fucking mumbo jumbo!" Kurt replied.

"This change they're so worried about, this stuff can all be engineered. Fuck that's what they do "ingenious solutions," engineers. We just move the water around in canals; the fucking Romans figured that out." Black Jack was tapping his fingers, looking at Stone a little, trying to get a read on this young gun. "What do you think Stone about Bloomberg stirring things up?"

He knew he had to be careful and make sure Black Jack found what he said acceptable. "There's always risk for any enterprise on this planet; alarmists are always going to be worried about all sorts of things, I don't buy their argument. We've been building a great economy for a hundred and fifty years and it's only going to get better with all the new technology that's coming on line. I agree, there's nothing we can't engineer for. We're making things all the time that improve on what nature has created."

Kurt tapped his titanium bracelet on the table, Black Jack wore one too, they had an interesting logo on them; something that looked like an eye, but he didn't get a good look.

"You can't find this in some crack in the ground. Strong as superman and light weight." It was a reminder to him of man's dominance over the Earth.

That's exactly what Black Jack wanted to hear as it resonated with his mechanistic view of nature. It was all understandable, it could all be modified to whatever ends really brilliant humans like him decided on. Why were so many people not able to understand that? But some would argue that he was missing the bigger picture.

"They don't have the trillions of dollars in the ground that we do. What the fuck? Do they think those refineries, and pipe lines and tanker ships just got dropped on us by the tooth fairy? Fuckers! We had to build 'em, pay for 'em. We put billions every year into maintaining and upgrading our infrastructure. We've got "return on investment" we need to make back; decade's worth. You know, fiduciary interests."

Black Jack continued, "There are millions of people in the US alone invested in this industry, where do they think their retirement pensions and 401k plan money is gonna come from if we don't use that coal, oil, and natural gas?" Black Jack's mind was rushing ahead, already running through the gambit of rationales he had created in his own mind for the ongoing of the fossil fuels industry and the agricultural industry it so much supported.

Black Jack adjusted how he was sitting and continued, "We've got our media people working the sheep every day. There are millions of them listening to us now. We gotta keep our common folk quiet, and on our side. As long as we have their votes we have our leverage in the government and it doesn't matter what the 'enviros' do." He said that word slowly and with distain in his voice. "We've got to keep an eye out for any socialist-populist uprising thinking they're going to change the status quo."

"We've got to make sure we don't lose it...we need to stiffen it up. We've been god damned successful keepin' that Muslim we have in the White House from getting much of his bull shit passed. If we can keep the sheep pointing at him for all the problems in the country, maybe we can get enough of our people in the right places by 2016 and take control of the government! That's what our class needs to do: *permanently take control of this country!* The sheep don't know what's good for them. We gotta make sure that the cream just keeps rising to the top."

He stroked his dark hair again, his testosterone was rising as he was gathering a deeper thought, a slight look of disgust animating. "There are sixty million people in the US who are just dead weight, Mr. Roosevelt and Mr. Johnson made sure they had a way to suck on the mamma's tit to and get their 'entitlements.'" He said the last word slowly, adding emphasis. "They just don't have what it takes to be a part of this modern world. Survival of the fittest! Whose pockets do they mostly pick for their 'entitlements'? "

"The cream!" Kurt answered, deeply enjoying the notion that he was a part of that class.

"That's right," Black Jack settled back into his seat, "we gotta cut 'em loose. Get 'em off the tit." His lips were full of animosity, almost spitting. The moment settled in. There was something very gravitational about what Black Jack had just said. Some weight of his deepest motivations; visceral!

"What can I do?" Kurt then asked, a certain excitement stirring in him. Stone was struggling a little with the conversation as it was unfolding, but he kept that thought to himself.

"We gotta keep feedin' our people red meat. Keep them stirred up. They gotta see how those enviro nuts are threatening their livelihoods, their jobs. That'll get 'em going. We've got to double down against Bloomberg and his ilk; if the people start listening to them," Black Jack bit his lower lip slightly, "Shit, they'll start taxing carbon. That's what the enviros want to do. Tax our gold that's in the ground. Who knows what other shit we'd deal with then? It's not happening!"

Black Jack ran one hand through his hair again. "Look how effective we've been just naming that health care law, Obamacare. The little people bite all day long on that. We could get 'em to eat shit with the right marketing campaign. Forty five percent of the electorate, that's all we need to keep this shit wagon government constipated; we can't let these enviros start nipping away that base. We need something to tie Bloomberg to." He took a good drink, and then looked very directly at Kurt, "You ever heard of the Green Shadow Cabinet?"

Kurt shook his head that he had not.

"These green fuckin' dicks: the Greens?" Black Jack's eyes deepened with a very deep distain and a question in them.

Kurt started shaking his head and acknowledged he knew of them; the Greens.

"They have what they call their Green Shadow Cabinet. They watch what the actual Cabinet does, then their Cabinet releases some statement telling the nut cracks that listen to them how they'd do things differently."

Kurt was getting the idea. "We connect Bloomberg to this Green Shadow Cabinet?"

Black Jack was shaking his head slowly, "ah hah, exactly."

"How do you hook them?"

Black Jack sat up and leaned in towards Kurt.

"They want to cut the military budget by up to 50%. There's a lot of jobs hooked with that 50%, huh?" He was shaking his head in defiance. "The gun people won't like that. Look how they stood up to the cracks after that Connecticut shooting thing. Shit, those fuckers are nuts." He shook his head a little not liking something about that thought. "We need to get God and country into this mix. There's some red meat. We get that connection and we might get this dog to hunt!"

He offered Kurt a cigar, and they both lit up. "We need something to hang the enviros on through 2016, so we don't lose control of those people we got in Congress." Black Jack said.

"We need a fund raiser?" Kurt knew that would be his part.

"You did a great job on the oil spill. Maybe something like that."

Kurt thought for a moment, "I have some people I'll give this to." He saw himself as a soldier in the battle.

"There's a very big future for everyone on our team, you just need to be very committed." The multi billionaire took another sip of his drink; his view of the world was secure, for now.

Black Jack had a corner of his consciousness, a door, that he kept a padlock on. Long ago he'd thrown the key away, it was the door where he could actually see the true effects of his actions on others, and the world in general. But that door was not convenient for satisfying his never ending need for "*more*; money (power) especially power!" The doors he chose to enter were filled with all manner of things to fill a longing in his spirit; for more.

He wouldn't refer to the people as sheep if he didn't actually realize he was a player in their manipulation. The uncurious are the sheep, the border collies run them around, herd them together and hold them with nothing more than thin air. The sheep never realize they can simply walk past the collie or kick it in the face. It is only their irrational notion that the dog has control over them that holds them. Knowing this, the wolves then lick their chomps.

~~~~~

Sport fishing was not allowed within twelve miles of Socorro and the other islands in the Archipelago. These high rollers could afford the very best to get them into some great fishing. Marlins' were the most desired catch; so big and strong and beautiful. Displaying one in your trophy room made a lot of balls tingle.

One large sixty-foot commercial fishing ship, designed specifically for deep sea fishing, pulled up close to Black Jack's yacht, they'd have the group out to the fishing waters by 10:00. The plan was to fish until 3:00 or so and then come back with enough time to make a dive to some caves off the south side of the island that attracted a lot of very beautiful fish. Both Kurt and Black Jack had been scuba diving in these waters before but had never been to these particular caves as they were pretty deep. But new submersible transport technology, and they had all the best, made getting to them a lot easier and safer.

There was ample room for everyone across the back of the boat. Black Jack had let the captain know that there would be a bonus for him directly if he got him into a big blue marlin; something over five hundred pounds would be good. He knew they got twice that big; at least they used to, but one that size would be a great battle. Black Jack would pay $20 a pound for any blue marlin over 500 pounds. The crew knew to rig Black Jack and Kurt for marlin; the others would be rigged for other fish: blue fin or yellow fin tuna primarily.

Marlin fishing was Hemingway-esque; man battling the sea creature. A picture of the writer and his family in 1935 with four near record setting marlin hanging behind them was displayed on the ship. What they did not explain was that heavy fishing of the great fish had severely reduced the number of such large creatures. Big marlins these days were about half that size.

Black Jack wanted to get to know the young scientist who headed up the research division of the company he was a silent investor in, his financial involvement was not even known to Stone. Black Jack was a visible extension of a much deeper union of wealth that, in fact, had aggregated together since at least the 16th century. Old money, like a very old and valued wine, holds a mysterious status like something from a different world. Not even Kurt, truly, understood "the family" Black Jack was a tentacle within.

At six foot three, slender, but strong, and tanned already-ruddy-skin, Black Jack stood out among the others. "I'm curious to know why you go by Stone?" he said, reaching out to shake hands.

The main man was talking to him, Stone liked that. "Just a name I got in college."

Black Jack shook his head; he wanted to know a little more about the story. "Did men or women choose this name for you?" Black Jack wore a faint grin.

"Just a couple of guys I play golf with." Stone answered.

"Hum, this sounds interesting, tell me more."

Stone nodded his head. "We were on the 18th hole, a par five, I was down to both of them by a shot; the hole was already worth $250 because of some carryovers. I was feeling confident, just had this edgy feeling that I could smoke this hole. I'd done it a couple of weeks earlier. I said I'd eagle, and if I didn't I owed them both the pot, which would be $300 each, rather than just one of them getting the pot. But if I did make eagle and they didn't, they'd both owe me $300. If two of us or all three happened to eagle then we'd just split the pot. I was the only one at risk to pay out $600."

"That would be a lot of money to some college guys," Black Jack said. "So how does it play out?"

"I'd checked the pin placement before we headed out; it was in the easiest location, down in the front. I knew there was a pretty high percentage chance to get on in two and below the hole where the putts were all straight in, no break to deal with. The second shot was the most important because you had to hit the ball low and get it to feed down the slope, I knew if you could just get it in about a twenty foot wide corridor the ball will always feed to the bottom of the green. Two of us had drives that set us up for the second shot, but my friend Skip tried to hit a high fade and drop it on, that shot is hard to keep in front of the hole. So my second shot worked and I had about a fifteen footer below the hole, straight in, they both had long putts, but with lots of break. Mine went in and theirs didn't. Skip started calling me Stones, and it caught on."

Black Jack was amused by the story. "So Stones was better than Balls, I take it?"

"Yeah, but I dropped the 's' my girlfriend at the time didn't like it with the 's,' so I just dropped it to Stone, and that stuck."

"You're a bit like my friend who goes by the name Ace. You have to live up to it."

Stone was wondering what that might mean.

They talked for about fifteen minutes; it was curious how much this Black Jack seemed to know about his research, and the interest he was showing in it. Stone suspected there was more to all that, maybe Kurt would shed some light later. For now Stone decided he'd just make sure he didn't say anything that couldn't be found in the company prospectus or that was generally available on the internet. Just in case it was some sort of test Kurt had cooked up for him.

"Fish on," Stone looked and it was his pole that was responding to the pull. He'd been through the drill before, getting the pole out of the rigging holding it; now it would be his strength against that of the fish.

"Probably a yellow fin tuna," the guide told him. "Pretty good size judging by the bend in your pole. That's what I had you rigged for anyway. We'll see. If it's a yellow fin we might see him make a few jumps. He should run fast on you too, they can swim at fifty miles an hour."

The drag was set to keep a four hundred pounder under twenty miles an hour; at the rate the line was going out it would seem just such a fish was hooked. Several more that were rigged for the tuna quickly were in action. They'd obviously gotten into a school of them.

An hour passed, good sized tunas were brought on board, their displayed bodies would make good trophies as well.

"Holy shit, look at that," a guide near to where Stone was standing said. "Looks like a sperm whale just surfaced. You don't see that very often." Several hundred yards off the east side of the boat the distinctive squared head of the beast could be seen; it was blowing water out of its air supply blowhole. "Must be a big male, look at the size of that fluke," the name for the tail.

"How big do you think he is?" Kurt asked.

The guide responded, "Those males get big, fifty five maybe sixty feet long, I'd imagine. Probably thirty five maybe forty tons, a big animal."

They watched as the whale seemed to just be resting, not moving very much, it would blow a little water now and again. Then it disappeared from the surface only to come back up forcefully a few seconds later, the bottom of his body rose up out of the water, even from this distance it was an amazing site. "He's headed for deep water," the guide said, "they'll go nearly ten thousand feet down after squid if they think it's worth doing." He was interestingly speculating on an animal's thoughts.

For a moment, Stone imagined what it must be like at the head of the great mammal heading down through the darker and darker water, passing quickly from where any surface light penetrates, going where their biological sonar would direct them. It did not occur to him, but to some it was fascinating, that this creature looking so different, and living in a completely hostile environment to that which humans are adapted to, still shared over 98% of the exact same process of evolutionary emergence as any human had. We shared so much in common, but this was not of interest to anyone not curious enough to contemplate the possibility.

"Fish on. Big Fish!!" Black Jack's pole, even with its massive line size and bend control, showed to those who knew, a large fish was now attached to the end of the line. Even before Black Jack could get hooked to his harness and get the pole into his hands the marlin took to the air. "Mother fuck, look at that fish!" Black Jack was, well - jacked! "Yeah, baby!"

He'd landed many a large fish, getting into the harness and getting control of the pole was easy for him. He loved the feel of the huge fish at the end of the line. The longer the fight would go on the more their two bodies would become entangled with each other; one fighting with all its energy for the freedom it had always known; the deep drive in all life forms to survive. The other end of the line the taker of freedom pulled with all his might. There really were just two wills attached to either end of the line. For one there was the immediate pain of a hook imbedded in its flesh but there was a deeper pain still, one the animal had no direct name or concept for. It had no understanding of what was impeding its normal flow of life, it only knew that something wasn't right and it needed to get away, it fought for its freedom, its life.

On the other end the will of a man, a human being, filled not with the need to satisfy his caloric intake for food energy. No, he sought something else…the simple, ancient, and visceral satisfaction of winning the competition; the heart pounding, adrenaline, and testosterone driven, even egotistical, emotion of winning.

Deep in the battle was a primordial element, a vestige of an ancient time when there was no "knowing" only pure reaction through instinct, a haunting memory from billions of years of predator and prey fortunes we all share, that through association we were all players in.

Slowly but surely Black Jack was winning the battle. His competitor had lost a great amount of strength in the several hour struggle they had already waged. With every drawing in of the pole now, Black Jack would bring the great blue fin marlin eight or ten feet closer to the boat. It was not a matter of if Black Jack would win, that was virtually settled now.

But there was a moment, several hours earlier, when the marlin made a decision to "take the bait." It had fallen for an illusion, what was not real, and what would eventually destroy it. Was the creature simply incapable of discerning the bait from the truth? Had it simply not evolved a consciousness capable of this distinction? Or, did it simply not review the dashing fish closely enough for unnatural signs? All that is known was that it had bitten hard and was now hooked so completely that no struggle it could muster could save it from its final demise waiting at the boat. Its story was now done.

A dorsal fin suddenly showed up on the surface not far from the boat. "Sharks, probably Tigers," a crewman said, close to where they were swimming. "We don't need them nipping at this big guy while we're trying to bring him in. Let's bait them up near the front of the boat, get them out of here." They threw some tuna heads out in front of where the sharks were circling, they soon moved that way.

Bringing the beautiful creature on board, it looked like it should pass the 500 pound threshold Black Jack set. "That fish could be worth 11 or 12 thousand dollars to the captain," one of the crew members was thinking. They had it up on the scales momentarily; yup, 573 pounds. Everybody would be happy about that; except of course the marlin.

~~~~~

They'd come to do some diving too and the sun wasn't getting any higher. Socorro is known for the quantity of big fish you can swim with, in particular the giant manta rays. The underwater landscape is not particularly colorful, so it is the fish that the divers are interested in; they are colorful and exotic. Black Jack had been here numerous times to swim with the mantas and loved that. He'd swam up under a number of them and blew bubbles on their undersides, they seemed to like it and it got his rocks going.

Big, aggressive great white sharks were rarely found in these waters. They hung out mostly farther north around Guadalupe Island where seals lived. There was always a chance some might show up, as they had many years earlier, but the divers just moved over near some of the underwater rock outcroppings and stayed still. They soon moved along.

Both yachts had been moved around to the southeast end of the island. They stopped at a location about five miles out from land's end. Satellite imagery showed the long trail of deep sea bed that extended south from the island for hundreds of miles. The cartography made it look like the island had been drug through the mud carving out the trench behind it. And of course it had, inch by inch over millions of years. The valley's and crevices created certainly offered sea life desiring such depths a sanctuary from the otherwise rather featureless bottom, with connections south for thousands of miles.

It was in these waters where the rock mount fell away steeply into the great depth of the ocean that Black Jack wanted to dive. He'd learned of a spectacular cavern where exotic fish lived. Few had seen the cavern from the bottom, illuminated by the light several hundred feet above, the view would be exotic and otherworldly, and an experience very few others have had. These were the sort of dives men such as himself dared to undertake and untold bragging rights followed with them.

When diving in these waters, at one moment you might have 20 or 30 feet below you to solid earth. And then quickly in another moment thousands of feet fell away beneath you into the void. Experiencing that sudden change was very-very eerie. It was here that divers had been reporting seeing a whale shark feeding, one of the great fishes in the ocean. Docile creatures that can grow to 30 even 40 feet long, they are filter feeders living on the zooplankton. Getting the chance to possibly swim up next to one would be an added benefit. It was also a pretty good bet they'd find some mantas to swim with.

Everyone had a small bite to eat, not too much before going into the water. Kurt's team crossed from his yacht to Black Jacks on a smaller boat they carried with them for trips to shore and these sorts of rendezvous. Black Jack had the latest in diving amenities, including a submersible cargo carrier which was basically a machine to carry them around under water. There were 12 divers, 3 of whom were exceedingly experienced guides and had the responsibility to keep track of everyone. Each guide was responsible for 3 of the divers. There was a location about 65 feet below the surface they'd ride the submersibles to. There was a rock outcropping they knew was there that the submersibles could rest on and be tethered too. Visibility was still reasonably good at that depth, especially with the angle of the sun as it would be for the next hour or so.

The two high tech subs with six men in each moved carefully down through the water allowing the divers to acclimate to the changing pressures and temperatures. It took about five minutes following an arcing descent path to reach the place they wanted. The four guides worked to tether the crafts securely. With the submersible safely attached, the divers then spread out along the edge of the sea mount as they'd agreed. It was very much like being on a very high mountain and all around is the sky and falling away was the Earth, but mostly there was just sky. A rope was run by the experienced divers in each direction from the submersible. It was brightly colored and the divers would always have it as a guide as to where they were. If they found a crevice they were interested in exploring the guide would attach a rope to them so they couldn't get lost or possibly get caught in some current and pulled away.

At this depth the light from the surface was rather diluted, and was much like dusk feels on the surface. Each man had a light on his helmet if needed. They planned to be down for about an hour, it would be nearly 6 by the time they came to the surface and lower light would be falling onto the dive zone.

Stone was grouped with Kurt and Black Jack. Before going down, Black Jack told them of an interesting crevice he'd found the last time diving here. He had found a group of white tipped sharks just lying on top of each other. "If we get lucky a group of hammer heads will come by, seeing them always gets my balls tingling a little. Just hang near the rocks, they'll just move along." He'd said.

With the high-tech helmets they wore, they had state-of-the-art radio contact between each other. Stone was anxious to get into the water and start experiencing in person what he'd been watching video clips and listening to stories about. Of course there's always that little voice of apprehension lingering, but that's good as it keeps you alert.

It had felt like something out of Star Wars as the submersible launched from the mother ship. The diver simply sat on a chair with water all around. There was something of a cage that would keep the largest, mainly great whites, at bay. Anything else could basically swim right through.

'What a jaw dropping site,' Stone was thinking to himself. Having the mountain of island at one side of you, providing a sense of scale and then looking off into the vastness that stretched out and down for immense and unseen distances. It made him feel vulnerable and small, but at the same time wildly alive.

The guides quickly set up the ropes that stretched in either direction for several hundred yards. The dive groups then spanned out keeping the ropes in site.

"Jesus, how did we get so lucky, up to your right Kurt." Black Jack was the first to spot the immense blue tip manta ray, Kurt and Stone quickly saw it too.

"What a beast," Kurt said, "it must be twelve or fifteen feet wide." And it was, it was circling above them.

Everybody was quiet to begin with; awe had overcome them. The manta looked like some flying space ship, the tips of its wings just moving enough to keep it on whatever course it was intending. The guide was motioning to them to follow him up to where they might get closer. Like a flying fortress, the manta glided along showing only a faint comprehension of the strange creatures that had entered its world.

"I want to swim up underneath of it," Black Jack told Russ, his guide. Russ nodded. Together they floated slowly up towards a point where they thought they could intercept it. As it approached they began swimming hard and secured a place just underneath the creature. The manta seemed to welcome the bubbles that streamed up on its lower side. On its back side parasite eating sucker fish were attached in a symbiotic relationship that had certainly evolved eons earlier through unknown generations. Kurt and Stone followed behind Black Jack and took their turns nuzzling up close to the giant. One of the guides carefully documented the encounter on video so the experience could be relived later.

After a few minutes Black Jack motioned that they should head back to the rocks and look for more of the interesting fish that could be found there. There were numerous schools of fish swimming around, most the guide had a name for. Monster looking green eels could be seen backing their way into short crevices. There were weird fish with heads that looked like a cross between a crocodile and a horse, fluttering by with their fins that looked something like those of a humming bird.

About a half hour into the dive, Russ told them to look up and to their right. Stone felt a chill go through him, it was a school of hammer head sharks, thirty or forty of them. They looked like they were on patrol, silhouetted by the light color of the sun-soaked surface above. They moved along and were soon out of site.

Nearing the end of the rope line Black Jack turned his body so he was looking at Kurt and Stone. He pointed down and below. "Down there, that's the spot. Tie on to the line with your ropes and we'll head down. I remember there was a little bit of a current. The water seemed a little colder as they headed down, maybe another twenty five feet. Stone could see the effect of the current on Black Jack and Kurt and then passing into an opening he felt it on himself as well. Good thing he was tethered, as it could be difficult to swim against.

Black Jack motioned for them to follow on down farther to where he was at. He was looking up. They both reached to where he was hovering, the world seeming to drop away to an eternal abyss below, but above was what looked like the core of an old volcano shoot. It was perhaps fifty feet wide and stretched all the way to near the surface. Swimming around inside were schools of brightly colored yellow, green, and white fishes. Stone found it mind-blowing, a perspective he'd never imagined, like something from a drug-induced dream. This was an experience he'd never forget. Their guide, Russ, was still back behind the corner. He had the camera.

"Russ, you think you could come down here and get a picture for us?" Black Jack asked.

A few moments passed and there was no reply. Black Jack checked the frequency monitor and it looked right. Maybe the rock outcropping was interfering with the signal. He swam back towards the corner as Kurt and Stone continued to revel in the spectacle. Suddenly Black Jack's body started to squirm and his head moved quickly one way then the other. He dashed himself up against the rocks. Stone saw his movement and tapped Kurt on the shoulder. About then Black Jack motioned to them to move closer to the rocks, and then come up to where he was.

As they approached the fear in Black Jack's face was obvious. "Something," he didn't finish his sentence, his jaw was clutching with fear. Kurt moved passed him to look beyond the rocks. "Fuckin' jesus," about 40 feet away what was left of Russ's body was drifting in the blood and inner-fluids-soaked brine of seawater surrounding his lifeless body. He seemed to have only half of a head.

The first thing Kurt thought was sharks, but as far as he could see there was nothing. He adjusted the frequency to that of one of the other guides, "Do you hear me?" Kurt's anxious voice queried. Ten seconds passed and there was no answer. He tuned to the next channel, this time he heard a voice respond.

47

"Stay in the rocks," the guide warned him. "We've got at least three shoals of Humboldt squid circling us."

Kurt knew that a shoal could have as many as twelve hundred individuals, which meant there could be three or four thousand of them nearby. They lived much deeper though so why would so many be at this depth? 'Had the squid attacked Russ? What was going on?' He looked back to where Black Jack and Stone were still hovering near the rocks.

There was movement just at the edge of where the water was clear enough to see detail. Then the water seemed to pulse with a red color. The ghostly color varied in intensity and moved around. Stone could see it, he suddenly remembered the story he'd read about the fishermen in Mexico who were pulled into the water and eaten by the squid and how they were called diablo rojo, red devils, because of the bioluminescence they could emit from their bodies. The sinking notion passed through him that it was thought they used the pulsing of their skin colors mostly for communication when they were hunting.

Kurt looked at the other two. "We've got to get back to the submersible. It's too far to try and swim back to the ship from here." Getting close to Russ's body would probably be suicide now as it had drifted out to the edge of sight; his bloody body would certainly be attracting sharks soon too. They moved through the water, close together staying tight to the rocks. It didn't occur to them that the lights on their helmets could trigger a response from the squid. They were within fifty yards of the submersible where two more bodies were drifting in a manner as Russ had been. That pulsing of light showed again from the waters just beyond where you could see. Just as they got to the submersible several hundred of the squid spotted them and were heading in their direction, and then stopped.

The enormous sperm whale rushed passed where they were attempting to protect themselves in the rocks. The water around them moved like a vortex pushing them hard against the crags and boulders. The squid were scattering realizing that their number one predator was streaking through the waters looking for them.

Reaching the submersible, Black Jack hit the button telling those on the surface that there was an emergency. "Black Jack, this is Everett, what's going on? We're seeing all sorts of bioluminescence in the water."

"Squid," he said as forcefully as he could. "We've got dead people down here. I don't know who's alive. A fucking whale just swam past us; a fucking monster!"

"You want us to put the other submersible in?"

Black Jack's first thought was to say 'yes, like bring all the cowboys, but that could make things worse, stir more things up, and probably get more people killed, like himself.'

"Do you have contact with the other guides on your radio? Russ is dead, there are at least two others who are dead, I don't know who they are. Fuck!"

About fifteen seconds passed. "We've got contact with Ed Spaeth and he's got his two people protected in a crevice. Nothing from the other two guides."

"Tell them to get to the submersible. Maybe that sperm's got the squid heading for deep water." Black Jack replied.

Kurt, Stone and Black Jack got into the submersible and pulled the protective cover around them. It would be little protection from the squid but it was something. Bubbles from the other three divers could be seen 30 or 40 yards distant. The divers were still behind a part of the submersed mountain. When they could be seen Kurt waved at them to hurry.

Stone was the first to see it again. It had surfaced once then dove and was rising fast again. The grey, blunt head, reminiscent of a train's locomotive thundering up from the deep, was coming towards them. It seemed to be traveling at an unnatural speed. The way a person can look that is running faster than their true fitness would carry. The great beast passed perhaps thirty feet out from where they were still tethered. They could see it more clearly in this pass. It appeared to have slashes on its side and blood was swishing out. There was no eye contact as the whale appeared hell bent for reaching the surface. Momentarily they could see as it broke the surface, probably clearing two-thirds of its body out of the water before crashing back into the sea. Those on the mother ship watched in pure awe as the whale spectacularly surfaced so close to where they were holding.

Ed Spaeth and the two divers with him quickly got into the craft and started to pull the metal cage around them shut. The tether was untied and they began their ascent. The view below was virtually black, everyone's eyes were fixed horizontally and above watching for the Humboldt squid. Suddenly there was some flashing of light from below then the submersible was hit very hard from the bottom, the craft lurched and everyone tumbled inside. Black Jack's hand smashed against the throttle and in the process the engine stopped. An enormous wiggling appendage rapidly bolted through the opening in the cage and took hold of Stone's right leg; adrenaline already running high in his system, spiked dramatically. He instinctively reached to try and remove the snake-like arm. It was then he saw the multitude of suction cups and sharp hooks along its length. A part of his brain was registering that this must be a super squid, a freak of some sort. His head rolled to the edge of the submersible, just then the central body of colossus was right in front of him, one of its 11inch wide eyes was staring at him, like that of the executioner.

49

As the submersible was spinning Stone's mind suddenly seemed to slip into another dimension. Everything was moving as if in super slow motion; the bubbles, the swirling water, everything seemed to move just barely perceptively. Then something spoke in his mind, but there was no sound, only a message. *'What do you believe?'* For a moment he felt calm and then it was gone. As quickly as he had left, Stone was back in this dimension, the reality of the horror that was occurring resumed.

What he could not know was that this attacker was a vanguard member of the genus and species Mesonychoteuthis hamiltoni also known as the colossal squid. They had moved their range north, or towards the equator from the Antarctic polar region, into a new niche that had opened up in recent years due to an imbalance in the oceans fisheries mostly caused by over fishing. Being about 45 feet long and weighing nearly 1,600 pounds, the colossal squid was absolutely enormous. It had followed the sperm whale up from about 7,200 feet below the surface. The squid had locked itself onto the whale when the whale attempted to consume it. A struggle had ensued between the two until the whale at last freed itself and headed to the surface for air. The squid had followed the whale up from the depths for reasons nature could only explain.

All around the craft the arms were now grasping. Andy's face mask had been knocked off and the beast had a firm grip around his head and the rest of the sub. The squid, thinking he had his sperm whale adversary firmly in tow, began heading back down into the abyss. The sucking-clinging arms seemed to have totally engulfed the sub.

Ed Spaeth, dazed but somehow reacting in a flurry, realized they were descending. He looked to his wrist band that told him their depth. They had gotten to within 30 or 40 feet from the surface when they were attacked and they were now back to 50 feet and descending quickly. Very shortly, there would be no light. Ed grabbed his knife and cut the arm off that was holding the cage next to him; the creature rolled in pain which made it even angrier. It ripped with its other seven tentacles. Andy was nearly unconscious as one vertebra in his neck had popped loose. Ed cut two more of the arms which allowed Stone to finally overcome the strength of the beast and pry open the cage doors. They were now below 70 feet and it was getting very dark, fast. The divers were able to get their head lamps going which startled the squid even more and it moved slightly away for a moment.

Five of the divers were able to break free from the craft and attempted to figure out which direction was up. Ed quickly knew and the others followed him. The submersible fell from site along with the beast and Andy in tow. As fast as possible they ascended, their systems were already under immense stress, getting the bends by rising too quickly could kill them even if they made the surface. Ed read his gauge getting the others to stay near him in a controlled ascent. They kept a constant eye below and could see nothing.

The group finally broke to the surface. The sea was rolling and there was still a lot of light but the sun was getting quite low on the horizon. They were several hundred yards from Black Jack's yacht. Just as soon as they did break surface they were spotted and a rubber boat headed their way. There were a few fist bumps between the divers seeing the boat heading towards them. But for the next two minutes or so, they hung over the depths where an angry creature now lurked with Andy likely still in its grasp. Each of them knew this and each in their own way had to control the feeling of utter horror of what had happened to their friend and what was below them. And where were the rest of the squid?

The boat drew alongside and quickly started assisting them out of the water. Everyone was nearly safe but then just as before, a luminescence pulsed all around. Two of the divers were already in the boat and started reaching to pull the others to safety. Black Jack and Kurt propelled themselves out of the water and onto the side of the boat, slipping inside quickly. A hand came for Stone and he was in. Ed was the only one still in the water. He was following duty as best he could but he wanted in now too.

But he was not quick enough, one of the creatures still workable arms sucked up around Ed's waist. He felt the hooks penetrating through his wet suit as his body was being pulled towards the center of the beast and its parrot-like mouth with razor sharp teeth. It could take off a man's hand or half his head in one bite. Ed still had his knife in one hand. With all his primordial instinct to survive he cut and slashed, he felt the pressure ease on his waist. He pushed away and swam towards the boat which he could see 15 or so feet above him. He selected his angle well and burst from the water with enough speed to propel him over the edge of the craft; one more kick and he was in. "Get out of here," he yelled.

They started to move, but not soon enough. This beast had not given up. Four arms grabbed up over the edge finding Black Jack and Kurt. They had both removed their masks but still had their tanks on. They were dragged out of the boat. Black Jack managed to pull his mask and mouth piece on to his head. Kurt was struggling to do so, but one of his hands was in the grasp of the suckers and hooks on one of Colossi's still working arms. Again the animal was heading for depth, its instinct telling it that the prey would die during the dive. The creature had rolled them up and was holding them close to its belly, Black Jack's ears were popping, from this angle Black Jack could see the grotesque 11 inch wide eye as it studied its prey. He could see he was being pulled head first towards the mandibles of

51

the beast's mouth. Kurt could see nothing as the sea water stung his eyes; he had all but given up.

Black Jack grabbed Kurt's right arm and thrust it into the beast's grinding mouth. Kurt coiled in pain, in doing so he took the swallow of water he'd been resisting taking up until then. The squid sucked the hand in further, this time hitting the titanium wrist band Kurt wore. Several of the beast's teeth were caught; its natural instinct was to expel and both divers were released. Kurt's body had gone into shock; he'd already swallowed water and was drowning. Black Jack was barely able to think as it was and just headed towards the surface as fast as he could. Everything was exploding inside his head. Looking down once to see if the beast was in pursuit, he saw Kurt's listless body drifting slowly into the abyss but he could not see the squid.

The boat had been circling not knowing if the divers would surface again. Black Jack screamed at them as soon as he broke surface. They headed towards him. He kept looking down to see if the creature was coming but he could see nothing. Momentarily he was on the boat. "Is Kurt …" Ed was interrupted.

"Leave, he's dead, get me out of this fucking ocean!"

(Cabo San Lucas, three days later)

"How about over there?" Stone pointed towards a walkway that led to the nearby beach. They'd just completed an interview with law enforcement officers in Cabo San Lucas where they relived the experience they'd had three days earlier off Socorro Island. Seven of the twelve men that went on the dive were dead. Four of the brutally destroyed bodies were eventually found floating on the surface, after two days of searching the effort to find Kurt's body ended.

Ed Spaeth, who was employed by the guide service, had been in discussion with the authorities for nearly four hours. Stone was brought in to verify the story Ed had told them. It all seemed so outrageous. It wasn't the sort of story the locals needed for business so if possible it would be best kept quiet.

Having survived, Black Jack quickly moved to limit the media's attention on him and the story in general. A few calls were made to some well-placed people in the effort to limit the exposure to the press. Families were quickly paid off and the truth of the story, it was hoped, would not go far.

~~~~

"Have you been able to sleep?" Stone asked Ed as they leaned against the rail, medium sized ocean waves were crashing on the nearby rocks.

Ed grasped the rail with both hands and leaned his body back looking towards the blue sky. "Yeah, a couple of hours each night, I'd guess. I've been doing a lot of walking too."

Stone leaned over the upper rail and placed one foot on the lower one. "I didn't sleep at all the night before last. By last night I was so exhausted I finally went out hard. But I must have been reliving it all in some nightmare. When I woke up the whole bed was a mess, I'd kicked things everywhere."

Stone stood up and looked at Ed, "Where the hell did that thing come from? I thought they were confined to the polar ocean and had never been seen up here."

In addition to being a very experienced diver Ed had a great deal of understanding in oceanography, especially concerning the living organisms. "This world is changing a lot. The populations of over eighty percent of the bigger fish in the sea have either gone extinct or are just hanging on. Things change. Creatures that are still alive move into new niches that are opened up by the ones that are gone. The colossal must be moving towards the equator. The Humboldt squid that they feed on have been moving their range so maybe they're just following them?"

Ed continued, "Did you see that picture of Hemingway and his family with the four really big marlins hanging behind them? It was on the charter ship. I think it said it was taken in 1935."

Stone shook his head that he had. "That doesn't happen very much anymore, if ever. The big ones just aren't out there in those numbers. You take away their food supply the way industrial fishing has the last fifty years. Well eventually the bigger fish can't make it because there is not enough to eat. It's going on all around the world. It's part of feeding billions of humans. Between scouring the oceans for fish and growing continents of plant food stocks and humans have exploded in numbers." Ed continued. "There are already 700 times as many humans on Earth compared to hunter gatherer times. Some people think there could be ten billion people by 2050 or 60. How the hell do you feed them all when we're already doing this to the oceans? A billion and a half people are already not getting adequate food; mostly because they can't pay for it."

Stone wasn't sure what to make of the comments Ed was making. He sounded like an enviro. "Hum. How did you get out of the submersible so fast?" Stone asked, remembering the massive confusion just after the squid rammed them and surrounded them with its arms.

Ed had to stop and think for a moment. "That was really strange, after the collision I saw those arms coming in everywhere." He stiffened a bit and shook his head. "My daughter was in a pretty bad wreck a few years ago. The car rolled three or four times. Scared the hell out of me when I got to the scene and saw that car even though I'd been told she was okay. A day or so later I was talking to her and she told me that while she was rolling it seemed like everything was going in super slow motion. All the stuff in the car, like her purse, the can of pop, stuff from the glove compartment, a jacket, etcetera, was floating all around but really really slow. Some voice supposedly told her 'everything will be okay.' Whatever that was?"

Stone was still listening, "I didn't know what to make of what she was saying, I'd heard that other people have had similar experiences." He looked more directly at Stone. "Well that's what happened right then, on the sub, everything went into this super slow motion, I could see how to move my hands, and the best way to cut the squids arm then get the sub hatch open. There wasn't really a voice but it seemed like something else was doing the thinking for me. It's strange that I can remember that segment of time just like I do the part that was going at the speed of life. But obviously I can."

That jogged a memory for Stone, "Geez, I guess, I mean." His mind was working back to that moment too; something had happened to him as well. He turned around and leaned his back against the rail, some people were walking past on the path, "The same kind of thing happened to me, huh. I remember the bubbles were all going really slow and it felt - well, like I could have stepped outside of my body and just watched or something, but I didn't. Hmm?"

"Huh, you too?" Ed remarked.

"So when you thought something else was doing the thinking for you, did you hear anything like a message?"

Ed shook his head that he had not. "No, it was so still, quiet, like nothingness."

Stone then told him, "I didn't really 'hear' a voice either, like a sense of sound, there was just this thought."

"What was it?" Ed then asked.

"What do you believe?" "That was it, 'what do you believe?'" Then it was like the motion picture started again and I was trying to get away from that barbed arm of that thing and follow you out of the sub."

Ed was silent for a short time. "You know that experience has happened to so many people. There must be something to it, something about the way our mind or brains work. Obviously, but what?"

"I don't know, I don't know." Stone reflected.

Ed had one more observation. "Something's not right with our world, it's out of balance." He thought for another moment, "It's us you know, something's out of balance in us."

Chapter Two

(Late May, 2013)

Louis could see the light on his mobile phone begin to blink and then the simple A minor tone sounded on and off, repeating until he answered the call. He could see it was from his brother's wife, Yvette; they had met several times, briefly. The two brothers had grown in such vastly different directions in early adulthood that interactions had basically ended about 20 years earlier. Kurt had decided his brother was an environmental nut case who did not appreciate wealth.

"Hello."

A sullen voice replied, "Louis?"

"Yes."

"This is Yvette."

Louis was silent for a moment; as he suspected that something was wrong. "Hello, Yvette." Louis's voice was tepid? Kurt and Louis' parents had both passed. Other than calling Kurt's other children, Louis would be the only person she would have to contact.

She hesitated for only a moment. "Yes, please steady yourself, Kurt has died in an accident." She was very still. Louis felt his blood pressure suddenly rise. "He drowned in the ocean, diving someplace south of Cabo San Lucas." There was again some silence, Louis was thinking to ask a question, but Yvette continued. "They were attacked by squid," the grotesqueness of the vision sounded in her voice. She relaxed, "I don't know anything else."

Louis felt another shot of adrenaline course through him. The idea that his brother had been attacked by animals in the sea and caused his death led to a deep, nauseating and visceral reaction. He did not even have words to respond with.

He sat down, though Louis was not close "now" with his older brother, there were those times so long ago when they were boys, when they were close. He had to think for a moment to recall his brothers two youngest kid's names. It came to him, 'Sasha and Ian.'

"I told the children just a little while ago. "They're so young, these things are so hard for them to grasp; it's not very real for them yet. Their father was not always so close for them. I don't know."

"Are you at the villa?"

"No, we're actually in Milan." There was some silence. "Louis, his body was not found. The accident occurred in a deep dive, we probably will never have a body to bury."

The vision of his brother's body sinking into the depths of the ocean was very troubling as well. Louis immediately replaced the image with that of his brother as a young boy when they would play.

"We'll have a celebration of his life when we get back. I'll let you know when." Yvette said.

"Yvette, I loved my brother. I did not understand or agree with him very much. I just want you to know that."

"If you really knew, Louis, I think Kurt in some part of himself wished he could be more like you."

Louis was silent as that touched him, "Hum, you think? How do you mean?"

It took her a moment, "In a word, satisfied. He was like someone who could never get enough to eat as he was always hungry. Oh, I'm guilty of it too, I suppose."

"I wish he could have directed that drive in a different way. Oh, let's not go there."

"Louis, Sasha just came in to my room so I'd better take care of her. When I get back to Bakersfield I'll get with you on all this."

"Okay Yvette. I will be thinking about you."

~~~~~

It wasn't that Louis lacked ambition or thought making money was evil. But somewhere along the line he'd come to understand the difference between knowledge and wisdom as it related to money. And he knew that wisdom was elusive and because of that our civilization was now in great danger.

What differentiated him from his brother most were the values Louis had chosen to live by. He was just like everybody. In our daily lives we are continually confronted with forks in the road, we hardly know them as they appear, but little by little they edge us this way and that. Some are bigger and more obvious, many not so much; pick up this book or that, read this article or that. Little by little we form our opinions, what we believe to be true, it's what we call our model of reality. This model can continually morph and grow, sometimes is gets radically modified when we reach "epiphanies." Sometimes we wander down roads that are dead ends and we have to back track; or we just get stuck. And sometimes we go down poorly chosen roads so far it's just not possible to ever get back to the right road. Or at least it doesn't seem worth the effort and the willingness to admit we were wrong. Louis would sometimes think about that when reflecting on the great difference between himself and his brother.

It was in the summer of 1959, when Louis was ten that something extraordinary happened to him. Since he was about seven, he'd been taking the family dog Sasha with him for long walks in the orchards and fields that stretched for miles around their home. His mother Mary kept a close watch and gave him limits within which he was allowed to wander.

Kurt did not seem to share the same interest in wandering. Reading books on science fiction and war, especially the mechanisms and how they worked: machine guns, bazookas, hand grenades, tanks, the list goes on, they all captured Kurt's imagination? By age ten Kurt began working for his dad, he liked the money and the list of things he wanted grew; more and more. Being two years younger Louis was happy to wait to start working.

But Louis had discovered something quite different, just by serendipity, and it wasn't immediately apparent to him. In his wanderings among the rushes, the reeds, the songbirds, the smell of fresh soil, the warmth of the sun or coolness of a breeze, something began to emerge within. It was like the sound of a distant drummer and it drew more near with every adventure. It was closeness to everything around him. Louis had no direct understanding or name for this comfort he felt, but it was like a favorite blanket or color, very soothing. It drew him back.

For hours Louis would often lay in the long grass just looking to the sky, Sasha would lick him on the cheek, then wander a short distance and wait. Sasha found the joy in "stillness" too. There was simple bliss in not thinking, just being.

One late sunny afternoon Louis had wandered a little further from home than in the past, there was a ridge beyond which his mom had asked him not to go. But that was a year ago, he was now ten, it shouldn't be bad if he goes to the end of the ridgeline. There was a grove of scrubby oak with lots of shrubs and grasses growing in and among them that Louis found a little mysterious and enjoyed poking along next to.

A pheasant, a rooster, suddenly jumped, he was startled. A rush of adrenaline raced through his body. As quickly as he was startled he was amazed; the bird was so colorful and metallic; greens, reds, rust, brown, and white around its eyes. How different from the common sparrow, but still a bird.

Walking just a little further, he came to an opening in the grove and then saw someone just on the other side of the barbed wire fence. The person was dressed funny, with a large hat that had a net hanging down over their face. Louis figured out quickly that the person was working with the many boxes that bees were going to and fro from. The person, he couldn't tell if it was a man or woman, did not see him directly. Louis just watched, curious of what the person was doing. Sasha saw the motion and barked.

The man looked his way and smiled. He finished moving the rack in his hand that was filled with honey to a storage box nearby, and then replaced it with a new one. "Hang on there young man," he'd said. Louis started looking around, this place looked far different from all the other farm land around. It seemed to be overflowing with colors and textures that he'd never seen before. And what were those big trees down there?

The old man had noticed Louis out walking around a few times as he stood near the back of his property. He had a well-worn path he'd wander his land on, this area was about as far from his house as he could get and still be on land he owned. The top of the old wooden house could be seen through the thickets and briars about 300 yards distant. He walked up close enough to Louis that the young man could see through his beekeeper's hat and gear, the long grey hair of the man falling down across his forehead, and some of it extending down to about his collar. "What's your dog's name?" the old man asked.

"Sasha," Louis was petting her on the head.

He thought for a moment, "I like that name for a dog, makes her" he'd already noticed how the dog peed, "kind of gentle, I'm thinking." His voice was that of an older man, it wavered just a little, but was friendly and direct.

Louis shrugged his shoulders. "My mom and dad named her when I was two, so I didn't get to say. She's just always been Sasha. Are you getting honey from the bees?" Louis continued.

The gentleman turned and looked at his row of boxes. "Yes, that's exactly what I'm doing. They've been very busy congregating it here for us." Louis assumed by his answer that the man must have a wife. He might even have some kids or grandkids or something, he was getting the honey for.

"I've seen you before, down there near the creek with Sasha. I like to come up to this point with my binoculars and study things. You've been down there a few times while I've been here."

It had never occurred to Louis that someone could be watching him from afar as he wandered around. Hum?

"Where do you live young man?"

Louis pointed back across the valley towards a house he could just barely see.

"Okay, you must be a young Mr. Krastle? I've met your mother and father; very nice people. "Your father," he hesitated for just a moment, "um, he's been quite successful farming. I can see that he works very hard. Your mom too, I'd assume."

Louis just nodded that he agreed. "I guess. Are those sheep down there?" Louis pointed to where some small animals were grazing a few hundred yards away.

"Well close, they're little pygmy goats. They're just pets. We have three of them and they do a good job keeping the grasses down in areas we want them grazing with our chickens. We raise the chickens and sell them."

Louis looked to see if he could see any of the chickens. Yeah there was something moving around down there. He looked beyond, trees went in each direction up and down the valley the man lived in. Louis knew it was Tijera Creek at the bottom of the hill. He had passed over it on the bridge several miles from his house, every once in a while when riding with his parents going somewhere to the east.

"What is your name young man?"

"Louis. My mom named me that but my friends call me Z because I don't like Loueeez very much. It can sound like a girl's name."

"Oh, I don't think so," the old man responded. "There are lots of names that men and women have: Terry, Jody, Lynn and I can probably come up with a lot of others. But if you like Z, I'll call you Zee."

Louis nodded his head.

"If you're not in too much of a hurry, I'll show you a little more of the farm." The old man was gathering up the buckets he'd brought along to carry the honey trays in."My name is E.O. Williamson by the way. I don't go by my given name either."

"Why not?" Louis said, just after helping Sasha get through the barb wire fence.

"Well, E is for Elmer and O is for Olaf. When I was your age I didn't like either of those names, so to my friends I'm Al, but to the rest of the world I'm E.O."

"Those names sound kind of oldish," Louis noted.

"Exactly."

"Do you like learning about plants, Zee?" E.O. asked, as he walked a short distance ahead of Louis and Sam on the gravel-covered walk.

"Yeah, I like knowing the names of plants. When I was a kid, I just thought there were trees and grass and that's all. Now I know that there are different kinds of trees and grass and they have names."

"Okay, well let's stop right here and I'll explain the plants and why they are here." E.O. found a little bit of shade from a nearby tree, Louis and Sasha walked over near him.

"All these plants you see are for our bees. Oh there must be 20 or more annuals and that many biennials. Those are plants that live just one year or two years. There are numerous shrubs that live for many years and then a few trees. Over there, on that sign, there's a list of them all. If you're interested some time we'll botanize and I'll teach you as many as you'd like to know."

Louis just had to stop and look. He didn't have a name for such a setting. A cacophony of color, texture, shape and form would come to mind from a trained artist. However, for a young boy who had never experienced such a place, it was simply awe inspiring. All kinds of bees were buzzing around and none of them bothered him and there was also a hummingbird that whizzed by. In reality there was so much life interacting here that a Ph.D could be earned coming to understand it "just a little" because to "know" the true extent was not possible.

The closer they got to the house, the wider the trail seemed to get. It branched every 40 or 50 feet and led to where more plants were growing.

At each of the branch points E.O. would stop and explain what they had growing down that trail. There was a trail for grapes and raspberries, one for miniature trees with fruit. Then there was the vegetable garden area which was terraced and all kinds of things that were green were growing there.

"Go ahead and pet his head," E.O. said when they reached where the pygmy goats were grazing. They'd been treated with such care since they were young that they had little apprehension to letting the boy touch their heads.

There were a bunch of little chickens running all around nibbling on stuff in the grass. "See over there, the big one with lots of color?"

Louis nodded his head that he did.

"That's the rooster. He's got about 50 hens he keeps an eye on, watching out for predators: owls and hawks. There's two more roosters running around the orchard somewhere with their bunch of hens."

"What do they eat?" Zee asked.

"With everything we have growing around here we have all kinds of seeds of course. Then there's the little bugs all over the soil, and worms. The trick is to get a really healthy soil. You can grow all kinds of things if you have that."

"You mean the dirt?" Zee knew it could be called soil too, though he usually heard the word dirt.

"Well, let's just say there is a huge difference, actually, between those two words, but yes, what you think of as dirt is something like soil." The old man knew he could easily overwhelm his young guest with too much information now. He had a gut feeling that this charming little guy might have that spark of intellect necessary to stimulate his curiosity to understand what he was surrounded by here. Hopefully Louis would get that tingle in his mind, that thing that makes you smile inside, that would excite his imagination and bring him back to learn and "feel" more.

A woman was working in a garden area. There was a gate that protected it so the pygmy goats couldn't get in. "Lou, we have a visitor."

She had been on her knees harvesting some asparagus sprouts and had a basket full of other greens sitting next to her. She stood up, some of her long brown hair streaked in quite a bit of grey fell down from under the wide-brimmed hat she was wearing. At 5 feet 8 inches she was a fairly tall woman. She walked over and extended her hand, "I'm Lou."

It confused the young boy for a moment as his name was almost like hers. "I'm Louis," he had to giggle just a little.

Her full name was Emma Louis and she'd settled on Lou when she was still a young girl. "Well, you have a fine name young man."

E.O. interjected. "He goes by Zee with his friends. Do you suppose Lou can call you Zee too? That would be a little less confusing with her around."

"That's okay," Zee replied.

"Young Mr. Zee and Sasha there found me up with the bees."

"Do you live on the other side of the ridge?" Lou questioned.

Zee turned and pointed, "Ah ha, probably about a mile and a half that way from the top of the ridge."

"His folks are the Krastles'. You know where there place is I think," E.O. said looking at his wife.

"Oh yes, of course," she replied, looking at Zee with a large smile.

"I have a little something I want to show you Zee, then I suppose you'd need to make sure you're getting back home before you're folks start worrying about you."

"My mom told me I always have to be home before the sun is three thumbs above the horizon." Zee lifted his thumbs to show how he'd calculate it.

E.O. smiled, "Yes, that would get you about 45 minutes to sundown, I'd think." He knew of the 15 minutes per thumb rule too. Size of thumbs would play into that some. "That's a handy rule your mom gave you there."

Zee followed as they walked over to the barn, primarily a wood structure with just some stone worked in around the base. The door opened easily, "There's where the chickens roost at night, they need to have their safe place." They walked through another door and into an area under a roof, but open to the air; often seen on barns. "This is where all our magic starts," E.O. said with a grin.

Louis followed the old man but he wasn't quite sure why he'd said magic. Zee saw the four boxes that lined up next to each other, each one was about the size of a kid's bed and there was room to walk in between each of them. E.O. opened up a steel grate cover that allowed air, water, and light to get through but not the chickens or other critters that might wander by. Keeping a very natural air supply to these bins, Zee would later come to understand, was critical to ensuring all went well in these composting boxes.

E.O. put his glove-covered hand down into the brown soil that looked very fluffy and pulled out a large handful. Right away Louis saw the worms and his nose and face wriggled a little at the sight.

"Worms!" Louis said, a bit of disgust and a young boy's joy in his voice.

"Yeah, worms," E.O. responded. "Those little guys are what make this place as productive as it is. That's why I call them magic."

Louis's eyes enlarged and stared more intently at the old man, "How do worms make all your plants grow so good?"

"I can't tell you why. Scientists need to study these little guys more. All people like myself know right now is that if you feed these guys the food they like to eat then they'll poop out for you some extremely good compost and it doesn't smell like the poop you're imagining. And when you spread that on your ground, it pretty quickly starts turning into very productive soil. There are a lot of things I'll need to explain to you about that, but we need to do that later."

Louis smiled at his new friend and shook his head briskly, "Yeah, it doesn't smell like poop to me."

E.O. continued, "My father started building the soil around here over 50 years ago. He told me that there was only a little tiny bit of good soil down along the creek bottom when he started. Everything else was just thick sandy clay. But he knew how to change it some. My father didn't know about the worms though. He's the one that cleared a lot of the pasture area of the small native trees that were here before, and then started making compost to add to the ground to build it, and make it so you could actually grow things. I worked with him when I was a kid about your age. We dug the canals to get the water from the creek to where we needed it. If you come back sometime I'll show you the walls I helped build so we could get flat ground for growing things on. Pretty flat ground makes irrigation a lot easier."

The Williamsons walked with Louis back to the top of their property where the bees were still working, following some intrinsic pattern of life they were born to lead. "Come on Sasha," Louis said as he passed through the barbed wire fence E.O. was holding open for the two of them.

"I'm usually around here in the afternoons. If you see that old green pickup down there by the barn then it's a good bet I'm around. If you want to learn more, just come and find me. We'll do a bit of botanizing and study some plants and bugs."

~~~~~

There was barely one thumb's distance left for the sun before it hit the horizon. Zee was running a little late. "I saw you hiking way out there along the ridge, Mr. Dreamer, and then I couldn't see you for a while. Where did you go?" Mary asked as he came in the back door.

"I met a really nice old guy, his wife too. They live on the other side of the ridge. They've got all kinds of stuff growing over there I've never seen. It's pretty cool."

Mary laughed, mostly for her little son's way of describing this new landscape he'd discovered. She knew that the Williamsons had a farm on that side of the ridge and supplied local people with chickens, and other food stuffs, grown the old-fashioned way. She thought it quaint, but not quite as practical as the newer ways her husband had adopted using more machinery, but still organic.

Louis was intrigued by what he'd learned about the worms. His curiosity would draw him back many times through the coming years as he learned more and more from E.O. and Lou. The fact that they fed him scrumptious food didn't hurt!

~~~~~

Louis stretched himself out across his leather couch and stared at the stain glass window he'd designed, fabricated, and installed in the house he and Minori had built together 15 years earlier. The conversation he'd just had with his sister-in-law triggered the need in him for a stiff drink and silence. As he sat there in the stillness he pondered his life and that of his brother's. He was deeply aware of their differences. Why, in the end, were they so different, he wondered. His mind drifted to earlier times.

This house he sat in, built with a central shinbashira column, similar to the Horyuji pagoda in Japan, making it exceedingly earthquake resilient, was a part of their dream of some land, a few kids, and a way of making a living done to the beat of their own drummer. At many levels "it" reflected the difference Louis sought to understand between himself and his brother. The structure was designed to harmonize with nature, to accept that people are embedded in it as opposed to being a detached force with its own rules and agendas apart from nature.

Shortly after returning from his time at the Rodale Institute in the mid 1970s where he learned the basics of agricultural ecology, Louis had attempted to explain to his brother, Kurt, what he'd learned and how he thought it made so much sense for food production and for the planet. There were already those calling into account the wisdom of using these synthetic chemicals and what the detrimental effects might be.

His mind wandered further back. The final episode that had tipped Louis to follow the principles he learned from Mr. Williamson, was being shown a flock of birds by E.O. that had been killed by DDT, a commonly used agricultural chemical at the time. By late in high school Louis read Rachel Carson's *Silent Spring* and became convinced that his father to some degree, and brother were following the wrong way to grow food. His mother, Mary, was open to her 'little man of the south' and his convictions but she saw no reason to stir things up with her husband and preferred to leave well enough alone. She was proud of Louis though, for being his own man.

E.O. had convinced Louis by the time he was headed for college, that to pursue the life he now dreamed of, he should go to the Rodale Institute in Pennsylvania and learn the latest science of organic farming and animal husbandry. By then, Louis felt deep within him that it was the right path to follow. He knew there was already a growing niche of consumers wanting the better tasting, and reported more nutritional, food. And there were already those beginning in the 50s and 60s and into the middle of the 1970s that thought eating food that had been sprayed with chemicals meant to kill pests, might not be a good thing for people.

~~~~~

Louis and Minori had met while they were both doing some of their undergraduate work at San Joaquin Delta College near Modesto. He had always thought himself the product of some rather exotic union between his German father and Mexican mother. There was something about someone of a far different ethnic group that can be very seductive. Minori sat several seats distant from him in their biochem class, but from the first day she was in the room, Louis had found her gravity to be significant. They would soon fall in love.

The two had decided that Santa Rosa, in the rich valley north of San Francisco, would be the place they'd make their home. Though the wine industry was burgeoning, Louis and Minori decided they would take a different way. Their niche would be high quality food grown purely the way nature had intended. They felt they'd talked to enough people who showed a sincere interest in such products that they'd pursue that angle.

Shortly after finishing their studies at San Joaquin Delta College, both Louis and Minori had headed east to Pennsylvania to attend some of the early classes the Rodale Institute provided. It was there they learned of the now famous book by Sir Albert Howard: *The Soil and Health*. This book taught the relationship between a truly healthy soil and the plants and animals it can support and create. The book introduced the early notion of a *soil-food-web*, where a dynamic interaction of trillions of microscopic organisms in only a few square feet of exceptional soil worked symbiotically to create food stuffs of extraordinary nutrition for those wise enough to enter into this relationship.

Louis and Minori learned the vast difference between this ancient holistic approach to agriculture and the new synthetic and reductionist view of food production. At the nexus was the notion that the farmer or rancher's first order of business was to build the most diverse soil possible, brimming full of micro flora and fauna well-adapted for the geographical location. These were the agents that created and cycled the nutrients and worked in concert with nature's greater players. This "elegant soil" would then propel the synthesis of extraordinary molecular compounds that the body of those humans eating it would nourish their roughly 75 trillion cells into the greatest level of health possible.

These are complex ideas and require people to think about nature, including humans, in an emergent way. They must visualize reality beyond the ordinary and seemingly obvious of everyday existence. Imagine the interaction of atoms, in quantities beyond imagination, guided by forces we only barely can attempt to understand, but manifest in ways that construct us. Imagine just one of your trillions of cells, composed of billions of atoms, where 10,000 biochemical reactions transpire about every second. How do they "know" what to do, what unseen code do they follow?

Louis came to see nature in this wondrous and holistic way. Many times he'd ponder its mysteries. This was something Kurt never did.

He was propelled further when meeting E O. Williamson who shared with him the very curious capacity of some little red worms, to create by passing other materials through their bodies, highly nutrient- enriched soil. Louis had been awe struck that something so small, and kinda funny looking, could be endowed with so much capacity. 'Did they "know" what they were doing?' He sometimes questioned.

Coming to a deep understanding and use of these principles was analogous to building a proper and strong footing for a house: build it correctly and the house will serve you well, build it poorly and it won't. There was a great deal to understand in building great soil, Louis and Minori were eager students and learned much. They returned to the west coast with their new-found knowledge, spirituality, and dedication to their land. This led them to many other revelations about life and living and their levels of consciousness and then to the people they became.

~~~~~

Minori's father, Lester, had grown up in the 1920s on a small farm just to the west of Santa Rosa off of Cherry Ridge Road. Lester was full blooded Pomo Indian – the native people of the area. Minori's mother, who was Japanese, had moved to the area after World War II, leaving the San Juan Islands near Seattle. Minori was their only child and she had been raised on the same farm her father grew up on. Louis and Minori had returned to Santa Rosa in October of 1974 and announced they intended to marry the next spring.

Louis sold his stock in Krastle Enterprises to Kurt shortly before he and Minori married. Their father, Carl, made sure the price per share was reasonable for both sons. He'd hoped that they would both take over the company together, but he understood the difference in philosophies that had emerged in his two sons. "They really couldn't be business partners, as far apart as they were in what they believed," he reconciled.

Money from the stock was enough to put a substantial down payment on the 20 acres of land Minori's parents owned. Once the land was directly theirs to control, Louis and Minori then began intensively improving the soil. It took a few years before their crops began to flourish as they had to figure out the most profitable plants to grow. But eventually they did and so too did their overall business that led to more land and more organically grown plants and animals.

Louis always remembered the free ranging chickens running around with the pygmy goats at E. O. Williamsons place, and as soon as Louis and Minori could, they got into that business too. It was hard work and required ongoing creativity to grow the business, but through the years EEO Farms did grow and so did their brand. The niche areas in the local markets carried their many products all with the label and the funny little red worms on it.

Contrary to his older brother's early notion of Louis' business acumen, he and Minori had been quite successful. They weren't multi-millionaires, but they were comfortable. Louis and Minori first capitalized on the research that showed the reduced nutritional value of food stuffs coming from the industrial agriculture sector. This problem was primarily due to the diminished capacity of the soils to supply the needed micro nutrients after being assaulted with the synthetic chemicals that disrupted the life processes in the soil.

Also, industrial agriculture's selective breeding of plants to provide greater yield, pest resistance, and climate adaptability, seemed to have created plants that were not as capable of assimilating the nutrients as plants from 30 or 40 years earlier were capable of. Significantly so! Louis and Minori quickly marketed this information to their growing customer base which triggered more sales.

Throughout the Bay Area they found many customers for their growing line of products. In addition in her studies, Minori learned of the cutting edge research into "just-in-time" food: the idea that foods, especially the fruits and vegetables, had a quickly diminishing shelf-life for their deep, nutritive, and metabolic system-wide optimum-health-generating qualities, in antioxidants and micronutrients. This is often measured in a few short hours. Humanities early ancestors ate plant matter, eggs, shell fish, and other food stuffs just as quickly as they were found. The concept is that for our foods maximum potency, eating it as quickly after being taken from the ground or the vine the better.

The idea that there was a "window of time" to consume the food, measured by a few hours, in which one gains the most health advantage, resonated with a significant number of people. They became the base for Louis and Minori's "Just-in-time-Greenhouse-foods" enterprise. It started with the greenhouse on their land and grew from there. They fed themselves and a few neighbors' great noon time salads. It caught on quickly and they soon saw the ability to expand. The great knowledge of building "elegant soil" was the corner stone of the business. Their little greenhouses started popping up all around the Bay area with the little red squiggly worms a prominent part of their branding logos.

What people eat, it is proposed, is more than just building blocks for cell material. It also carries vital nutrients and other "information" for the systems in our bodies that protect us from agents that would diminish our health, or our homeostasis. The life Louis and Minori created became pretty much the antithesis of Kurt's. Their paths diverged as Louis had discovered a door to a new level of consciousness, one his brother could have entered too, but he didn't. The longer someone goes past a door, or a fork in the road, the more difficult it becomes (even if there is some part of them that might want to) to back track. They become so invested in the path they have chosen that, considering they might be wrong, is nearly impossible for the ego to accept. This is where so many get stuck.

~~~~~

Minori placed the basket she had in her hand, filled with flowers she'd just cut in the garden, on the top of the bar counter top. "You seem distant," she opened.

Louis sat up and put the glass he'd been sipping the drink from on the small table next to the couch. "There's some bad news. Kurt has died."

"Oh!" Her voice trailed off as if struck in the abdomen. Her hand went over her mouth. She looked at him as her eyes were conveying the question.

"A scuba diving accident, somewhere south of Cabo San Lucas, near some island. Jesus, they were attacked by squid; I can only imagine."

Minori moved over and sat on a chair next to him.

Louis glanced at her then looked out the window, "His body was not found." There was something even darker in the notion that his body could have been consumed by sea creatures or is simply a part of the detritus that accumulates on ocean bottoms normally."He was always looking for the next big thing to thrill him," Louis observed.

Minori stood up and walked over to the window and looked out to the landscape they had built, "Kurt could be so charming. At times, you know, he really could."

"He had that flamboyant side of him, like my dad. He was always a ladies' man. God he must have gotten laid a lot!" There was a touch of jealousy in Louis's voice.

Minori gave him a bit of a blank stare.

Neither said anything for a while then Louis began again. "My mom would sometimes say how Kurt always wanted something more, like he could never get up from the dinner table without still being hungry. He could never be satisfied very long."

"He had a hole in the bottom of his emotional tank?" Minori offered. "How do you think you got the bug to be a wanderer, a day dreamer, and Kurt didn't? You two grew apart although it did sound like you did a lot together when you were little."

"We did, in grade school anyway. His being two years older was a little stretch, and it probably made me work a little harder to keep up. We rode our bikes, played army and through dirt clods at about everything. We were just kids. When I was about eight or nine he'd started working with Dad more. Kurt would hang with him working on the tractor or anything mechanical that needed fixing. That was always just a chore as far as I was concerned, especially by about the time I was ten or so and I'd learned about wandering in the fields. I just loved it. It would just about make me shake with some kind of weird happiness, just wandering through the weeds and the brush." He laughed, "Kurt thought I was nutty wanting to wander around like I did. I don't know, maybe I was." Minori had heard a lot of this before, but it was good to let Louis reflect.

His train of thought stopped for a moment, "Yeah, then when Dad started paying him for working around the farm, that's when we really stopped doing much together. I'd do some work, I needed a little for movies and the arcades, things with my friends. Kurt would get bigger ideas about what he wanted. I think he bought a motorcycle when he was about 15."

Minori had gone to the kitchen and returned with some meat and veggies for them to share. She didn't say anything, but thoughts were formulating in her mind. Her voice was soft, reflexive, like that of a mother carefully explaining to her young daughter the perils of her monthly cycle that was just beginning. "The world asks us, every day many times, who we are, and what we believe. How we answer, thousands of times, becomes who we are. I think your brother didn't hear the questions or feel the tickles that come from the stillness. His ego was turned up too loud. You can't hear or feel that which comes from the stillness if you are too loud. I fear that so many are like Kurt, their own drummer beating so loudly that they don't hear that voice in nature calling to them, and our world suffers greatly."

Louis thought there was something extraordinary in what she was saying, "Those levels of consciousness we've been studying and people's world views, those are the real things that differentiate people, aren't they? They're at the root of why people are so out of control around the planet. It's what they know, and what they believe to be true."

He took another small sip of his drink, "My brother never listened to the stillness, like you say where you get drawn to the truth. It's really through grace you experience the joy of just looking at a perfectly-formed flower." He was stuck; the world to him was something to control, to dominate. I can remember him telling me about American Manifest Destiny when we were just in our 20s. It gave Europeans the supposed right to dominate the native people and nature as well. He saw nature as a commodity to control and break up into little pieces to sell, rather than the unfathomably complex holistic spiritual system that it is. He missed *completely* what it truly is and our place in it. In my opinion, Kurt's values, were about the opposite of where they needed to be and I don't think he was ever truly happy because of that."

Minori then offered, "Our world, certainly can be a very dangerous place, and you always have to be aware of that. But you can also learn to love and live in awe of creation, its complexity and elegance, and live like a respectful guest. Maybe that's the biggest thing your brother did not understand, we are all just guests here."

Louis gathered his thoughts for a moment. He was formulating a way to complete his feelings towards his brother. "When we were young my mother would sometimes tell him he was trying to turn stones into bread. You know the first temptation of Jesus. I never did understand why she said that, and it never occurred to me to ask her before she died. But I think I know now what she meant: there are limits to the tinkering with nature we humans can do wisely and there's a point where we have to recognize when we don't know what we don't know. To me, we are all embedded in nature and we need to understand and respect our place. We have to move with exceeding caution using this brain and mind we have inherited. It can serve us well, and it could very well lead us to our demise. I think we're like some dinky ephemeral part of an eternal dance made up by something else. We can learn the steps and fit in and dance with the creator, or ..." He looked towards Minori, slightly shaking his head, "We can ignore that and continue to see ourselves the way my brother did, as separate and in charge of the dance, and see what it gets us. I think the creator would opt for a new dancer."

Part Two: Hopes and Dreams

Chapter Three

(Washington D.C., February 2013)

"Looks like snow." Helen spread the drapes a bit wider and stood for a moment looking out across the grounds of the White House towards a sky that was rapidly melting into blue, purple, and black; punctuated by the fluffy particles of ice falling straight to the ground. They could be seen into the distance illuminated by the lights of the city just initiating for the evening.

Troy leaned back, adjusted his squarish-brown Italian glasses to a place a little higher on his nose, and looked outside, "We're going to get quite a bit it looks like. When I was a kid that was good, I'd rather not battle driving in it now."

Helen looked off to the distance and continued, "I just love watching it fall. I remember sitting upstairs in my room, years ago in Buffalo, watching it come down and cover everything. It makes the world look entirely different. There are so many soft lines." She continued to gaze. "I hear this is going to be a big storm, people are really hunkering down in Boston," saying that made her think of her friend that lives there.

"When are these storms going to give us a break?" Helen said, mostly to herself, Troy's head and concentration was still stuck on the letter he was reading.

Helen walked back to her desk where she could continue to read through the volumes of letters that were sent to President Obama every day. They were his contact to the ordinary people, his way to take the deep pulse of the country. With 65,000 paper letters coming to the White House every day, picking out the ten that should be chosen to go to the President each day was a challenge. She had a large staff who sorted them as to the topics: health care, jobs, the wars, environment, how they spent their stimulus checks, it went on. Helen's job was to get them whittled down to a reasonable number that Mike could go through and make the final selection.

There had been a lot about jobs lately; the lack of them. Like the kind of jobs that a man could raise a family on. The last one in particular had hit a nerve. 'Was it really like that in America,' she asked herself?

Dear President Obama,

I don't know if this letter will ever get to you, it doesn't matter for me I guess as I'll probably be gone by the time it gets to you anyway. But maybe by you reading this somebody else might not end up like me. I've never written a letter to somebody that's as important in this world as you are. I hope I sound reasonably intelligent, I do try.

Well, anyway, here's what I want to tell you about. A month ago I turned sixty one; I started working full time in about 1976. I guess I'm pretty much an ordinary kind of guy, I didn't set the world on fire in school, I wasn't ever very sure what I wanted to do "when I grow up" like they always say. I always liked building things though, so I worked in the construction trades in the seventies and eighties doing carpentry mostly. In the early nineties I learned that you could get a degree in computer drafting. I liked that idea because it still had to do with building things, kind of creative I guess too, and it was a lot easier on your body. I did that and got a good job. I was doing pretty well at it too, that is until the recession hit.

I went through a divorce in the late nineties that set me back. But things got going again and I was able to pay off my little house. When the boom was going on I decided to invest in an office building a developer was doing. I borrowed the money against my house. Everybody was saying it would be a good investment, like a retirement nest egg. I talked to all the people I could think of: real estate, my 401K advisor, the bankers, they all said it would be a good deal. That was in the fall of 2006.

I lost my job in about June of 2008 and with it my health insurance. We were hearing we'd be back to work in a few months. That's not what happened. I didn't have a lot of free cash, that's some of my own fault in all this. But you know the story. I went through my unemployment insurance, when that ran out I started drawing on money I had in different funds. It's not like your bills stop coming. I was in my late fifties then, it's not like you can just get another job real easily. I'd been taking a risk that I wouldn't have any-

thing happen that cost me much; I've been pretty healthy all my life, so I gambled that I wouldn't need that expensive health insurance. At $500 a month I couldn't pay for it and everything else. Well, I gambled wrong. I started getting this ache in the back of my neck, I put up with it for a few weeks but it wouldn't stop, I couldn't sleep. So I finally went to the doctor. They did their tests and told me to come back in a couple of weeks. The pills they gave to help with sleep cost a bunch, which I had to pay for in cash, and after a few days they just made my head feel like a lump of cold meat.

I could tell when the doctor walked into the room he had bad news. He told me I had cancer and it was in a real bad place to operate on. He asked me about what sort of work I'd done years ago and in particular wanted to know if I'd ever built anything using railroad ties. I told him I had, for a couple of summers I worked for a landscaping company; those kinds of walls were the big thing back in the seventies. I learned later that he'd had some other guys that had my kind of cancer that had done that kind of work. We all just thought we were getting all buff and a great tan, nobody told us that stuff could give us cancer and kill us.

They've told me about a few procedures that might help but I'd have to pay up front for them. Which if I was going to be alive would take me five years to pay off ... that is if I had a job. The value of my house is less than what I owe on the of-fice building, so even if I could sell my house I wouldn't have enough money to pay off what I owe on the office building. If this damn recession hadn't happened I'd have my health insurance and I'd probably be able to pay for the procedure I need, but now the doctors know I don't have the money. So I get to check out earlier than I'd planned. I do believe in personal responsibility and tried hard to live that way. But it just seems that sometimes things other people do, like sneaky screwing up the economy, cause unforeseen and unfair problems for pretty innocent people.

I sure hope there is something else after we die; it's been kinda rough here. So, Mr. President of the United States of America, I think you are a good guy, I think you care about people like me. I hope you will keep this in mind as you are

*working on health care reform and everything else that af-
fects people's lives. Do you think those jerks on Wall Street
ever think about what they do to people out in the world? If
you can throw a few of those guys in jail I'd sure appreciate
it.*

*Very truly yours,
M. James Mallard*

Helen walked back to her desk and put the letter from Mr. Mallard in
the "to the President" pile. She sat down and took a sip of water from the
glass she kept near during the day. "The world is exceedingly beautiful
and it's incredibly mean all at the same time, don't you think Troy?"

Troy turned his head from the reading he was doing, "What?"

"It's beautiful and it's mean, and indifferent. I almost think that indifferent bothers me more. It's like nothing is at the wheel." She'd answered.

"Yeah, you read enough of these stories, you get pretty numb." Troy
turned back to what he was doing.

"I liked the world a lot more when I was ten; I hadn't lived long
enough to get a little jaded by everything. A fresh blanket of snow was
even more beautiful then."

~~~~~

The effects of two large glasses of red wine were making her mellow,
just the feeling she liked after considering all the voices coming from the
country every day. Helen was sitting on that large rose-colored reclining
chair she'd spotted and purchased years earlier. The snow was still falling
two hours after getting home. The small meal she'd fixed was settling. It
was a good time to drift her eyes across the pictures of friends and family
that were displayed above the book case. She stopped when she reached
the picture of the blond haired young lady standing by herself next to a
waterfall, a mist rising behind her. Helen had been thinking she needed to
call Joan, her friend going all the way back to their days at Boston College.
'What a beautiful campus,' she was thinking. 'It must really be snowing in
Boston, maybe Joan would be at home on a Friday night given the severe
weather?'

Joan's number was speed dialed. It rang four times before her old
friend answered. "Hello."

"Are you decent?" Joan knew the voice as they called each other every
two or three months.

"Only when I'm forced to be," Joan answered.

Helen was laughing, knowing how Joan liked to tease. "How've you been?"

"Oh, busy, but I've had a few days off here recently, been doing a bit of house cleaning, organizing. It's kind of amazing the things you find stuffed away. I found a card from Harry he'd sent me a few weeks before nine eleven. He sounded so good." She stopped for a moment to let the emotion pass.

"Is it anything you can share with me?"

"Oh, yeah, well kind of," her voice dropping remembering the part about an intimate time she should keep to herself. "I think he was just happy, he'd had that awful divorce, and I think I could just hear the sunshine in his writing. We both knew how easy the connection was for us. Oh, I shouldn't." Joan was shaking her head, knowing for her own sake she should not spend much more time there.

"Have you heard from this David?" Helen knew she should move the conversation forward.

"Yes!" Her pitch changed and she seemed up-beat. "We talked the other night for several hours. He is very interesting and bright. I've been learning a lot about his childhood. He lost his mom when he was really young and of course it had a huge influence on him. He thinks that had she not died he might not have got the deep bug about science. But that's hard to say for sure."

"Why does he think his mom dying had the affect of him getting the bug for science?"

"It gave him a place to put his anger and anxiety. He was just in grade school. I can't imagine having lost my mom then. Kids go different ways at cross roads like that. He just decided he was going to be this great student."

"Well, he had to have some natural talent, lots of effort and desire doesn't always mean you'll have success. Are you going to see him anytime soon?"

A smile emerged on Joan's face, though no one could see it. "We've actually got a trip planned. We're going to meet in Salt Lake in March and then drive down to Moab, Utah. He says it's an incredible place. We plan to rent a big four wheeler and do some touring around. Some other people might join us, it sounds like. I'm excited!"

"Sounds maybe a little serious?" Helen was speculating.

"I try not to let my mind wander too far from the present. Relationships are light and fun, and then they're suddenly muddy. But the alternative is emptiness; so we fail and we fail and we still try some more. Gluttons are we all." Joan's voice again seemed to depart to another place.

"Oh, did I tell you that he's been invited to be involved in the Human Proteome Project?"

"I don't think so, sounds interesting."

"It's an international effort, Dave says there are teams from China, Switzerland, Italy, I don't know and I think France, probably others. He's with a group here that's working on Chromosome #17. That's about all I really need to know, it gets pretty heavy to understand, but he tells me a little."

"How's work?" Helen asked, moving the conversation in a new direction.

"Oh, I'm with the group now that's focusing on the student loan debt crisis, another of our fine nation's debacles. So I've been traveling all around the country gathering information for Jill, my boss. We're trying to get a real clear picture of what's going on; uh, these poor kids."

"How so?" Helen responded.

"They're now at collectively over a trillion dollars that's owed. Something like two-thirds of the graduating seniors are in debt, and pretty serious debt."

"What do you mean by serious?" Helen asked.

"Twenty-nine to $30,000, and some a lot more," Joan responded. "That wouldn't be such a big deal if there were actually jobs for them that paid a salary they could live on and pay back their loans. They're not all like me and have a silver spoon to feed them with." The fact that her uncle had left her a small fortune was not lost on Joan's conscience. She knew she was just very very lucky.

"You've always been so aware of that Joan. If only a larger-portion of the rest of the world's elites would see themselves as you do."

"Some do. And I'm not a saint, Helen. I spend plenty on myself. I just try to keep it all in perspective. I love the work I do, but most of the stuff I work on shouldn't even exist since they are always about some group taking advantage of another group or just really bad policy. But I don't think I could do this if I didn't have the financial stability my family gave me."

"So what are these kids up against?" Helen continued.

Joan thought for a moment, "What aren't they up against?" She said that with her mind fixing on the bigger picture of the world. "Well, they're all being told they need a college degree and probably a graduate degree if they want to be able to have a good job these days; have a middle class standard of living. So they've been doing that, the problem is they get out of school and there aren't the jobs, like I said…with good salaries. Oh there are jobs for some of them for sure, like the jobs where you design robots and software that replace workers. The people with money really like those kinds of jobs."

"There is this idea floating around that the government should purchase at least some part of the loans; get these kids out from under such crushing debt. There's more student loan debt in the country than there is credit card debt. You know we bailed out the bankers to the tune of billions of dollars. Then they took the money and in a lot of cases paid themselves bonuses. One top Wall Street executive said 2009 may have been their best year ever. The gaul! It didn't substantially get directed back to where jobs would be created. These people are guilty of the worst kind of fraud but because of their tentacles in the government they get away with it!"

"I've heard that most of the loans have been paid back, and early in some cases." Helen observed.

"Yes, but that's little consolation for everyone that lost their houses and often times much of their life's savings because of the crash and don't have the time left in their life to make it back."

Joan had another anecdote to share, "I met this one kid, he'd got a degree from a technology school to do networking, when he was done he had about $40,000 of debt and couldn't get a job. Maybe he's not that good, but if he wasn't why did he get through school?"

"Cause they wanted his money," Helen answered sarcastically.

Joan was shaking her head that she agreed. "He has a job driving a school bus for a nonprofit organization now. Not exactly what you need if you're going to pay off that much money and have an apartment, or God forbid, buy a house. In Europe so much of this schooling is paid for. It's all about how a society shares the wealth. Anyway, that's what I'm working on." Joan was walking towards her window, "My goodness the snow is really coming down. The weathermen have been saying we could set some records. I know Dave would say this is to be expected with climate change."

"Anyway, how about you?" Joan then asked, wanting to know more about her friend.

Helen had just checked the snow falling also. "We're going to get quite a bit too it looks like to me." Joan's question settled in her mind. "Oh, reading all these letters from people, you really get a much bigger picture of what's going on out there in the world. You start seeing how the thoughtless actions of some can reverberate through society and cause enormous suffering to total strangers that had no idea how those actions would adversely affect them. There can be so many chaotic ramifications of things. Some of it is so heartbreaking. There was a letter from some guy in the Portland, Oregon area that I read just before heading home tonight. He's going to die from cancer. He knows it, and it's likely that had his insurance not lapsed he could have received the surgery that would have saved him. How horrible. Evidently his cash flow got very bad due to the recession so he took a gamble that he could go without it for a few years. Sometime after he let it lapse, he learns of this cancer."

Helen was shaking her head and pounding her fingers on one knee. She had more to say. "Those bastards on Wall Street, those greedy little bastards, they could care less what they do to people in their ugly quest for excessive wealth." Her voice was filled with indignation.

Joan thought of something to share. "I know of a young gal who lives in Reno that my sister Rene knows. This gal is actually a good friend of her friend Dana," Joan continued, "She might be one of the poster children for the recession."

"How's that?" Helen asked.

"Oh, Rene tells me that she had gone to a technical school and got a degree in computer drafting. It probably entailed more than that, but in essence that's what she studied.

From what my sister tells me when the collapse of the housing market came she and her husband lost their jobs. Like most people, they went on unemployment and rather half heartedly looked for new work, which, to be fair, didn't exist."

"This starts in 2008. By 2010, they are pretty much out of unemployment and of course, they didn't have any real savings. Here's the tragic part that nobody really knew: her husband, who was just in his early 30s had lost a little boy in a drowning accident years earlier when he was in his early 20s. He'd left the kid with some friends and they failed to watch him properly. The mother of the child was gone and he was raising the kid himself; and from what I hear he very much loved the child. I don't know the details, but I'd guess he had a dead son on one side and some friends on the other. That's got to make for a horrific nightmare. Lidia, that's the gal who was married to him, says he was drinking too much when they met but it was tolerable. She loved him and they got married."

"So the recession starts and they can't get work. The debts pile up that they can't pay, so eventually the bill collectors start calling. He starts drinking a lot more. Finally, Lidia can't take it anymore and they separate. She's living virtually day to day. She gets food stamps, borrows money from anyone that will help her. Rene says she truly was looking for work. She went to 20 or 30 job interviews with follow-ups, but couldn't get hired. Then, late last year Rene hears that Justin was killed. He'd been riding home with some friends after a party. Of course he and his friends were very drunk, and they somehow manage to hit a telephone pole. I guess the other two in the car lived and Justin was the only one killed. People say he never got over the loss of his boy. How do you if you have any kind of a heart?"

"Of course they should have been wiser with their money, but the severity of the recession was caused by people who could care less about how their activities affected the vulnerable, like those kids. The root of all these problems is people who just don't care about what they're doing to others. It's all about them."

Helen's breathing had slowed and she gazed with more penetration into the snow falling just outside her window. "How horrible! Life can be so totally unfair. You have to put those kinds of things out of your mind if you want any joy in your own life."

"Yes, but, well sorry, it goes on, poor Lidia is still married to the guy. They just aren't living together, so she's a widow. For several months after all this she still is living off the generosity of others around her. And then one day she just disappears, like she just fell off the planet. The fear is she died. Rene has no idea where she went. Who knows what forces caught up with her?"

"That story, though, can probably be told a few hundred thousand times where the details change just a little bit. The dynamics of a system that gets a little out of balance, can, for some people, be deadly; depending on your circumstances."

"I don't think we'd have near as many problems if so many people hadn't left the farms. If you have some descent land with water, at least you can raise your own food; just think how much more stable our society would be if those tens of millions of people living in the cities hadn't been driven off the land over the last hundred years. It was a definite plan by business people to get control of the land. Once they had control of it, a pretty small number of people, could then sell commodity crops around the world and make outrageous amounts of money. Again, it's all about them." Joan said.

"Hum, how about we change the subject a little bit?" Helen asked.

"Okay." Joan responded, and then asked. "Have you done anything more with this Frank guy? It sounded like you enjoyed going to dinner with him."

"We've talked a few times on the phone. He's gone a lot with State Department business; it doesn't make it very easy to have a relationship. He interacts with Hillary every once in a while so it's fun to hear the details that he can talk about. I have very much enjoyed the times we've gone to dinner; he's very considerate and interesting. Every once in a while you'll see him stop in mid sentence as he's thinking if he can tell me something or not. Washington is filled with secrets you know."

"Yes, the mind game capital of the world, wouldn't you say?" Joan queried.

"Probably," Helen responded.

A few moments passed, "what do you think we expected for our lives by this point back when we were in college? What, 15 years ago?" Joan asked.

Helen laughed, "I couldn't tell you exactly, I probably thought I'd get married and have some kids, and maybe a white picket fence like my mom always talked about. One very big problem though, finding Mr. Wonderful."

"Yes, so true." Joan's mind slipped to thinking about Dave. "This guy's very interesting."

"Oh, a little more about your new guy?" Helen's voice had that 'I'm pretty curious tone to it.'

There was a little smile in Joan's voice as she began. "Have you heard of this organization, or maybe movement, it's called *The Kingdom of Good*?"

"No, but that sounds familiar."

"It should, it's a tweaking of the Christian concept of The Kingdom of God."

"Just a second, I'm going to get more comfortable in this chair, this sounds interesting. Okay, so *The Kingdom of Good*. Sounds, what, I guess big. I haven't heard anything about this."

"It's a pretty big idea alright, I'd say. Okay, let me explain. So, I think it was in 2010 my friend Dave was touring Europe with a buddy of his from college, a guy named Matt Lundquist. They start seeing these posters on the walls of the train stations they were going through talking about this lecture this Dr. Sherman was giving all over the continent. It was about the climate crisis, but even more it was about the crisis of human consciousness, that this Dr. Sherman said was the true root of the problem. I guess I should say problems as he outlines all these things humans are doing that, taken together, are just not sustainable and leading to, well, in the worst case he says, a massive loss of our population 95, 98 percent, and at the very worst our extinction."

"Extinction?" Helen's voice rose distinctly. "This Dr. Sherman thinks we could go extinct? In how long?"

"Well, that of course is not knowable, but supposedly some pretty knowledgeable scientists think by the end of this century things could be really getting bad if we don't change dramatically what we're doing. And if things really spiral out of control, which they think is possible maybe in a hundred, hundred and fifty or two, three, four hundred years. There are so many variables that could happen like pandemics or nuclear war because of breakdowns of civilization. Or maybe something we're missing entirely right now. It's really scary."

Joan moved from where she was sitting so she could take a quick glance out the window. "Holy cow, the snow is still really coming down. The lights are so pretty glistening through the snow. Makes you wonder if there will be any snow in a few hundred years? What a crazy thought." She moved back to her chair. "There's this really great website *The Kingdom of Good.com* where all this information has been put together. It's really well done and fascinating. It explains and uses these very intuitive graphics to help.

Joan was thinking. "What, I guess it helps to visualize where we're at ecologically, based on our evolution of consciousness. It sounds haughty, but if you just take it slow and think about what this Dr. Sherman is saying, it eventually seems to really make sense."

"So how does he say we're going wrong?"

"Umm, mostly I'd say he thinks we just didn't understand the world, you know, how it works biologically and ecologically. The industrial revolution began in the 18th century, and then exploded during the 20th century. We built this new civilization without truly knowing the limits that we had to live within, and now we're living with the consequences of that. Oh, I saw this one analogy where he says that humanity was something like a thirteen year old obnoxious boy getting hold of a Maserati. He terrorizes people with it to begin with and eventually totally trashes it because he has no idea or desire of the need of how to treat or take care of it."

"That could be one of my nephews," Helen quipped.

"It's the immature mind: our, let me think … biological urge to reproduce and control more space, ancient motivations that nearly all creatures seem to have." She laughed, "I read that some place and I think it's funny. "Well, we have that too. This Dr. Sherman said because of our unique bodies and brains we gained this level of thinking power and the ability to create stuff that when it's not used wisely, we end up tearing the planet apart. We're destabilizing the balance, he says, and the balance is what we're adapted to and we're just screwing it up. Industry started doing all kinds of things before our science and understanding of how things fit and work together emerged. Our science was behind our industry."

"So he says that "sin" is really just not living in "the way" and the way that comes from the Buddhist teachings is all about how to live in a holy way. And holy can be thought of as "holistic" which sees life and existence as a whole. Something that's all connected, and if you treat it like it's just a bunch of independent pieces, like a mechanism, it's like pulling parts out of a car engine, the whole thing is eventually going to break down."

"Who is this Dr. Sherman anyway, I've never heard of him?"

"He's English, he's like a professor and a theologian; he taught at the University of East Anglia, it's near London."

"And so what is this *Kingdom of Good* then?" Helen knew this was all leading to something.

"Okay, so did you know that scholars think the main message Jesus was conveying was this idea of The Kingdom of God? That's how we've all heard it called, at least I did." Joan explained.

"I guess I didn't know that, huh, what sort of Catholic does that make me?"

"Well, not many people do. So, anyway, this Dr. Sherman somehow makes the connection that this Kingdom of God should actually be called *The Kingdom of Good* since it's the action in our minds, the goodness, that's the central quality which is most critical for our survival. And he explains this part where when Northern Europeans learn about this concept from early Christian missionaries, their word for good is "godt" which of course just sounds like the way we say God today. So, that's where he says the meaning kind of got changed. He says that true goodness is like God or the divine entering our sphere of reality through our consciousness. Dr. Sherman thinks that without goodness, which he says is like …" she had to stop and think. "the deep reverence, awe, respect, for the divine and all its creation, and the sense of responsibility to carefully and lovingly care for everything and everyone. Something like that. Then beings with our ability to manipulate the world just won't be able to live sustainably on this plan-et. We'll just trash the environment, like we're doing, and then kill our-selves off as our ego's rule our decision making process; we don't let goodness enter and guide us in a way that works. Just look at the problems in the Middle East: the root of their conflicts are complex, of course, but simple too. Ecological breakdown is already happening there. Part of the Syria thing really started with farmers crops failure and the government not helping out. A critical number of people there simply have not emerged to exist emotionally in *The Kingdom of Good*. Though I'm sure there are quite a few that have. It must be incredibility frustrating for so many there."

Joan went on, "So there is this one graphic that shows these seven lev-els of consciousness that across humanity seem to exist. For example a new born baby is at one extreme level, and maybe a starving one at the extreme of that level. And let's say Albert Einstein or some Nobel Peace prize winner, the Buddha or Jesus, at the other end. You move up through the levels based on a lot of things; like your native intelligence, curiosity, richness or scarceness of the environment around you, how much love you encounter, things you choose to grow and learn about, lots and lots of things. And then there's like this major break level he points to, I think it's from level four to level five, that's the critical jump, he says when you are ready through learning and experience and the freeness of your spirit, and you naturally make that transition. *You pass from the ego-captured organismal level to the transformational spiritual level.* And when you do, one of the critical things that occurs in your consciousness is that you come to see all humans as just one part of the whole of nature, not separate."

You see all of nature this way; it's all connected through what's called the Akashic Field. This is where it gets very esoteric, some people say this "field" is the mind of God or divinity and it connects everything across the entire universe, and maybe beyond. How can we know? But something must be connecting everything, how else does everything "know" how to work with everything else? Do you get what I'm saying? How do these uncountable number of particles *know* what to do?"

He came up with this other really interesting idea where he simplified what are considered the 2 most important commandments: love god and all people with all of your heart, mind, and soul. You remember that from catechism don't you?

"Yes." Helen replied.

"Well, he simplifies that to just one short sentence: Love Creation Entirely. It seems so simple and elegant to me. Of course, if you love something you hold it in the highest esteem and creation is the most tangible expression of divinity which includes all of nature including us. So if you love all of that entirely you must take care of it. He calls it the central moral ethos for humanity. Everybody has to decide for themselves, but it seems like a really good way to organize your life and civilization if we could."

"Oh my, I will have to review that. What an idea!" Helen seemed truly inspired.

Joan continued. "I love the graphics he uses to depict all this too. He has one where life is shown like a river moving along with all this incalculable interaction and evolution (little and always ongoing changes) in the parts. All the parts are ultimately connected and dependent on the whole. But humans didn't understand that well enough and so now we're off on a stretch of the river that's headed for a thousand foot cliff. And too many people just aren't paying enough attention to how turbulent things are getting, though huge numbers of people are waving their hands and warning everybody else."

"But the scientists say we're running out of time to get out of this diversion stream and back onto the one that goes on far into the future. To some sort of nirvana that potentially awaits humanity out there. Somewhere in the future, if enough people cross into the consciousness level of *The Kingdom of Good* where they accept the problems and our responsibility to react to them, we might reach this nirvana."

"But we have to wake up real soon and not go over that cliff. He has the idea of a Mephistopheles Moment where we pass some temperature threshold where we lose all control of the heating and our future. It's really scary. To avoid that cliff takes letting go of the false notions a lot of people have had about how things are. And a lot of people have to give up on a massive amount of wealth and power they have. Of course "that" right there is one of the biggest obstacles. So many people will just deny reality even when some part of their mind is telling them the problems with our civilization are true. Like they say, these facts are real inconvenient for certain people."

"It all sounds very complicated," Helen had now moved to her own window to check on the snow, she had the same feeling as Joan, seeing the lights as they twinkled through the snowflakes. "What is it going to take to keep some horrible future from happening? What kind of world are we leaving to the kids?" Helen's voice was worried.

Joan was thinking deeply about Helen's very prescient question. 'What will it take?' Joan had to stop and think for some time before answering.

"Well, I think it will take enough people to let go and wake up and do the right thing regardless of how much money or power they have to forfeit. Those that resist and deny the most are either tethered to something they think they can't let go of. Almost like when you're first learning to ride a bike and your parent is helping you keep it balanced, then at some point that leap of faith happens and you break free from the bond. Or they are simply evil and would rather destroy the planet, and let people in the future deal with the cruelty that will unfold. But they just deny that will happen in their own minds. That's the convenient thing to do. Rather than give up on what they see as their wealth and power base."

Helen reacted, "Oh my, it's all connected isn't it? How much so many just think about themselves or how little they think about everyone else, including those that haven't been born yet."

"*The Kingdom of Good*, hum. I'll take a look at that website. I think there must be a lot to be learned there." Helen said.

There was a smile on Joan's face, "Oh yes, it's like taking a class in philosophy and ecology, politics too. So interesting, and I'd say it all makes sense to me. But that's just me as it's going to take millions of people to resonate with it, and respond. God I hope they do!"

Time passed and the beautiful snow continued to fall. Their conversation moved to memories from college, and a lot of frivolous things which was fun and easy and allowed for some joy to slip in; it was the joy that was most precious. When they both finally hung up each realized how wonderful it is to have a truly trustworthy and dear friend!

Chapter Four

Matt filled his plate with some baked chicken, yams, cranberries, mixed greens, and a scoop of his favorite guacamole. 'Uum,' he loved that Hepe's mix that he always seasoned it with. There was a glass of red wine and ice water too. It was Friday night and he was settling in to listen to the rant coming from MSNBC; he liked Ed in particular. The night before, the 14th ,Valentine's Day, he'd spent most of the evening on Skype talking to Maria. She was back in Bilbao; their meeting in Boise had gone well. Their feelings for each other had grown even deeper. Now they would have to plan the next time they could be together.

The phone rang, Matt hit his mute button. He could see the call was from David Herrick, who was now back living in San Diego.

"Poncho," Matt answered.

"Matt, I haven't heard myself called that for a while, takes me back to college."

"Hey man, yeah it's just fun to call you that; good to hear your voice. What's goin' on? "

"Did I get you at a good time?" Dave asked.

"Yeah, good enough, I'm eating a bit, but that's alright I need to take little bites. What's up?"

"Just missed you man, thought we needed to bond." Dave said, with a grin in his voice.

"How sensitive of you; you been taking pinky pills or something?" Matt teased back.

"No, but I've been smoking dope with a hippy girl with dreadlocks. What do you think?"

"Did she smell better than your dog?"

"Actually, I have to admit there is something pretty erotic about the smell of a woman that's like that. It's musky, but whew I'll tell you my inner Neanderthal started poking his head up some."

"Did you get a knee knocker with her?" Matt thought his friend might find that one fun.

"Getting ahead of the story aren't you?"

"Maybe, but I want to know before we're done. Where'd you meet her, what's the deal?"

"Okay, yeah I haven't told you about this. Here's the short version. I had this conference in Eugene last summer, so instead of flying I decided to drive. As I'm driving through the Salinas Valley, I start hearing on the radio that it's the Summer of Love reunion in Haight-Ashbury. You know in San Francisco?"

"Ah, yeah I think so." Matt was eating, taking tiny bites.

"So I get there and start wandering around and stop into a Ben and Jerry's ice cream place. I get something and as I'm leaving this Amazon Hippie girl with dreadlocks comes up to me and asked if I'd ever had a schweddy balls."

"No, really? Make your tummy turn?"

"I'm pretty sure I felt something. Anyway, she has this idea to go wandering off around this park that's real close."

"What's this girl's name?"

"Alicia, like Alice, it'll make sense in a sec."

"So we find some nice place in the park and start smoking some of her pot. I don't know if it's just me or if what she had was some super duper pot. All I know is that I went off on a trip pretty fast. Funny thing is that I remember this trip better than I do most of my normal dreams. Somehow my brain synthesized what I'd recently learned about the near extinction event for humans about 74,000 years ago."

Matt interrupted, "Really, I hadn't heard about that, but it's interesting. Sorry, go ahead."

"Well, actually you did, Dr. Sherman talked briefly about it. You were probably studying Maria about then. But anyway, so this girl Alicia is in this dream, but she's even more rustic than the way she looks now, like more hair on her face. She was skinnier, hard defined muscles, and her skin was brown and red, and she had those dreadlocks. You know that song White Rabbit by the Jefferson Airplane?"

"Yeah."

"So I"d heard it recently, that's going in my head and that lyric that goes 'remember what the door mouse said: 'feed your head, feed your head' that's going along. And then I realize what my kooky mind was whipping up for me; what I'm supposed to be getting from all this."

"What's that?"

"She figures out a new food source, well mostly she figured out how to capture a new food source, with a trap the fish would swim into made out of branches. Then I get it: feed your head, feed your head. Bottom line is you gotta eat, you need replacement energy."

"So what's the point of it all?" Matt questioned.

"I've been trying to figure that out myself. Then the other morning I was just sitting quiet with my coffee and what it might mean comes to me. That girl represented the force that got our human ancestry through that bottleneck when we almost went extinct. She made the difference. She had the imagination and insight to figure out a way to get the food they needed to survive. It was her will that made the difference. Maybe just one person tipped the balance for the entire species and for all of us that exist today, because she imagined what she did."

"You think it could really have come down to that?" Matt was gazing off to his ceiling trying to visualize that setting.

"We'll never know of course, but my bet is that it wasn't too many individuals that made the difference. For some reason I had that dream. Where did it come from?"

Matt started to hum the repeating line from The Twilight Zone. "We're a couple of nerds you know," Matt said, understanding how ethereal he and Poncho could be in their conversations.

"I know, we have these conversations that anthropologists have. I guess we're sort of closet anthropologists." Dave acknowledged.

"After having this dream I've been looking at *The Kingdom of Good* website and I saw where that bottleneck occurred. I know Dr. Sherman talked about it, but it's been long enough that I don't really remember it very well now." Dave noted.

"So *The Kingdom of Good* website had information about all that stuff?" Matt asked.

"Yes, when they study the human genome they find that we have a very low level of diversity of genes as compared to most all other animals. There are about 23,000 human genes and we all have 99.9% the same genes, so one tenth of one percent is about 23 genes. Evidently, across all of humanity, they only find about twenty three different genes that we don't all share. That's across over seven billion people, so for you and me having mostly northern European ancestry we probably have just a few different genes. But here's the deal, it's the epigenetic part of the chromosome, all those on and off switches that regulate the genes that create so many of the differences we see. And some really new research is saying that our genes actually are influenced by interactions with the environment around us. It's like we're actually connected with some strange filament to everything that's there. How weird is that? Just a few years ago scientists didn't have a clue what the epigenetic area between the genes was there for, some thought it was of no use, like junk. Now they're getting a better understanding."

"They think the numbers point to various bottlenecks, but the most serious was about 70,000 to 74,000 years ago. That time frame coincides with the eruption of Mount Toba in Indonesia which was about a hundred times more powerful than when Mount Tambora erupted in 1815 and caused the year without sunshine. And Tambora was a lot more powerful than Mount Saint Helens. Anyway, they think Toba caused a severe drop in temperature and sunshine got seriously blocked out for 10 or more years. That had to put huge pressure on the humans alive at the time. That was a really close call for our species. I've seen estimates that there might have been as few as forty adults left or up to twenty thousand."

"Either way it means we almost went extinct. And just think of that, the Neanderthals would be the most evolved beings on the planet and they'd probably still be hunting the same old way they had been for hundreds of thousands of years. And the planet wouldn't be heating up like it is, getting ready to get rid of whatever is causing all the problems. Funny how that's a lot like when we get sick and we run a temperature, and just a few degrees can make a huge difference in how we feel. I'll have to remember that the next time I'm trying to explain to someone why just one degree of average temperature can be so important."

Matt had another take on it, "Boise wouldn't exist, cell phones, mountain bikes, guacamole, you and me, Maria too. Think about that Ponch; we humans were never a for sure thing. So many people think we're here because God ordained that we would exist and made us in his image and all that stuff. How does that square with almost going extinct?"

"Yeah, I know." Dave responded and then continued. "Or how about the mutations that allowed our heads to get bigger, you know where the muscles on the tops of our homo erectus ancestors heads go away, the muscles they used to grind green matter shrink, skulls expand and the cerebral cortex emerges that gives us this extra ability to imagine and reason. What if that hadn't happened? Did the divine cause it to happen?"

"Bbbbbb," Matt made a blowing sound with his lips flapping. "It's hard to believe it's just all random."

Dave continued, "I don't think it's all totally random, there's gotta be some underlying," he stopped, he had to think for a few moments, "algorithm, yeah, some kind of algorithm." His voice was a little distant, sort of detached following the thoughts in his own head more than directing them towards Matt. "Something's tying this all together." Dave's mind went racing after that thought. "I've been reading a book the *KOG* (Kingdom of Good) website suggested. It's about that quantum field Dr. Sherman was talking about; the Akashic Field. The idea is that everything's connected by it; you and me, the neighbor's dog. This one analogy is that we're like islands in the ocean, we look separated but under the water it's all connected. I remember when Dr. Sherman talked about that, I just couldn't get my mind around it then. I don't know, maybe I can a little more now. I think it all fits in with how Dr. Sherman was emphasizing The Kingdom of God ... or Good. When we first listened to him I didn't get it. I kept asking myself why he thought this *Kingdom of Good* concept was so important for dealing with the problems we have today? I'd think, why can't you just say here's the proof of what's going on, like the physics and biology you can measure of heating of the planet and species extinction rates."

"What do you mean?" Matt questioned.

Dave was thinking, "I struggle with all this but okay, I'll do the best I can. So, scholars say that the primary message Jesus came to give and brought to this world is that this Kingdom of God, as Europeans have called it for who knows how long, was planted by him, he was like the original mustard seed, so the idea now exists among us. But you have to seek admittance, and there are certain rules to that. See, humans are the first life forms on this planet to have the ability to question what we are, how did we get here, why are we here? It's like we climbed this virtual ladder and passed through a level nothing else ever has before. Try to picture coming up through a trap door to the rooftop of a building to a place where no other species has been. We are an entirely new force, but we carry along with us all the instinctual baggage of millions of years of evolution where our ancestors were much more "animal" than we are. Don't you see, it's all about consciousness levels? The message Jesus brought was for this new animal on the earth and about our consciousness level."

"Why would we need some message brought to us?" Matt was following closely."I remember Dr. Sherman talking about this, but go ahead tell me what you're thinking." Matt continued.

"Okay, there were just more dots I needed to connect for it all to make sense to me." Dave went on, "It's connected to those two most important commandments." Matt knew what he meant. "And when you combine them into just one short phrase you get: *Love Creation Entirely*. If you live by that simple thought, truthfully, the rest just takes care of itself. We live sustainably on the planet."

"I don't like using the word love, it seems awkward somehow, but if you hold someone or thing in the highest of esteem; that's pretty much what we think of as love. So if you seek that connection with the ultimate source, the divine, and then you hold it and all people and nature in general around you in the same state of mind, then this "goodness" binds the whole thing together. Does that make any sense to you?"

Matt was thinking for a short while, "Yeah that simplifies it. And the product of the Divine: is nature, which we find all around us and includes all people, you hold in the same reverence. Something like that?" Matt's voice rose as his answer had a question in it.

"I think so." Dave made a slight sound of a laugh, "Humans emerged from the eat or be eaten world. We needed a strong sense of self protection, which is probably the ego, to help shield us from everything out there that could do us harm. It was a source of motivation too: greed and power have their place with lower animals but in certain people they've become lethal. The ego was a necessary tool while we emerged through all that time. And the thing is, it's still very much alive in us today. It's the strong sense of "I", preserve me, and enhance me. I feel it all the time; me, me, me. And I'm pretty sure just about everybody does, to varying degrees. But it's that very me, me, me that gets in the way so often from being able to see the "we." I think that's a truly essential quality of *The Kingdom of Good*, you truly embrace the "we" part.

"Do you think the agnostic types, and there's lots of them, are going to accept Dr. Sherman's point of view; that the message from Jesus has something to do with solving our problems two thousand years later?" Matt perceptively asked.

"Well, I'm not sure; they'd have to make the decision that Jesus was somehow divine and brought this message. Maybe, as more people hear about it and study the website, maybe it would connect."

Dave continued. "And why wouldn't his message be relevant to our time. We don't need everybody to buy in on this, but we do need a critical number of highly motivated people to do so. Something like 4 to 5% of the adult population I've heard. If they are motivated by believing the KOG connection or just believe in this cause for reasons they have, it doesn't matter. We just need highly motivated people."

"And to the best of my knowledge Jesus was the only spiritual figure that had the KOG as their specific central message. All I can say is that, at least for me, it seems plausible. I wasn't there when he was alive or was crucified and then was resurrected. Is it too much to believe that it hap-pened? That's for everyone to decide for themselves; I don't "know" that it did, but I "think" it did." Dave finished.

Matt realized how close to the heart of the matter they were getting. "And that's why Dr. Sherman was so emphatic that *The Kingdom of Good* was the essential tool for us now; it's the key for dealing with the climate crisis and all the other problems."

"The climate crisis is just one symptom of our dysfunctional and un-sustainable civilization. But it is also the most pressing symptom of the deeper malfunction in the human spirit, and all the problems we have emerged because of that." Dave answered.

"There's more to keep in mind too," Dave went on. "Remember then how Dr. Sherman was saying that the three temptations of Jesus were in fact the same ones we all face, like not living in "the way" or by the Ten Commandments. Turning stones into bread, the first one; that's just doing things that go against common sense and reason or are lacking wisdom. Not living within the limits the physical world sets for us on Earth is a tragic example of that."

"Some ideas in the Bible sound like they were made up by men." Matt said.

"Have you ever heard of the Jefferson Bible?" Dave then asked his friend.

"Maybe, that sounds familiar."

"Thomas Jefferson went through his Bible and cut out everything except those passages that sounded to him like they came from Jesus. I'm with him; I think it's with his words you find truth and wisdom."

"What are the other two temptations again?" Matt questioned.

"Well, the second one is about desiring high status and expecting that God will catch you when you fall, or things don't work; the pinnacle of the temple. That's like the unwise seeking or use of power. Having power is an enormous motivational factor in the animal world of course. It can just be very dangerous in us. Jesus told us not to expect God to intervene when we abuse power. And the third one was greed, wanting to possess great wealth... ike the entire world. Jesus told us that all you really need is to love God and you will find happiness."

"What would greed look like in the animal world?" Matt questioned.

"Wanting more bananas to eat, I'd guess." Dave answered.

"What would power be then?" Matt followed.

"Sex. Mating, parenting the next generation. When you think of these things in an evolutionary context it all starts to make more sense." Dave added.

Dave smiled to himself. "If you step back and look at the climate crisis you see where we're falling into the trap of the three temptations and missing the essence of the two most important commandments. Somehow our moral relationship with the divine and with the Earth has gotten way off track."

"How do you think we managed to do that?" Matt was in agreement with the symptom, but what was the cause?

Dave thought again for some time. He was shaking his head, "Dr. Sherman said we just got too clever before we had time to be wise. Our technological ability outpaced our collective ability to grow and live wisely. Remember him talking about the mentalist level of consciousness that really got going right after the microscope and telescopes were invented around 1600? People begin to see this much vaster reality than what they can see with their eyes. It must have been incredible for them to imagine. But it also starts the idea that nature is mechanistic, like little separate parts and not a holistic system. That fundamental misreading, false premise, gets us in big trouble now. At least in some of the things we're doing."

"I guess I'm not up on that, but I'll trust that you are." Matt responded.

"I've been going to their website a lot, it's not like I just remember all this from when we listened to Dr. Sherman. But what happened is that the reductionists or mentalists, those that truly thought nature could be understood like you do the workings of a car motor, got ahead of the holistic vision of nature where the quantum world and all its weirdness is really animating what we experience. And here's the thing: we are just barely beginning to grasp what it's about. What are the true depths of dimensions in nature? We don't know."

Dave went on. "We're like pre-schoolers with it all and need to be post doctorates or better. Dr. Sherman liked to say, our cleverness has outpaced our wisdom; especially in food production. And now we have SO many people whose wealth depends upon our clever, but unwise thinking in energy production, and food production is a part of that. So even when common sense tells you that what we're doing is wrong; well, there's another little voice that just says to deny the obvious. It's just too inconvenient to believe."

Matt wanted to say something, "Every time I start to think that there must be some spirit, okay God involved with us, I ask myself about all the really shitty stuff that exists like birth defects, plaques, wars, the evil in people, and think how this spirit fits into all that."

"What's your answer?" Dave followed.

Matt didn't say anything for awhile, "I don't have a certain answer for that. You've got to admit that the shit really does happen. But maybe it's all just emerging as best it can; we're a part of the emergence. Maybe the only way to get away from the shitty stuff is to get to a higher level of consciousness. Holy cow, I sound like the scarecrow when he gets his brain, don't I?"

Dave laughed, "Yeah," as he remembered the scene from The Wizard of Oz.

"Without a doubt," Dave continued. "It's not a perfect system; but maybe, just maybe, that's part of what we are about. It's up to us to hopefully make it more perfect? You and me and everybody else are all a part of the emerging of consciousness that could do that. It's like; it's the consciousness stupid and our bodies just carry it around."

"I need to take a break Dave, can I call you back in ten minutes?"

"Sure."

~~~~~~

Matt began. "That's a lot of concepts to get straight in your mind. I think it's really hard for many people to move past the simpler explanations of how and why things are. For example; God made the world in seven days, Adam and Eve, the flood. A lot of people just can't live with ambiguity. Ponch, that's why they make up or adhere to a creation story that makes them feel comfortable, it's not ambiguous. Like Dr. Sherman said, 'it's what those people believe to be true that is our real enemy in dealing with the climate crisis and what they deny to be true.'"

Dave responded, "Well I know one thing: if we humans didn't exist the world's ecosystems would be healthy and balanced. We wouldn't be pushing everything towards this edge." Dave was imagining the really big picture.

Matt had another take, "I wonder how many people see the world like this and realize all the dynamic forces that had to occur for them to have ever been conceived? Just think how unlikely it was even a few hundred years ago that you and I are talking now."

"Do you think any of those fundamentalists-type religions you have would buy any of this?"

Matt was laughing, "I suspect there's a few, believe it or not. But they're the ones who don't believe they will get their own planet when they die either or plan to invite their wife to go with them to heaven. I mean come on."

"So, the Akashic field," Dave knew he needed to finish the original thought, "I was reading where anthropologists have observed some of the last hunter-gatherer tribes on the planet and they supposedly can communicate telepathically, like being miles away from each other and not making a sound. How does that work?"

"So you believe it's true?" Matt asked.

"Well the guy who was writing about it is a much respected scientist. I guess in my rating system I give it a pretty high chance of being true. So it just makes me wonder if this deep matrix or field they're now talking about could it be the same thing that *The Kingdom of Good* flows within?"

"I need to do some reading, so I'll have to get back to you on that." Matt said, just before taking the last small bite from his plate.

"Well for me, that's what Dr. Sherman based his premise and his entire lecture on. That the most important tool we'll have to confront all our problems, and especially climate, is *The Kingdom of Good*. Those five principles lead to it: the three temptations and the two most important commandments, and if you truly live within those bounds then you will be in *The Kingdom of Good*.

"It's come to make so much sense to me. Goodness is divinity flowing through anyone into the world. This goodness interacts with others and starts the virtuous spiral upwards." Dave paused for just a moment, "I read one time where somebody asked Albert Einstein why he believed there was a God, and you know what he told them?"

Matt answered that he did not.

Dave continued, "He said because there was beauty in a flower. I read that years ago and at first it didn't make much sense to me, but the more I thought about it the more I think I know what he meant. What other creatures on this Earth have the ability to perceive something as beautiful? I really doubt even the chimps or bonobo's do. So it's most likely just a human thing. We can't eat the flowers we think are beautiful. So it's something more abstract. Is it a gift to our consciousness? It's like a very subtle hint; a nuance, the sublime. Is it *grace*?"

"I think I know what you mean," Matt followed. "There was this old guy and his wife in our neighborhood when I was growing up, they had the coolest little house they'd been fixing up for years. Every time you'd see them they'd smile and wave and if you were close they'd say you're name and ask you how you are. Every summer they had extra food from their garden they'd give away. People were always gathered on their front porch, just chatting. There was this great feeling that just seemed to come from their house; I just loved to look at it. You know the house and all the plants they had growing around it. It all just made me happy. Then just a little ways down the street there was a house where you'd never see the people, the front yard was just rock and weeds, I'd walk past that house and want to get past it as fast as I could. I think that's kinda what *The Kingdom of Good* is all about too; it can just be a feeling. It's like happy and hopeful, living is good and worth cherishing and fighting for. It's that feeling that will save us, I'm thinking Poncho; that's why Dr. Sherman thought it was so important."

~~~~~

This time Dave asked for a five minute break. "I need to get going pretty quick, but there are a few more things I wanted to let you know about." Dave said as they resumed the conversation.

"Did you know that Al Gore has a new book out?"

"Yeah," Matt was thinking, "What's he call it: The Future, I think."

"That's it. I just finished it. The last part is called "The Edge" in that and his conclusion I pretty much hear him challenging us."

"How so?" Matt asked.

"In the first part of the book he talks about Earth Inc. which is the new emergent corporate dominated business model that's world-wide; all linked together by telecommunications and the Internet. He also explains what he calls the Global Mind, which is a metaphor for how we're all so interconnected by the Net. He talks about so many of the problems in the world being caused by certain unwise human industrious behavior and then makes the connection that there is Earth Inc. not really grasping or taking responsibility for the effects of what they're doing. And then there is the Global Mind which is all the rest of us tied together to potentially confront and redirect Earth Inc. so that it doesn't destroy us. And just like Dr. Sherman was saying, 'It's the hand off from his generation, the World War II group and the Baby Boomers, to our generation The Millenials, that will either rally and change the direction of things or else for hundreds or thousands of years if people manage to hang on, then we'll be cursed for not recognizing our responsibility to them and reacting."

"He's pretty much framed the issue hasn't he; tee'd it up?" Matt observed.

"Pretty much," Dave replied. "Do you know how much heat energy we're trapping every day because of the pollution of the atmosphere we've been generating?" Dave asked, having a very important quantity in mind.

"No."

"The equivalent of four hundred thousand bombs, like the ones dropped on Hiroshima and Nagasaki. Every day! That's jaw dropping to me. At least a major world figure has put it out there like that now." Dave paused and then continued, "It's up to us to either believe we have this responsibility to act or not. I say we do!"

"Okay man, what do we do? I know you've already been giving your lecture, that's more than I've been doing." Matt said.

"That's been okay, but Al Gore has an army out doing that now. I think we need to get linked up with him, and then we need to help him and like the 350.org people all get linked up into one unified movement. Remember Joan, the woman I met in San Diego, she's a liaison with the Green Party?"

"Yeah, ah ha."

"They have a worldwide network already set up; we could link with them too. There are probably hundreds if not thousands of groups: the Sierra Club, the Cousteau Society, the Union of Concerned Scientists, the Natural Resources Defense Council, on and on."

"So the idea would be to get all these groups from all around the world to link up into one unified group?" Matt was thinking out loud. "Isn't there one already?"

"No, I don't think so; there are just all these different groups."

"So why would they link with this group you're imagining?"

Dave had a simple and elegant answer, "It's as old as humanity Matt. We've come together around fires for over a million years to strategize our good and fair future. Remember what Dr. Sherman said; that this negotiating is the hallmark of our species: it's part of our fundamental strategy for survival."

Matt's mind was moving quickly, "We need a fire for everyone on the planet to come together around, that's what you're saying, I guess, huh?"

"Exactly, I see an exceedingly powerful website where anyone on the planet can go to post ideas and discuss problems and solutions. The most important thing we have to do is take on the American government."

"What do you mean?"

"Like Gore says, the United States has to lead. The moral leadership has to come from the US. There are 535 members of Congress, in the House and the Senate, if they all believed we are facing this crisis and were dedicated to acting, things would change in a hurry. We'd build on the information already on the site, I see a new part of it where every one of the congressional districts in the US is identified; then we'd identify the critical information about those districts (population size and demographics, voting history, employers, how the local economy works, probably more). Then we'd lay out everything we know about the individuals that are representing those districts. Then you have to focus on the people that vote and don't vote, because a huge number of people don't vote. A lot of those people you'll never get but if you can get enough maybe you can change the outcomes of the elections. I still hear Dr. Sherman saying the politicians aren't the problem directly, it's the electorate. If enough of them believe what we believe, things change. That's the challenge Matt."

"What's it called?" Matt then asked.

"We don't need to reinvent the wheel. I think Dr. Sherman's name for this thing would be best: *The Kingdom of Good*. We get those people that are currently running it in England to see this bigger role to play. It seems corny at first, but it's so simple and it links what Jesus was saying with what modern science says is the essence of our species; that we evolved negotiating a common future that was good and fair for everyone in the group. Of course it got bastardized eventually by people manipulating things to their greater interests. But still, within it is the closest thing we have to a species-wide ethos. Remember: *Love Creation Entirely*. And if enough people truly take that to heart, then maybe, just maybe we still have a chance to get ourselves on a sustainable path."

Matt was thinking, "Ponch, you're a nerd, but a good nerd."

"Well, it's far from complex scientific or engineering thinking. If I didn't think of it, someone else would, I just hope it can be effective."

"You know what else Poncho?"

"What?"

Matt knew he'd sound a little corny, but he also knew some of the deeper workings of his friend's mind. He'd never mentioned it before, maybe now was a good time. "Your mother would be very proud of you. I have a little idea of how much her memory must mean. I don't know if your dad ever thought to tell you that? My mom, every once in a while, will tell me that my dad would be proud of me and I know how important that is to me. Anyway, for what it's worth man."

Dave cleared his throat a little, "I was just thinking about her yesterday. I was out for one of my long walks and I spotted a lady tending to some flowers. It made me think of a time I remember my mom out doing that very thing. It's been so long now that I can think about her and it doesn't hurt as much as it used to. It's almost pleasant, like I'll linger on the thought, and maybe it seems just a little like she's there."

"I kind of know what you mean, every once in a while something will spur a thought of my dad and I'll actually enjoy thinking about it," Matt added.

"That's life, right?"

Matt continued, "Yeah, life. My mom says we're all little actors in this enormous production. We all have some part we play out. The roles we play aren't preordained, they emerge. Luck, both good and bad, hard work, vision, all these factors and plenty more converge into the act that we play out. Somehow you have to care about doing good and fair things. It's not the easy thing to do lots of times, the easy thing is to decide to let someone else do what you know is needed, but you can't be bothered to do it. That's one of the biggest hurdles of all, I'd think, just our own reluctance to care or be bothered."

"Dr. Sherman said he feared most that we'd only respond half heartedly to the climate crisis, without the deep resolve it's going to really take. I think that's very true. It's like when the English didn't want to believe the Nazi's actually represented an evil force they had to respond to. Since World War I had been fought only twenty five years before, and they didn't want to think they had to go through that again. But reality is what it is. There's a revolution already started. It's not a question if we'll respond, we are. The real question is will we respond with enough intensity to matter? And the truth is you and I will never know because it will continue to play out for a long time after we're gone. My selfish side hopes we have that much time. How much do we care about those that come after us though? That's really the question, isn't it?" Matt finished.

"Pretty much," Dave answered.

Dave had one last thought he'd been holding and needed to share with Matt. "I think we need to have a rendezvous very soon, somewhere with a few really smart people we know. We'll figure out our strategy for what we've got to do there. I know a guy that used to work at Google who I think has a lot of connections in the media tech world. Here's what I'm thinking, what if we all meet in Moab, Utah in like late March. The weath-

99

er is pretty warm by then, and we can do some mountain bike riding and then sit around a fire and hatch a plan. What do you think?"

"I agree, we need to get something going." Matt responded.

"Okay, I'll get some details figured out; specific time, where we stay, food, and I'll get back to you. I think we need to produce some sort of video to put on the web, but I need to think about that more. I'll get back to you," Dave said.

"That sounds good. I'm thinking I might hit up my Uncle Dan for his travel trailer, he's told me I could use it for something like that."

"That would be good. These guys are pretty well off, they'll probably stay in hotels. But if we find a place to have a camp that's out someplace it would give us a frig and toilet wouldn't it?"

"For sure."

"I think I like your Uncle Dan!"

Chapter Five

"Hold it up and I'll tell you what I think," Maria chastened Matt to show her the picture he'd been painting. They were connected via Skype and had found a much richer way to engage each other. This was typical of their generation, sometimes referred to as the "Digital Natives" having been born after 1980 and had for all of their lives engaged with the new digital world of technology.

"This one will be for my mom. I'm not going to tell you what I'm painting for you. You'll just have to wait and see."

Matt set the picture on an easel so it wouldn't move around which allowed Maria to study it closely. "That really does look like your mom, but a long time ago." The woman dominated the picture as only a very small piece of what was meant to portray Matt showed in the corner. Her arms were folded, and she had the gaze of someone listening intently to someone else. "Okay, what's it about?" Maria asked, having studied the picture long enough.

"Okay, well after I saw the pictures that Brooks Dryer and George Good Elk painted I decided that was a really good way to say thanks to someone or just to honor them. I've wanted to give my mom something. So, after thinking about it for a long time and dismissing a lot of ideas, I remembered this one time when Dad wasn't around. I was having some troubles with a kid at school. I'd always assumed that I'd get in trouble with my parents if I got in a fight with some kid, so I always tried to avoid fighting. But this one kid kept saying things that really made me angry. Well, once I was kind of telling my mom about him and she just spoke up and told me to stick up for myself and to not let him bully me around. That's all I needed. So the next time that kid started his needling at me I challenged him to a fight. I was serious. He wasn't expecting that from quiet little old me. So what do you know, he shuts his trap and I didn't hear from him anymore. That picture is of when Mom told me it was okay to stick up for myself. You wouldn't think someone would need an approval for something like that, but from the culture I was raised in I guess it just made me that kind of kid. Anyway, I can just remember how empowered I felt after she told me that. I guess this is my way of thanking her.

"Am I dating Leonardo da Vinci?" Maria asked smugly.

"I hope, maybe a little part of him."

"Obviously not the gay part!" Maria was laughing. "I wonder what sort of chocolate Leonardo liked? Do you think there is gay chocolate?"

"Would they have had chocolate candy back then?" Matt asked, realizing the little things like having chocolate so readily available was probably not something even Leonardo would have had. Times do change.

"Oh, I haven't told you about the video I watched yesterday," Maria had something new to talk about.

"What's that?" He stretched a little, Maria watched as he flexed his muscles 7500 miles distant.

"Let me grab it." She returned quickly and held the cover of the video up to her camera so he could get a good look at it. There was a character image of a young woman with a bandanna wrapped around her forehead. One hand was pulling it back so one of her eyes could be seen. The word "Robust" read boldly across the cover.

"Looks interesting," Matt offered. "What's it about?"

"Basically how the New World Order, you know the richest people in the world are supposedly manipulating all the rest of us, is what the guy is suggesting. He talks about the world's financial system, energy, agriculture, medicine; you know, just how the world works. He says there are eight or ten families that have control of these mega corporations and they think they're smarter than all the rest of us and need to control everything.

"Do you think we're getting manipulated?" Maria asked her boyfriend.

"Oh God, at the level he's talking about, I don't know. It stretches credulity some."

"Does he talk much about carbon and pollution of the atmosphere?"

"Not much, though I think I remember seeing windmills and solar panels."

"I think George Good Elk made a good point."

"What's that?"

"Well there's this handoff going on between our generation and the Baby Boomers and some things are pretty messed up like the economy, healthcare, military, even some things to do with the environment like toxic waste and nuclear waste. Lots of bad things that have to be dealt with, but getting the pollution in the atmosphere way out of balance and then have the climate whack out, flip; like he says, billions of people could die in the process. There are already climate wars going on. Did you know that?"

"Kind of, what do you mean?" Maria questioned.

"Well, like all over Africa. The energy system is changing because of the temperature rise and so what happens is the rain falls in different areas which leads to droughts which leads to food shortages. Africa is like the canary in the mine shaft, life is already so on-the-edge there that just a little change in rainfall, or weather in general, and they have food shortages. And the next thing you know they are fighting each other. That will only get worse. What happens when millions of people can't get the food they need? Especially countries like Pakistan and India that have nuclear weapons?"

"Or the water," Maria interjected. "I saw this reporter on CNN the other day he was showing where all this water had been depleted in northern Iraq and through a lot of the Middle East."

"Surface water?" Matt asked.

"No, it's ground water, like the aquifers are just shrinking. They've been pumping it out way faster than it gets recharged. So they create a food bubble that creates a people bubble. What happens when the bubble bursts?"Maria said.

Matt continued, "Uh, that place is already a tinder box; it's hard to understand how people can even continue to live there."

"Can you imagine what it must be like to try and live in Syria right now?" Maria had begun munching on some chips; her voice was a bit tangled.

Matt had something new to explain, "I was talking to Dave a few days ago about what we need to do. He thinks we need to plan a gathering with a bunch of friends and make a video that we load to the web where we tell everyone "we're in" on confronting the crisis. He thinks we should go to Moab, Utah to meet and make the video."

"He's already giving lectures isn't he?" Maria responded.

"Yeah, like mini Dr. Sherman lectures, but he's not sure where it's all supposed to lead. He thinks we need to hook up with Al Gore's people, the Climate Reality group. Dave has gotten to know a few people from the tech community, some of them have already retired. Can you believe it? They're in their mid thirties and are already retired."

"Right company at the right time," Maria responded.

"I don't know very many architects that have done that; the ones that do usually have gotten into real estate development. When it works they can do really well." Maria got the drift of what Matt was implying.

"When's this going to happen?" Maria continued.

"Poncho, I mean Dave, was thinking late April; they say it gets nice and warm then. Can you make it?"

"Back to America?" Maria quickly asked, "I was just there! It would be fun to hear you call Dave Poncho again," she smirked.

Matt laughed slightly. "Yeah Ponch."

He continued, "I think this is going to be a pretty big deal, with Dave's connections, he knows people that know people."

"What is it that they know?" Maria chided.

"The internet, I think. This thing gets down to a battle for people's minds, what they believe. Like George Good Elk said, we have a democracy in America and every two years there is an election. Supposedly about 88% of the congressional seats are voted on. Just imagine if a movement could sway the minds of the electorate to vote in candidates who believe we've got to change the way we are doing business, which right now is not sustainable? Just think, every two years there's change: people die, young people get to the voting age, some people might be swayed in their thinking. And there's always all those people who just don't vote. Forty percent of the eligible voters don't vote! How many of those could you get to turn out? In one election a lot can change."

"Maybe two cycles." Maria thought out loud. "We're the digital generation: YouTube, Skype, Face Book, Twitter, we just have to get people to listen." She was silent for a short while, she was thinking about this rendezvous. "Okay, I want to be there. I need to talk with my boss and see if I can get time. When will you know the particular dates?"

"Let me get a calendar and see what might work." His slightly ghostly image moved from Maria's screen and he returned in just a few moments with a calendar. "The weekend of the 27th and 28th might work, that's Saturday and Sunday. So, if say everyone got to Moab on Wednesday night the 25th, we could have three days to hang, and then everyone heads home on Sunday the 28th. What do you think?"

"Well, that gives me two months. We'll just have to see what my boss says. Promise me chocolate when I get there?"

"Lots of chocolate, lots and lots and lots of chocolate!" Matt was smiling.

Chapter Six

Micky, Matt's mom, had her television tuned to CNN getting the latest news on the sequester of funding for the government that had begun that morning. The economy was already weak, at least in creating good-paying jobs. It was limping along trying to gain momentum after the crush of the Great Recession and now this. Of course, a certain part of the economy was doing just fine. It would only be a few weeks and the Dow would break through to its highest point ever. Record profits for corporations, but of course sharing a little more to help the US budget issues or getting more people working just wasn't going to be an option.

As if talking to the television the auburn-haired woman began. "This is just what the Republicans wanted, grind the economy to as slow a pace as possible and hope they can pin the blame on Obama and the Democrats. Cynical bastards, all of them!" Matt's mother was indignant about the GOP. They had one mission as far as she was concerned: protect the already rich.

Micky's second husband, Jack, had his smoker going out in the backyard. He was turning some steelheads he'd caught on a trip to Lewiston and Orofino into some tasty meat. He had his brown bib overalls on and a cap he seemed to wear a lot. It had a patch on the front left that looked like a fish jumping out of the water.

Micky decided to join him. She had two beers, one for each of them. She tugged at his belt and he leaned over a little to where he could kiss her. "Smells good. You'll have the neighbors over here before too long."

"Has the country fallin' off a cliff yet?" Jack was as spittin' mad about the whole sequester thing as Micky. It still wasn't known for sure if his pension from the BLM would eventually get hit by the whole thing. "Boehner been telling more tall ones today?"

"Of course, he's saying Obama hasn't had a plan and of course he does. What a mess."

Jack took a swig of his beer, "I wish Obama was better at getting out and explaining his strategy, give us the big picture, use some charts and graphs to make the points. If he understood how to do that better then the Republican spin machine would be easier to see through and give everybody out here the facts they need to support him. But for some reason he's not getting the message to do that. Makes me wonder if any of my emails to the White House ever get read?"

"I know, you've sent a lot of them." Micky put her arm around his waist and gave him a hug. "Lucky I found you in this big old world, Mr. Harris."

He opened the smoker lid just enough that he could check things out. He thumped his chest playfully, "Me good fisherman, bring food for wife." Jack wrinkled his nose at Micky. "I'm the lucky one," he said with sincerity. Micky lightly pinched his side.

"There's Matt," she said, seeing his little pickup pulling into her drive. He was by himself and had decided to take up his mom's offer to stop by for dinner after work.

"Hi Honey," she said, giving him a hug as he walked up.

"Smells good," Matt observed.

"Hopefully I have the recipe just right on the marinade. I think last time I had it too strong." Jack replied.

"How was your week?" Micky asked.

"Kind of a grind. We had a deadline this morning on some tenant improvements at the new shopping center being built out in Meridian, at Eagle and Fairview. Have you seen that?"

Micky nodded that they had, "We were by there a few days ago, lots going on. That new park is really something too; we stopped in and walked around. Amazing to think that was just this big flat piece of ground a few years ago, and now look at it with the lakes and the big ... what do you call them, the big mound type things?"

"Berms, is probably what you're thinking of."

"That's it. Really really great though."

"Want a beer, Matt?" Jack asked. "Or maybe it's time for something with just a little more bite?"

"Whiskey on the rocks?" Matt responded, knowing that was probably what Jack was thinking.

"You want one too, Honey?" Jack said looking at Micky.

"Sure, but about half as much as you gave me last time. I don't like getting too much of that in my system."

The steelhead would need several more hours before being ready so that would give them time to have a drink and a little to eat, before Jack needed to complete his task.

"Have you been following all this stuff going on back in Washington, this sequester thing?" Micky asked her son.

"Yeah, some," Matt responded. "It's kind of confusing, seems like they're just screwing things around, and everyone is blaming the other guy. How are we supposed to know what to think?"

"And we jump from one hot pan to another. The next thing we'll be hearing about is the debt limit again." Micky opined.

"That's the one where were messing with dynamite," Jack began, "we suddenly send a message to the rest of the world that we aren't going to pay our debt, the bond market will tighten up real fast, and that will send everything into a frenzy."

Jack finished pouring the drinks. Matt took a very small swig as he'd learned how to let the strong whiskey just kind of melt into his mouth. It took just a second before a warm sensation seemed to pass down through his body.

"Hits the spot," Matt smiled towards his step father.

"It has its place. Just a little bit, too much of this stuff and you have your head in a toilet." Jack said.

"Remember my friend Eric?" Matt asked.

"The school teacher, football coach guy?" Micky responded.

"Yeah, that's him. When Maria was here we met him and his girl-friend downtown. He told us about this book he'd been reading, it has to do with the social behaviors of different species. It's really what Dr. Sherman was talking about too; in fact, it ties in with where the name of his lecture comes from."

Matt had already been telling them about the KOG. *The Kingdom of Good*, which is all about the strategy we agree on for dealing with the future basically. I guess implicitly it includes this kind of idea. It's really interesting, especially as I've been thinking about it more. Everything that lives has to somehow strategize about its future; how it's going to live in the future. I'd never thought very much about that before, but when you look around the animal kingdom there are different strategies animals use to exist. Some herd up, some wander around in small bands such as predator types like wolves and hyenas, and some are very individualistic like grizzly bears. What's interesting about humans, I guess, is that were what's called 'eusocial.' We live in groups and defend a nest. Like dung beetles do." He laughed. "I guess that would be a cave in the really old days. And we use the concepts of good and fair as part of our socialization and how we plan for the future."

Matt continued, "So we live together in these big groups because we have better lives, but to do that you have to have goals. So the thing is, everybody is still an individual and we all have our own…well honestly, selfish goals." Micky nodded her head that she agreed. "So the reason humans have created the world as we have is because we work together at some level. Nobody can do great things all on their own. There are "always" connections with other people to get things done, make things happen."

"It makes you wonder how eusocial our current members of Congress are?" Micky lamented sarcastically. "I think President Obama needs to stick on his leader hat and get those guys in a room and get things figured out. I believe that when people get things really explained well, like with real-clear-thinking, you can bend some minds. I think this eusocial thing is exactly right, the vast majority of people want good and fair solutions to how we live together. It just takes someone that knows how to really get to the meat on the bones about things, to get agreements."

Matt's step dad chimed in, "I think a lot of clear-minded people are starting to wonder if Obama has it in him to parse the really stingy parts. Like Medicare, how much is fair for society as a whole to pay for any one person?" Jack didn't like moochers either.

Micky continued, "The cost of health care, like the expense for the doctors, hospitals, tests, treatments, all that stuff; that's where I'm hearing the costs have been growing way beyond inflation. That's the main driver of the deficit. I don't know about the wars in Afghanistan and Iraq because I heard they put them on a separate credit card."

Matt wanted to add, "And we have all these people eating this un-healthy food, getting obese, and having all these health issues: cancer, heart disease, diabetes. Just think if all those people were just reasonably healthy? Healthy people don't go to the hospital and rack up bills."

"I think we need to get eusocial and figure out our dinner for tonight!" Micky was having fun.

Chapter Seven

A pleasant light filled the work area. Matt was sitting across the table from one of the structural engineers assigned to his project along with the electrical engineer. They were discussing some tricky framing and how the electrical system would need to integrate with all of it.

It was a space intended to project the vision of today's structures, responding to the energy and environmental challenges of the early twenty first century. The ceiling was exposed revealing the large pre-fabricated beams that supported the roof. They were made from recycled materials that had given the design special LEED points in the recent remodel of the building. The firm wanted to project the theme of sustainability. The mechanical duct work as well was a noticeable element adding to the "techy" feel of the office.

"What's the depth of that beam?" Matt asked.

"Eighteen inches," Frank Lutz the structural engineer replied.

"Is that big enough to create a chase and get all your electrical through there?" Matt asked, looking at Terry Shields, the electrical engineer.

"I have two four inch conduits and two more that are two inches, so twelve inches … I guess we're fine."

Matt was pointing towards a column on the plans, "When you hit this column you can run everything down to the basement. We have a one hour rated wall right here so code should be fine for putting the control panel about here." Matt was pointing to a place in the basement noted as Room 003. "What do you think, do we have it?"

"Let me go back and update my CAD file, I think that area has just been in a hold position for a week or so. We'll get it tightened up." Terry said.

"I need to get an update to McEllhenny by tomorrow morning, is that going to work? I need some pricing from them ASAP." Matt asked.

"Yeah, no worries," that was Terry's patented way of answering an affirmative question.

"Good, well I'm supposed to get with Mike on something, so if everybody's okay it's getting close to five and I need to scoot." Matt told his group.

~~~~~

Matt returned to his work space and grabbed his light jacket and then headed down the short hall to his boss Mike's office. Mike was standing

109

next to his throw table studying some drawings. Matt tapped on the glass. Mike smiled and waved his hand for Matt to come over and take a look. "You think we can get this built for twelve million?" He was looking at the preliminary elevations for the new Hogan Outdoor Adventure store planned for one of the remaining lots along Front Street.

Matt raised his eyebrows, then lifted his thumb and acted like he was scanning the drawings. A magical number would just come to him. "$11,750,000 is my estimate."

"I've got to go to the partners tomorrow with the numbers. McEllhenny says definitely not more than $12,250,000. They've got everybody in town working for them. It's probably a good number."

"Are they just negotiating with McEllhenny?" Matt asked.

"Yeah, I guess unless someone comes in and thinks they can pound all the subs down some more than old Mac. Anyway, you good for a couple of hours? I'm meeting an old friend at Bardenay and I think you should meet him. We went to school together and I'm thinking about bringing him on. He's a damn good designer, but he's been going through some tough times."

"Couple of hours, is that what you're thinking?" Matt didn't want it to be too late getting home.

"That's about right, Dana's expecting me by eight, so I've got to be out of there by 7:30 at the latest."

"Let's go." Matt tapped the window again as they left.

It was a pleasant early April afternoon as the two crossed the walk on Front. "My friends name is Bob Granger. We met up at the U of I in Moscow in about '82 I think? Yeah, '82. He worked at the firm years ago. I think he got laid off in the downturn in the early 90s. He went to Portland for a while, but came back because he just didn't like it over there."

"He was doing alright here until the recession hit. Bob was with a small group and they just couldn't get any of the stimulus work that kept most of us going. His wife at the time had a job with Blue Cross so they had some stability that way. Like a lot of these guys around town they just pick up little things here and there. Then the recession-divorce hits."

Matt looked at him as he hadn't heard that one before. "The recession-divorce?"

"I don't know if it was caused by the recession. There obviously were some cracks in the marriage, but they ended up going hand in hand. So this guy's my age, mid fifties, and then boom! Half your wealth is gone, and you're out of work for several years. It's brutal. I've been hearing this scenario a lot. I guess the pressures of the recession push some of the shaky relationships over the edge."

"He's in damn good physical shape though. The guys up in the foot-hills running all the time; ski's too. That's why I thought it might be good to introduce you two, he has a son about your age and he's into all that stuff like you are."

~~~~~

The place was a bit noisy when they entered as sound was echoing off of the rafters, but that added to the experience. "Let's get that tall table over there." A waitress was coming towards them. Mike met her and asked if they could have the table near the window.

"Sure, just the two of you?"

"No, one more."

"Can I get you something to drink?"

"Just a beer for me, something light."

"The same," Matt smiled at the waitress.

Mike spotted Bob coming through the door; he stood up and walked towards his friend. They shook hands and moved over to where Matt was sitting. "Mike Granger, this is Matt Lundquist." Matt slightly nodded as they shook hands. "We just ordered a couple of beers. What do you think you'd like?"

"Um, maybe something dark?" Bob looked for the waitress and nodded at her. She knew he was ready to order.

"Do you have a good smooth dark beer?" She ran through a list. "Oh, I've had that Kokanee Dark, let's go with that." Bob said.

Mike got the conversation going, "Matt joined the firm in 2009, wasn't it?"

"Yeah, dead on at the bottom of the recession," Matt explained.

"So there was nowhere but up, huh?" Bob commented.

Matt looked towards Mike to get his reaction, "I think it was pretty much the bottom," Mike acknowledged.

"2009 was definitely a very tough year." Mike went on. "Most of us took major pay cuts, like down fifty percent or so. We had to layoff thirty percent of the firm. Had a lot of nights where sleep was pretty scant. The bills don't stop, we have that set overhead. What, we had grocery store work for you, that's what got you going wasn't it?"

"Yeah, good thing people still needed to eat." Matt answered.

Mike continued, "I got Matt on my team about a year and a half ago, we needed help on a big project and that group was a little slow, so I nabbed him. You went to Europe for a short time in there didn't you?"

111

"Yeah, for two months in 2010; September and October," Matt answered.

"My sons there right now," Bob said.

"Oh, where's he at?" Matt asked.

"Germany." Bob said.

Matt was curious, "What part, I have some friends that live near Munich."

"Well he's kind of close, he's in Ingolstadt. I think he said it's a little over an hour north of Munich."

"I think we went through it. We met some people that lived up north near Hannover, so we went north and south a few times. It seems like I remember stopping in Ingolstadt at the train station. So is he touring or working?"

"He's actually studying their windmills. He has a degree in mechanical engineering and thinks the wind energy business will be good one day over here."

"I sure hope so. It's clean, you know, no carbon." Matt knew he could talk that slightly politically sensitive issue with Mike around. Mike was totally for the renewable energy that was clean.

"So are you the environmentalist type?" Bob asked of Matt.

"Absolutely, especially when it comes to the carbon and the polluting of the atmosphere. We're getting really close to a threshold where there's so much carbon we ensure the two degrees of temperature rise that the climate scientists are saying is like very scary." Scientist Matt was emerging.

"Matt's our in house expert on climate change." Mike took a sip of his beer, nodding towards Matt.

"My son, Randy, told me that the Green Party is pretty influential in Germany. At least Germany seems to be leading the way with a lot of green innovation." Bob said.

"They do green roofs and green walls a lot. I see them in the trade magazines." Mike added."He's going to be here in a couple of weeks, maybe I can introduce you two? Sounds like you may have things in common."

"Is he into sports?" Matt then asked.

Bob smiled, "Kayaking and skiing. Sound familiar?"

"That's pretty much a Boise standard. Yeah, who knows, maybe we're on the same page." Matt said.

The conversation moved on to the office and the work that was coming up. Bob would be hired to be on the team with Matt. They had a good shot at a hospital project in Eastern Oregon. If marketing landed that one, they would start there.

By 7:00 Matt mentioned that he'd probably better be going. He actually wanted to get home so he could watch the English Premier League Soccer game. Manchester United was playing Liverpool and he didn't want to miss any of it. He needed to call Dave and an email to Maria would likely be in store too. With Matt leaving, it would give Mike and Bob a chance to discuss more personal things.

~~~~~

Mike motioned to the young lady. He was thinking some finger food to go along with their beers would be good. "How about these?" He was pointing to a line for the chicken wings.

"Sounds good," Bob replied.

"Would this be on your tab, sir?" the waitress asked.

Bob started to tell her to put it on his then Mike interrupted, "This is mostly business, let me get it." Bob just nodded to him and took a sip of his beer.

They'd known each other a long time. Earlier in life, they had been very good friends … at a level like Matt and Dave. But during the years Bob had been married to Stevie, their friendship had waned some though after he left the firm. Bob had gone out on his own thinking a little better life could be had in the fast-paced growth years of the late 90s through 2007, which added to the distance. They'd kept up some through the past three years since Bob and Stevie had split. Mike knew some of the challenges his old friend had been working through.

"So have you bought your dad's house yet? I know that was your plan a few months ago." Mike queried.

"Not so much buy, my siblings and I own it jointly, it's in a trust. I've spent some to remodel it, I have the option to just stay and start buying them out. Kind of hard to do that though when so little money has been coming in. Fortunately they're on my side, giving me some time to recover."

"Pretty hard to go through a divorce in the depths of the most severe recession we've ever had, I'd guess?" Mike offered.

Bob had leaned forward and had one elbow on their table, "It added a lot of confusion to an already very difficult time. Like figuring out how much things were worth, like the house; it was assessed at quite a bit in 2005. By the time we're doing all this it was down by half or so. But it's just a number, what someone might give you for it could be a lot more. It didn't matter because if we tried to sell it then we'd both have taken an enormous loss. You know we'd worked like hell to pay off the house, so we had the value there. When everything was clicking along we decided to get that new office space. Since the house was paid for and its value was set at about what the loan for the office would be we were able to put the mortgage on it rather than on a commercial loan. The monthly payment wasn't any more than what our mortgage had been, so we thought we were good."

"What we didn't know was about to happen was this popping of the housing bubble. I asked everyone I could think of: bankers, realtors, my financial guy, if they thought it was a wise move. They all said yes, things were fine and you couldn't go wrong with real estate, especially with the spot we were putting together. Of course, we know now that those bastards on Wall Street and those hedge funds were fueling the whole thing and driving prices up. I just read where there was one hedge fund out of Chicago called Q-Exeter that became exceedingly active right before the crash. This guy was saying it made the crash 30 or 40% harder than it would have been otherwise. They cost me tens of thousands of dollars. Just imagine what they did to people all over this country: millions and millions. They're some of the worst kinds of criminals if you ask me. They figured out how to make money on the way up and the way down, and none of them went to jail. Go figure. Or is the Justice Department just lame?" He stopped to take a bite of one of the finger wings that had just been set down in front of them. "I'd like to stick one of these up the ass of a lot of those bastards." Bob had a tough-guy grin on his face.

Mike then responded. "Yeah, they were making money selling the securities around the world and then betting against them to fail and collect the insurance on them. That's what you're saying, right?"

"Exactly. And they were clever enough to get into the government and massage the regulations so that they couldn't be held criminally accountable. Pretty slick deal, huh? I wish they'd take those top guys at Goldman, Chase, Bank of America, hell there's all kinds of them responsible, and put them in a 6 by 9 cell all together, see how powerful they feel then."

"The consequences of the crash played out for people in various ways, depending on their situation, hasn't it?" Mike observed.

"Oh, there's got to be millions of stories. People probably died as a consequence. You know, like lose your health care because you don't have a job and can't make the premium payment, and then get really sick, that sort of thing. It reminds me of when you're out on the water in a little boat, minding your own business, fishing maybe. And then some ass hole in a really big boat goes by and sends waves that screw you all up. That's what those bankers did, hedge fund managers, their ilk. They go off doing all the crap they can get away with and we're here in the dark and have no idea what they're up to. But sure enough we get hit by the monster wake they send out around the world." Bob was shaking his head.

"Is there blame to go around between you and Stevie?" Mike asked rhetorically, moving the conversation to the divorce, knowing that there always was.

Bob answered, "You can't be with someone for twenty six years without having some "things." Of course, I sit around in the night at times and think about this and that, I'm not perfect. But here's the deal in my mind: there was this person I knew when we were dating; that was the person I was placing my bet on. I remember the night I decided to ask her to marry me. I just kept thinking about the *trust* we both would be putting into each other. Life is filled with all the unknowns, all the stuff that's going to come up. The question I had was: can you trust that person with that unknown future? What would she have done had I come down with cancer? Would she have just taken off? Time changes people too. If somebody doesn't love you anymore, it's just tough, it's just really really tough."

Bob was thinking for a moment, "Mike, why is it that you've had this steady marriage since you were what, twenty three weren't you? And I've had all these different relationships; and then this catastrophe when I'm in my fifties?"

Mike chuckled a little bit. He understood what Bob was asking and he'd actually thought about it before so had an answer already formulated in his head. "It's a lot luck, but I think I also understood who I am when I was really young and so did Sue. A lot of what dating is about is telling the other person who you are. If you don't know that yourself, well you can't very well tell someone. Things haven't been perfect for us. We've had a few times where one or the other was wondering if it was what we wanted, that is being together. We talk effectively though and don't leave things where they fester. Problems are kind of like physical wounds we suffer. If you don't take care of them properly they can turn into something far worse than what the original issue was."

Bob set his beer down on the table and moved it around a little on the coaster. "Truth is there was always that distance between us. Like a door or something." His mind was drifting to another time. "Behind that door is this place where you really connect…I don't think we ever could get there, really. Before I die I just hope I can meet someone that gets me and I get her and we can go into that room." Bob smiled, "Sorry, a little soapy there."

"No, don't be, I know what you mean. It's rare, even with me and Sue, we can go for months sort of off in our own place, but every once in a while something sort of shakes things up and if we don't go to that room, at least we know it's there. Huh, there I go."

Bob went on, "You know the really hard thing, and I imagine a lot of people struggle with this, is remembering all the good and really great

115

things we did together. We travelled and hiked, talked, shared great meals and sunsets. There's all the things you do for someone in that length of time, and the things they did for you. You just think they mean more, like glue to hold things together. I was reading a while back that some guy speculated that the reason for World War I had mostly to do with people's levels of consciousness. I think that was part of our situation, I was becoming more open to certain things and she was getting more closed. So something ultimately gives. She isn't a bad person; she has what she believes to be true about things. I guess we just got on a different page. But it doesn't matter now. All I have is the future, and I've got to do the best I can with what I have left in it."

"That's exactly right." Mike said. "Just don't forget to allow someone to get close to you. Sometimes it takes a bit of time to recognize that spirit."

Mike was looking at his watch, "Well, Bob I tell you, at least you have your health and that will go a long way to get you bouncing back."

"Yeah, that's what I've been focusing on. I work out and run all the time. It's pretty cheap entertainment too!"

Mike pointed to Bob to take the last of the chicken wings. It was time they called it a night. Mike knew Bob would be a real asset to his team when he got on board. Now they just needed the overall economy to remain somewhat stable, and for the recovery to stay on track. But given the politics of the country and the great deal of instability around the world, that would be an ever and ongoing question.

Chapter Eight

The phone rang six times and still no answer, then there was a pause 'You've reached Dave Herrick. Please leave me a message at the tone.'

"Poncho, hey it's Matt, just getting back to you on the timing for Moab. I'll be up till 10:30 or so if you get this."

Matt had his headphones on and was glued on the game. He heard a buzz in his ear as his phone was programmed to forward to his headphones. He paused the game, but he had TEVO so it would keep recording while he took time to answer the phone.

He could see it was Poncho, "The very brilliant Mr. Herrick. Hello."

"Hey Matt, I was in the shower."

"You in there by yourself?"

"Yes, unfortunately."

"So is this Joan going to make it to Moab? This mystery woman you've been telling me about."

"I think so. She has a meeting in Seattle the Thursday after we're in Moab, so she's been lining up a flight from Salt Lake." He was quiet for a moment, "I really-really like this woman Matt."

"Ohhhkay, I think I catch your drift. I'm looking forward to meeting her." Matt was feeling happy for his friend.

"I think I have everybody pretty much lined up." Dave said.

"Who all are you thinking?" Matt asked, wondering about these worldly types Dave was meeting.

"Overall I think there will be nine of us: you and Maria; me and Joan; Ron Witten, he's retired from Google, he's loaded, of course and I think he just needs a new challenge. His wife is Sally Hyde. She's an administrator in a school district down here and has a Ph.D in Education. "Then there's Aiden Filer and Heidi Bloomberg. I think she has connections to the big money back east, but I don't know the details. Aiden works with me in the lab; he's a specialist in protein folding and is a brilliant guy. He comes up with the most amazing ways to create experiments to figure out what's going on. I think being able to imagine those experiments is a sign of really deep intelligence. They can be very abstract, and you've got to have real grind to work through them, to get data knowing that you might be totally on the wrong track."

"And I also invited my cousin Nathanial Herrick, long for Nate. He's a specialist in film and has worked in Hollywood and all over. I think he has a latest girlfriend who might tag along with him. But I'm not sure. He'll be great for filming, editing, and all the connections we need to get what I'm thinking about creating out on the web."

"Aiden and Heidi can be pretty intense at times. They both raced bikes: he did mountain bikes and she was a street racer. She's been rich all her life, so underneath it all you can pick up on the dominance thing they have going. But it's under control, they're very likeable."

"I think my friend Eric Mays and his girlfriend Aubrey will be coming too. So I think that's eleven people." Matt told his friend, adding two to Dave's total. "Oh, I talked to my Uncle Dan and he's good with me taking his travel trailer along. It'll be good to have something like that at a base camp. It's a good place to keep food and it has a dependable toilet in it too. Maria and I will stay in it. If people want to camp there that's good or they can get rooms in Moab. We just need a good place to congregate and build a nice fire so we can get around it and talk."

"That's a great idea." Poncho said. "Say thanks to your uncle for me."

"What's the goal for this thing anyway Poncho? We can't just get together and talk and dance around, howl at the moon. We've got to produce something don't we? So that's the video you've been talking about, right?"

"I've been thinking a lot about that and I've got an idea. We can't start this revolution; it's already begun. Organizations like 350.org, Occupy Wall Street, Climate Reality, the Union of Concerned Scientists, and others, they've already got it started. Even the Tea Party in a way has started it. They were manipulated by big money a lot but some of those people realized that big business is ripping us off. They just didn't know the details. Well the truth is coming out now, slowly for sure. But it's getting clearer how the money interests have been manipulating things." "What I see us doing is this. We need a list of grievances kind of like Martin Luther nailing the 95 theses to the door of the church in Germany. We've got to say these are the certain pre-eminent activities people are doing that have to stop. We'll call them the Moab Manifesto. Has a ring to it don't you think?"

"Ah hah, pretty catchy. It's kind of like the Declaration of Independence, too. They were just revolting from tyranny and that's pretty much what were saying too. But I like the name, so what do we do with it?" Matt asked.

"Make a YouTube or Vimeo video like I mentioned, and it's got to be really good." Dave answered. "That's where my cousin Nate comes in. This thing really needs to pop. Nate's been around all those people doing these shorts and is a strong environmentalist too. He grew up in Montana. He's my dad's brother's son and is a big guy, kind of brawny."

"Are there any YouTube videos right now on the climate stuff?" Matt asked.

"Yeah, I've looked through a lot of them. There's this guy from NASA, Paul Adair and his presentation and graphics are really great. He

118

mentioned this website called climatecrocks.com. Holy cow when you go there you can find like over ninety little videos. Some explain the concepts and others are the deniers, which are the crock part of it I guess. They work to debunk the denier's points."

"I watched two videos this morning, one really lays out the problem, particularly the melting of the ice in the Arctic, it's one that NASA put together. They show the changing ice over ten years or so. It looks like a slushy. Like chunks of ice, thin ice, then water all moving around. You can tell as it changes from winter to spring to summer to fall. The big heavy chunky ice that's white which is the stuff that lasts all year long doesn't ever melt: well it just keeps getting smaller and smaller. Then in a light blue is the ice that forms every year, but then melts. Then there is the open water that's like a real dark blue. They say that permanent ice could be all gone in the next ten or fifteen years. I hope they're not missing something on that. Sea levels haven't risen drastically yet, only like 8" in all the last hundred years or so. That's because the Arctic ice is on water so just like ice cubes in a glass when they melt the water level stays about the same, it's just changing form. The real problem with sea level rise is when the ice on Greenland and the Antarctic really starts to flow, that ice is sitting on land, well rock, so it's not displacing water right now. This guy said we'll probably see three to six feet of rise this century. Think of what that means to all of the coastal cities."

"Is there ever any good news about all this stuff, Ponch?" Matt had that nervy feeling you get every so often when life seems so indifferent even meaningless.

"Actually, yeah two things."

"How's that?" Matt asked.

"Huge is that the cost of wind and solar, and particularly solar, are falling so fast that they'll be cheaper than getting your energy from coal, even with all their subsidies, in just a few years, like 2017 or 18 or so. Wind power is growing really fast too. And even geothermal should be coming along fast. Of course, the fossil fuels industry doesn't want us to believe in it. But like the guy says, even deniers will sooner or later have to face up to the fact that all the clean energy is much cheaper than the dirty stuff. That's where a big tax on coal in particular could knock it out."

"There's still oil and natural gas, right?" Matt noted.

"Yeah, and it's a myth that natural gas is so much cleaner than oil because all kinds of methane gets released in the process of getting it out of the ground and processing it. All kinds of nasty chemicals are put into the water they use, taking it totally out of the hydrological cycle, forever in any realistic timeframe. We're really getting conned on that one."

Poncho paused then began again, "And Matt, I just watched this video where this guy, what's his name I wrote it down. Found it, Alan Savory who was on the TED talk thing. He's showing how we can use livestock grazing to actually mimic nature and stop desertification and in the process sequester all kinds of carbon."

"What, you mean get more animals mulling around? I thought that was one of the big problems in the first place." Matt responded.

Dave went on. "Remember when it comes to ecology you need to keep in mind how nature has worked in the past. He starts out by showing land around the world where there are no more herd animals moving across it anymore. Where that happens a surface algae starts to grow. Turns out that's not good, he called it a type of cancer, because that film of algae actually works as a barrier for water to get into the ground. When it rains the water doesn't penetrate and then evaporates back to the atmosphere. When that happens then all the soil microbes disappear, they can't live without water. So you get this sterile land."

"But here's the amazing thing: he showed pictures of where he'd managed grazing of livestock back across that land. The animals hooves broke up that layer of algae and then they pooped and urinated which is nature's way of cycling nutrients. In just a year or so he had pictures of the very same places with grasses, plants, and small trees starting to grow. That's good for a lot of reasons, but hugely it's a way to sequester carbon. He said that some calculations have been done that say if we could change just half of the areas of the Earth that have been changing to desert back to places with grassland and shrubs, we could sequester massive amounts of carbon into the soil. It's a little counter intuitive, but it's hard to challenge his pictures."

Dave continued, "But at the end of the day the number one goal has to be to keep the giant glaciers at either end of the Earth in place, if we don't, oh God."

"What do you mean?" Matt asked.

"It's not just the flooding Matt, that's bad enough and will kill millions of people. But it's what happens when those huge ocean currents get shut down. What happens is you don't move heat from the equator up to the north, which is all that keeps northern Europe from turning into Siberia. And you don't get the mixing of oxygen into the ocean depths that keeps the organisms down deep alive. That's the ultimate killer Matt. The oceans become anoxic, which means 'without oxygen.' They turn puky green and belch hydrogen sulfide which is deadly to most everything living on the land. It's when the oceans turn on us totally, Matt. That's when we're really done. Our pale blue dot Earth becomes a pale purple- yellow-green-gray dot when seen from several billion miles away. It's a Carl Sagan thing; I'll maybe explain it more when we get to Moab."

Matt was thinking, "Okay, I think I know what you're talking about. And that grazing thing, yeah that sounds good. But the next thing you know, the fossil fuels guys will get a hold of that idea and they'll say look there's no problem we can just poop and pee ourselves out of this mess."

He went on, "I think it's mostly like George Good Elk said, "It's not so much that we don't know we have a problem or that we don't know what we might do to deal with it. The biggest challenge is just reacting aggressively enough, overcoming the drag of the deniers.' We're up against this huge problem and we don't know the limits. And when will we cross the line we can't come back from? That's the unknown; the really scary part of this whole issue. Don't you think?"

Dave was processing that question, "Yeah man, that's really it. We're messing around with this contraption, the earth's biosphere system. We don't really understand it, but were pushing it around. Why would we do that? Why wouldn't we take the conservative approach?"

"Ponch, I really need to hit the sack. I'll get it all finalized with everyone here. We'll get to Moab on Wednesday night the 24th of April and plan to head home on Sunday the 28th. I'm really looking forward to it man! Two days after Earth Day which is kinda good timing I'm thinking."

"Sounds good. I'll get things organized on my end. Hey, be thinking about some music too, something with the theme of "what do you believe." I'll call you the weekend before just to make sure everything is set."

"Okay, maybe I'll talk to my Uncle Dan. He's creative that way."

Chapter Nine

(Salt Lake City airport, Maria is landing, April 24th, 2013)
Matt left Boise at 7:00 pulling Uncle Dan's travel trailer. He knew it would take a little over six hours to get to the airport in Salt Lake City. Maria's flight didn't land until 3:30 that afternoon, so he figured he'd have a good buffer of time before she landed. It was a reasonably clear day so the view to the Wasatch Mountains that lined the eastern edge of most of central Utah could be seen and were always appealing to Matt.

As he made his way along the freeway, his mind wondered back the two and a half years that had passed since he'd gone through Utah on his way to San Diego to meet Poncho before their trip to Europe. He remembered wandering the streets of Park City with his architect's eye, studying the artistic atmosphere that had been created. It was a response to the environment and the sensibilities of the people that chose to live there.   From there he had gone to Sundance and then further to Saint George. He had to smile, remembering the round of golf he'd played with the two brothers, the one who was so competitive he'd even cheat to end with a better score than Matt, and the other brother who saw through his brother's short comings.

His mind continued to retrace the journey from San Diego on to Europe where he and Poncho had first met the young Germans, a few of whom he still communicated with. His mind moved on, remembering when he first met Reno in Switzerland. Whoa, that gelato and cappuccino had tasted good, that crisp and sunny morning in Interlachen.

Then there was that awful feeling he'd get thinking about those climbers of the Matterhorn, the first ones to ever reach the summit in 1865. That was just a few months after the American Civil War had ended. How ecstatic they must have felt being the first ones to have ever made it there. And then a few minutes later four of them fall thousands of feet to their death. What a horrible feeling it must be when you know you have *lost all control of your life*! A spooky thought came over him, 'could it ever get that way here, could conditions get so out-of-control that we lose all control of our future? That was very troubling.'

But then he'd met Maria in Rome. She was like a four leafed clover, so rare. He could have searched a life time and never found her wittingly. But through serendipity, she appeared. There was something about Matt, different than many his age. He knew what a precious gift had appeared to him. He could learn from the mistakes of others that were not as aware and not lose sight of the gift that had been placed in front of him. But he could not know now the challenges he would face, the unknowables of a chaotic future.

~~~~~

Just as in Boise a few months earlier, Maria was one of the last ones to appear at the gate. But from his vantage point Matt caught a glimpse of her in line behind five or six others. His heart palpitated seeing his dark-haired lover.

Maria was dressed nearly all in white, even her boots that pulled over her pants up half way on her calf were a tan-white. She had a powder-blue low-cut shirt on and a small necklace Matt had given her when she last visited. The one thing that stood out was her black backpack. She smiled broadly seeing Matt. He gave her a hug and a brief kiss, and then whispered something in her ear. Maria rocked back, her eyes widened. "Promise!" she said.

Matt just lifted his eyebrows and shifted his nose a little; that was a promise he'd savor keeping.

He held her hand and they started talking about the flight, she'd left her room in Boston that morning at 6:00 am to make the connections she needed.

"I got quite a bit of work done on the flight, I've been working with NOAA, you know of them don't you?"

"Aren't they like NASA, but deal with the Oceans?" Matt observed.

"And the atmosphere; it's the National Oceanic and Atmospheric Administration. It's where more the biologists and chemists work; NASA is more the engineers; but I think there's a big overlap. I got a draft of a letter from the Royal Society of London about some recent work they've been doing on acidification and the affects up the food chain from the crustaceans, which are the first organisms dealing with the effects of the extra carbon dioxide mixing in the oceans. There's some data emerging that's getting some people a little anxious. You know the fish we harvest need something to eat. If the food chain underneath them starts to break down of course we feel it up the food chain. Just something else for us to talk and worry about at the meeting." Maria suggested they stop at one of the food vendors, she was feeling a craving for some chocolate.

~~~~~

Matt headed south on I 15, he was heading for Spanish Fork where he'd take Highway 6 to Green River. Then there was a short stretch on I 70 to where he'd then head south on Highway 191 to Moab.

"Everywhere seems so big here in the western US," Maria observed. "You can drive for miles and miles and never pass a town. And look how far you can see." They were nearing Green River, having crossed the stretch from Spanish Forks that is a very arid and vast landscape. "It's a little like Spain here, the aridness at least."

"You'll think you're on a different planet as we get closer to Moab. It's really different. There's a huge amount of this red rock, and then when you go a little south of Moab you start seeing this weird banding of white and red rock, like a zebra pattern."

"Is there much vegetation?" Maria asked.

"I don't remember very much, maybe some grasses and shrubs. I don't really remember trees at all. There's probably some trees growing down along the Colorado River. It flows right past the town."

"So are we mostly going to mountain bike, or just hike?" Maria had her seat moved back and had her feet resting on the dash. She adjusted her sunglasses and stuck her right hand out into the wind whistling by her opened window.

"Okay, I haven't told you yet, but look at this." Matt pulled a flier he had in the storage box between his seat and Maria's. On the front was a picture of a Hummer being driven down through some rocky area, there was a caption that told of four wheeling adventures.

"Are we going to go on a trip in one of these?" She asked, thinking that sounded like a lot of fun.

"There's room for six people, so I'm hoping Poncho and Joan and Eric and Aubrey will go with us. They've already committed actually, I just wanted to keep it as a little surprise until now for you."

Maria was silent for a short time, "Does riding around in one of those huge vehicles match up with the values we're trying to promote?" She looked towards Matt.

"Or driving this pickup pulling that travel trailer, we're adding our carbon footprint right now. How do we live and not do that?" Matt replied.

"I know I've had this discussion with others; it's a paradox. We had no control over this huge system we were born into. We have to be a part of it just to survive. But at the same time if we don't change it will destroy us." She was grinning, "I guess it's like a bad date, you just have to put up with it until you can get home. We just have to figure out how to get home fast!" She started laughing and pinched Matt in the side.

Matt was resting his hand on the gear shift between their two seats; Maria moved hers over and set it on his. "My man's lookin' out for me! He's earning lots and lots of chocolate."

Matt pushed on the accelerator a little, "We need to get to our room!" He looked hard into her eyes; she was taken back just a little. Once she recovered she had to tell him, "I agree!" He'd decided that for the first night they'd get a room in Moab then find a place to park the travel trailer for the rest of the time. First things first!

"Chocolate?!!!" Maria said in a seductive voice, looking at Matt with her bedroom eyes.

~~~~~~

They showered together. Maria loved the feel of their soaped-slick-bodies rubbing together. Their love making began there and soon moved to the bed. It did not take long before Maria began making the sounds she had not held back when they were in the cabin in January. Matt softly put his hand over her mouth, she giggled and pulled the pillow over her mouth and continued her expression of pleasure. "Matt!" her fingers pushed more deeply into his back. Then sounds that were not words began to spurt from someplace that even Maria had no name for.

"I love you," Matt said as softly and controlled as he could.

"Ohhhh," Maria roused, she was biting on part of her lower lip.

"Uh,"

The pleasure and closeness that drew them near and near continued for some time. Chocolate, there were rivers of chocolate.

They were young and a second round would follow shortly.

~~~~~~

It was only late April, but Moab was already quite warm, even at breakfast time. Matt had his tan shorts with a light green and light weight REI body tight shirt on. He didn't like to wear sandals so much, he preferred the new designs of open shoes that wrapped your feet. They protected your toes but still let the air breath easily through them. Maria was in her shorts as well, she had a white blouse and a sand-red wind breaker like top on. Her hair was quite fluffy having just been washed and wind dried.

Matt was eager to see his old friend, it had been over two years now since they'd seen each other in person. Meeting Joan and all the others was going to be invigorating, he imagined.

"I think I see Poncho," Maria announced as they were getting out of Matt's pickup a block or so up the wide street in Moab they had chosen to park along. Maria had not seen Poncho for the 2 ½ years since the days in Rome. She was eager to see him as well.

Matt and Maria crossed the wide main street meeting Poncho and Joan on the other side. Maria quickened her step so she could get to Poncho just a little more quickly. They hugged and Maria gave him a quick kiss on his

125

cheek. Matt and Poncho hugged the way guys do. There were those smiles and sounds that come when special friends meet after much time apart. Poncho (Dave) set to introducing Joan just as soon as the initial phase of greeting had passed. He turned and took her hand, Matt was smiling he could immediately see the connection to his friend in Joan. She had a sense of being reserved, but holding much behind the eyes.

"Okay, this is Joan Labeau." Matt extended his hand and they shook.

"This is Maria Laducci," Matt then said, allowing the two women to connect.

"I've been hearing about you for what a year or so," Maria began, looking towards Joan.

"And I learned of you very soon after I met Dave," she laughed, "I mean Poncho."

"God, it's good to see you," Matt said, putting his hand around Dave's head as if to give him a Dutch rub. Poncho punched him slightly in the stomach. Matt acted like it hurt.

They had their eyes set on a restaurant which opened to the street and had a feel of indoors and outdoors. The four of them were first getting there and so worked with the waitress that seated them so as to get a large enough area for the eleven people they expected for breakfast.

"Um, it smells good," Maria noted as they were sitting down.

"They must have the barbecue going already." Matt said.

"Your hair and beard are a lot shorter than the last time I saw you," Maria was smiling looking towards Poncho.

"There are plenty of people with long hair at my company, especially around the lab. I guess it's just not me."

"Poncho has that black wingtips quality about him, don't you think?" Matt was being a little sarcastic, but he knew Dave well enough to know it was about true.

"It's funny to hear you calling Dave, Poncho." Joan began. "He told me that you did, but it doesn't seem real until you actually hear someone say it. Wasn't it you that came up with that name, Matt?" Joan questioned.

"Yup, he had that old Mexican poncho he'd wear around campus. I mean how could I not nickname him that?"

"Do you have any pictures?" Joan asked.

Matt looked up scanning his memory to think of any photos he might have of his friend from their days at the University of Idaho. "I remember one, but I haven't seen it for a long time, maybe it's in some of my boxes. I might have printed one out. I don't think I have one still on my phone. I'll try to remember to look when I get back."

"I'll get your email so I can remind you," Joan was smiling.

"There's Eric and Aubrey," Matt announced. Matt stood up so he could wave to his friend. As they approached the table Matt went about introducing everyone. It made it easier that Dave had sent an email out with everyone's name and picture on it. It made getting names and faces connected a lot faster.

Almost right away Ron Witten and Sally Hyde, along with Aiden Filer and Heidi Bloomberg showed up. Everyone was pulling out their little sheet of paper with the names and faces. He'd also given a very brief bio on everyone. Dave was good at thinking ahead, anticipating things that would be helpful.

Dave continued, speaking to everybody, "I think my cousin Nate is going to meet us up at Lone Mesa; he won't get here until later this afternoon. He might have his girlfriend with him, Liza. But that was up in the air when we talked a couple of days ago. He's a free spirit for sure. He has this long, pretty thick auburn hair, and a beard with a little grey streak in it." He paused for a moment, "So everyone's here. Rebels with a cause!" He lifted his glass of orange juice.

Everyone took to chatting, getting acquainted for this rather unusual gathering. Based on the strength of Dave's charm with them all, and his conviction that something really important needed to happen, they'd all agreed to come.

Dave and Matt had worked out a basic itinerary, there needed to be a certain amount of order to how they spent their time. But they of course also wanted everyone to have time to spend as they wanted.

For this first day they scheduled a walk where everyone was together, as much as possible, so they could get to know each other a little more, and just get settled into the new environment. The plan was to go to Dead Horse State Park and then do some hiking along the trails that offered such great vistas of the Earth's geological history.

~~~~~

"There's the one we have reserved," Maria was pointing towards a large shade structure just a short distance away.

"I think I'll just park right along here. Good as any don't you think?" Maria just nodded her head that she agreed.

Matt stopped so he could talk with the others about the location, it's the place he'd reserved, but they didn't actually have to stay here. This would be where they'd spend the next three nights planning how to save the world for humanity, so getting a place everyone would be happy with seemed a prudent thing to do.

It was barren, but that was true just about any place near Moab. The views to the distance were spectacular. Most everyone was staying in town so it didn't need to offer a lot more. Matt, on second thought, had decided that he and Maria would rent a room most nights anyway, a good shower and chocolate was nicer that way.

Dave's cousin Nate had spent the night on the Mesa in his camper just a short distance away. Dave had called him and he easily met them as they were gathering at the camping site.

"It's a plan then," Matt said, after talking with everyone about the location. It would be fine as far as everyone was concerned. Group dynamics didn't cause too much of a stir on this first order of business.

Maria guided Matt as he backed into a nice spot they'd agreed would be better. She was signaling lightly with her right hand, her dominant one. When the back of the travel trailer was where she and Matt had agreed would be a good spot, she waved her hand telling him to stop.

Uncle Dan's travel trailer was one of the clean-lined Euro-style types, an Airstream. It was 10 years old and Dan had gotten it from a woman he knew for a few bucks and some barter on a very large framing job he'd done. "This baby could sell for over $45,000, just as it is," Matt told Maria as they were unpacking and setting it up.

She looked around and noticed that it seemed to be rather simple in its finishes, and it was just a nineteen footer, it seemed small. "$45,000, really?"

"Yeah, absolutely. These travel trailers are built really well, people just want them. Uncle Dan did some horse trading to get it; you know like a labor swap thing. This lady wanted a remodel more than she wanted a travel trailer."

"You Americans and your travel trailers," Maria was shaking her head.

"Looks good," Nate had appeared at the door. Matt smiled and extended his hand so they could shake. He recognized him straight away from the photo's Dave had provided.

"You don't look at all like Dave," Matt said, knowing that Nate was Dave's first cousin.

"Do cousins ever look anything alike?" Nate flipped his long auburn hair to one side and adjusted his sun glasses. He was brawny just like Dave had described. He looked ready for a volleyball match and he'd be spiking some hard ones down on you.

"This is my girlfriend, Maria," Matt was leaning back against the stove and nodded in her direction.

"Hi," Nate said, thinking to himself how pretty Maria seemed. He liked her faint accent when she told him she was glad to make his acquaintance.

"These Airstreams are great, built to last." Nate's eyes were scanning the interior.

"My uncle let me use it. I couldn't come close to affording one of these, it's almost like buying a house to get one."

"Yeah, that's what I've heard."

"Are you going to hike with us?" Matt asked.

"Oh sure, we're going out to Dead Horse Point I was told."

"Not a very nice name," Maria observed.

"I was reading about it," Nate continued, "It said that some horses got blocked out at the end of the Mesa and couldn't get away and ended up dying of thirst. That sucks."

"How awful!" Maria said with a woman's empathy for animals in her voice.

"Let's make sure to take water," Matt was holding a bottle in his hand.

~~~~~

Everyone had gathered under the large shade structure. Just to one side of it was the fire pit. "Nate has enough firewood in his trailer for us to stay here a month." Dave observed.

"I'm seeing a pretty small fire; don't want us to be hypocrites straight away." Matt smiled and punched his friend lightly on the shoulder.

"Pretty hard to live in this world without releasing carbon," Ron Witten said, "If you flush the toilet your releasing carbon somewhere.

Heidi was laughing, "I'll just hold then." This caused everyone to giggle a little.

Dave started. "Before we get going on this hike, I just want to thank everybody for getting here! I hope you've been reading my propaganda," Dave had been sending out emails telling everyone about what he hoped they would accomplish. So it wasn't like there was a great mystery of what this was all about: saving the world for all the babies to come, human and others, basically.

Dave had changed into a shirt with a decal on the left side. "I decided I'd wait until we were starting out on this hike to show this to everyone. Like I told you in the emails, Matt and I agreed that we need some iconic symbol for this whole movement. It's climate change, it used to be global warming, but the thing that stood out to a lot of us is this one symbol, these glaciers. They're the iconic symbol of our time. We exist as we do because they are there. If they go away, so do we very likely. And about everything else that exists with us. If we save our glaciers, if they are still sitting there about the size they are now in a hundred or two hundred years then we will have been successful in what we are doing here. If they are gone or can't be saved…well, I don't want to think about it."

"Looks great!" Aiden said, he'd only heard a little bit about the idea. A few drafts of it had been sent out, but until now only Joan had seen what he'd actually come up with. Everybody else was agreeing. "Awesome, way cool," Dave heard.

"I have like five patches for everybody. We want the world to start seeing this logo everywhere! Let anybody that asks know they can go to www.saveourglaciers.com and get the website where they can order these logos."

"Oh, did you guys watch the movie that 350.org released last Sunday, on the 'do the math tour'? I hope you got my email about that." Most everyone was nodding their head that they had. "I've got it on my iPad. I think it'll be good to watch. Anyway, let's go for a hike, we can get to the heavy stuff later."

Maria and Joan had quickly started a conversation, they of course both knew of the other but this was now the first time they'd been able to meet. They each shared half of the intrepid duo that had forged such a deep friendship between school and their adventure in Europe. There would be so much to know about the other.

"Let's go through the visitor center," Joan said to Dave. "I'm sure there will be information there that will make the hike that much more interesting.

"I agree," Maria added.

Outside the building all sorts of desert adapted shrubbery had been planted, a fairly long stairway led through the plantings to the horizontally and layered looking building that of course echoed the landscape all around. Tall windows seemed to be everywhere in it.

Joan stood near the rails gazing off to the vast panorama before her. The red canyon walls, punctuated by the sage green of the indigenous plant life stretched for sixty or more miles to the horizon. It was the first time she'd seen the deep desert canyons. She took the needed moment to just let it sink in.

After they'd all gone through the visitor's center they congregated at the starting point for the trail. "Well it's a little over nine miles to make the loop out to Big Chief Point. I'm guessing three and half maybe four hours at the most to make the loop. It depends on how much time we spend out at the end." Dave was saying. "There's a couple of other viewpoints along the way. I think it's pretty hard to get lost."

A group of eleven people can't all stay close together for very long. Conversations had already started between different people and as they began walking those conversations just continued.

Maria, Joan, and Sally had formed one small group. "If I remember correctly you are from Oregon, am I right?" Maria asked looking towards Sally.

Sally smiled, "Dave's list of everybody was pretty cute wasn't it? Good memory. Yes, actually I grew up in Eugene. I've got the web toes like they say."

Maria continued, "I need to tell you, I took the list and searched the different cities people call their home towns. I'm from Spain so I didn't know where they were all at. Eugene looks very green."

"Oh, it's that way all over the Willamette Valley, its green for a reason, we get lots of rain."

"A lot different than here, I'd think?" Maria responded, holding one hand over her eyes so she could dim the reflecting light some and see to the far horizon.

"Oh my, this place is the antithesis," Sally responded with emphasis. "But this place has its own kind of beauty, I think. The red cliffs and the sky that seems to go on forever are wonderful. The sky doesn't feel as big in Oregon. You always seem to be in a valley or on a hillside with lots and lots of trees which makes things seem not so expansive."

"If I had to choose, I'd live where it's greener," Joan piped in. "It's very green on the east coast, that's what I've seen most of my life, so it feels like home. I like this big expanse, but it seems a bit like Mars."

The trail was quite wide and another group passed them on their way back from the loop. There were always a few that would catch your eye and say "hi". Most people on hikes are in a good mood.

"You're working on a Ph.D, didn't I read that?" Joan questioned looking at Sally.

"Oh, I've started. It's going to be a few years getting through it I'm sure."

"What school?" Again Joan asked.

"Oregon State, that's Corvallis. We're pretty close to the University of Oregon which is in Eugene. Were about fifty miles apart. So as you might expect all of central Oregon is an amalgamation of Duck and Beaver fans. Ron loves sports, he graduated from the U of O so he's a pretty big Duck's fan." Sally sighed just a little, "So we're at most all the Duck's home football and basketball games. I like going with him some of the time, but I have my own things too. I let him be the sports fanatic in the family."

"Any kids on the horizon?" Maria questioned, it was a subject she was running through her own mind a lot these days, and she was curious what other young women were thinking. With Maria's more visionary knowledge of what the future might be for children she might have, she was questioning if she wanted to bring them into the world.

Sally looked towards her new friend, her eyes were moving around a little as was her head, "I'm like most women, I have my dreams of children running around; needing me, all that. If you're paying much attention these days though, you have to wonder what sort of world I'd be bringing them in to."

"How about you?" Sally turned the question to Maria. She smiled faintly, "With Matt, I assume you mean?"

Sally laughed lightly, "Oh of course, you and Matt aren't' married. But yes, let's say Matt's the father."

"I'm like you, I'd love to have a child with Matt. Of course we practice making them a lot," her eyes widened and she smiled broadly. "But I'm like you, I'm very concerned about what sort of world they will have when they are our age or a little older. What's it going to be like?" It was a topic they'd return to later.

A short distance away Aubrey adjusted her sunglasses and pulled her hat a little tighter down on her head, as she negotiated a turn at the trail head. Heidi was walking next to her. She touched the leaf of an arid-looking plant as she walked next to it, finding its sage green leaf and lavender flowers inviting.

"That sun is pretty intense," Aubrey told her walking partner.

Heidi looked towards Aubrey, "It feels different, a little less intense but maybe more piercing than on a hot day in Boston. We have so much more humidity. It can feel like you're boiling a little bit. This feels like... I don't know, maybe like little arrows hitting you." Heidi responded.

"Ugg, let's see did you grow up on the east coast? Aubrey questioned.

"Yeah, in New Jersey, a town called Newton. It's in the north west corner of the state. We have lots of rolling hills, trees, and humidity."

Aubrey had pulled out the paper Dave had put together with the brief biography on everyone. "You play the piano. Like play-play?" Her intonation suggested the question of whether Heidi was a serious pianist.

"There was a time when I had dreams of being a concert pianist. My teachers were always telling me if I worked hard enough I could do it. I had an interview with Julliard, but it didn't go well. Working hard isn't enough. There's got to be something in your spirit that gets you to that really high level. I had to finally admit that I just don't have that. I was always good at math and people told me to focus on finance if I wanted to make good money. They didn't tell me about some of the people I'd have to work with." Heidi laughed at her own comment.

"No one can prepare you for the personalities you'll meet along the way," Aubrey followed.

"How about you?" Heidi asked. "What part of the country are you from?"

"Upper mid-west; Watertown, South Dakota to be exact. We have lots of rolling grass lands and not very many trees; and wind, lots of wind. I went to school in Brookings at South Dakota State. It never even occurred to me to try and go to Harvard. I see that's where you went."

"Yes, my dad went to Harvard, he's a Harvard man. I guess in a way I never had a thought I wouldn't go to Harvard. It was always just pretty much assumed I'd go there. Trust me, I understand connections and a silver spoon, I'm guilty. But it wasn't like I could just sleep and go there, it was hard work."

"I'm sure it was. Are the buildings old and Gothic and covered with ivy? That's the picture I have in my head, where did I get that? That movie Love Story, I'm thinking. Remember that, with Ryan O'Neill and Ali McGraw. Oh, I loved it."

"You've got it, lots of red brick buildings and bronze statues."

"I want to see the east coast some day. A trip out there is one of those things Eric and I talk about taking every once in a while. I'd like to see the Civil War sites. I'd love to see the trees all turning color. Actually Idaho has some great fall color if you know where to go."

"Oh that's right there's like four of you from Idaho. From Boise, right?" Heidi queried with a question in her voice.

"Yes, I live in Boise now after about 3 years in Rapid City, which is in South Dakota too. I'd been teaching school there. I really love it in Boise. The weather is mild and there's just a lot of great recreation really close. Lots of trees have been planted throughout the city so it's actually nice and green through the summer. And there is lots of great fall color in the trees and shrubs. But what I really like is going over to near Sun Valley in October. Oh the aspen are an intense yellow and the brush is often red and orange. It can be so striking with the green of the big conifer trees. Eric knows the trees, he taught a lot to me about them."

"What got you to Boise?" Heidi continued her query.

"A job, mostly. I'm an English teacher and there was an opening at a junior high. I have to admit that I had a bit of an in for the job. I went to graduate school with the gal that was the head of the selection committee; in fact she told me about the opening. I probably would still be in Rapid if she hadn't called."

"Did you meet Eric in Boise?"

"Ah ha, Yeah. And we'd never have met if I hadn't got the job."

133

"Chance is just always at play in our lives, isn't it?" Heidi responded with a certain ironic quality to the tone of her voice.

"It's almost spooky that way or maybe even sad. You wonder what doors you missed passing through." Aubrey's voice was almost melancholy. I guess we only get to experience the doors we choose to enter." She smiled and looked towards Heidi, "I hope I'm not being obnoxious with my "profound" observation!"

"Not at all…very good, actually!" Heidi responded.

"And you?" Aubrey then asked.

Heidi gathered her thoughts for a moment, "Meeting Aiden was just this chance thing too. He was studying biology and I'm in finance, our classes never really crossed. It just turned out that we both had this desire to learn how to throw a pot on a potter's wheel. It was only worth one credit as I remember. It turned out that we both needed an elective in the arts. So through some serendipity we both chose that class at that time. And you know it just sounded like fun. I'd seen a few plates and cups a friend of mine had made, so I just decided to take the class. And poof, there was Aiden." Her voice faded some, it was a special memory.

"Tell me more." Aubrey said, the way girls will when romance creeps into a conversation.

Heidi smiled at her. "It's funny what you notice and remember about someone," she laughed slightly. "I liked his shirt, it was this purple-plaid thing. It was quite old, it looked like it had been washed about a thousand times, and there was even a small rip in one shoulder. But it looked really good on him. Our eyes met at one point, he smiled at me. He has a nice smile…at least to me. I distinctly remember I felt something stir inside. I was dating a guy already, a Harvard man from a well-to-do family; Hmm." She was remembering.

"Then you were wondering if he'd try to talk to you, right?"

"Oh my of course, you know what that's like?" Heidi looked towards Aubrey for confirmation.

"Oh yes. The guys think it's so hard for them to approach us…so they think it's easy for us to sit back and wait for them?"

Further down the trail Aubrey moved the conversation to the more timely and relevant topic. "You have a good job in finance and you were a serious bike racer. So what gets you interested in this meeting Dave and Matt have put together?"

"Well, Aiden of course. He and Dave have become really good friends through their work. They're both molecular biologists, they work on all this cutting edge stuff. It's actually really interesting. I understand just enough that I have a vague idea of what he's telling me. The lab actually has certain things he can't even share with me. I'd be clueless about it anyway. Aiden says Dave reminds him of John Kennedy. They say Kennedy had some ethereal quality that other men admired and would follow him instinctively, a natural born leader. I think he's right, Dave has some sort of gravity. He's seductive to both women and men."

"I hope for Joan's sake he's not like Kennedy in his womanizing." Aubrey noted JFK's reputation that way.

"My instincts say no, that was kind of that generation. I heard JFK's father was the same way and expected his sons to be like that too." Heidi said.

"I hadn't heard that, I guess it would make sense though." They walked for a short distance and nothing was said. Aubrey continued, "Matt and my Eric are good friends, we've hung out quite a bit with him. Being a bachelor he's been really faithful as far as I know. He seems to be very dedicated to Maria. Maybe there's a generational thing going on, do you think more of the guys our age really are dedicated to relationships? Staying still and not wandering off?"

"Oh, that's so hard to say. Hmm, maybe…maybe life has changed in some way that leads a little higher percentage of them to want what most of us girls mostly want: "relationship." I think they must have a lot of the old time male motivation though. You know, impregnate as many different women as you can. And most of them don't have the vaguest clue why they have that motivation."

Aubrey had to comment, "You sound a little like an anthropologist."

Heidi laughed, "Yes, you're right, I do. I read a lot of that stuff."

Something occurred to Aubrey, "a lot of the problems we seem to have in our society…our whole civilization, it seems is from people clinging to old obsolete ideas about how the world does and should work. Don't you think?"

"Definitely that." Heidi shook her head affirming the notion. "It's the money too. I've seen the influence of big money on people up close," she shook her head again. "It turns people, it's the power and certain people love their power, and their stuff."

Heidi had been studying the rationale that Dave had sent along to everyone to think about before coming to the rendezvous, she'd reached that kind of magical point where she had become very firm in her belief, passing through the wishy-washy stage. She, probably even more than Aiden, had crossed that point where she now thought of herself as a warrior in the cause, an activist.

Heidi continued, "Look, I know quite a few people that are a part of the so called elite in America. They know we have to change. They know it, but they're being like kids you call in for the night to get a bath and go to bed. They know it's inevitable that they have to change. But what they're doing is just so engulfing, and for many of them the source of much of their wealth. They just do everything they can to look the other way and not listen to the voices of those telling them that things are going way wrong. And it's them; the elite, that have to change. It's just so not convenient for them to do so; I swear. They'll drag their heels until we all go over the cliff with them, and I don't want to do that."

Aubrey had studied history quite a bit and could see the correlation with our time and past conflicts between the ruling class and the rest. The difference this time, though, was that not only were there political conflicts over wealth and power, but the very balance of life on the planet is in jeopardy. Sort of the ultimate stakes are on the table. "A large majority of people with inherited wealth and power often feel entitled to their positions, like it was ordained by God." Aubrey smiled, "Dave and Matt would say the "divine" since God actually means the goodness of the divine."

Heidi's face showed a question.

Aubrey continued, *"The Kingdom of Good,"* the virtuous circle of goodness" the Dr. Sherman lecture dealy?"

Heidi shook her head, "Oh, yes, of course, I've studied the website a lot."

Aubrey went on, "Look at the French Revolution, the American Revolution, and about any other revolution. It required massive change to an entrenched social order. If history teaches anything it is usually bloody. Look at the Civil War in America, it was about slavery and basic human rights. That didn't change without a brutal blood bath war. The civil rights movement in America was generally peaceful, but even with it there was blood spilled; and it's really still being played out. It's hard for me to see how getting the elites that control our world's politics today to massively change, as the scientists are saying we have to, will happen without a similar bloody war." Heidi could see that her new friend was quite observant. She was rather enlightened. But was she right about that? Will it take a bloody revolution?"

They neared a place where the others had stopped to take in a particularly impressive view. Heidi had one last comment to make. "I know, the old and entrenched does not give way to the new easily."

Joan and her new friends walked up to where Dave and Matt were already standing. Dave had his binoculars out and was studying the walls of the canyons. He put his arm around Joan and gave her a kiss. He was holding a flier, "It says that the rocks exposed down at the bottom, right next to the Colorado River were formed about 323 million years ago, give or take a few million years. Right here, where we're standing is part of what they call the Kayenta formation and it was formed about 144 million years ago. So at the bottom our ancestors are amphibians living mostly in some shallow seas, and here at the top they're some sort of little mammal living in burrows trying to keep out of the way of some dinosaur. Plus or minus three thousand feet of geologic history exposed here. Really fricking incredible!"

Joan punched him lightly in the ribs, she wasn't much for his using words like that even if they were changed a little. Dave nodded his head that he understood. But then grinned, he would reserve his right for emphasis.

Maria had sat down on a nearby rock and with her binoculars studied the landscape. It was vaguely like some parts of Spain with its aridness. But in Spain she had never seen 180 million years of geology laying out for display as it is here. A view like this had never been explained to her there.

Matt sat down next to her, "When you think about it the way Poncho just said, you know 144 million years…you touch some surface of rock and it's been just there for all those years or whatever. When it formed our ancestors were huddled up in some little burrow someplace chomping on the roots of some tree that was shading some dinosaur. Geez, think of that, there's some unbroken line of life that leads all the way back to those little creatures."

Matt's mind drifted for a moment and then returned to the conversation with Maria. "The life in me or you has been going nonstop since the beginning; if you think of the life force itself, like a separate thing, it just inhabits various individuals–countless organisms–through all of time. So in that way it has never ceased. Like a flame that just gets passed from torch to torch."

Maria wiggled a little, there was a part of her that wanted to be sarcastic to her lover; she decided to just pinch his ear lightly. Matt laughed, he knew what she meant.

Nate was tagging along with Ron and Aiden, the three of them were already down the trail some. They were all interested in mountain bikes. Aiden had actually spent two years on the American tour. He'd briefly ridden in Europe as well.

"Aiden, so you raced some on mountain bikes?" Nate had seen the mention of that on Dave's introduction sheet.

"Yes, I did the XCT cross country tour for two years. I just couldn't do well enough to get sponsors to back me. I was paying for pretty much everything myself and getting to the events, covering entry fees, room and board. I loved it though; it can be such a rush."

"Was that before you met this lady you're with now?" Nate was wondering how all that traveling would impact a relationship.

"Oh yeah, it was before I went to college, I was like nineteen or twenty. It's easy to just head out then and do whatever you want to do, nothing tying you down."

"Yes, for me it's been nineteen and twenty over and over; like Ground Hog Day." Nate knew what he was all about and wasn't tepid to state it. "I live by my own rules. My way of life probably isn't what a lot of people would choose, going all over the continent doing photo shoots. But I like it. It's not always real glamorous, but from time to time I get to do something really great and creative. And when you see your work out there and people are saying like that's cool. That is cool! That keeps me going!"

"Do you ever shoot mountain biking?" Ron asked.

"No, I never have."

"What sort of things do you shoot?"

"Corporate stuff mostly, advertising videos, videos for bands with some song they're trying to push. And I do some website videos for businesses. Dave has something he wants me to shoot for his company. They've got some hot new product they want to create some buzz for."

"I saw that you're retired from Google," Nate said looking at Ron. "Most people our age are still trying to get into some mid-level management job and make the payments on a car and a house, and you're already retired?"

He nodded his head and raised his eyebrows which sort of conveyed the thought that it just is what it is. "I am 39; I have eight or ten years on most of you. I hit the timing right and had the right skills they needed just then. We're not stupid rich either. I don't think of myself as retired. I've got some other ideas I want to explore, I'm just taking a couple of years and thinking about what I want to do with the rest of my life."

"Like what?" Aiden then asked.

"Well, to be honest, something to do with why we're all here. I got the programmer bug when I was in like high school. My friends were the nerds and we learned how to do some simple programming and I came up with this little video game. That got me hooked. I'm pretty lucky Sally stuck with me considering the kind of hours I worked. We grew up together. A lot of people don't grow up together well. I guess we got lucky. But you asked me what I'm thinking about doing. You've heard of fusion power, haven't you?"

Aiden answered, "Every time I hear something about it though it's like fifty years before it can be a viable energy source."

"I used to think that," Ron said, "But I learned of this Fusion Energy Consortium. I really think this group has it worked out. They call it their SPOS or Solar Power Operating System. Because it is like the fusion that goes on inside stars. This would just be moving the process to the Earth and controlled in a very small area. It's safe they say because there's no radioactive material to store for thousands of years. They say they can put a plant right in the middle of a city and have no safety concerns."

"No kidding?" Nate said.

"Yes, that's what they say. So they plan to use the heat they generate to boil water that drives turbines just like we do now. They say they can also use the massive amount of heat generated to create hydrogen. Which is the primary molecule needed that can then be combined with carbon dioxide to create gasoline that can be burned in the cars we have now. That's a big deal since there are already hundreds of millions of cars around the world with engines designed to use gasoline."

"But doesn't that just make the whole global warming problem worse?" Nate asked right away.

"That, of course, was the first thing I thought of too. But, if again they're not full of shit, they have a process that is carbon neutral. On their website it says they can create a machine that extracts carbon dioxide from the atmosphere and then combine it with hydrogen they create as a by-product of the fusion process to make various hydrocarbons including gasoline. That is very alluring as I just said since it would work with the engine designs we currently have. So they remove from the atmosphere carbon dioxide that is equal to the amount emitted from all our vehicles. That's the carbon neutral idea. I admit that I need to know a lot more about it before I get too involved, but if it's true, to me that's extremely exciting! I guess you do have to wonder about the carbon dioxide that is already there."

"What would you be doing?" Aiden asked.

"To be honest I haven't even begun talking at any depth with them. But it sounds like they will need programmers, and people with skills in advanced IT. In about a month I have my first meeting with people in their human resources group to start the conversation. It may end up being a dead end. I hope not. I think this is just the sort of breakthrough the world really needs right now if we're going to skirt around this crisis with the environment. I've had a lot of time to read, Dave directed me to a lot of good articles, even to the information from that lecture he attended in Rome. I was your typical skeptic a few years ago, of course that's before I began educating myself in earth and life science. I see this bigger picture now that Dave talks about. It's a little bewildering, really, how people can have a lot of ability in really pretty advanced technology, but still not have a real foundation in how the Earth works. I used to be one of them. But I was curious and started educating myself. I like seeing the big picture... and it seems the big picture just keeps getting bigger and bigger the more you learn."

"Now that sounds like Dave," Cousin Nate said.

Further back Dave and Matt were hanging close to Maria, Joan, and Sally. They were just a few meters away, but their conversation was more specific to everything they'd been thinking about the past few months and what they wanted to accomplish with the rendezvous, besides a lot of fun.

Dave began, "I think we need to start thinking pretty quick about where we want to take the camera shots. We don't want to get stuck on the last day scurrying around to get some great photography. I want to get images of everybody enjoying this world; loving it for what we get free of charge. I'm seeing some shots of mountain biking, a little rock climbing and then maybe we'll get lucky and find some people doing that and get a quick interview. Everybody's going to have a different take on what they want to project. Let's pass it around for them to be thinking about. I think Nate can get some shots at the end of this walk so we can use this experience some."

"Are you still thinking we'll call this thing the Moab Manifesto?" Matt asked.

Dave shook his head in affirmation. "I like the ring to it. It sounds kind of sporty and political. Huh, I see Karl Marx on a mountain bike."

Matt chuckled, it was a funny vision. "So how do you see this whole thing coming together? Like, what are the first part, the middle part, and then the end?"

Dave had a piece of paper in his back pocket and pulled it out and handed it to Matt. "Here's what I'm thinking." Matt took a moment to study it. He was nodding his head noting that he was getting the idea. It used the: who, what, why, where, etc. approach. It starts with Dave describing the crisis humanity is facing, focusing explicitly on temperature change and how that impacts the biosphere.

Dave began. "Climate Change, actually, is too limiting in its description. It is just one aspect of the bigger picture of human activities around the world that are leading to disastrous effects and certain calamity if business as usual does not change, and very-very soon."

He had a series of images that showed the exponential and massive rise of humanity in the last 150 years powered by fossil fuels and the so-called green revolution. There were pictures of the "stuff" we produce and don't recycle sustainably. Pictures of our polluted air, water, land, and food supply. Pictures of some of the 200 species that go extinct "every day" when only about one a month would be normal. What more proof is needed that humanity is killing the planet? Pictures of storms and people and other life caught in the path of the destruction humanity is causing.

The outline went on noting that Maria would do the lead in to each of the "cast" of eleven that would make their short eight second appeal. The last person to speak would be Joan; she will make a closing statement and ask everyone to join the Green Party in their country, as it is the only existing "world-wide" organization capable of uniting people around the world to the cause. She would also ask that others make their own video too, which could be linked to this one. Joan would close with a suggested moniker "One Green World."

"Great idea man," Matt began, "I'll bet that within two weeks after we put up our video, there will be the next one, and within a few months there will be hundreds. You know like the Sun Valley Manifesto, and the Spokane Manifesto, the Eugene Manifesto, it could go on and on."

"Some of them will most likely be better than ours, give people the chance for some creativity and see what you get." Dave added.

Matt had another topic he wanted to discuss with his old friend, "I was thinking about that story with you and the girl with the dread locks in San Francisco."

Dave chuckled just thinking about his alternate universe interactions with the hippy girl several months earlier where he was given some all-too-powerful cannabis that got him hallucinating about some pretty weird stuff. Dave had to stop and think back kind of hard. After all, his visions came by way of a drug-induced trip of the mind. "Oh yeah, Alicia, Alice …you know "go find Alice" Grace Slick?"

"That was it. I was trying to remember what the girl's name was. 'Feed your head; feed your head…that's what the door mouse said.' Pretty cool how you made her into Mitochondrial Eve."

Dave made a low laughing sound, "cool dream though, it was like I was alive in the world 74,000 years ago. What a trip."

"You think we could be heading towards another bottle neck, like we did then, when humans almost went extinct?"

"I don't know, I look at that graph of human population, you know where it goes along at pretty much a flat line just barely going up over that last 10,000 years. Then, "zap," like a hockey stick, it shoots pretty much straight up, starting about 200 years ago."

Matt was nodding his head.

Then Dave asked, "How does that graph go over, let's say, the next 250 years? There are all kinds of possibilities, right? For now it just keeps going up, we're over seven billion now, heading to eight billion by about 2025 or so. I read recently that it's a pretty sure thing we'll at least go over ten billion by around 2065. That is if nothing critical happens before then that slows the population growth. There's already all these under nourished people. There are millions of them. It's just insane. If we were a sane species, world-wide, we'd have a plan to control our numbers. But that's not the way it is."

"You had that dream that this Alicia was some girl that invented a trap for fish and because she did her little tribe survived the population bottleneck." Matt remembered.

"Just a dream, but something had to of happened, their world went dark for several years, scientists think, because of the volcano going off in Indonesia. Food would have gotten very hard to come by with sunlight vastly limited and the cold must have been really tough too. Figuring out how to catch and eat bigger or different fish that were high in protein, and probably very minimally affected by the volcano's pollution, would have been a bonanza for any group that figured out how to capture them easily. I did a little digging and found that anthropologists think humans, going way back, probably over two million years, were living along coastlines and estuaries and gathered food like frogs, and clams, bird eggs, even small fish; cat fish probably the most. That behavior, along with scavenging kills by other predators for meat, probably worked together to push brain growth in those early people. I guess iodine is critical for our brains and sea food is a great source for it. People that moved too far from where they could get those kinds of food would suffer health problems associated with not getting enough iodine in their diet."

"It's just pretty profound I think; the idea that we almost went extinct. What would the Earth be like had we not made it?" Matt posited.

"And what will the world be like if we truly go extinct in this crisis."

"If it gets bad enough that we go extinct," Dave was shaking his head; he looked out across the vast landscape the horizon being 50 or 60 miles distant, "probably something like this…but everywhere."

Matt looked around, this landscape suggested things to him. The first being there were no trees or at least very few. Forests, at least ones we are familiar with, and all the varied life forms that depend upon then, would most likely vanish for many, thousands if not millions of years. Evolution would need vast amounts of time to cause new life forms to re-emerge to fill the many niches vacated by life forms of our times. A new balance would establish; one without humans.

"Do you think it's possible Ponch? Do you think we could really destroy the world?"

They walked on a short distance as Poncho was thinking, "Yes!"

~~~~~~

The groups mingled and mixed on the second half of the walk. They'd gotten to know each other substantially more by the time they returned to the visitor's center. Dave had spread the word that they'd go back to where the travel trailer was parked and have their first group discussion before everyone would head for dinner and to their rooms for the evening.

Dave had asked Nate to bring firewood for them. He had a small utility trailer and had actually brought the wood with him from Montana. That was a long ways to haul wood, but what was a gathering if you couldn't sit around a fire. It was just the human thing to do.

Dave had printed out the timeline that you could get from the *Kingdom of Good* website, because he thought it would be food for stimulating points for conversation. It encapsulated the big picture. It was the same timeline Dr. Sherman had used in his lecture Dave and Matt had listened to in Rome, where Matt and Maria first met.

But there were plenty of other things to talk about: fun things, things about living and loving our lives. That was what Dave hoped would happen, everybody in their own way getting turned on about this place. For how cool and mysterious it is and for how it made them feel.

They'd feel the warmth of the sun and maybe a cool breeze. See a great sunset and beautiful rocks of unimaginable age. And a dark night sky filled with thousands of stars; the ones you could see anyway. It's the sublime that so often is the most satisfying element of our experiences. Often there are no words, just some feeling. This tickle of a reward in just living. By the third day he hoped they'd all have their little corner of reality to share for their eight seconds of fame on the video they'd produce.

Chapter Ten

(Day two, Friday, the next morning, April 25th, 2013, going mountain bike riding and hiking)

"What was that guy's name that found me?" Dave was looking at Matt.

Matt had just taken a large bite of the eggs and potatoes from his plate. He was thinking back, he had to visualize the event again from when they were on their European trip and before they reached Rome. He could see himself coming up on the place where Poncho had wiped out, and saw his friend in the rocks and brush fifteen or twenty feet below the trail. He remembered leaning down next to his motionless friend saying his name. It brought back that same sense of being scared. A voice came from behind him. Matt took a swig of his orange juice, he could see the guy's face, then in an instant his name associated for him: "Rainer Ahl."

Dave was telling the story of when he and Matt had last gone mountain bike riding together in and around Interlaken, Switzerland. "You know I never really got to talk to him, I was so woozy as we got off the mountain, we just never really spoke."

Matt continued the story, "He helped us get to the hospital, and then he had to leave to see his girlfriend I think. Probably never see him again; people just pop in and out of our lives. That helmet you were wearing probably saved you from some really bad head injury. We might not be sitting here right now if you didn't have it on."

"Well I would just say that you guys better be careful where you go riding today, stay away from places that are over your head." Aubrey, who had that sort of motherly directness, told them. Eric gave her that look 'okay mom.'

"Have you guys decided what trails you're going to ride on?" Maria asked.

Matt had the map he'd got at the visitor center and pointed to the one he was thinking they might start on. "How about this one, it's a part of the Klondike Bluff trails, one called Dino-Flow? It's rated beginner to intermediate, I think we need to get a feel for what the different levels are all about."

"Okay, we can start there. Everybody's going to have their idea of what they can handle. We'll probably break up into smaller groups depending on what level of trail we want to try." Ron noted.

Having ridden mountain bikes at the top level Aiden had a vastly superior ability level than the other guys. But since they'd never ridden together the guys didn't really have an understanding of that. They'd all ridden enough to be familiar with the new bikes and being clipped into the pedals. But just like when you get around others that have pushed into new orbits of ability in say playing a guitar, or alpine or Nordic skiing, whatever discipline you choose, you typically discover that things move a lot faster and require an upgraded mental and motor set. Mountain biking certainly fills that requirement. The learning curve can cause you a bunch of hide, broken bones, torn tendons, and probably some other ails. It's still a blast!

The girls had all headed to Arches National Park for some great trail hiking. The guys were all heading out on the mountain bikes; maybe a bit sexist but nobody was complaining.

Nate had told his cousin they'd better reserve bikes or they very likely wouldn't get the ones they want. Aiden was the only one who brought his own bike. It was his baby, and he was its master mechanic and kept it in top shape. He knew that on day two when some of the others were planning on four wheeler rides, he knew a trail he had learned to ride years earlier, and he would head there. Several hours of nirvana awaited him.

After breakfast they had headed to Poison Spider Bicycles to get their rentals. The consensus had been, excluding Poncho, to get the 2014 Ibis Mojo HDR 650B. It sported the 27.5" wheel size and was very popular. Poncho had already ridden one of the Ibis Mojo, he wanted to try something new, so he went with the 2014 Ibis Ripley 29er. It had the new 29 inch wheels. He'd give it a try.

The weather was fabulous. There were only faint streaky clouds that you might think were in the stratosphere punctuating an otherwise baby blue sky. The sun was still a quarter of the way above the horizon when they left the rental office and headed towards the trail head. They had all gone in together and rented a big four wheeler they could carry themselves and the bikes in to make it easy getting to the trail heads. The sun's morning shadows, stretching to the west, gave the ochre landscape depth accentuating the canyon walls, boulders, and arid plants it's photons interacted with.

Klondike Bluff trail system was the first area they'd head to. There was a good parking lot there and the trails offered varying levels of difficulty. They would start out on Dino-Flow and just see what other trails might seem alluring.

No matter how mature young guys might seem, they nearly all have a competitive streak in them they love to tap, in something of an adolescent way. When you get in a group it just seems to naturally come out. It can be a good thing for the most part; it adds some dynamism to the experience. It just has to be reasonably controlled.

Aiden had ridden here before and suggested that they take the route that started on the Midline trail, then connect with Baby Steps and return back on Dino-Flow.

As they headed out, Matt reminded himself to not let his mind wander too much, as he was prone to do, stay in the present…connect with the mountain. It was a little mantra he'd say to himself as he got going and throughout the ride.

~~~~~

At some point in Matt's discussing mountain biking with Eric, who he rode the most with around Boise, the idea of "what is it" about mountain biking that they liked the most, came up. As they came to find out, that can be a virtually never ending discussion, or a very short one. To begin with, there is just the obvious: movement; being outside with nature all around; the challenge of the varying terrain and speeds; the challenge to your body to balance with the bike and the world. As in all activities there is an ascendency of skill that must emerge if the person's spirit is to be drawn to greater proficiency. It is just like the will or desire to play a musical instrument, it requires the person to challenge themselves to take that next step along some, in truth, never ending pathway towards perfection, to nirvana.

In one of his mountain biking magazines Matt had noticed an article titled "Zen and Mountain Biking" it intrigued him greatly so he had sought out more information on what that meant. If a person seeks out the meaning behind Zen, you are then introduced to the teachings of Buddhism and eastern philosophical thought in general. In that process he then remembered the part of Dr. Sherman's lecture that discussed the spiritual philosophy that emerged in the Hindu Valley of what is today called India. But he did not follow up right away with what Dr. Sherman had explained, so those teachings had not become a part of his life in a meaningful way, yet.

A year or more had passed between when he'd returned to Boise after the trip to Europe and this period of spiritual investigation began. Nothing in particular was pushing Matt along some road to spiritual growth; he'd just drifted like so many of us do. No one thing had struck his rudder that would cause him to react. At some point along life's journey though, if a person lives long enough, their rudder gets hit by one thing or another which leads them to some reaction. What that reaction is varies between people and where their life experiences to that time places them. As it was, Matt was far enough along in his question and answer process with life that he was then ready to seek out the meaning of Zen.

The process of discovering the underlying meaning of Zen was like discovering a book that leads you into a room you'd never knew even existed, and had never even thought to look for the door. This is a door that can only exist for you when you are ready to look for it. Matt was there, his father's death was probably the first really big rock to hit his rudder. It had knocked him around plenty, it might have gotten his attention but he wasn't ready yet. Then there was Monica's death and the ugly part of human nature it revealed to him. Followed by Dr. Sherman's lecture and Poppy's death in Rome, in 2010. And then the incredible bond with Maria that emerged. And then the knock of the other rocks and debris that littered the river of life he'd been travelling. But it wasn't until he sought out the meaning of Zen and Mountain Biking that this intuition about living revealed itself to him.

In his reading Matt learned again of Siddhartha Gautama, who is considered the first Buddha; or awakened one. Siddhartha was born in 563 BCE in what is today Nepal. Through circumstances in his life he'd been drawn to try to understand "being" at a much deeper level. The art of meditation was already established in the area where he was living, it would be from the knowledge and implementation of this knowledge that Siddhartha would eventually announce to the world that he'd discovered a great truth at the center of being. At its core, Zen unites you with your true spiritual self. Only a very, very, very few begin to truly grasp what that really means, or to be more precise: how it really feels. It is when the analytical and observing mind quiets itself to the realm of the "don't know" mind. It is where intuition dwells. It is the mind in the natural flow of the universe. There are many teachings associated with this central thought and are relevant to everyday living. But for the activity filling Matt and the other guys consciousness today, the Zen of mountain biking was all that mattered.

A day on your mountain bike, given a reasonable challenge, can be in many ways analogous to your river of life...a condensed version. Matt had found an article on the Internet that was so on target with the analogy between living and being, and riding his mountain bike, that he had saved a copy, and read it several times. The first thing discussed was just the idea of starting your ride. There is always the possibility for something to go wrong. You could fall and hurt yourself; you could run into a tree. There are just things that are not knowable at the start. If you let the chance that something bad might occur stop you from beginning, then you get stymied altogether and never get to experience the joy that's hiding in the ride. Likewise, if you try to plan for every possible diversion that might pop up in your life it is as hopeless as trying to see every rock, brush, and change of surface along some trail in advance and hold an absolute set path. It's not possible and you'll soon wreck for sure.

The best thing to do is to just keep your mind on going the general path you want and let your front wheel bounce around a little while making sure you do slow down if you get to bouncing to some rate you really can't deal with. Go with the flow. And the last thing, probably more than the others that resonated with Matt, was the ability to let go of your failures. All those things in your past that no longer truly exist, but some part of you keeps trying to resurrect. The best and most positive thing you can do is to, as is the case in mountain biking, embrace the difficult part of the hill you are on, learn from those things in the past to help you in the present, but separate yourself from them so they do not shackle you now. In that way you are open and ready to the new experiences that are waiting for you just around the bend.

The true fun and joy of mountain biking, as in the experience of being, can't be held in your hand, it has no form, it dwells in the place of "don't know." It's like trying to hold beautiful or invigorating in your hand, they are feelings, reactions to experience. They say Zen is being aware of your oneness with the world and everything in it. One great way to try and discover it is on a great mountain bike on a great trail!

At the start everyone just needed to get warmed up, get their blood flowing and any tightness in their muscles loosened up. Dave had asked Aiden to take the lead at the start. The trail wasn't too wide so they'd end up in single file.

Matt ended up the last of the six of them as they headed out, he lagged behind some as he was experimenting with the gears, getting a feel for how they changed and the sense for at least what the middle range had.

There was little conversation going on as the riders enjoyed settling into the connection of themselves the bikes and the landscape. Aiden would spot something every-so-often they could catch a little air on if wanted, not everyone would try it. The group stayed together for several hours following the various trails. Some on the dirt then others, particularly EKG, challenged them with the slickrock … basically riding on reasonably flat surfaced rock. They enjoyed stopping and taking pictures of the ancient footprints that dinosaurs had left in what was then mud, many tens of millions of years ago.

The group separated in the early afternoon. It was apparent that Nate and Aiden were more advanced riders; they wanted to find some trails that challenged them a little more. So they headed to the Sand Flats Recreation Area where the Slickrock Trail System was located. Everyone else stayed and rode more of the trails around Klondike Bluff.

"Looks like we have company," Nate said, nodding his head in the direction of the lone rider approaching them.

Aiden was quiet for a reason. Dust kicked up as the rider slipped to a stop just short of where Nate and Aiden were standing with their bikes. The rider was silent as he lifted his goggles up onto his helmet. Some long blond hair fell down across his dusty and sweat-beaded face. A smile began to form, but there was an odd bend to it due to the heavy scar through the right side of his upper lip. "Thought that might be you," he nodded towards the parking lot, "saw you earlier; I guess you just never forget how some people move around. How you been Aiden?"

Aiden's mind was buzzing with the memories associated with Rocs Swenson; the one rider in the country he had competed with most, head to head, for the five years he was on the circuit. Rocs had won a slim majority of the time. But there was that one big race where Aiden had got the best of him by a gutsy move on a dangerous part of a circuit. Aiden became the talk on tour; at Rocs' expense. To a small degree the score had been settled in a later race, but as it stood neither knew which was dominant.

"How you doin' Rocs?" Aiden began.

"Good," Rocs nodded his head and formed his funny grin, "bitchin, actually, found some great rides around here."

Aiden looked towards Nate, "This is Nate, he's a cousin of a good friend of mine. There's a bunch of us here hangin' out."

"Sounds cozy," Rocs tone and grin was a bit sarcastic. "I'm headin' up to the mesa," he looked up towards the flat-topped mountain a half mile or so away. "I was up there all day yesterday," he spit some of his chew on the ground, "you want to go?"

Aiden looked towards Nate, "you good?"

Nate was wondering what was up there, 'why would Rocs describe it as bitchin?' There was a part of him that was questioning the idea, but he quickly over rode that thought. "Sure, let's go!"

The first part of the trail was easy; the hardest thing was just busting your torso through the willows and other vegetation that was covering a lot of the trail. But that changed soon enough; the grade started getting steep and rocky. They all had some of the best mountain bikes available with gears and drive systems that quickly allowed for adapting to the change in conditions.

About a third of the way up Nate could see that they were going to pass through a section where the trail crossed a large and sloping rock face. Most riders would stop here as a loss of balance could easily lead to a several hundred foot fall. Rocs was leading and didn't even slow down a bit to discuss the upcoming terrain. This was just a taste of what was coming, but Aiden and Nate couldn't know that.

Rocs had pulled off the trail at the top and waited briefly for Aiden and Nate to join him. Nate was breathing harder than the others, his conditioning had never been to the level they had reached and still had to some degree.

"Looks like Mars," Aiden commented as the three grouped.

Nate was scanning the landscape beyond and below them; it struck him how on the mesa there was virtually no plant life…rock everywhere.

Aiden knew there was a tension of competition between himself and Rocs. In the next hour or so some old scores were likely going to be worked on, he figured. He looked towards Nate, "Don't' go anywhere you aren't comfortable with, some of this is going to be really gnarly." Aiden had witnessed some bad wrecks in his time and didn't want to have to life-flight his friends' cousin off the mesa particularly.

Nate shook his head, feeling like he'd been put in his place a bit. Maybe he'd set Aiden straight on that?"

Having ridden the mesa the previous day Rocs went about explaining some of the terrain they could somewhat see. There was a few hundred yards of slight downhill in front of them, you could get some pretty good speed, and at the end there was a ledge you catch some air. "I'll go first, you'll see," he said, then tightened his helmet a bit before taking off.

Aiden and Nate watched, they could see the point where Rocs would launch from a high point and catch that good air. It wasn't long and he was flying. Aiden was counting the seconds he was in flight. He was just starting to mutter two when Rocs landed. "Forty or fifty feet?" There was a question in his voice directing towards Nate.

"I might slow it down a little, but I'm good." Hate understood Aiden's implied question.

Shortly they were both standing with their bikes next to Rocs having finished the jump. Nate had definitely taken some speed off and had actually hit a little harder as his flight trajectory was more out and down rather than out and away. After a short time analyzing that jump, they continued. The route was taking them higher and higher on the mesa. There was no real trail, but there was a general obvious route that avoided the deep ravines that segmented the rather wide mesas top. Nate stopped and looked over the edge at one point, 'Whoa, you don't want to go over there,' he thought to himself. That would be , and eight or nine hundred foot fall would be a life ender.

Aiden and Rocs were nearly out of site as Nate followed them; they were competing with each other as they climbed through the slick rock towards the summit of the mesa. There were many places they past where a fall could be disastrous. They reached the top well before Nate; there would be time for them to talk now.

"You hear what happened to Drew?" Rocs began, taking off his helmet.

Aiden's mind moved back seven or eight years to a time the guys on tour were meeting a lot of the same girls. Rocs had met her first, but she had taken a liking to Aiden. Knowledge of Aiden's rather wealthy family of course was commonly known, and to Roc's mind was most likely the reason she had found him alluring. In those days Aiden just took advantage of his good looks and whatever other attributes girls would like about him, so that he didn't sleep alone much. Drew had come and gone.

Aiden looked at him, "Drew Laird, you mean?"

Rocs nodded his head in agreement, looking back towards where Nate was making his way towards them. "Yeah, that Drew!" There was a dismissive quality to his response.

"Somebody told me she died…a fall or something?"

"Yeah, a fall. I was there when it happened. She was trying to get a better look at a waterfall; she slipped." Rocs went silent for a short time. "She liked you a lot, you know? Hum. I lost track of her for a few years then ran into her down near Taos, she was living with some guy who made pottery…kind of weird. We hooked up for a couple of months, then that fall. It's been two years…."

Aiden could tell by the tone of his voice that it was hitting a raw nerve.

About then Nate got to where they were waiting, so that subject ended. But not in Rocs' mind.

"Now we have to get back down." Rocs' voice and body language suggested competition. "I have a $2,500 bill that says I'm the first one back to touch your car." The wager could be read in his facial expression; he had something to prove…or settle.

Nate was just catching his breath and looked at the two of them. 'Something's goin' on,' he thought to himself. "That's too rich for me." He knew it was personal between Rocs and Aiden anyway. It was no time for questions now.

Aiden had been processing the wager as Nate had joined them. He realized there was very likely some of their history woven into that wager: unresolved dominance in their racing career; rich boy poor boy feelings; and probably something about Drew. There was something else, but that didn't occur to him.

"I've got it in cash in my pickup. It's yours if you beat me." Rocs' voice was very focused.

'Wow, something really personal was goin' on here,' Nate was again thinking.

"I'll have to get it from a bank if I lose, but I'm good for it." Adrenaline was really starting to spike in his system as his subconscious was considering the implication of what he was entering in to.

Nate decided he should try to back them off; he had just seen all the wicked places where they could fall...they could get killed. "Hey guys, this might not be the best place for this?"

Rocs looked at him and commented, "Thanks, that's what my mom might have said, but she's dead so I don't care."

It was a pejorative statement and Nate didn't like it. He looked towards Aiden, Aiden's glance was dismissive. 'Okay, he thought, at least he'd tried.'

Twenty five hundred dollars wasn't much to Aiden anyway. It would be good to win, but if he didn't...at least it would be a good story. Those thoughts moved through Aiden's mind.

But not so for Rocs, it represented just about all the money he had in the world. But to beat this guy...uh, the desire to win was visceral. That can be dangerous.

Rocs faced his bike downhill, Aiden did the same. Rocs handed a stone to Nate, "when you drop this we go, crazy time."

Nate wasn't sure he should even do that; 'I should puncture someone's tire,' he thought. 'Surely they both know their limits and won't do something that gets them killed. Self preservation surely would take over?' Okay, he would drop the stone.

Nate looked at them, "Are you both ready?" They both nodded they were. Nate held the stone up high so they could both see it well. His grip opened and the stone fell.

The grade dropped away very quickly for the first thirty yards or so; their speed built quickly. Through the first three hundred yards the slick rock was wide and the riders separated six or eight feet from each other. Aiden had thought through the route back, he knew that to win he would very likely need to be in the lead by the time they got to the cross slope area; there was no way for two riders wide there. From there on, you could just block the path of the other.

They were quickly coming onto the deep crevasse; wrong decisions now could get you killed. Aiden was looking for a line down through the next two hundred yards or so; 'this is where the race will be won or lost,' he was thinking. Suddenly Rocs veered sharply to the right on a route Aiden thought was just a dead end as you could never cross the crevasse as far as he could see. 'What was he doing?'

Aiden stopped, 'had he been duped, did Rocs know a route down he couldn't see?'

What Rocs' had not shared was that the day before he'd found a place to jump the crevasse. From Aiden's location nowhere looked like it could be jumped.

Nate had been following and had now joined Aiden. "What's he doing?" Nate asked immediately.

"I don't know." Aiden's voice seemed lost in thought.

Momentarily Rocs had swung out wide and was now heading directly towards the crevasse.

"Holy Jesus, shit, he's going to jump the crevasse!" Nate was animated. They both watched, stunned. From their angle it was not possible to see the landing point, there was a place just beyond though that if he made it they would see him right away.

The day before Rocs had spotted this place and had done some of his old calculations and decided he could make it. Missing would be bad; but what the hell anyway. He'd screamed the whole way across...it was bitchin! He had landed with plenty of room to spare. The afterglow of the adrenaline rush was worth every ounce of the fear he actually had felt. Little did he know then how he would be able to use the short cut the next day.

Aiden knew that if Rocs made the jump he would have his money. All there was now to do was watch.

Rocs had taken the same route up the incline as he had done the day before...everything should be the same, he assumed. His speed was building as he neared the take-off point. 'Was he going as fast as yesterday?' He was slightly undecided but trying to stop now he would almost certainly slide into the crevasse...go for it!

His intuition was right though, he was going slower than yesterday, he had picked up a goat head and a slow leak had been flattening out his back tire which created drag.

Half way across he could see he was too low; he was going to hit the rock wall below the landing edge. His intuition said get away from the bike. And just as quickly he could see a tree growing from the side of the rock, he was headed right for it.

Smash, Rocs hits the Netleaf Hackberry and the rocks. Self preservation filled every inch of him, he grabbed for the branches of the tree. His left hand hit the biggest branch. As fast as he could he grabbed with his right hand. He was slipping through the branches. He gripped harder and his momentum stopped. He looked down and nearly lost his grip from the terror. The branches were cracking from the weight. He could not see, but the branch he was most dependent on was nearly ready to break entirely. Pain and shock was gaining on him.

Realizing that something had gone wrong Aiden and Nate had moved as quickly as possible to get to where Rocs was at. As they approached they could see the tree and that Rocs was somehow hanging onto it. Aiden stretched out on his belly and crept near the edge. He looked over; the view made his stomach churn and made him want to freeze. He moved his mind passed that. "Rocs, can you hear me?"

Rocs lifted his head, blood was streaming from his nose, and he was very pale and looked like he could pass out at any moment. "Looks like you win," Was Rocs' muffled reply.

"Nobody wins, we're even man. We're going to get you up here, hold on."

Nate had made his way down near to Aiden. "Do you have any rope in your pack?" Aiden asked quickly. Nate shook his head that he did not; Aiden expected that, but thought he should ask. "Okay, the only thing we can do is lower a bike to him; he's too far down to reach with my hand."

Nate's face showed a question. "We can lower a bike to him, he can grab the tire and we pull him up. That's the only thing I can think of we can do."

Rocs could tell that the roots of the tree were nearing a point where they would give; the branch he was holding onto was nearing that point as well. He figured he was dead, but about then the bike wheel lowered next to him.

"Grab on Rocs, we'll get you up here."

Right at that moment a weird sensation passed through Rocs body, some sort of epiphany actually, it would be days before he processed that moment. Someone was going out of their way to help him.

He grabbed the wheel with first his right and then his left, he was now totally in their hands. Aiden could feel the weight and see Rocs hold on the wheel, he started to pull. Nate was holding his legs and had his feet firmly under his arm pits. Rocs reached a point where his feet could push on the tree; his hands momentarily then reached an edge he could grab. He scrambled and reached safety. They all collapsed. A half minute passed before a word was said.

"Why man, why did you take that jump?" Aiden at last asked, now feeling some angst because of the whole deal.

Rocs was feeling sheepish, he knew he looked foolish…he wiped some more blood from his nose and face. "Kicks, I guess."

"Huh?" Aiden responded.

"Thanks." It just came out of Rocs. "Thanks…" that was all he could think of to say.

When they reached the parking lot Rocs was showing the signs of being nearly in shock, and he had lost a lot of blood. "I'll drive you to the

154

hospital," Nate said. Rocs could barely get himself in the back seat, he shut his eyes and was out.

'What's that?' Nate thought to himself as he got into the driver's seat. On the passenger seat was a small bag, it had the medical logo on it. 'Is he diabetic?' Nate thought to himself. He opened the bag, there was a syringe and needle and a couple of bottles of liquid: Fentanyl and Methadone were written on the bottles. Nate knew what they were for: pain medication, primarily for cancer. 'Maybe there was another reason for Rocs extreme risk taking,' he thought to himself.

Rocs was barely conscious by the time they reached the hospital. He was wheeled into the emergency room. The two explained what had happened. Quickly they examined him and found he was not in a life threatening condition. Aiden and Nate said they would check back the next morning.

~~~~~

The two returned to camp, poured themselves a stiff drink and joined the others to discuss what had happened.

After about ten minutes it was Heidi that made the observation, "His risk taking is a lot like what we're doing around the world. It sounds like a guy with an ego issue; kind of like our civilization."

"If he has terminal cancer it explains a little more too; sort of the 'what the fuck' attitude." Nate said.

Then Maria spoke. "But in the end, when he has the choice to live or die, he chooses to live. Pretty much like Rocs we all have to not give in to the idea that it's all hopeless…like it's too big a challenge and there's nothing we can do. We've got to reach out and grab that bicycle wheel and pull ourselves to safety. I know we can if we just try hard enough. But will we try hard enough?"

~~~~~

'With a little coaxing from Maria and Joan, the five women grouped together and went to Arches National Park to take a long hike. It was a pretty easy sell that they go to the Devil's Garden Primitive Loop and take the long trail which was noted at being about 11.5 kilometers, and should take them about four hours to complete. The trail head was at the far end of the park, so they got a nice view of the general landscape just as they drove through.

Joan, actually, had come up with the idea that the women might hike together and discuss a women's point of view on the climate crisis and human impact on life in general. Mothers are endowed by nature with their unique physical and emotional tools in the tool chest. Evolution had honed the mothers of humanity to what they are in broad cross section today. Joan was looking forward to hearing how the various ladies juxtaposed their female intuitions with what many feel is the greatest challenge our species has or will ever confront.

With her light blond hair blowing slightly in the wind, Joan clicked the button on her key chain and heard the lock of the doors on the Subaru she and Dave had rented in Salt Lake. "I'm going to use the potty before we head out." Joan said to Maria and Sally who were standing comfortably near her.

"Good idea," Maria followed.

"It feels even more like being on Mars here than it did yesterday at Dead Horse Point," Heidi observed as the five women now began the walk towards Tunnel Arch.

"It's really a wonder that there are places like this on the planet," Sally added. "I was reading about how this formed. Where we're at is part of what they call Paradox Basin, it's been a low area for over 300 million years."

Heidi was walking right next to her and showed interest in her eyes.

"There was some huge mountain range to the north of here, ancestral mountains to the Rockies. So there was a shallow ocean to the west that would fill in here during wet cycles, then in dry cycles it would evaporate and leave salt layers behind. That's those light colored bands you see. Then the material being eroded out of the mountains would cover over the salt, that reddish-brown material. That cycle repeats many times and that's how we get the funky bands laid one on top of the other."

"It's amazing what can happen over long periods of time," Heidi observed.

They all went up to Pine Tree Arch, then circled back to the trail so they could head next to Landscape Arch. This was such a unique area where the rock and weathering worked together to break the stone into these formations that eventually left only an arch spanning in some instances several hundred feet.

"Our planet is always changing, I remember when it finally really settled into my mind how that is," Joan began. She was walking pretty much in the middle of the five heading up the large stone and sand pathway. "It's like an epiphany isn't it … you can learn the basics in school and maybe you kind of get it, but until you really think about it a lot it's still kinda abstract. There are just so many factors involved in the creation of the world…its pretty mind boggling actually."

Maria had a point she wanted to make, "And there's the biology too that's always being influenced by the geology. It all interacts and changes. Very few people, really...let's be honest, truly get the deep interplay between what's happening geologically and how that influences biology."

"Mutations," Sally said, "Sort of the invisible hand of creation. I don't like to say God, that seems confusing."

"Would you mind explaining mutations to me," Heidi asked, "I've spent most of my life doing financial analysis; I remember the concept from high school. I guess I'd have to admit I don't really know how that's supposed to work."

Maria smiled, knowing even she found the mechanism of evolution weird. "It just gets down to little changes in the DNA sequence. What seems odd to me, maybe bizarre, is that they're supposedly just random. Sometimes the bonds in a base pair just breakdown, some of them happen during cell division, radiation from the environment, and even from outer space, viruses can cause them too. I don't know, it just seems like there has to be some deeper system at work."

"I think that Dave's going to talk about this more tonight because it's so important to what's happening right now." Joan pointed at several plants nearby, "Every living thing exists because it fits with the current balance in the environment, and that includes the average surface temperature. What I didn't know, but what Dave's been explaining to me, is just how finely adapted the plants and animals are to that average surface temperature. It doesn't sound like much, but just one degree of average surface temperature can mean the difference between a species thriving or going extinct. All that has to happen to a species is for it to not be able to make babies for the next generation, and very quickly it will have a population collapse. Maybe Dave will explain that to you, he's done a lot of research and thinking about it."

By about 2:00 that afternoon they had made it to Dark Angel Spire. It supposedly looks like a woman with dark hair gazing to the distance.

"It just looks like a big phallic symbol to me, I have to say," Aubrey was laughing. "It would be located just about as far out at the end of the Park as possible."

"I can see the guy's toes down there, and yeah there's his head over there." Heidi teased.

"He's got short legs and a long torso," Aubrey returned. All the girls were now laughing whole heartedly.

"God, isn't that just like a guy, fall asleep, get a hard on, and point to the sky." Sally observed.

"Well, he's had that one for about a million years, it's probably time he calls his doctor." Heidi said. "That's a little more than the four hour limit you here about on the adds companies selling boners warn about." The laughing continued; real, honest, laughing!

Eventually they tired of their phallic jokes and began to head back. A little ways past the Double O Arch they found some nice boulders just off the trail that could serve as seats, so they decided to sit down and chat before heading back to the car.

"Just think of all the people that have walked up to the end of this trail to see that big spire sticking up there. What do most people get out of seeing it? Is it worth the walk? Is there something people get from seeing something that's just different than the ordinary? I mean they've set aside this whole area and said it's so unique it should be owned by the people of the United States." Joan was asking, mostly to herself, but to the others too.

"I always like seeing things that are different, things that are unique." Sally paused for a short time then added, "I think the wonder in it all is "how" did this or that get there. There's a story behind everything and this spire or that arch has a different story. To me that's what's fun thinking about."

Maria had some insight hearing that, "Well, that's everything really. Everything has a story; the butterfly, the mosquito, the ocean, the single mom living on the street. Everything is a story that's played out over time."

"And we're just seeing the story as it is right now; it goes on … what will it be? That's interesting to try and figure out." Aubrey continued the long thought.

"The past is buttoned up like a zipper. It just is what it is…the future though, well there are all sorts of possible futures," Joan added.

Maria then said, "We all play our part in the future. Little things we do now can ripple through to the distant times and have huge impacts in some cases. And what we don't do can ripple too."

"What can the estrogen do about that? The mother chemical; if she could talk what would she say?" Joan smiled.

"You're killing me, probably," Maria answered. "About two hundred species around the world go extinct *every day*. Like 50,000 a year, when normal is about one a month. If that doesn't strike you as something killing the world, it's hard to imagine what would." Maria had seen Dave's outline for the video and had been exceptionally moved by the number of species extinctions…how telling.

"Have any of you read Silent Spring by Rachel Carson?" Maria continued.

"I know of it," Aubrey replied. The others agreed they'd heard of it but had not read it.

"When I was little, growing up in Spain, my dad showed me the book and told me about what she had written. How all these man-made chemicals, especially DDT, were being used in agriculture back in the fifties and sixties. And that those chemicals were causing all kinds of problems to life forms, killing them. He hated the idea of using those chemicals. He said we weren't listening to the world and that if we didn't change our ways we'd all end up dead too. I finally read it a year ago or so, there was one part where she says that 'mans war against nature was actually a war against himself,' "that pretty much sums it up."

"I was reading, where was it?" Sally rolled her lower lip in slightly, something she'd do when trying to recall a deeply buried thought. "It might have been NRDC's quarterly magazine, or maybe something else. Anyway, they were saying that there are something like 80,000 manmade compounds out in the environment now and that we don't really know what the long term effect of them will be. But they know that there's an increase in mental disorders associated with some of them. That's just really scary. Those chemicals are especially toxic to developing fetuses and to their brain cell development."

Weeks earlier while sitting in her apartment sipping coffee and listening to some soft music, a state of mind she often found insightful, Joan had decided to look back through some of Dr. Sherman's lecture material that Dave had given her. His point about the three temptations of Jesus and how they related to our modern challenges had piqued her curiosity. They were fresh in her mind so she decided to bring them up now. "Are we trying to turn stones into bread?" She looked at the other girls. Heidi was looking at her with a question on her face. "It's the first temptation of Jesus by the devil, which Dr. Sherman talks about it in his *Kingdom of Good* lecture."

Joan continued, "The first time I heard the comparison I wasn't sure what I thought," she paused, "but the longer that idea has had time to mingle in my mind it starts to really make sense."

"What do you mean?" Aubrey asked.

Joan continued. "So Jesus goes to the desert and he's tempted by the devil three times. Oh, it's not particularly well known but the Buddha, Siddhartha Gautama, evidently just before he reached enlightenment was tempted by the same three things it's said. Isn't that interesting? To some the temptations represent: fear, desire, and opinion. So Dr. Sherman takes it a step further and says there's a reason for "those" specific three things. He thinks they represent the primal motivations of all organisms and actually represent: action (fight or flight and how reason interacts), sex (power), and food (energy). They are primal drives needed for survival.

They've just taken on a whole different level of complexity among humans. And have become toxic and life-threatening recently."

Joan had to take a breath before continuing. "Individually we're tempted, and as groups we are too. Turning stones into bread, you can make all kinds of analogies with that. It's like satisfying unrealistic or even unethical desires. When we produce our food using synthetic fertilizers that then require us to use pesticides and herbicides that actually create poor quality foods, and make us sick, and help to destroy our soil and pollute the atmosphere; aren't we sort of turning stones into bread?"

She brushed her hair to one side while thinking of a little more she wanted to share. "I think the other two temptations are relevant to our global crisis too. The second temptation is to become an exalted person or elevated to high status. That plays on our motivation to hold high rank in a social group, which is old as old. That desire goes way back to even our pre-human times. And the third one is to rule over the world. That's territoriality, which is old as old too. We learned to want to control a territory for the food primarily we could obtain from it. Then of course later it is things like minerals: gold, silver, and others we want to control. They were the explicit temptations of Jesus and the Buddha. But more importantly they are the core/implicit motivations/temptations we all face. Around the world people have bitten hard on these temptations to satisfy these inner drives without wisdom guiding them. Now we're all paying the price for that indulgence."

As Joan was finishing they all had returned to the parking lot. "I've never heard anyone make that connection," Heidi said. "But you know it makes some sense. I think there's something very truthful about all that. It makes sense that it would be motivations from our evolutionary past that are at the base of everything. What does that bode for the future?"

Maria commented. "That big rock, you know where we were just at, Dark Angel Spire? It's supposed to remind someone of a woman looking off to the distance. She's kind of like all of us in that way, we're looking off to the distance, to the future. To everything we hope and dream for. It's like the hidden message. She's like us wondering what's coming and what's out there? It's just a normal thing to do. I just wonder how are all the things going on all around the world now going to affect how our lives turn out?"

Chapter Eleven

A nice fire greeted everyone as they converged for the second night at the campsite where the travel trailer was kept. The plan was to talk for an hour or so, enjoying whatever beverage anyone might want, and plan a bit. They'd reflect more on this day's happenings as they ate dinner in downtown Moab later that evening. Dave and Matt intended to use this time to update everyone with what they considered was the critical information from the *Kingdom of Good* website that they could use in the video-manifesto.

"I know you guys saw this timeline in the attachment I sent you," Dave began, "but I wanted to go back over it again, just to make sure everybody understands what it's all about. Okay, before I get going, does anyone have a question about just getting oriented to what this timeline is showing?"

Everybody had already studied it and they understood basically what it was depicting. They just needed Dave to fill in the details.

"I realize that for all of you, grasping that there was this enormous time since the Big Bang, is understandable. However, hopefully showing it in this graphical way helps to get a little bit better sense of the vastness of the time and where important parts, relative to all of us, emerge."

Sally spoke right up, "I've heard the 13. 6 billion years a lot of times, but never tried to imagine what that looks like in a graph. I'd say yes, this really helps me. This little short segment is one hundred million years and clear over here is the beginning of the universe? Geez, this is good Dave."

"Well, for all of these images we need to thank Dr. Sherman and everybody at the *Kingdom of Good* organization in England, they're the ones that put this all together, not me."

"See the faint image of the little four-legged creature underneath the overall timeline? I think that's just really clever. The tip of the tail is at the Big Bang and its nose is at the current time. They're showing the emergence of life, and more importantly, consciousness, through all that time. And that little guy represents the basic form of six appendages we all are descendants of. Our tails don't show up much now, of course."

"But just think about that a little: if you believe in evolution, you can't say it just starts with the first life forms on Earth. There had to be all these steps that were leading to it finally emerging here. Our galaxy forms in that first billion years. And then scientists think there had to be a mother star where all the heavier elements that we have on Earth get created. It finally explodes and that material gets incorporated when our solar system forms which isn't until a little after nine billion years after the Big Bang. Then there's the time until the first life form emerges, they call it LUCA, which means the Last Universal Common Ancestor. Every last organism that has ever existed descends from that first reproducing cell. That's around 3.8 billion years ago, roughly. What's driving or organizing all those gazillions of atoms to group and become what we think of as a living being? That's a mystery we don't understand but, quantum mechanics is giving us hints, evidently."

~~~~~

Dave held up a new diagram, this one said the *Kingdom of Good* at the top. "All the images on this sheet work to explain the variations in human consciousness. Dr. Sherman said that by understanding this you would understand the central problem that humans face: and that's our own instinctual nature."

He paused for a short while just letting that thought be absorbed some. "What this is really showing is two realms of consciousness. See where it says: organismal, ego-captured, at the bottom of the page? And then at the top just under *The Kingdom of Good* it says: Enlightenment and Transendent? You can see that right at level five this transition or transformation is supposed to occur. That color image that sort of looks like a tornado, represents the emergent population of humanity.

We emerge from the super-deep ancestry that is not even our species and consciousness is just organismal: ego-captured, where perpetuating the self is preeminent. But then about 200,000 years ago our species emerges with our much more complex brain/mind and for that you can see they've broken the species-wide consciousness into seven levels."

"Boy, can I ever see my dad in this level four, 'clever but sometimes tragically not wise.'" Heidi said, as Dave took a break in his delivery. Everybody laughed.

He continued. "Yeah, you have to study those little boxes with the information in them. It starts making a lot more sense when you do. See how they're showing that band right along the number five line?" There were comments that they did. "That's the major-realm transition line where a person truly breaks free from being captured by their ego to being able to recognize the ego's force and can rise above it. That's where a person begins the transformation to allowing their true spiritual being to emerge. And what Dr. Sherman is saying is that when you "truly" are on that path (he emphasized the word) then the larger understanding of creation and wisdom naturally emerges. You see the holistic reality around you, and become empathetic towards it all."

Maria raised her hand wanting to say something. "So this revolution of consciousness is from the fourth level to the fifth level. And that's why the color spreads out along that line because there are so many people just below it?" There was a question in her voice.

"Exactly," Dave answered. "You can be the top CEO of some Fortune 500 company or the most talented computer programmer in the world and still be stuck in the fourth level."

"What's stopping them from crossing?" Eric asked.

"That, of course, is the central question. Dr. Sherman says it's our ego, the sense of our self or I/me and how it is like a magnet that we have so much difficulty separating from."

Eric rocked back in his chair a little and muttered, "Interesting."

This is where the spiritual stuff comes in. You know Dr. Sherman wasn't just a scientist; he was a theologian too and preached at the Church of England. He saw this connection between the message of Jesus and the temptations he was given, and the human condition and what we call our ego. See on the right side the boxes that are in purple? Those are the three temptations simplified and then the two most important commandments simplified to one statement. So, he says the three temptations simply represent the primal urges we have inherited from our evolutionary ascent. The first one, 'action without reason, or just opinion' is just doing something that boils up in your mind and is usually motivated by fight or flight instincts. Interpreted poorly, those behaviors can ultimately work against you and others. It's basically action lacking wisdom. The second one is desiring high status, which can be simplified to 'power.' And power can be simplified to sex, as that was the center of power through evolutionary time. And the third is desire for great wealth, which can be simplified to 'greed.' And greed can be simplified to food, as food represents energy and acquiring energy to supply the body was essential for any organism to live and reproduce. Which in combination are the deepest drivers of all. You see, it's all about organismal consciousness."

"So how does this moral ethos then relate?" Heidi again asked.

In the Bible, Jesus is asked which of the Ten Commandments were the most important. He said there were two: love God entirely and love all other people entirely, which is the shortened version. What Dr. Sherman says is that since the most tangible expression of God on the planet is Nature or Creation, and since people are all a part of that, then the two can be reduced to one and you just say: '*Love Creation Entirely*.' And love can mean to hold in the highest esteem. Creation is nature and all of us. And Entirely is with all of your heart, soul, and mind."

"Of course," Heidi then said emphatically. She seemed to be the one all of this was connecting with the most. "And that's the central moral ethos. If you hold Creation in the highest of esteem you then must logically do everything to protect it! Right!"

Dave was shaking his head in agreement. "If Dr. Sherman is correct; Jesus was in affect warning us about our own animal instincts. They served us in our ascent through evolutionary history, but in this highly technological world they can become maniacal and work to our detriment. The power and greed hold onto the spirit of so many people. Especially with all of the material wealth that has suddenly emerged since we discovered how to use fossil fuels to run our economy and make stuff. It's all a vicious circle and we've got to get off this merry-go-round."

"Fossil Fuels are like black cocaine or heroin, I think." Eric commented. "They start out seeming like a good deal and suck you in. But then over time start taking you down a rat hole and turn out to be horrible. I think that's where we're pretty much at with them and their effect on our beautiful planet."

Dave continued, "The good news is that this gives us some kind of tool to organize around. It's an idea that we can use to recruit people that are almost there, but just need that little boost to get to the next level. If they can just see it this way and be able to say to someone, 'come on, let go of that animal baggage and let the real spiritual being in you emerge. Maybe that can be the key?"

"I love it," Joan then interjected. "We can explain the science stuff till we're totally exhausted and still not be successful in getting the political change we need. But if the right people come to understand that it's the evolution inside their own heads that is the most critical. Maybe, just maybe we can create the crack that we need to break the logjam and get the people on board that make the change."

"We need enough people to mentally transition to *The Kingdom of Good* to make that happen," Dave finished.

~~~~~

Having discussed the psychology, Dave moved the discussion ahead to focus on the science. He held up the sheet that explained the average surface temperature for the earth. This is the critical metric as it relates to a stable climate. There was a great amount of detail and everyone listened and learned. It was the same material he would present in a lecture in San Diego in a few weeks. It was a lecture Stone Fisher would attend and it would have an immense impact on his own consciousness and plans for the future.

"Just for reference," Dave began, "a little before half way in that last 100 million years the asteroid that wiped out the dinosaurs, except for the birds of course, hit. 70 to 80 percent of all large life forms on earth were eliminated. Keep in mind that our direct ancestors at that time were little mole type mammal creatures living in the ground. They survived and that's why we're all here. Our very earliest ancestors we think of as human emerge about 2.6 million years ago, or so. So we go from little mole like creatures to these caveman types over about 62 to 63 million years. All that time consciousness is evolving and emerging along with the body structure. Starts to give you a sense for how short a time creatures like us have lived on the planet. Anyway, this is all the stuff Dr. Sherman was showing, I thought it was quite interesting how he related the emergence of consciousness along with the timeline, until you see it that way you probably wouldn't think of it. But looking at this, how else could it be?"

Joan spoke up, "Each of us are like these point sources of consciousness aren't we. We exist because of this vast history of coming into being through billions and billions, probably more like trillions of organisms we emerged through. And the level of consciousness slowly emerged through them as well." She shook her head in amazement.

Dave had his copy of the graph on an 11" by 17" sheet of paper with a clip board that fit it underneath. "What I learned from Dr. Sherman was the need to get a big perspective. This next image is about the changing average temperature on Earth and how carbon dioxide relates. Of course since the changing temperature has so much to do with the imbalance that the Earth is going through now, it's critical to understand it in the big picture."

"Before I take you back in time, I need to explain the current situation with carbon dioxide and this idea that 350 parts per million is a safe amount we need to keep the atmosphere at or below so we can keep the temperature from rising and causing all the problems. So I know you've heard of 350.org which is the climate group this guy Bill McKibben and some other people started. The basic notion is that below 350 parts per million we'd be safe; like the livable and stable range of temperatures are maintained. And beyond that is real risky business. Currently, we're at about 400 parts right now and we're getting the average temperature rising about .02 degrees Celsius (~.036 F.) per year. That's when in a usual cycle it would be going down. So keep that in mind as I move through this other material."

"There's this process called the carbon cycle." He was looking at the others, they were nodding that they understood. "Carbon is everywhere; in all of us, the plants, the animals, the lakes and rivers, the trees, the rock, the oceans and…the atmosphere. The problem is there's just too much of the stuff in the air to keep things the way we need them and have a stable climate. Basically we're screwing up the balance of the carbon cycle and we need to get it back in balance. I'll get to how we do that later."

Dave held up a different sheet, "I'm just focused on carbon and the carbon cycle right now. But Dr. Sherman says that nitrogen and its cycle is just as, or maybe more important than carbon. He calls the two the 'Sixty Seven' challenge. Carbon is number six in the periodic table and nitrogen is seven. That's how he comes up with that. I'll explain the issues with nitrogen later."

"So for the vast majority of time that the earth has existed, our ancestors were micro organisms, fish, all kinds of different ones. It isn't until here," he pointed on the macro timeline to a point representing about 640 million years ago. "Scientists think the world was covered entirely in ice for a long time, maybe 15 million years before it recedes. So all life forms had to be living under the ice, including ours. But then there was a bunch of volcanism and the ice went away and the beginning of the modern world begins about 542 million years ago, which is the beginning of the Cambrian Period. This is when life starts to really diversify and eventually moves out of the ocean on to the land. But that takes millions and millions of years."

He pointed to the line on the graph that represented average surface temperature. "You can see its cold here, down around 12 or 13 degrees Celsius, that's about 53 to 56 degrees Fahrenheit, while the ice still covers. Then the world warms up a lot to what's called The Hot House Earth that's set at roughly 22 degrees Celsius, or about 72 degrees Fahrenheit. That's average temperature. Today we're around 59 degrees Fahrenheit, and less than one degree Celsius change, which is 1.8 degrees Fahrenheit, is melting the glaciers. Look across the graph; the Earth has preferred the Hot House Equilibrium to the Cold House we live in today. I'll get back to that. Then it dips down here to the Cold House, the first mass extinction happens. Of course this is all taking millions of years to happen so this graph just gives it a relative sense of time."

Dave moved his finger so he could note the other line that showed the relative amount of carbon dioxide in the atmosphere along with the temperature line. "You can see that around four hundred million years ago the carbon was getting removed from the atmosphere pretty quickly."

"How?" Sally asked.

"Mostly through mountain building; you know, plate tectonics moving the crust around. As they collide ground is pushed into the air and exposes rock. Carbon dioxide in the air bonds with water molecules making carbonic acid which, it turns out, bonds with a lot of different types of rocks very well. It attaches to those rocks and is held there for millions of years

166

until it gets cycled through volcanoes. That's why these cycles take millions of years. But here, from about 400 million years ago, until about 250 million years ago, the planet sort of reluctantly gets drawn down into the Cold House Earth. Pangaea was at its maximum, that's when all the continents were all tied together, which I read probably had something to do with the Cold House Cycle. Then, right here, massive amounts of volcanoes go off, this is when Pangaea begins to split apart. The east coast of America and Northern Africa were joined together, but now they're splitting up. Look how the temperature spikes; it even goes past the typical top of the Hot House equilibrium temperature, and then comes back down. Look at the carbon dioxide level: it doesn't go way back up, but just gets a little past where we are right now," he noted that point on the far right side of the graph. "That means it didn't take the carbon dioxide levels to get way up there to get these really high temperatures. What was it?"

Dave then showed them the picture of a section of the land and ocean where massive methane hydrates (frozen, like ice cubes but enormous) lay just beneath the surface. "See the spot where the temperature goes up above the top of the line, right at about 250 million years ago?" He asked. "That's when the greatest mass extinction ever recorded occurred. Science tells us that about 95% of all species alive at that time went extinct in a short period of time. The consensus is that some of the methane that had been sequestered in the ground, like it is now, was released when the temperature had increased by four or five degrees Celsius, caused by the carbon dioxide that had been released due to some massive volcanism. What's really scary is that with the one degree we've seen, methane is already escaping into the atmosphere. We could reach a tipping point in not too many years where we lose any ability to deal with it and that would be catastrophic." Dave paused, "But we're not going to let that happen." He couldn't move on just leaving that thought.

Everyone was busy digesting what he was telling them. There wasn't a lot of sound as that disturbing idea was striking a nerve.

"So you can see what generally happens, by about 145 million years ago carbon dioxide was being drawn down on a pretty steady line until it gets to modern times. The Hot House Earth held on stubbornly until about fifty to sixty million years ago, then the temperature starts going down pretty steeply until current time. Again, mountain building seems to have a lot to do with that. So we've now had this pretty short, but still millions of years of Cold House Earth."

Dave handed out another sheet of paper that read at the top, A *Climate Change Mammalian Population Collapse Mechanism.* The average Earth surface temperature is again the critical metric to keep in mind. That's what these graphs are all showing and how that temperature affects life.

"Right here, this is about 65 million years ago, that's when the six mile wide asteroid hit the Earth. All of us are here right now because it hit on the other side of the planet from where our little mole-like ancestors were living at that time. And it's a good bet they were living underground which gave them more protection from the weather problems that followed. And their food source was probably roots and lots of things that were already underground. They didn't have to depend much on living things above ground for food, most of which probably shriveled up and blew away. They were little, and didn't need a lot to eat. Whatever it was a significant number of the mammals alive at that time made it through and so we're here."

He moved around and pointed to two places on the graph, representing 65 million years ago and now. "Over this stretch of time the atmosphere and average surface temperature gradually changed. The ancestors we evolved from did too. They had to. How else do you get from an underground living mole type creature to someone like you and me without having all these intermediate metabolic and morphological changes and levels of consciousness? Species last about two million years on average, so that would mean there were probably 20 to 25 species we emerged through in just that time frame."

"Mutations?" Aiden interjected.

"Yes, that's the engine of change; DNA sequence changes caused by the environment: photon strikes and viruses are a few vectors, but I don't think we have a very good understanding of the "how" yet and maybe the "why." But there are all these little changes, some are beneficial, some aren't, some are like nebulous. Anyway, I need to make the connection to this article."

"What he's in effect telling us is that at least among mammals that there is a very critical ambient air temperature that pregnant female need for them to successfully carry an embryo to birth. All animals are embryos at sometime. When a females body heats up past a certain limit, its body is stopped from dissipating heat to the environment by internal mechanisms. When this happens there is reduced blood flow to the uterus. Uterine blood flow is an embryo's source for oxygen, water, nutrients and hormones, and also works to carry heat away from the embryo. When this shuts down, the embryo dies and is aborted. This is how a species can very quickly go extinct; you don't have to over hunt them."

"It seems that nature has something hard wired into many species, and in particular mammals' metabolisms to just shut down as the Earth warms. I've read where a number of scientists think the real reason so many of the big animals of the recent Ice Age went extinct was actually caused by this. See on the second page where he's talking about cows and how they have these optimal temperature ranges their internal metabolism allows them to reproduce within. Outside those ranges and the species population collapses."

He moved his hand back to the graph, "So all along here there's this gradual evolution of body types, consciousness too. But that's pretty static until way-way later when our species emerges. Just keep in mind how nature was constantly selecting for individuals that were in balance with everything around them, in particular the average ambient air temperature. 'Balance,'" he emphasized the word.

There was a line extending from the temperature line on the graph and all along it were the families of all the other life forms on Earth, plants and animals. "It's not just humans or mammals either; all these life forms in some way are affected as the temperature changes."

He noted the next diagram. "So this graph takes off where this one ends, about 500,000 years ago or so: again, its average surface temperature that's being shown. This oscillation of the line is being caused by the Milankovitch Cycles. Have you ever heard of them?"

Eric spoke up, since he was an Earth Science teacher he knew about them. "That's the name of the guy who worked out all the details showing the effects of the Earth's orbit, and tilt."

"Yes, and precession." Dave moved his hands around showing the various concepts of the Earth's motion. The Earth has been doing all these things since it was hit by that Mars-sized planetoid that created the moon, like 4.6 billion years ago. That's really the official beginning of the Earth, actually. But until the North and South American plates began to collide about 2.5 to 3.5 million years ago the ice didn't grow and shrink at the poles because enough heat was carried around the world to keep that from happening.

"So those red areas above the line, which represents the average of Earth's temperature in the last ten or so thousand years - about fifteen degrees Celsius – are the warm periods. They last ten to twelve thousand years or so, and then the Earth moves back into the colder phase. The glaciers grow and recede accordingly. So keep in mind, again, that all life forms need to keep in balance with that ever changing temperature."

Joan had been thinking that her man needed something to drink. She'd gone into the travel trailer and mixed him a concoction she knew to be one of his favorites, something called a fuzzy mother. She gave him a kiss and handed it to him. He took a good long drink; his vocal chords could use a little cooling.

Dave continued, "So you've heard about this 2 degree Celsius rise of average temperature above the preindustrial age average, haven't you?"

There were a few nods. "So the best I've been able to find for why that amount, noted by the IPCC primarily, is that would be the temperature maximum rise that we could incur and still avoid having the major ice sheets melt entirely. It's based on what they think happened in the Eemian period; I'll explain that in a second. The problem is though; I've been hearing that the scientists are saying that is too much, we only really had room for about one degree rise. We're going over that amount no matter what. We are going into uncharted waters I'm afraid. We are going to need a really good plan!"

Dave pointed to a new diagram. "Okay, so right here, this is about 125,000 to 130,000 years ago. This is called the Eemian. It was a more robust warming period, both longer and warmer than the one we're in now. Our bump here is called the Holocene, just so you get the idea." He hesitated for a moment collecting his thoughts. "You can see that the temperature was a little higher than the peak of the Holocene, which we past about seven thousand years ago. When the Eemian warming occurred, it peaked in warmth at about 125,000 years ago. At that time Greenland lost nearly all of its ice. Sea levels around the world were fifteen to twenty feet higher than now. Deciduous trees grew in northern Norway where there is only tundra today. Think about that, the amount of carbon dioxide in the air then wasn't changing noticeably. Our ancestors weren't digging it up and burning it. So all that change was just caused by the tweeks of the Earth's orbit and the little higher temperatures they caused. The water in the oceans was high enough that Scandinavia was an island. Denmark, Northern Germany, and parts of Russia were under water. The Neanderthals would have seen all that, our ancestors weren't even in Europe yet. Well, except some modern humans did mate with Neanderthals and Matt's living proof." Matt just grinned and rubbed his arm pit.

"There was no New York, or London, or Tokyo then. People were living in little hunter-gatherer tribes. They probably hardly noticed the changes. They just moved around. We have millions and millions of people now living along those coastlines. Just looking at this, it's hard for me to believe we won't get a similar rise." Dave pointed to where the temperature was right now, "See, we're already about here, well past the peak of the temperature rise. We should be steadily going down in temperature as we're at the end of one of the Milankovitch Cycles. We should be going into some rhythm like these other drops into glacial periods; slowly of course. I'm hoping that's maybe an ace in the hole for us but I don't know."

Dave had gotten up to stir the fire as it needed more oxygen. "What was I saying, oh yeah, where do those hundreds of millions of people go? Inland where there's already millions of people? That seems like an enormous problem to me. There are a couple of points along that line I want to note. You can see that somewhere around the warming period just before the Eemian, I don't know what it's called about 200 thousand years ago. That's when modern human's evolved and Mitochondrial Eve, who we all descend from, lived.

So we've been around for two full cycles it looks like. Then the other one I think is interesting is that at about 74,000 years ago, we humans almost went extinct. I've read where they think there were as few as 10,000 individuals, maybe even a lot less. Just the idea that we almost went extinct is pretty profound, at least to me."

"And then there's this," He pointed to the next graph. "This is the last 20,000 years. At about 15,000 years ago you can see we started up in temperature, then it went back down about 11,500 years ago. Then it shoots up to this pretty stable temperature starting about 10,000 years ago, which coincides with the advent of agriculture and human population growth. This is called the Holocene."

"Hang on, I'm getting there; just two more small charts and a few other concerning things and then I'll pass around the arsenic."

"Dr. Death," Aubrey half heartedly then said.

"I know, it's scary, and unfortunately the scariest stuff is what I'm about to talk about." He stopped and looked around at everyone. "I know some people think I'm just Mr. Negative; I've got that vibe from some people. Not you guys; I hope at least." A few of them wiggled their fingers at him. "But if you don't know what your enemy is doing how in the hell do you defend yourself? It's like the Allies in World War II, they needed to know everything they could about what the Germans or the Japanese had or were planning so they could develop the best strategy they could to combat them. We've got to do the same." There were nods of agreement.

He moved to the next graph that had quite a few different measurements being shown. "So what the KOG folks have done here is create a time line starting in 1750 which is when the industrial revolution really gets going. These different metrics – measurements of things – I'm showing them at the year they first started to get measured. What's showing are world population, carbon dioxide, and degrees Celsius in a line relative to time because it's important to understand them that way Dave pointed to the line representing carbon dioxide. So in 1750 it's roughly 280 parts per million. To make that a little easier to imagine that's like about 1part in 4,000. I can almost start to imagine that. So that's enough to keep the planet warm. If it wasn't in the atmosphere we wouldn't be here, no life could exist it would be too cold. So now were just about to 400 parts per million, so that's like 1.5 parts in 4,000." He looked at them shaking his head then he spoke more slowly to emphasize the point, "If one part in 4,000 keeps us just right, what will 2 parts in 4,000 be like?"

Dave stopped for a moment, letting that really sink in. He knew even really smart people who hadn't thought much about all this, might take a little while to ring a bell. "I get it, son of a bitch!" Aiden said, still a little shaken by the mountain bike adventure with Rocs. "I get what you're saying: if one little marble in a bucket with 4,000 does this, then what does two or three do?" Dave was glad that had connected.

Dave continued. "And the affect is on temperature. At less than 1 degree of temperature rise we're already seeing impacts on crops. What's that mean for the future? What happens when food prices start going up and up. What happens when we realize we're truly having difficulty feeding ourselves? How fast does a society start breaking down? How fast does the United States become like the Middle East?"

"That's why getting carbon dioxide back down to or hopefully below 350 parts per million is so critical. Each part is so incredibly powerful!!" Dave's voice was rising. "The atmosphere is "full" right now. So even slowing the amount we add is still over filling the cup."

He continued, "So here's the world population, a little less than a billion people in 1750, and then kabboom! Up it goes. We're adding a billion people every twelve years which is like 200,000 every day. The best estimate I found for a reasonable carrying capacity is about two billion. I think even that's too high. And we're over seven billion right now heading to eight, nine, ten? The so called Green Revolution, using synthesized fertilizers has been the driving force behind this."

He held up a new image, "Look at these two graphs. There is a lot to absorb in all this, but if there is one thing I hope you take away is this. In 1909 this German chemist, Fritz Haber, discovers how to synthesize a plant usable form of ammonia/nitrogen. We go through the war years and then right after the end of the second one, population explodes. There is one reason for that; the most limiting factor in growing stuff was nitrogen and now we had all we could use. There is so much to this, but there is all this other stuff to talk about. Just remember this is the real nexus, the discovery that changed everything and really is at the root of the climate crisis. We can talk more about that later."

He moved on, "So here's the temperature since 1880; it's not doing much then about 1910 it heads up. Of course a lot of wars are going on and all kinds of nasty-stuff was being released into the atmosphere. It stabilizes for a little while during the 50s to the early 70s. Remember that the oceans have been absorbing a lot of the heat, that's another fine problem we'll be dealing with. But then in about the early 70s when our folks were in high school, it takes off. It's rising at about one degree Celsius every 50 to 60 years, which is about .02 Celsius (~.036 F) degrees every year. We've already risen about .85 C.; so in fifteen to twenty years the temperature will have risen one full degree above the baseline, which is roughly the early 20th century average. But that's if the rate of increase stays the same!"

He let that thought settle. "The temperature rise scientists are saying is extremely dangerous to pass is 2 full degrees. So from about 13.73 degrees to 15.73 Celsius. Let's say 15.75 or 16 degrees Celsius for easy to remember numbers. That's about 59 degrees Fahrenheit. There are a lot of reasons why this temperature going up is a bad deal, but to me the critical thing is hitting a temperature where automatic feedback loops kick in. It's called a tipping point and, I don't want to sound too dramatic, but the truth is I don't think the consequences of hitting that tipping point can be said to dramatically. Okay, I'll say it.

"It would more than likely destroy the habitability of the planet for all life forms probably any bigger than bacteria. Nobody can tell us how it would all unfold or how long it would take. But just to make my point, I think there are scenarios where that could happen in maybe 150 to 500 years, and there's a spooky scenario I can imagine where it's even much sooner, but let's hope that's not true!"

"Okay, Dr. Death, you are really starting to scare me. I mean, are you kidding; nothing's left alive on Earth a hundred and fifty years from now?" Heidi said. That was a totally new idea to her, and there was a lot of questioning in her voice.

Dave looked at her with sincerity and reality in his face, "Dr. Sherman has a name for this threshold temperature, he calls it our Mephistopheles Moment. He says that humanity is mindlessly creating a Faustian Bargain of our own by not changing our current behavior. Mephistopheles is the name for the devil in the story about Faust."

"Holy shit! Really, there's a name for that temperature point?" Aiden was very animated in his response.

"Yeah, that's a way to think about it. Anyway, there's a lag time between when a molecule of carbon dioxide forms in the atmosphere and when the effects of it are felt. Scientists think it's about thirty to forty years. So right now we're experiencing the effects of the total carbon loading in the atmosphere "just" in the 70s. And we've added a huge amount since then. So thirty or forty years from now the effects of what's there today will be experienced. That's roughly, but you should get the idea."

Matt wanted to say something, "The temperature doesn't necessarily go up at the same rate. If we hit a point where methane starts burping out in enormous explosions, then it could be like putting your foot down on the accelerator and going from oh, twenty to sixty all of a sudden."

"What actually happens as the temperature goes up?" Sally asked. "I guess you talked about how species die off because they can't reproduce."

"Great question! If it just got warmer and nothing bad happened it'd be like no big deal. But it is a big deal. And just one degree Celsius increase can cause a lot of problems, like I've been saying."

Dave motioned with his finger. "Okay, these categories are shown on the timeline at the year they were first being measured. For example, this is species extinction rate. So, you can see that in 1910 we had just about the normal baseline of extinctions going on which is about ten or twelve a year which is one a month. Nobody really knows how many species exist, but a good estimate is at least 10 million plants and animals. And there's probably a lot more, but they're the small ones like bacteria which are hard to find. Scientists believe that as many as 95% of all species are microorganisms living in the soil and the oceans. So today, in 2013, it's at least 50,000 every year and some scientists think it could be a lot more. Humans are causing this! If we saw some alien space ship land on the Earth and we see them killing all this life on "our" planet wouldn't we accuse them of killing our world?"

"There's a lot of different ways we're causing these extinctions. Up until now we hunted or fished them into extinction or destroyed their habitat they need to live and reproduce. Pretty soon another phase will set in as the temperature rise starts to really affect their ability to make babies. Like Sally said, I was talking about it a little bit ago; where a species population collapses because they can't create new babies. Well that typically goes on naturally as temperatures fluctuate, we're just really accelerating it."

Dave moved his finger over to the next category, "I thought this one was interesting to note. In 1960 the entire world's gross product was $1.35 trillion dollars. In 2012 it was about $72 trillion dollars. The United States part of that was about $15 or 16 trillion. That's a lot of economic activity change in about fifty years, like 65 or 70 times as much activity. All that activity is powered by something; mostly fossil fuels. You can see why so much carbon dioxide has gone into the atmosphere in that short period too."

He raised his hands towards the sky acting like he was feeling something. "This is like the newest metric and actually it's probably the most relevant because it measures the energy change going on. You asked what happens when the temperature goes up, Audrey. So here's the light bulb example. As it gets brighter and brighter the surface it's shining against kinda does the same, right? If it was your hand you'll feel more and more heat. Agree?"

She nodded that she did.

"So that's measured in watts per square meter on the Earth's surface. So the Earth's surface is like your hand reacting to that increased energy that is released as more and more heat. It's absolutely normal to have a certain amount being directed back to the Earth's surface from the normal amount of carbon dioxide in the atmosphere. But since we now have a lot more carbon dioxide in the air we're getting more watts per square meter of energy created. This is more energy in the system. To give you an example, I recently read that the increase in trapped energy everyday as compared to normal is the approximate equivalent of 400,000 Hiroshima sized atomic bombs going off. Again, that's *every day*! So the amount of energy continues growing because we keep putting more heat trapping gases in the atmosphere. That increased energy has to release through the atmospheric system somewhere. And that's why we're getting the increase in extreme weather. And, unfortunately, it's only going to get worse if there isn't drastic change. And I suspect a lot worse."

"So a storm like Katrina, for example," Eric began, "It would have happened anyway, but from what I've read the water in the ocean was warmer than usual so as it was building it just had more energy to pack into it. That's the idea, right?"

"Absolutely, and then because there was so much removal of the delta wetlands that normally dissipate the power of the storm, it just mowed everything over. Then you have a few million people living there that a couple hundred years ago wouldn't have been there. Well, you get a disaster. And what you have to imagine is that those kinds of storms will keep coming. Look, Hurricane Sandy came along; it was outrageously powerful for various reasons, mostly the convergence of factors that were amplified by energy increases in the meteorological system."

"I have this last sheet," Dave said. "So I've been talking about the factors that are *affecting*," he emphasized the pronunciation, "the system. This sheet is a generalized list of the *effects* that are already happening. And like I've said, this is with just less than one degree Celsius of temperature increase."

"What's really concerning to me is that the supposed *acceptable* limit of temperature is two degrees overall, about one more than what we already have incurred. What will that bring? Some are even saying that two degrees will be catastrophic. In other words, they're saying that one degree was all we really had. We will go over that amount no matter what. The only question is can we stop the filling of the atmosphere and start the draw down? And I have to tell you, from what I read some climate scientists think it's not possible to stop it there. A growing number are saying four, five, and even six degrees increase by 2100 is possible. What would that mean?"

"Game over!" Joan said, there was defiance yet reticence in her voice. "We've got to get those soil vacuum cleaners going or we're going to hit the tipping point on methane release and then it really is game over." She was referring to a very new concept that Dave had brought to her attention earlier.

"Joan's talking about what I'm hoping may be a truly effective way to combat all this. I'll explain that shortly."

The sheet Dave had was titled *One degree Celsius of warming and effects seen and possibly anticipated worldwide.* "I want to establish the effects of the climate or environmental crisis we are now witnessing. It gives us a baseline to consider all of this from."

There were eight categories:

1. Melting of Glaciers: rising sea levels, salt penetration of land, loss of agricultural land and water.
2. More intense storms: Thunderstorms, cyclones, hurricanes, and lighting.
3. Variation in weather patterns and land surface changes: more deserts and drought
4. Species Extinctions: at least 50,000 per year (and probably more) compared to 12 typical.
5. Crop Failures: increased heat and carbon dioxide are already having significant negative effects. More heat and carbon dioxide will exacerbate the problem.
6. Human migration: massive numbers of people being forced from their lands as they become un-livable. Attempting to move where others already live ... genocide and localized war is predictable.
7. Insects on the move: Mosquitoes are now more numerous and moving into areas they hadn't been before, and are spreading dangerous diseases like malaria and dengue fever with them.
8. War of nuclear and/or biologically armed nations: wars using conventional weaponry and primarily driven by climate induced factors are already occurring. Extreme weather coupled with fragile societies could lead to war using the most horrific weapons.

Dave continued, "Each one of those eight categories could, and do, have full books written about them. They are all expanded upon on the *Kingdom of Good* website."

Dave held up one last graph. "I've been showing you a lot of graphs, but there's only one that really matters, I think. Everything we do over the next ten or fifteen years will come down to whether or not we control the heating of the planet or not. It's really just that; we either do or we don't. There are actually some scientists right now saying we are on a trajectory like this where by 2050 we're already over 5 degrees Celsius and heading off the charts. It's all over if that happens. I don't believe it. I wouldn't be here if I did. The green line, that's the hope line, that's the one where we bend the curve. If we control the heating and make the line look something like that, then we save ourselves and most all the other life on the planet."

"They've shown dots with question marks next to them above the line, those are the potential Mephistopheles Moments. They are representing the unknown possible temperature points where we lose control of heating. It's sort of like a mountain climber just losing his grasp on a ledge and then there's just nothing they can do. I don't want to get there. We've got to do everything we can to make sure that line gets bent. You can see where it says *Bend the Curve*." Dave smiled knowing that discussion was pretty loaded with angst.

"So in the note I sent out, I suggested that the goal of this meeting was to create this thing we'll probably call the Moab Manifesto.com; which you all get a little part in, by the way. I'll make a link to the *Kingdom of Good* website so they can see the graphs and everything there." Dave explained.

He went on, "To me this is the most important graph of all: the human population graph." He held it up. It showed the relatively flat line for the last 10,000 years, then rising slightly about 2,000 years ago, again 250 years ago, and then like a bullet it shoots almost straight up to over seven billion now. "If you could see this graph 200, 500, 1,000 years from now then what will it look like? What shape will actually happen? Will it hit ten billion then crash down as fast as it went up? Will it go up to eight billion and stay there? I don't think so. Will it move back down on a line that's not a crash but a glide? As in maybe we're working to control it or like we haven't lost control and "can" guide it? To me, that's the biggest of questions…how will it play out? Personally, I think that unless we get control of our breeding and "agree" to drastically cut our numbers and make the human footprint small and nimble; nature will just do it to us. It will be horrific if that happens; and in all the different ways that it could."

But there was a bright way to consider it. "Look, I know that all sounds so negative, and it is, but there is another way to think about it. If reason actually emerges around the world we could make a plan. We could take control of our destiny rather than just letting nature do it for us. If history tells us anything it's that some long-haired angel type won't descend on a cloud and wash all the problems away. We have to do it ourselves. We need a plan. I don't have one in my back pocket, that's what we have to work out. Just like our ancestors did for thousands of years, sitting around campfires working out what are good and fair strategies for their common survival. Scientists think that the ideas of 'good and fair' behavior between tribal members played a huge role in the social structure and evolution of early human groups. They probably sat around fires together and worked the details out. So, today we have the internet that allows us to talk to each other in big groups all around the world. It's like we have this sort of virtual big fire to sit around and figure this thing out!"

"Don't forget to mention Plan B." Joan told him, "and the soil!" The others looked at her funny.

"Oh, yeah, of course. The Earth Policy Institute has what they call Plan B. It's the best idea out there right now that I've heard of. Basically the government taxes carbon and then sends everyone a check. It's phased in, the cost of carbon fuels go up making the alternatives cost effective. There would be no way to track how people spent the money, but since their costs for everything with carbon in it was going up fast, they'd likely do the sensible thing and buy cars that run on electricity, or get solar panels for their homes, all of that stuff. Of course all the entrenched moneyed interests will fight this tooth and nail. But I haven't heard a better plan. The Republicans and industry just deny there is a problem, just like the tobacco industry did. But they probably have a lot more money. But it's a plan to get behind."

Heidi spoke up, "You mentioned something about nitrogen and the sixty seven challenge, or something earlier. What's that about?"

"Oh yeah, that's like a whole other discussion. Carbon is number six and nitrogen is number seven in the periodic table of elements. That's where the sixty seven challenge comes from. The short on that is this. Remember how I was just talking about that in 1909 this German chemist, Fritz Haber invents how to synthesize nitrogen from the air. It was "the" most limiting element for plant growth. When he figures that out the natural throttle on growing stuff, and most importantly…people, came off. It's really the starting point for the climate crisis." He held up that sheet and the graph, "See how the population just explodes around 1950? If our population had just continued to grow at the same pace as before then we might be to three billion people now. But look where we really are…7.3 billion and growing at about a billion every twelve years. There's so much to that, we can talk about it more later."

Dave went back to the original subject. "If the time comes that people can look back on our time and consider the ideas and innovations that actually were most effective. I think it will be that we finally realized how insanely we treat the land and the soils in particular. And most importantly how we can leverage what they do naturally to draw down the carbon in the atmosphere. What we know now that we virtually were clueless about just 25 or 30 years ago, and that includes the scientists as recently as the early 1990s: is the power of the world's soil microorganisms and plants for scrubbing carbon out of the atmosphere. It is what they've been doing for ever; it's their natural life cycle. We were ignorant of that and have gotten in the way. If we can get a solid hold on this idea we can turn the soils into the biggest vacuum cleaner ever imagined."

"Hundreds and hundreds of millions of acres around the world are torn open every year then left uncovered to the elements after harvesting the cash crops. The soils dry and wash away senselessly. What we didn't really understand thirty years ago, that we do today, is that numbers beyond numbers of soil organisms (billions in a teaspoon) when allowed to function as nature intends, sequester the carbon from the atmosphere that's released through the plants and down into the soil where it is stored. It is the base food source for the microbes. And given sufficient time, measured in only a few years, they will gather the carbon, which currently overflows a safe amount in our atmosphere, into the rich humus fertile deep-brown soils are known for. The carbon will be safely stored away in the soil. The microbes do it for us for free. No machine man has been or will ever be able to imagine can come anywhere close to that. And when you come to grasp the fullness of nature's true work, you realize it is "not" possible for man to transcend." Everyone was quiet as they just let Dave's ideas settle in.

Eric broke the silence, "What about solar, wind, geothermal, waves, breeder nuclear energy and carbon sequestration? Aren't those strategies too?"

"Of course." Dave said. "And in their parts they can and will play a major part to slow down the use of carbon. But unless we move like at warp speed, like we did when World War Two started, a lot of people including me think it will be too little too late. Just remember the Mephistopheles Moment, we don't want to get anywhere near it."

"I agree so let's get this manifesto thing figured out!" Eric said strongly.

"Are you going to make Vimeo stars out of us?" Maria at last asked.

"I hope so. I hope it goes mondo viral." Dave smiled at Matt, a little joke concerning the modifier Matt seemed to like to use at times.

"So what's your plan for this video?" Aubrey questioned. "Do we all have to talk?"

"Hum, well, I'll tell you what I was thinking and see if you all agree. For a while I thought that it would be good for everyone to have a part saying something, but it could get too long and repetitive. So the more I've thought about it I think if just one person , and I'm not thinking me on this, did the majority of the talking would be best. And then each one of us said our name and where we're from and then in, like, three to five words said they were behind what," he paused and looked towards Joan, a smile on his face, "Joan said, that would tie us all together…or hang us all together."

"Benjamin Franklin." Nate made the connection.

Joan was looking at him, her facial expression was saying "what, me?"

"You'd be great!" Maria piped in. Maria just had an intuitive notion about her new friend. She had some aura, but she couldn't quite place where it came from.

"I can introduce the group and why we're doing it, and then I just think it'd be great if you talked," his voice trailed off, "you know this stuff. There needs to be the female energy in this."

"I see this thing looking like we are right now, a group of people sitting around a fire, just hanging out and having a good time." Dave began to explain.

"And contemplating the end of the world as we know it." Sally crassly offered.

Dave shrugged his shoulders. She smiled, "I'll try not to be so negative."

"Okay, so I'll tell them what Dr. Sherman was saying about fires and people," Matt began, "it was pretty interesting when he was explaining that humans are, what is it?"

"Eusocial." Dave answered.

Matt continued, "Yeah that, Dave touched on it just a little bit. That's our social way of being. It has to do with multiple generations living together, and defending a nest. What is it, beetles do it too? Dung beetles; pretty good company we keep. So these scientists think that early humans adopted this way of being and fire was like the central thing. It offered warmth, protection from big animals, and food preparation. We probably started off with burned meat. Anyway, because we started living in these kinds of little groups with shared responsibilities the idea of good and fair emerges. So, like behaviors that were good for the group's survival and behaviors that were fair between members start playing into everything. It's our strategy for survival among all these other species. It's important to understand I think."

Dave looked towards Matt and Maria, "That night in Rome in 2010 was extremely special to me. But for Matt and Maria it was something beyond that. That was the night Matt and I bumped into Maria who was with her sister and a friend. This whole thing starts for us that night. I don't really know if Matt and I would have gotten into all this like we have if it hadn't been for listening to Dr. Sherman in the piazza in front of the Pantheon that night." He shook his head in that way we do when something seems distant and unclear. That was the big epiphany for me."

Chapter Twelve

(Day three, Saturday April 26th 2013, they four wheeled during the day and now are making the manifesto)

Dave and Nate had talked earlier about what the best way to shoot the group around the fire would be. Nate really understood lighting and how to capture the best effect for the shoot possible. The content of the video was important of course, but imagery can have a huge capacity to capture the attention and imagination of an audience. Nate had put into words as best he could the look he wanted to capture. It sounded good to Dave. He knew his cousin would do it well.

"Here's a chalk board you can make an outline on. You know this stuff well enough. If you just talk to those eight points then the words will flow." Dave gave his girlfriend a kiss. She helped it to linger.

"Nice," he said, and blinked his eyes at her. "If it's written in your own hand writing, it'll be easier for you to read." She agreed, and began writing down an outline of what "she" wanted to say.

Seeing the need to get everyone in a good spot, Nate began directing traffic. His light set up would be good for a half hour at the most so they needed to get going. Spontaneity in the production would be good, getting facial expressions and voicing that was heartfelt, would be the critical thing to capture.

"Okay, Matt move to your left a little, Maria move a little in front of him; there, that's good." He adjusted everyone around the fire. Dave and Joan sat in the middle on chairs only 8 inches or so off of the ground, with two couples on either side of them and sitting a little higher.

For good luck and a sense of unity, Maria had thought to sign the chalkboard and got everyone else to do it too. It was one of those little ideas that emerge sometimes that help to inspire the group.

~~~~~~

Two last pieces of wood were added to the fire, everything seemed set … it was time to roll. Dave knew he needed to set the tone: smart, honest, heartfelt. Nate nodded, the camera was going. He leaned in towards the camera, he was engaging his audience.

"My name is David Herrick, I'm sitting around this fire on this very nice early evening with some friends of mine; Moab, Utah is just a couple of miles away. We're all here because we think something's wrong, way wrong on our planet. Things just aren't like they were when my folks were young or for that matter when I was young in the late 80s and early 90s.

Like when the seasons change, or the intensity of storms, how much snow or rain we are getting, how hot and even cold or not cold it is during the various seasons. There are extreme fires, floods, droughts, hurricanes and tornadoes. They carry force well beyond the normal levels. If you're paying attention at all you must be noticing the differences. And if you're listening to the voices of the scientists and other concerned people you really know something is wrong. Something is causing this."

"Scientists tell us that "we" are polluting our atmosphere with heat trapping gases. The heat builds up in the land, atmosphere and the oceans; and this is energy that has to be dissipated. The dissipation of that energy is what is causing what is called climate change. Scientists also tell us the effects of this growing energy imbalance will get much worse than that we are already dealing with. If you are hurting yourself by beating your head against a wall, doesn't it make sense to quit beating your head against the wall? Of course it does. As a force on the planet we humans are beating our heads on the wall. Unfortunately, too many of us for various reasons, some extremely immoral, will not stop. Our futures are all bound together on this tiny planet. Those who will not stop, must be stopped. This is a task far more easily said than done. This video and manifesto is our attempt to do something to stop them."

He paused briefly and looked both left and right at his friends. "All of us here are American, except for Maria, she's from Spain," she waved her hand briefly. "Some are from the east coast, the west coast, and parts of the heartland. We all agree something is wrong, very wrong, and somehow we've got to fight back. This is our attempt."

Dave looked to his immediate left, "This is my friend Joan Labeau and she's going to tell you a little more." Dave leaned back and Joan leaned forward. She exaggerated her lean a little more than Dave had. She reached out and grabbed some sand, then let it fall slowly down around her ankle-high hiking boots.

She began, "These grains of sand were once, millions upon millions of years ago, bound in solid rock someplace in the Earth's surface. The molecules that make up the soil particles that are falling with it were at one time bound in a plant that was eaten by an animal, the animal died and here is part of what's left. Those dust particles could be me someday, or you. We are the Earth as surely as this sand and dust are," her voice had risen, it then fell quieter. "We humans are just one manifestation of life's seemingly infinite possible forms here. And we are different from all the others in one extremely important way; we know. That's what homo sapiens means "man who knows he knows" or "wise man.""

"And what is it exactly that we "know" that all the other millions of species on the planet don't? My answer is; we can affect the nature of things, not just be affected by nature. That's why we can do everything from chip a rock to be used to scrape meat from a bone, to building space ships that carry men to our moon. We know. So how is it that a species this clever is now poised to cause its own and millions of other species extinction? To me, that is a staggering question."

"Surely, if every human around the world believed as the 11 of us here tonight do, that our way of living upon the Earth is not sustainable, and in the worst scenario will lead to our extinction; certainly we would do whatever was needed to change. Our population and subsequent draw on the resource base of the world has absolutely exploded in the past 100 years and in particular since the end of World War II. Our numbers are growing by a billion every twelve years or so. We will soon be eight billion, some think we could reach ten billion before," she stopped and ran her hand through her hair, "Before nature's harsh and unforgiving rule takes control."

She stopped for a breath before continuing, "We can only exist in the numbers we do because of a food production network that is not sustainable. The fuel sources we use to produce our food and allow for our mobility and other comforts produce by-products in heat trapping gases that pollute our atmosphere and cause more and more energy to be trapped and dissipated. That's what we're seeing in extreme weather patterns." She moved herself slightly to a more comfortable position.

"The basis for our destructive behavior relative to nature is the false premise that humans are separate from and above nature. Many believe we were instructed by God to subdue and have dominion over all living things. We have unwisely "interpreted" this to suggest we can use nature in any way we find desirable, however unreasoned."

"Observation and reason tell an open-mind that humans are but a part of nature and entwined in its web that we only vaguely understand. The complexity of nature and its unfathomed depths should give us great pause whenever we seek to manipulate it. This fundamental notion that comes from the Judeo-Christian orthodoxy is so much at the root of the sins in our ways. We must face up to this wrong-headed idea and admit we must live in harmony with the rest of nature. Or we believe nature will ultimately prevail and remove us."

"The negative effects of this are all around us to be seen, for those willing to look. But seeing the errors in one's ways requires moving the consciousness to a slightly higher level, as dear Doctor Einstein told us."

"This is my answer about our clever but unsustainable behaviors just posed. There are many that know we must change. Their voices have been rising for many years. Yet their pleading so often falls upon ears that have no desire to listen. This is humanity, a great cross section of consciousness ranging from instinctual to transcendent: from focus on separation and only the moment or the bare minimums of survival; to a sense of connection with and divinity in all things."

She stopped again, and then drained some more sand and dirt through her hands. "My friend David told you briefly the what. I am trying to answer the why. So the "why" to me is this; our problem is the way we think as individuals and what we believe to be true. Taken all together that represents our "model of reality" we hold in our minds. It is our level of consciousness."

"So this is what I believe to be true. This is my model of reality, or my level of consciousness:" Joan began her ending.

- I believe human behavior is the sole agent leading to the climate and entire biosphere crisis.
- I believe that it is a false premise that we can grow our food sustainably using industrial agricultures methods. The colossal and catastrophic mistake of moving to synthetic fertilization and all the follow-on consequences is central to our moral breakdown of not seeing nature in its entirety as holistic "Holy" and is the crucible of our dilemma.
- I believe we have a very short period of time measured in a few years, ten maybe fifteen at the most, to dramatically change our ways or we will lose complete control of ours and our descents destiny on this planet.
- Being the most egregious polluting society and contributor to the ill, I believe that only the United States of America reversing this mindless path and "leading" through its federal government to a wise and sustainable path, can the world be directed away from this impending catastrophe. If we don't lead the others cannot and will not. It is likely a new political party will need to emerge in America to lead this effort. As the two existing parties appear captured to varying degrees by the moneyed interests that have no motivation to change their destructive ways.
- My dream is for One Green World, sustainable and existing for many millennia into the future."

"I hope that millions of you will see this video and feel as I and my friends do and create your own manifesto from whatever town or group you want. Perhaps the beating of an ancient drummer, the one that led our species to survival all those thousands of years ago when we nearly went extinct…will grow and grow like an army coming to free us. Just maybe, whatever it was that got us through then will emerge again, now. My name is Joan Labeau, and that is what I believe and wanted to say. The rest of my friends have a brief message too."

One by one the camera panned to each of the others. They said their name and where they were from. Each one endorsed what Dave and Joan had said. Nate took his break from behind the camera and added his voice as well.

Dave finished, "This is what we call The Moab Manifesto. It's a simple statement of what we believe and what we want done. To get a lot more information please go to *The Kingdom of Good.com* and you'll find a link to our manifesto and the science behind what we're saying. Please, anyone and everyone that agrees with us, create your own manifesto. Put it in your own words. This is the "what can I do about it" answer so many of you have been asking. Please, DO IT! So, from Moab, Utah, mountain bike capital of the universe, thanks!" They were all waving as Nate faded the scene to black, the fire being the last thing glowing.

Nate played it back on his iPad so everyone could see the first draft before he edited it. He would fine tune it for a great look and sound quality. Everyone was so amazed at the presentations both Dave and Joan gave, just off the cuff.

"That was, uh, really great." Aubrey told Joan.

There was a truly humble place in Joan. She'd felt the sting of life's existence enough to keep a grounding about herself. "Dave and I have talked about this stuff so much, I've read nearly every book he's told me about. I guess at some point it just gets thick in your head. I know there are plenty of subjects I'd be totally unable to talk about like that."

"Nate thinks he can have it edited and loaded onto Vimeo in a week or two, no later than the first of June," Dave said. "Once I get it I'll send it to all of you, then you start attaching it to emails to everyone you know. And then we'll just have to see what happens. Will people agree and do their own? I guess we'll listen for the drummer."

Chapter Thirteen

"Hey man, how about meeting for a Christmas drink? Let's say Pengilly's at 4:00. Let me know if it works." Matt left the voicemail for Eric that morning as he thought that Eric might be free that afternoon.

Matt heard the bells on his iPhone ringing and he could see it was Eric calling. "How's it going man?" Matt had been reading some downloads from the Internet while laying back in one of his comfy chairs. He had a cup of coffee mixed with some hazelnut flavored Bailey's Irish Cream going.

"Got your message. Yeah, that sounds good. I got my shopping done yesterday. It was brutal out around the mall, glad to have that done."

"What's Aubrey doing?"

"She's cooking up some pastries and they smell pretty good, too. I asked her and she's fine if I slip out for a few hours. So I'll see you about 4:00."

"Sounds good." Matt went back to looking over some articles he'd downloaded. It was all starting to piss him off. He'd been a big supporter of President Obama, especially since he had made comments in the 2008 election cycle that made it seem that he would be a true advocate for changing our dependence on fossil fuels. But it hadn't been going that way. In fact; it seemed he'd sped things up for finding and developing fossil fuels. 'What the hell?' he was thinking.

There were a few piles of snow still around from the four or five inches that had fallen a little over a week earlier. Matt was the first one there. He recognized a few faces who always seemed to be around.

Eric saw him sitting in one of the booths. "A little nippy out there?"

"Better than it was a couple weeks ago, geez that below zero stuff is not much fun." Matt responded.

"So much for global warming," Eric just had to make that observation.

"You working for the man now?" Matt responded. They both laughed a little. Matt slid a few pictures across the table to him. "Remember that spot?"

Eric studied the picture, "Yup, that's when I got into the big one at Louie in October. Great fish!"

Matt gave him a few more pictures. The others had been taken in Moab, mostly on the mountain bike trip. "Those trails were great. This picture was obviously taken before Nate took his fall." A faint smile formed on his face having experienced bike wrecks himself, "no rash on his cheek."

"Yes, had he been hurt more it could have messed up the meeting. Anyway it worked out."

"What do you hear from Maria?" Eric asked.

"Oh man, this long distance relationship thing sucks. She's back in Spain for Christmas. And then she's up in Norway in January doing some more research on salmon populations for her company. She's got some time in late February, so we're planning to meet Dave and Joan in San Diego then."

"How long do you think you can keep this long distance thing up? Seems like it would be hard."

"What we're hoping is that she can convince her company to let her live in Boise and fly around as needed. Norge is investing in salmon farms on the Columbia up in Canada. Maria thinks she could get a position working on that. We're crossing our fingers anyway."

Matt slid some more papers across the table, "Here's where we need some real help."

Eric picked them up and glanced at the topic statements: Policy Pro; get ready for climate tipping points; Obama administration and Climate Change. The True Story; Former Oil Industry VP Warns of Fracking and Climate Change; there was also a copy of the November, 2013 NRDC monthly.

"Those are for you. Some real uplifting reading for this Christmas. That one there, the one by the former big oil VP, helps to get a better understanding of what's going on behind the scene with Obama and how he's opened up everything to big daddy oil and gas."

"How's that?" Eric was quickly looking over the topic sentences in a few paragraphs.

"It sounds like people think Obama has accepted the reasoning of the fossil fuels industry that the effects of climate change can be dealt with through engineering: levee's, dikes, canals, dams, I suppose."

"You're kidding?"

"Well, that's what that guy thinks anyway. Like most things, we just don't know for sure. But they make it sound like it's just an engineering problem and, hey, the tax payers can pick up the tab for all that. The ones by McKibben and NRDC are pretty much the same, telling how Obama was talking about confronting climate in 2008, but now he's on a different page. I remember some speech he gave, oh quite a while ago. It sounded to me then that he was hedging his position saying that we would now do what we had to, to deal with the "worst" effects of climate change. I was wondering then what he meant by that. I guess we're starting to find out. It appears he has no intention to try and radically confront the fossil fuels industry: like in a massive carbon tax. If we're going to adapt we need to get going. We could get the money to build a new energy infrastructure. No, we're kicking the can down the road even further."

Eric was shaking his head as he quickly read on through the documents. "Have you signed this petition to the President on Fracking?"

"A couple of days ago. I already sent it in. Like it will matter."

"What part of "over 350" don't people get?" Eric said, his voice filled with a degree of anger. "When scientists tell us that the atmosphere is "full" at 350 parts of carbon dioxide per million, and we're now at over 400. What don't they get? The glass is already overflowing and we're just turning on the handle, cranking it in more and more." He looked at Matt, his mouth and his eyes were even more filled with consternation, "What is it about so many people, Matt, that are just sitting back and letting this be done to us? Too many sheep?"

"That's part of it. So many people I think who would care just don't have much of a background in science, so it doesn't really make sense to them. There are so many people who are disengaged; this stuff just doesn't get on their radar."

"Well, I think there are ten or twelve other manifestos out on the Internet now, which are getting legs." Eric said.

"I was hoping there'd be more by now." Matt added.

"Maybe this spring more of them will go online."

"I was talking to Dave a few days ago, he thinks we need another short video that works to link all the others. He's also talking about trying to get some really big rally going, probably on Earth Day. That's the first of April. There's not enough time to organize something really big by then."

"2015 or 2016?" Eric said.

"That's what I'm thinking. It will take some time; but have something really big!"

An hour and a half passed and they both needed to get going. "How about some racquetball next week?" Matt asked.

"Sounds good!"

~~~~~

Matt was driving his little pickup and took the far right lane exit, passed the car wash to where it intersected with 16th street. A car had stopped in front of him, waiting to make the turn. He realized there were some people standing near the curb. Looking closer he could see that one of them had a sign in their hand. This was always an awkward moment for Matt; who are they? Do they really need some help? Or were they like the lady who walked the street with her shopping cart, neatly dressed and seemingly normal, but waiting to catch your eye so she could make her pitch, and then return each night to a comfortable apartment? So the newspaper article had said.

The car ahead pulled out, Matt pulled forward. 'Geez,' he thought immediately to himself. It was a young couple, probably in their late 20s like himself. And something he'd never seen before: a young child in a stroller was placed in front of them. The sign read, 'baby hoping for a Christmas.' Matt looked directly at the child, the child looked warm and healthy, he glanced at the other two and their eyes immediately connected with his. He could go, but there was no one coming but a car was coming up from behind. He rolled down his window. "I'll be right back." They nodded at him.

He found a parking place and then walked back to where they were. They looked so normal, was this all an act, could this be like a horrible form of deceit?

The young girl spoke first, "God bless you." Injecting God into their communication straight away has some visceral appeal; the notion that some force of goodness was bringing them together. A part of Matt wanted to know their story. How in the world did they get in this situation and with a young child? He had already dug a $10 bill out of his wallet. If he was going to this effort, he thought, anything less would be insulting to them both. Handing the bill to the young girl, Matt felt a warmth suddenly flow through him. Quite vicariously a man standing on the other side of the street, watching the interaction had the same feeling come over him. Instead of continuing on, he crossed the street and offered money to the young couple as well. It's hard to say who received the greater gift that afternoon.

Chapter Fourteen

(Dallas, Texas; early January 2014)

A thick smoke was circling above the ash tray holding the Cuban Cigar that had been left while the grey-haired man poured himself a drink of Fighting Cock Whiskey on the rocks. He was a large man, over six feet four, but slender and firm. He'd had a strong baritone voice when he was young, but it was rarely used for singing. It did serve him though, in his years rising through the layers of management in the oil industry. It commanded attention with those he worked with. In his rise he'd had to get dirty some out in the grease with the rough necks.

Frank was a mining engineer. He'd followed his own father into the business. He'd left Odessa, Texas for balmy Moscow, Idaho in the late 1970s. By then he was already in his late twenties. After four years he graduated with honors in 1981. School was not particularly difficult. Mostly it was a time for him to grow out of his cocky-ways he'd carried around northern Texas to the honky tonks between Lubbock, Amarillo and Abilene. The scar above his right eye told a bit more of the story too.

"Uh huh, I've seen it." His answer was in no hurry and low, a sip of his whiskey moved slowly down his throat as he answered. He crossed his long legs and put his cowboy boots up on the low table across from his desk. "It's gettin' some legs huh. Hmm. This fuckin' Internet, it's sort of like water or gravity, it can be your friend or your enemy, just depends on the situation. Well, which color card do we need to play here: red or blue?"

The intermediary on the other end of the line said she'd need to consider that. She would talk it over with her father and get back.

The game had been getting trickier recently, for the family, keeping it sorted out whose political career needed some oiling to keep their best interests in line.

It was entertaining watching these kids make their do-gooder plea to the world. 'Misguided little shits,' he was thinking. The thought even crossed his mind that the blond haired bitch was pretty good looking. The dark-haired kid needed to get his ears whopped.

Denial had been working with the sheep for ten years now. There was certainly more room for discussing the issue on the red network. Let the sheep know that the science was still out; there was no consensus on this climate bullshit. It always amazed him how easy it was to just throw that line out there and how the sheep just settled in behind it. They loved their red team and anything they got fed that the red team wanted them to eat. They just sucked it in.

His mobile phone rang again. "Yeah, yeah I heard Black Jack got into a pickle down there near Socorro Island. Is he in a mood for this sort of thing?"

Frank listened to the member of the family, "Ah huh, so we'll play a blue card on this one. They know, they're not listening to the Eco nuts. We got years and years to deal with this thing. We've got a big investment there to get fully paid on. These confused little Eco nuts need to get the idea there little protests are getting them nowhere. Yeah, okay, I'll get with Black Jack; we'll get some blue oil goin'.'"

There was a little more the woman needed to tell him. Frank didn't say anything, just listened for several minutes. "Haven't done any of that for a long time," his voice was pensive. "That bad? Hmm, I'll need to talk with Black Jack on that too. I think he's got the artillery around him to take care of that sort of project." He listened a little more, "Okay, particularly the blond bitch. We'll get 'um all, it'll be a clean job, I know how Black Jack hires." He listened, "Yeah, yeah tell your dad it's good as done. Tell him I hope he had a very happy Christmas too. Okay, bye."

'God dammed, weasel fucks,' Frank was thinking to himself. There was a part of him that didn't like passing along the message he'd just received, but he knew he had to. Black Jack's very private line, which even the NSA had not figured out the code for, was quickly accessed and a call placed. It was early January of 2014 and Black Jack was at his home on Maui where he spent the greater part of his time and directed his part of the empire. With the families', which some referred to as a cartel, private satellite system, they could direct their operations around the world with the comfort their conversations were secure. At least until some high school kid on summer break offered the NSA a different angle to break their code.

Black Jack was just finishing a long shower when Frank first called. He'd now settled himself under the light morning shade of the palm trees around the upper deck of his veranda. The view to the ocean was spectacular this morning. "Frank, you called?" His voice was direct, slightly hurried as 18 holes of golf were scheduled with a tee time in an hour and a half and he needed to warm up some.

"Yeah, pard … Oh, hey, I heard you had a scrape down there near Socorro. You doin' okay?"

Just the thought of the whole ordeal made Black Jack's skin crawl a little. "Think of the worst fucking nightmare you've ever had, and then have about 10,000 mosquitoes biting you to wake up. That starts to get you close to that thing. I have 4 spots on my neck where the fucker's claws ripped out some pieces of my skin. I had some graft work done so they're not too obvious."

"Some kind of squid, I heard?"

"Yeah, had to be one of the colossal squids. The fuckers aren't suppose to live that far north. They're supposed to be down around Antarctica. But they've found them up around Japan. I need to just not think about it. It took me several weeks to get to where I could get to sleep and not have some sort of nightmare. Jesus, what's up anyway?"

"Well, looks like the sheep got a few goats makin' noise a little louder than the family wants. Did you get the video link Pricilla sent around?"

"I know there's something I'm supposed to watch. I'll take a look a little later. I'm headed to play some golf shortly."

"You still scratch?"

"I was but I seem to have something fucking with my mind lately. I'm struggling breaking 75 most days. It's lookin' God damn nice today. I'm gonna shoot me a good low score."

"Well, I won't hold you up too much more here. Look Pricilla says the family wants these kids gone. Poof , no more. They think two of them in particular could end up being some big phenomenon leaders. We don't need that shit; another John F. Kennedy. We need to grease some blue first. You know which senator I'm talking about? His wife's' company needs some good contracts. Have him make some greeny eco statements, but make sure he votes the way we want it. I know you have some good hires around you to take care of these loud mouthed kids. Make sure it's clean with no tracks."

Black Jack finished drinking his Bloody Mary, "Okay. I gotta hit some balls."

Chapter Fifteen

(San Diego, just after the New Year 2014)

Gezana opened the refrigerator door looking for the cucumber, onion, and tomato she would need to prepare one of her favorite cold soups, Clear Gazpacho. She then cut the cucumber and onion into bite sized pieces and put them in a pan to boil. She knew the receipt by heart. When the veggies' were cooked just right she'd then blend them with the tomatoes, some coriander, capsicum, and Tabasco sauce. Strain it a little and serve.

She'd just been to the gym and was dressed in some rather sexy black tights and a light blue lycra top. She was not excessively bosom, but nice. When Gazena moved in with Stone, she'd asked if they could remodel the kitchen just a little to get a feel she was more at home with. The look was Rachel; bold bright colors and maybe just slightly retro. A fresh bouquet of flowers was usually somewhere in and around the kitchen.

She and Stone had spent the Christmas and New Years break in Sun Valley where his parents had a great second home there. He went alpine skiing at Baldy, but had also discovered Nordic skate skiing a few years earlier and found he liked that a lot too. Gezana just liked the beautiful scenery.

There was a new email from her younger sister. Gezana was eager to see what she was saying:

> "Gezee, (they had nicknames for each other) it was so great when you were here. I loved learning about your life in America now, even though I wished you didn't live so far away. Momma cried the night you left. Nobody could see her because she went into her room but I could hear. Don't feel bad, she was laughing when we watched a movie later that night. You have to go where you find love, I think. I dream about a boy that will love me the way Stone loves you. How lucky you are. I know one boy, I wish he would call me and take me for a ride on his scooter. What does love feel like, Gezee? How do you know if you love someone or they love you? Oh. I was looking for some new music on the Internet this morning. People were saying try this song or that song, and then one of them said to look at this video. It had music from Pussy Riot in its lead in. So I watched it. It's a bunch of people your age sitting around a fire in some place...I don't know where it is. America maybe. If you watch it you'll get the place. I know that Stone is

some kind of scientist. It is cool with the music and how everything looks. Gezee, please send me a nice long letter all about how you know you are in love, with lots of details please. Write to me! Bruna (BB)

As she sipped on the soup she'd made for herself, Gezana decided to take a quick look at the video. It begins with a very serene setting with the horizon of a distant bare mountain in reds and some light greens. The light seems to be that of the early morning. Then there's this distant sound, it's going very fast, Gezana can tell its punk rock. Then bobbing along the horizon is what looks like four heads. Then quickly you see that they are heads with balaclavas on. One in light blue, one in purple, one in dark blue and one in bright raspberry. Their heads are shaking around to the beat of the music. Right after them come more and more other heads dressed the same way, their balaclavas are in every color imaginable. 'Looks like a protest statement to me,' Gezana was thinking to herself, "Hmm?"

It was then that the picture turns to Dave and everyone else making the Moab Manifesto. Gezana continued to listen. Anyone that would tie Pussy Riot to their statement deserved a quick look at least, she thought. When she was done she forwarded it to Stones' computer. She wasn't very sure what he might think about it. He was a scientist, but what she'd heard him say about the climate situation was very little and mostly that he felt it wasn't proven to be a problem. Oh well, her sister had sent it so she'd do the same.

~~~~~

Stone moved up rather quickly behind her as she was doing the dishes, he put his hand around her waist and kissed her neck. She smelled so good. "Six birdies today, no bogies, sixty six."

"Well, if you'd had three birdies it would have been my favorite number." She pulled one leg up and curled her shoulders and smiled at him mischievously.

He nodded his head grinning also. "I'll remember that."

Looking around the kitchen, he could see Gezana had some kind of specialty meal going together: olive oil, chopped onions, a red bell pepper, some garlic, paprika, some rice and white wine and then the meat, some chicken. "Arroz con Pollo," Gezana told him, puffing her plump lips. "I wanted to get a little more protein than I had in my soup for lunch."

"Works for me," Stone responded.

"The wine is over there next to the computer. Before I forget, I got an email from BB this morning with a video attachment she thought you might like to watch."

"A video? About what?"

"I took a peek. They're protestors, I guess. There's a group of people about our age, maybe a little younger, sitting around a fire. They're warning us about climate change. You should get a kick from the lead in."

~~~~~

Following his often normal routine, Stone left the bedroom and his lover who was now sound asleep, having enjoyed her man. He was wearing only his shorts and a lycra running shirt. He stopped at the frig and looked for a little snack. Gezana had an assortment of veggies for them to nibble on. He sat down at his computer and briefly scanned the New York Times and Rolling Stone Magazine for any interesting articles. Opening Rolling Stone a picture of Ron Burgundy was on the cover since "Anchor Man 2" was now released. He was looking forward to catching a showing as the whole premise made him laugh.

'What's this?' He brought up the article. "Obama and Climate Change" there was a new little voice in Stone's head, which had been getting louder ever since his adventure with the squid and the moment where time seemed to drastically change. And then there was that message in his mind 'what do you believe?' He was still wondering what that was all about. Six months earlier he'd have skipped this article, considering it inconvenient to his career path. Not tonight, something said, read it.

An interesting graphic was featured at the beginning of the article: it was a hand drawing of a mountain landscape with a fossil fuel processing plant set in the middle. It sets the tone. He scanned it briefly before reading the whole article: Global Warming's Terrifying New Math. Greenland and Antarctica melting: Climate Changes Dangerous Effects; The Fossil Fuel Resistors. 'Alright,' he thought, 'read it through.'

Stone mixed himself a drink and then wandered out into his landscape. The night lighting added an aesthetic dimension he very much was drawn to. He sat down on one of his large wicker chairs and just settled in. He looked up into the somewhat hazy sky. The lights of the city tended to dampen the contrast of blackness to the stars he knew when in Sun Valley and other remote mountain type areas.

Like the battles so many of the service guys coming back from Iraq and Afghanistan (Vietnam, WWII; on and on) Stone too had his PTSD to come to grips with. Visions did keep slipping into his consciousness of the squid attack, even during the day. His escape was to force himself to insert an entirely different vision into his mind. One where he had control. Such a moment had just passed and he'd successfully placed the altered vision in his mind. Having just read an article where some were suggesting we might be nearing a planetary melt down where we lose control of our future, might have tipped him to those horrifying visions.

'What do I believe?' He could handle that. The notion washed around inside his mind; much of it being processed at a level slightly below typical awareness. 'Was it reasonably possible for the earth to spiral out of control so we couldn't live here? It seemed preposterous, how could a system so huge possibly change like that, especially in any amount of time that would matter? But some inkling of curiosity bubbled to the surface of his mind: 'Do a search on: climate change and tipping points.'

He scanned the possible links for what looked most interesting: one from *Political Machine* caught his eye. As it opened, a large ad from Big Oil noting that the energy industry supports 9.8 million jobs, was at the top of the page. Another Big Oil advertisement was to the right of the article. 'Report, get ready for climate change tipping points.' He read on, "The American Research and Review Council...so-called tipping points...result in "abrupt" impacts...need for an early warning system. Right now we don't know how many of these thresholds are...James White...University of Washington, Seattle. Blah, blah,...International Energy Agency...green house emissions to surge in the coming years...20% more each year by 2035...trajectory...far above 2 degree Celsius increase internationally agreed safe level."

The article he'd read just before going to Socorro Island while he waited at Cabo San Lucas, popped into his mind. The part noting the change in the oceans balance of life, due to the vast over harvest of the large and medium sized fishes, was leading to a new balance. Or tipping point, he wondered. 'Why was that fucking Colossal Squid so far north?' A thought from his subconscious told him that the balance in the oceans was already drastically changing. And what else was happening?'

~~~~~

Stone went on and checked his emails, not much from the lab, just updates on the experiments. 'This day-to-day stuff can be pretty mundane,' he was thinking.

He spotted the email from BB, Gezana's younger sister. He briefly read the note and thought it was cute how the 14 year old was so interested in "what love was like?" Good question. Did he even really know?

The opening of the video was entertaining. He thought he got the meaning behind the bobbing balaclavas, and the many more that followed. They represented dissidents, just like Pussy Riot. By the end of the video Stone was starting to have a funny feeling in his gut that something was changing. And it was in him.

He sat quietly again staring at the now motionless computer screen and his drink was empty. He could see the number of times the video had been watched, now well over a million. People were obviously listening so it must be resonating with more than just the geeky Eco types. He was starting to believe something new about the climate. He didn't know it, but his consciousness was moving ever-so-much closer to a new level. He also thought the guy doing the talking looked familiar, but he wasn't sure where he'd seen him.

His mind drifted back, years, and then some more. There he was in his 6th grade class explaining the development of a chicken egg to everyone. He was very proud of all the sketches he'd done copying pictures from the encyclopedia. That's when he'd learned what a cross section was and it bent his mind figuring that out. But it was right then, right then when the teacher was making such a big to do about his science project that he'd decided he wanted to be a scientist. He was going to figure out some big things and make a real good living doing it. He wanted to have a house with a swimming pool just like the Hansen's who lived a few blocks away had. Kids vary when they start contemplating their future life, but if you ask them, at least here in America, most have a pretty big expectation for what they will be doing. Stone certainly did.

And like everyone who made the Moab Manifesto or the other manifesto's now being made around the world. The hopes and dreams of a happy and healthy future they all assumed should be theirs, was pre-eminent.

Part Three: Epiphany

Chapter Sixteen

(San Diego, February, 2014)

"You gonna go?" Oscar asked, popping his head into Stone's office. He had the printout in his hands with the lecture time scheduled at San Diego State University by a member of the research group that had recently released a very damaging review of the chemical glyphosate, the active ingredient in their competitor's herbicide. Stone had read the article the day before. It was just one more nail in his growing consternation with his path in life. He was shaking his head slightly and it grew in greater intensity. "Yes, what the hell. Better to know what the enemy is up to then be blindsided, I guess."

"It starts at seven. I'll meet you by the front door at a quarter 'til?"

Stone nodded his head. At least he was feeling refreshed from the intense work-out he'd done that morning. The trainer he worked with at his gym had him strap on a vest that weighed 35 pounds. He'd gone through his circuit 4 ½ times until he was wiped. That last sprint put him on the floor. It hurt then, in that good way. It just felt great now, and his muscles were all glowing, rewarding him for doing the right thing.

It was Gezana's night out with her girlfriends and they'd actually joined a bowling league. Together they'd designed their own team tee shirts and had decided it was actually great fun.

"I'll be at a conference at the University tonight," Stone told his girl-friend, via his blue-tooth phone connection, as he drove down Mission Valley Freeway. Gezana blew him a kiss. Stone knew where he wanted to park. He'd take the off ramp to College Avenue then to Montezuma, take a right down to 55th and take another right. He'd find a spot in the semi circular parking lot across from the Public Safety Building. There would be a little shade for his BMW under the grove of palms in the adjacent landscape island. It was a short walk from there. Stone was a bit uneasy about what he might learn this evening. Could his schooling and everything he'd been working on for years be a fool's errand?

"I might be a little late. This talk runs till 8:30, then I might have a beer with Oscar. I might need one." He told Gezana just before hanging up.

"Okay?" Gezana answered, "Why do you say that?"

"I'll tell you more tonight or in the morning. You have a good time with your girlfriends. He had his code word for how much he loves her:

"mucho bombon." It actually carried another meaning between the two of them as well.

"Promise!"

"Always!"

For Oscar it was already shorts weather, even in the middle of February. His darker skin complemented the Tommy Bahamas palm-tree-inspired blue and yellow print shirt he was wearing and sandals finished off his gig. Oscar's sun glasses were sitting on his forehead while he looked over the syllabus for the lecture.

"Are we dressed about as incognito as possible?" Stone inquired of his colleague as he arrived.

"I look like a prof, don't I?" Stone nodded.

"Here, you might want to read over this. It's a little more than what was on the invitation email." Oscar handed him several pages to read.

'DK Herbicide May Be Most Important Factor in Development of Autism and Other Chronic Disease.' And a little further below, 'The Horrible Truth about Cleanse.' Stone looked up at his friend and shook his head. He then looked down through 'the story at a glance.'

- There are two central problems relating to glyphosate in the human and animal diet:
-    Nutritional deficits develop, particularly mineral.
-    The molecule is toxic to a vast number of benefi cial microbes that inhabit our bodies.
- The glyphosate molecule may very likely be the key factor leading to a vast number of diseases common in the western world.
- There may be a toxic affect by glyphosate on the vast mix of bacteria that inhabit our gastrointestinal system as they have the same biochemical pathway that glyphosate inhibits to kill weeds. It disrupts the functioning of the microbes and it is especially negatively preferential towards our beneficial bacteria, which then allows the pathogenic bacteria to multiply and cause health issues.
- The exploding epidemic with autism may be associated with glyphosate exposure; problems with gut disbiosis (imbalance of gut bacteria, leads to leaky gut) and sulfur metabolism and transport.

The key word in everything he was reading was "glyphosate" as that was the chemical his group was attempting to alter just enough to get around DK's patents. DK was the biotech giant Stone's company most wanted to beat. But these guys are saying the basic chemical disrupts the viability of all the bacteria in humans, 90 % of our body's cells, and other life forms it comes in contact with. It didn't sound good. How could their new molecule get around that issue?

"Good evening everyone, my name is George Huff and I'm the Director of Communications for the San Diego Distinguished Lecture Foundation. It's our mission to bring recent and relevant topics important to the general public to our lecture series. Tonight Robert Jones, author of *What Biotech doesn't want you to understand*, will share with us the results of a recently released, peer-reviewed paper authored by Dakshi Mohinder and Dr. Sidney Sedlecek, a research scientist at Harvard University. They will be telling us how their research has revealed how glyphosate may likely be destroying human health."

Stone sat forward in his chair, listening intently. The presenter began by suggesting that DK must be taking their inspiration on product information from the evil one itself. As they pretend there is no problem with Cleanse though as Dr. Sedlecek states, 'glyphosate may likely be one of the most important elements in the outbreak of multiple chronic diseases and conditions that have recently been developing in European and North American societies.' A graph showing the list of likely influenced diseases appeared on his Power Point screen: autism, cancer, Parkinson's Disease, Alzheimer's, ALS, Multiple Sclerosis, were a partial list.

Jones went on, "It's only recently that research has discovered the true extent that bacteria reside in our bodies. We now know that for every one cell with your DNA in it there are about nine or ten others that are not even you. They are bacteria and exist on and inside of you by the trillions. Now DK has claimed for years that Cleanse is safe and is harmless to animals including humans because the mechanism it uses to kill weeds-disruption of the shikimate pathway-is absent in animals. Well the 'rest of the story' is that the shikimate pathway **IS** present in bacteria. The bacteria resides in our bodies for a reason, they are performing very important functions. When they are healthy we are too. If you kill or drastically inhibit the bacteria there can be serious consequences. Illness often develops in humans and other life forms coming in contact with this chemical."

He went on to explain gut disbiosis which are imbalances in gut bacteria, inflammation, leaky gut, food allergies such as gluten intolerance and other systems in the body being chronically impaired. The bottom line was that genetically engineered food that required Cleanse or any other herbicide that interfered with the shikimate pathway, was potentially poison food. How could a person of conscience get around that fact?

Stone had read down through the rest of the hand-out. Virtually the entire study was screaming out that what he was doing would be just as bad since they were just looking for an alternative way to disrupt shikimate. It wouldn't matter; another mechanism would have the same effect on the bacteria and human health. If this research was right, and his gut was telling him it was, he'd certainly been a sucker for a fool's errand. 'How could his education not have included this,' he asked himself?

Stone didn't want to stay around for the Q and A period. It would feel like iodine being poured onto an open wound. A line had already formed though for Q and A. Stone looked at the second guy in line, a tall slender fellow with dark hair, maybe a decade younger than himself. He looked very familiar, then it registered: this was the same guy who was in the video he'd watched a few days earlier. He couldn't remember his name and it sure seemed like they'd met somewhere else too.

"Oscar, let's listen to this guy. I recognize him and I'm curious to hear what he asks."

The first guy in line was definitely a geek. His question was way too technical, asking about biochemical pathways relating to cytochrome P450. Jones had to take a pass, suggesting the question be directed to Dr. Sedlecek.

Dave was next, "Mr. Jones, I don't have a question," he began, "I'd just like to make a statement that I think is relevant to the entire genetic engineering food debate." He stopped, looked from side to side at those around him, "Has anybody ever just asked the simple question 'why do we need all this food?' I know that on the surface it seems like a dumb question. We have to feed all these people on the planet. I've read that the true carrying capacity of Earth though is probably somewhere around two billion people if all the reasonable arable land was cultivated using organic farming methods. Some think organic could feed 7 billion, but why?"

"Organic methods that would soak carbon out of the atmosphere and head us back to a sustainable climate. Okay, so we'd have 2 billion people rather than seven, soon to be eight, nine, or ten? *Um, so what's wrong with just two billion people?* Wouldn't that make the experience of life better for every human?"

"We're cutting down rainforests that are actually the lungs of the planet. And for what good reason? To grow more food for people we don't have room for already? And what about all the water it takes to grow that food! Getting dependable water from year-to-year is already an enormous problem. My point is this: if we just had more discipline controlling our population we wouldn't need to grow this food-from-hell, which actually makes us sick in the first place. That's all I wanted to say."

As soon as he was done others began applauding followed quickly by nearly everyone else in the room. Dave smiled, raised his hand, thanking them.

"We need more like him." Stone heard a woman say that was standing nearby.

Outside the hall, Stone walked over to where Dave was standing. One of the ladies that had heard his observation had stopped him and thanked him for making the comments he did. He never missed an opportunity to hand out a card noting the dates of his lectures. "I can make the one next Tuesday evening," she commented. She studied the little map showing the location where he gave the lectures.

"Can I have one of those?" Stone asked, coming close.

"Sure," Dave handed it to him.

"You're on the video, the one from Moab?" Stone asked, his tone implying a question.

Dave was aware it was getting a lot of viewing. He nodded his head, "Yeah, that's me."

"I like the balaclavas," Stone noted, grinning.

"My cousin, who shot the thing and edited it, put that in. It gets people talking."

"My name is Stone Fischer. I recognize you from a conference 6 or 8 months ago. You were talking about proteome research you're involved in. It was in Eugene."

Dave had a brief flashback, remembering for a moment the experience he'd had in San Francisco getting a little too high with a hippy girl. The memory was connected with the trip to Eugene in his brain.

"Are you in Biotech?" Dave then asked.

"Yes, I work for NewGenoBio."

Dave nodded his head acknowledging that he'd heard of the company. He knew they were primarily a genetic engineering company associated with large industrial agriculture.

"What got you to the point to make the video?" Stone then asked.

"Well, that's kind of a long story. It had to do with seeing a lecture by this retired professor. The professor's name was Dr. Sherman. He had about a two and half hour lecture on the climate crisis and about every stupid thing people are doing. His points were intense and I came away and just knew I had to get involved. The more I learned the more radical I've gotten. My girlfriend, Joan, was the other person doing the talking. I thought she did a great job. We weren't singing or dancing, so it's a little more of a challenge to do it someway that gets people to watch, and most important to listen."

"Well, I'll plan to be at your Tuesday presentation," Stone told him.

"Good, please bring anyone else you think might be interested or at least open to hearing the material."

Stone couldn't think of anyone in the company he could share with about his concerns. He was going out on a limb with this himself by acknowledging a human caused problem with the climate was not a part of being on message in his company. He'd keep it quiet that he was going.

Leaving the plaza, Stone noticed a face in the crowd who was just leaving the lecture hall. It seemed very familiar to him and he couldn't place it for the moment.

A few minutes later, his subconscious mind must have been working on solving where he'd seen that face before. Suddenly it occurred to him that it was on Black Jack's yacht. The guy he'd seen was one of the security guards Black Jack had in hire. He had such a prominent nose and the look of a body builder, and Stone had a knack for remembering detail anyway. It seemed like an odd connection.

~~~~~

Stone closed the glass door to his office. He had some emails needing to be read and didn't want any distraction from the hallway. He took a look briefly at the pictures Gezana had sent him taken on their Christmas and New Year's vacation ringing in 2014. 'I look drunk,' he thought to himself, looking at one of the photos.

He worked his delete key on several more knowing the content from meetings he'd had in the last few days. Then the topic line really stuck out for him on one of the emails: We're killing the planet! This was a very secure email address known to only a select few. If this was some sort of environmentalist email he'd know they'd been hacked. There were no attachments, but still, if there was a bug in the email it could cause some real problems for his network. He thought about it for a little bit and he was curious what it might say. Especially with his growing concern about his own research. It occurred to him to just forward it to his home computer, the one he rarely used. If it got hit with a virus there would be little concern.

~~~~~

The work outs his personal trainer had been devising for him were getting insane. Now he was wearing fifty extra pounds in an armor suit that weighed down both his chest and his legs.

"Five more Stone. Give 'um to me!" Mick said, clip board and stop watch in hand.

Stone knew this was where he made the jump in fitness level, maximizing the effectiveness of the work out. He drew in more air and focused his mind to the end just three more lifts away. Complete, he sat down next to the wall and put his head close to his knees.

"Way to nut it out man. We'll be seeing some real improvement in a few days with that. Don't forget your electrolytes!"

Stone nodded at him, still working to catch his breath. He quickly showered and slipped into some fashionable post workout garb and headed home.

A quick stop at the refrigerator for some carb loading was prominent in his mind upon arrival. He sat for awhile, relaxing, letting the food and electrolyte enhanced beverage settle. Gezana wasn't home yet as she'd mentioned doing some shopping with one of her girlfriends. She should be home soon though, he was thinking.

He remembered the email he'd forwarded to himself earlier that day and this was probably a good time to check it out. There it was, along with a few others from vendors he allowed to drop their sales announcements to him at. We're killing the planet. 'Okay, what's this all about? Hmm, someone must be trying to convince him that glyphosate was a bad boy he assumed. How did they know to send this to his work email ?' Stone was thinking.

That wasn't news to him. Of course the new Ag could be tough, but he had been convinced that the up sides certainly outweighed the down sides. He knew that the name of the game was to just keep ahead of nature's re-actions to their tactics and strategy. He read on. There was one article heading though that did stand out to him: DK's Cleanse Herbicide May Be Most Important Factor in Development of Autism and Other Chronic Dis-ease. He'd just seen all this at the lecture the night before. Where was this coming from? Who ever had sent it wanted him to focus on this article, as the heading was highlighted. He looked down through 'the story at a glance' with the five most important concepts in the article condensed to a few sentences. They had been highlighted too. The connection with the body's bacteria was troubling to him. He'd been of the false impression that glyphosate had no effect directly on the human body because the cells of our bodies don't have the shikimate pathway, and they don't; but the 90% of our bodies bacteria cells that work in tandem with those that have our DNA, do; according to the researchers.

In fact, they can be destroyed by the molecule. How he had missed this in his education? He wasn't sure. Well, even when he was doing PhD work a decade earlier, the understanding of the vast ocean of bacteria that inhabit the human body was only beginning to be unraveled. Their stagger-ing numbers were somewhat known. But until DNA analysis reached a point where the different species could be revealed, the potential problems there were simply not known. But that now seemed to have changed.

He opened another attachment, this one was dated in 2006, and it was titled 'Human Gut Bacteria and the Shikimate Pathway System.' He began reading and eight minutes later he was complete. What he had just read deeply disturbed him. In fact it made him feel slightly nauseous. 'How could they?' he thought.

There was one more attachment and this one was a jpeg. It was a picture with several people standing and talking to one another. Right away he recognized the man standing at the center of the picture. It was Dave Herrick and the blond looked familiar too. She was probably the one in the video. There were two more people: a guy with a girl with dark hair. They all looked to be in their late twenties or early thirties. There was a second page of hand written scribbles. It looked like a sheet of paper that someone would have been taking notes on over time, as there were doodles and squiggles to get the ink to flow markings. One in particular had been highlighted; 'eliminate per Family directive.' The word eliminate had been underscored and a note added next to it. 'They intend to kill them! These are notes made by Kurt Krastle. I believe you should be aware of certain images he liked to sketch.' A line stretched to one. 'The Family order is still in effect!'

'And what's this? Another attachment?' He opened it and there was a video clip from the Wizard of Oz. He touched the play button. "Toto, come back here," Dorothy called to her little dog, being terrified herself by the three dimensional image of a man's head shrouded by smoke that had been speaking to her and her companions. "Toto!" A curtain was pulled back revealing a man controlling gadgets that quickly connected him with the ephemeral head she was being scared by. Stone was laughing, remembering the scene.

Then it moved to another scene; the one that scared him even more when he was a little boy. It was Dorothy, the scarecrow, the tin man, and the cowardly lion being chased by the wicked witch of the west, the castle guards with their big hairy hats, and those dreadful monkeys. The witch lights the scarecrows arm on fire. Dorothy is terrified, thinking only to save her friend. She grabs a nearby pot filled with water and throws it on the scarecrow's arm, hitting the witch at the same time. The witch had tried to avoid the water, but could not and begins to melt, and melt, and melt. She cries in despair, to no avail, banished from her beautiful world. At first, Dorothy is terrified that the witch's armed men and the monkeys would attack her and her companions. But to her astonishment the soldiers consider her a hero. 'Why did someone want him to see this? How odd?' he thought.

There was no more information. He was staring at the image, thinking. Then it just seemed to disintegrate as so did the other sheets. Whoever had sent them knew how to cover their tracks. Once the attachments were opened they had a short shelf life. Stone would have nothing to forward to anyone if he had become so inclined. 'Am I in some Mission Impossible time warp?' he again was thinking to himself.

The details started moving through his mind. The doodling definitely looked just like the pages he'd get from Kurt at times. The hand writing, it all looked the same. He wasn't sure what the Family meant. Must be a bigger organization? The 2006 brief was really bothering him. And most disturbing of all was knowing that his colleague and his assumed girlfriend and others were targets for elimination by who or whatever the Family is. Who wanted him to know all this? How did they think they could trust him with such information? Well, maybe they didn't trust him so much since everything had vanished from his computer.

Stone takes Gezana on a road trip to the mountains near San Diego)

"A little quick on that one, don't you think?" Gezana prodded him.

"I know this road," he looked over at her through his sunglasses, and then slowed down.

They'd left San Diego several hours earlier. Stone had a place near the Mount Palomar Observatory he liked to go to when he had lots of thinking to do. He had a great deal on his mind now and wanted the freedom that comes from having the landscape changing every moment around him. He needed to share with Gezana these concerns that had emerged the past few months and days.

It was a late February day, a little cool but clear. It would be like a nice day in May in other parts of the country.

"I think it's someone on the inside with a conscience," Gezana was saying. "Why would this 'Family' let you know they intended to kill those people? The only thing you've done that might be a red flag to anyone was going to the lecture the other night and that had everything to do with your work."

"Yes, but why me? I keep wondering if it's some sort of ploy. They want to test me to see what I do with this information. How did they know I would have any idea who Dave Herrick is? I listened to him at a conference in Eugene a year ago or so and then I talked briefly to him after the glyphosate lecture. I guess someone could have seen us talking there."

Stone was trying to think of anywhere else he might have interacted with Dave. Nothing was ringing a bell.

"Ever since the scuba diving incident you've been different, Stone. It seems like you've been detached, something is working through you." Gezana observed, as they took a fork in the road that seemed to be leading to higher country.

He looked at her, then back to the road. "Is it that obvious?"

"Some. Maybe, am I right?"

"Yeah, I did mention it." She looked at him with a puzzled expression. "The thought that went through my head when time seemed to slow way way down," Stone said, looking briefly towards Gezana.

She was shaking her head acknowledging the conversation they'd had. "The voice that you heard?"

"It wasn't really a voice. It was just a thought that filled my mind."

"Oh, it asks you what you believe. Right?"

"Yes, isn't that weird? Why that question and then?"

A short time passed. "What do you think it was?" Gezana then asked.

"I don't really know, I guess it was my subconscious talking to me. But what's that?" Both were quiet again for a while.

Stone began, "I've had doubt for sometime about what I'm working on. I haven't wanted to admit it, I'm so invested in this industry; my schooling and my working life. It's all been about feeding people by using synthetic chemicals. Have I been fooling myself all these years?"

Gezana had no answer for him.

"I remember my grandfather telling me about a guy who lived not far from where their place was, outside of Sacramento." He looked at her to see if she was recalling the place. She nodded. "The old guy was the last person in the valley to use horses to farm with; it was like the late 60s, early 70s, and still using horses. He said the guy plowed, and disked, spread manure, and even hauled hay in from the fields, all using horses. It must have been pretty brutal work, trying to compete with the farmers using tractors. I guess he actually was killed by his horses, some accident where the team pulled a wagon over him."

"How awful," Gezana said. "What makes you think of that?"

"Just the incredible difference in a couple of generations, I guess. This guy in the 70s, using horses. Today we have farmers with tractors as big as small houses being run by computers connected to satellites to put fertilizer or insecticides or whatever it is they need down on a per square foot basis. We work with satellites and computers and the weeds just keep coming at us. They grow faster and bigger. We get one type under control and three others come along. Hell, I know our chemicals kill the life in the soil, the micro biology. The industry I'm a part of keeps trying to go

208

around nature, like push it out of the way so we can do it our way. The Green Revolution and good old American know how."

Stone saw the location where he wanted to stop. "I found this place when I was about twenty six, I think. It has a pretty remarkable view. Stone had packed a small lunch thinking they could sit here and enjoy the panorama for a while. To the south and west they could see towards San Diego, directly west about thirty five miles was the ocean. "Three hundred years ago there might have been a 1,000 or 2,000 people in all the land you can see out there. There are millions down there now."

"So many people," Gezana responded.

Stone was silent for a few moments, "I think there was a reason why I heard that message." He looked more closely towards Gezana, "It's a miracle that any of us or anything exists," he walked a short distance away and motioned towards everything all around them. "How does a giant tree like that come to be on a planet that used to be a boiling caldron of magma, or the shrubs, or the birds, all of it?" He walked over near to where she was sitting, "or someone with your eyes?" He stepped back. "It's all a miracle."

He continued, "My industry started out with the best intentions, mostly. It was all about making a stable and dependable food supply. We learned how to synthesize all these different chemicals. A lot of them were used in World War I and to kill people. And then after the World War II we discovered how to spread these chemicals and amazingly we grew more and more plants. Of course the weeds and the bugs and the rodents and all the things that had always been there were still there. But we'd interfered with the natural balance that controlled them, so we had to invent ways to kill them. And then they changed and we had to find even more new ways to kill the new ones, and it goes on and on.

The only problem is now we find out just how much those synthesized chemicals are doing to us. We make ourselves sick with our food. Then we invent a part of the Pharmaceutical Industry to deal with our poisonous food. And then we get the government to pay for it. It's a vicious cycle to hell. I think that's part of what I'm supposed to figure out: "What do I believe?"

Gezana had not seen Stone in such a mood before, challenging himself this way.

He continued. "I watched a video the other night while you were asleep. It was a Nova special called Extreme Ice. They were showing how all the glaciers everywhere around the world are disappearing, very rapidly, and so are the continental glaciers on Antarctica and Greenland. We've warmed the planet and the glaciers are telling us so. Nobody thought the systems' balance was as fragile as it is. Just like we didn't see the unintended consequences in the way we've been trying to produce our food. It's all connected, it's the same confused way of thinking. We're not seeing the truly big picture! *We aren't living by some moral principle that keeps us heading in the right direction."*

They both sat for awhile, and then Gezana asked, "What are you going to do about letting that guy, Dave, know that the Family may want him and his girlfriend dead?"

Stone was quick, "I've got to let him know something might be up. The question is, 'Am I being vetted by someone with this family? Or is there somebody on the inside that knows me, and wants to use me to help avoid this murder?" Stone thought some more, "why wouldn't they tell me who they are?"

Chapter Seventeen

(Dave's bi-monthly lecture, early March, 2014) (note: much of the information in the next ten pages or so are very similar to Dave's talk at Moab. Points are being emphasized.)

The Southern California Conservation League had offered space to Dave in the basement of the building they occupied to deliver his bimonthly lecture. For nearly a year he'd been giving it, trimming out and adding where it made sense. Others were now doing the same, using the same set of images Dave had put together using material from the *Kingdom of Good* website and others he'd found. A few years had passed; more information had emerged, so it just made sense to update.

The room could hold 150 people comfortably. As the seats were filling up it looked like this could be one of the bigger audiences.

"There's a few seats up here," Dave said as three or four people came through the door just before he was to start, one of them was Stone. Dave nodded briefly towards him.

An 11 x 17 inch printed hand out was given to each person coming in the door. On it were a series of images. One by one they were intended to explain the big picture that too many people don't grasp.

~~~~~

"Good evening everybody. Thanks for coming out tonight. I'm Dave Herrick. Since you're here you must have some understanding of why I'm giving these lectures. I think this is about number sixteen or so. I started a little over eight months ago."

A high school aged girl near the front raised her hand, Dave acknowledged her. "You're on a video on the internet aren't you?" A few people laughed.

"Yes, that's me, and my girlfriend Joan. She's in Washington DC right now working on some related matters. Thanks for asking about that. Are the rest of you familiar with what she was just asking about? Which is The Moab Manifesto? Please raise your hand if you do." A lot of hands went up. "So, exactly what we'd been hoping would happen has been. I think at last count there were sixteen new manifesto's, including one from Point Barrow, Alaska. They're on the front lines in all this, so they were pretty eager to put their manifesto out there. Check it out as it's very creative."

He paused to see if there were any other comments. The content had not changed since he'd given it a few weeks earlier to his friends in Moab. It was so engrained in his mind anymore he hardly needed to look at the images to keep his train of thought. What he'd worked hard on was developing an ending that provided a sense of hope, a plan for action, something we could actually do. The basic consensus was that unless the United States of America's Federal Government somehow became the leading force in the effort to dramatically change our misguided industrious behavior, getting others around the world to follow would never be possible. We would be like some old drunkards who simply talk about the need to change their ways but always find the justification for one more night out. That is until the nights run out.

He began by briefly explaining the overarching situation we are facing. "Right now, we humans are like workers constructing the gallows we will be hung by in a few days." On the screen behind him pictures of our coal and gas fired energy plants spewing clouds of carbon dioxide and other harmful substances into the air, was projected. Then pictures of cities, cars, freeways, endless miles of fields growing just a few different varieties of plants, and forests being cut down all around the world. It showed the oversized footprint of our industrious behavior and our civilization.

A picture of people living a bucolic lifestyle in the 1850s then appeared. Dave continued, "In about 160 years we here in America and much of the industrialized world have transitioned from this being the status quo where about 65 % of the population are farmers, using no synthetic chemicals I'll add, to today where about 2 ½ % of the people are farmers. Worldwide population exploded from about 1.3 billion to over 7 billion today. This was made possible by two primary factors: first was discovering how to extract, fabricate, and combust fossil fuels to provide exponential amounts of new energy. Second was the so called Green Revolution which uses synthetic chemicals for farming: most importantly, ammonia/nitrogen."

A graphic showed on the screen of the carbon dioxide molecule. "When you combust any of the fossil fuels: coal, oil, or natural gas you release energy of course, but you also release numerous molecules such as carbon which immediately bonds with nearby oxygen forming carbon dioxide. And this is the molecule of greatest concern. If all these molecules we are creating could be captured and kept out of the Earth's biosphere we might be okay. But scientists and engineers have not been able to figure out how to do that for an economical price. So, it just gets dumped into the atmosphere/biosphere where it stays for many years. And that is a problem."

He used his light pointer to highlight the carbon dioxide molecule image on the screen. "The carbon dioxide molecule is "tuned" just right so that radiation bouncing back from the Earth reacts with it and radiation then emits from it warming the atmosphere. It only takes about 1 molecule of carbon dioxide in every 4,000 or so other molecules to keep this nice temperature we're accustomed and "evolved" to, in place."

Another graphic showing a cup with the number 350 labeled on it appeared. "For the last 10,000 years or so the carbon dioxide level in the atmosphere has been below or around 280 parts per million. That's about the 1 in 4,000 I just mentioned." He pointed at the 350 number, "This is the number of carbon dioxide molecules scientists now tell us is a safe limit to keep the Earth's systems in reasonable balance. Unfortunately we are already at or even above 400 parts per million. The fear is now that we are on track to go over 500 parts per million and higher. At that level very-difficult-to-control temperature increases would likely follow. That occurring could have catastrophic consequences for not only human life but nearly all larger life forms."

A picture of a different world of just rock and lichen in yellows and lime greens and an atmosphere that looked grey and dismal appeared. "This could be the normal surface of the Earth in just a few thousand years; perhaps even sooner if we lose in our battle to change the current trajectory. This is what we fear the Earth will look like, and we won't be here. This is what we "must" avoid!" There was emphasis in his voice. "The good news is that there are millions of people around the world that now acknowledge this potential and are trying to change our civilizations way. And the group I'm a member of; *The Kingdom of Good*.com (KOG) has a detailed plan of how we can do that. The end of this lecture is focused on that."

Some new graphics appeared on the screen. "I was fortunate to listen to a lecture given by this gentleman in 2010, Dr. W. W. Sherman, while I was in Rome. He had developed this concept of the *Kingdom of Good*, which is his interpretation of the central message from Jesus, which we know as The Kingdom of God. His main point is that the KOG briefly, is a level or even realm of consciousness that transcends our ancient animal level of consciousness. It's spiritual, and at that level of consciousness people would just behave in a manner that would be sustainable. The problem is that not enough people have crossed to that realm. This is all explained on the website, so I leave it to you to explore more there. My emphasis tonight is on what we can do now to change our course."

"I will say though, that I agree with his premise that the reason we face the formidable challenges we do, is because within our negotiations of our common future we are collectively, that's on the average, behaving like adolescents and not adults. We have an excessive number of adults who are stuck in an adolescent stage of consciousness. They're not evil, but just slow to make the transition. The evil ones are the people who know better but for reasons of wealth and power they refuse to change their ways. They must be stopped or we all, including them, will lose catastrophically."

I gave a condensed version of this presentation to some of my friends a few months ago when we met in Utah and created the Moab Manifesto. They heard some of what I'll be going over with you tonight. It was my way of trying to motivate them to help me and a few close friends make the video.

My approach is to step back and try to explain the big picture. To put the climate crisis in perspective you need to understand how average Earth temperature affects the biosphere which includes all life forms. To accomplish that, I take you back in time so you can start to get your head around it all. Average surface temperature, that's what I keep pounding on."

Dave's pointer moved to the first timeline graph. "It wasn't until I saw Dr. Sherman's lecture that I came to get the really big picture around all this. And since we are talking about life on Earth, particularly human life, having a reasonable understanding of what it took for us to emerge in this universe and on this planet is critical. This is important so you can appreciate what we are, and in particular our consciousness, and what we are fighting to not lose."

"The central premise of KOG as to why humanity is not living in balance with nature is that collectively we have not reached a level of sufficient consciousness or awareness to where our politics can effectively deal with the problem. That's why we feel it's so important to explain the bigger picture of human emergence and how that relates to our consciousness and awareness of the fragility of the natural world."

His pointer moved to the first bar of the overall page, "This entire page puts the timeline of human emergence in a graphical context. I'd read about all this and the various parts, but until I saw it this way I didn't have such a concrete method to visualize it. This top bar portrays the entire length of time "our" universe has existed, according to scientists. Keep in mind that some scientists think there may be many, and maybe an infinite number, more universes. That's speculation for now. This last little bit over here represents 100 million years. The genus homo doesn't emerge until about 2.6 million years ago, then our species Homo Sapien 200,000 years ago, with modern behavior only seen emerging between 125,000 and 50,000 years ago. This is all fascinating to study, please do, but I'll move onto the next page of graphics for now."

Another timeline appeared but this one was focused on just the last 650 million years of Earth's history. "The Earth and the Moon emerge about 4.6 billion years ago, so about 4 billion years passed before we even get to where this graph begins. But it is not until this point that large life forms appear on the planet, so it makes sense that we pick up the story here. Before this time life was evolving in the oceans of course, but now it is set to move from the shallow seas to the land."

A picture of the Earth covered in ice is shown at the left side of the timeline. "You may not be aware but scientists now think that around 650 million years ago the Earth was entirely, or nearly so, covered in ice. Then, through volcanism they speculate, additional carbon dioxide enters the atmosphere and over time the planet warms and the ice melts. Eventually land is exposed. Over millions of years first plant life emerges on the newly exposed land and then after many more millions of years life forms capable of transitioning from the shallow seas to the land begin to do so."

He moved his light along the timeline. "Around 400 million years ago the first amphibians appeared. Moving along, about 225 to 230 million years ago both the first mammals and dinosaurs emerge. Due to some interesting morphological reasons the dinosaurs developed large bodies, while the mammals did not. They lived along side each other for about 165 million years. Many of you know that an enormous asteroid hit the Earth about 65 million years ago and put an end to the dinosaurs, except for the birds of course. Their kind made it through this event that nearly wiped out all life, but our little ground dwelling ancestors somehow survived, or we wouldn't be here tonight. Fascinating, I think."

His light pointer moved back to the beginning of the graph. "Critical to what we're discussing is the major temperature ranges. We're showing temperature and carbon dioxide levels together on this graph so you can get a sense for how the two interact and have changed over time. The two extremes were shown in red and blue, "It seems the Earth likes certain high and low points ranging between 10 to 12 degrees Celsius at the low, we call this Cold House Earth, and 22 to 24 degrees Celsius at the high end, this is called Hot House Earth. You can see that the Earth has spent the majority of time in the Hot House Earth range, and temperatures in between. You can also see when the five previous mass extinctions of plant and animal life occurred; unfortunately we are right now in a sixth great extinction event and it is being caused by us."

The pointer moved, "Here, about 55 million years ago, 10 million years after the asteroid impact, and coincidentally about when the primate lineage begins to emerge, I want to offer some observations. At this point our ancestors are some small, maybe a foot long with an equal tail, squirrel-like creature living in the trees and eating the small fruits that they bare. They are of course not the only creatures on the Earth. There are many others though their numbers are only building back after the near total extinction caused by the asteroid."

"The modern world of plants and animals as we know them today truly emerge from the catastrophe of the asteroid impact. Think about it: the large land animals today are all mammals. When the asteroid hit mammals everywhere were tiny little mouse-like creatures, or nearly so, living underground mostly. That likely played heavily into why they survived. So the past 65 million years is really the mammalian lead up to our current world."

A picture of the Earth without any glaciers and the continents in their relative positions from that time era was shown on the screen. "The Earth, 55 million years ago, did not have any glaciers; it was still in the Hot House equilibrium. These are the Appalachian Mountains the ocean extends clear to their base, what is now our east coast is under water. On the west coast about half of Oregon is ocean and California is a shallow sea. This is about what the world would look like again if the Greenland and Antarctic glaciers melt totally. This would be catastrophic of course, but even worse would be the scenario Dr. David Leonard explains in his book *A New World*. He explains that if the currents of the oceans shut down and cause the oceans to move from an aerobic oxygen producing equilibrium to one where they flip to anaerobic and belch the poisonous gas hydrogen sulfide, which is deadly to nearly all plants and animals living out of the ocean, all large organisms would be done. This would be one possible final nail in the story of life as we know it. Of course this is what we have to avoid and I wouldn't be standing here if I didn't think we had a chance. In a little bit, I'll be explaining what I think we have to do."

He moved his pointer back and was comparing the temperature and carbon dioxide, "You can see here, at about 145 million years ago, the carbon dioxide level starts to drop. Temperature seems to take a considerable amount of time to follow but eventually it does. Scientists think the uplifting of the Himalayas which exposed a vast amount of rock for carbon dioxide to bond with was exposed, thereby removing it from the atmosphere. This then eventually draws temperature down. Something to keep in mind is that it's not that life can't exist when it's a lot hotter, like with Hot House Earth temperatures, but life forms have to evolve and adapt to that different balance. If the change happens slowly enough some species will evolve and balance with the change, but if it's too fast they go extinct. That's one of the big fears now; it will happen so fast that our species and others won't be able to adapt quickly enough. And that's even without runaway heating, which is the biggest fear."

The pointer spotted the area along the temperature line from 55 million years ago to about 2.6 million years ago. "Between here and here our lineage changed from something like a squirrel to an upright walking creature that used rocks to clean meat off of bones. This temperature change along this line was contributing significantly to changes in our morphology and to our consciousness. This is a critical point to remember. Our bodies and all the other creatures on the planet now are finely tuned metabolically to exist within a small window of average temperature. Scientists now understand that any species weakest link relative to air temperature is at reproduction. Females of all species lose their embryos when air temperatures put extra stress on them at critical times in their reproductive cycles. Even a few degrees can make all the difference. This is already affecting mammal species around the world. What happens if the temperature rise is not halted? We are already experiencing species loss, thousands of times greater than normal, primarily by over hunting and habitat destruction."

Dave continued. "How fast will we start losing larger species as this factor takes hold? For example, there were many large predator species that lived during the latest ice age but have now gone extinct. Some have speculated that human hunting caused this. But recently some scientists are rethinking that, considering now that the temperature upswing from about 15 to 10 thousand years ago may have had a greater part in that happening."

He pushed the button for the PowerPoint program to move to the next image. "This graph moves us closer to the present showing temperature relative to time. Here we're going back 415 thousand years. About 2.5 to 3 million years ago, the North and South American plates had collided sufficiently to block the flow of warm equatorial water to the northern part of the planet. Until that time glaciation cycles had not been occurring. This changed things because warm water and air no longer could be carried to the northern polar area."

An image showing the Milankovitch Cycles appeared. "Variations in the Earth's orbit around the sun, lean, wobble, and precession have all been happening since the Earth first formed. When the two continents merged those cycles were then sufficient to cause the growth and then reductions of the glaciers over approximate 100,000 year periods. Those areas shown in red are the time frames when the average temperature was above the average for the past 10,000 years, which is about 15 degrees Celsius."

He moved close to the screen, "About here, at this bump or maybe a little afterward modern humans emerged, plus or minus 200,000 years ago. This is when so called Mitochondrial Eve, a single female we all can trace our lineage back to, lived. The mutation that allowed for the enlargement of our brain case and speech is most likely the common factor that leads to her. There may be an even earlier last common ancestor to all people alive today because most non Africans have some Neanderthal heritage. It might be more like 500,000 years ago to reach that individual. But it is to Mitochondrial Eve that we "all" most recently connect."

"Getting back to the graph, then a deep cold period occurs. You can see how fast the temperature rises beginning about 135,000 years ago. This red area is called the Eemian and it lasts a little longer than the current Holocene period we are in now which has been going for about 10,000 years or so. But during the Eemian it actually gets warmer; maybe one or two degrees warmer than the current periods peak.

"But here is the critical thing to keep in mind: those warming periods were driven "only" by the Milankovitch Cycles, just additional heating from the sun. And the carbon dioxide levels were not being exacerbated by the additional combustion we are contributing to the atmosphere now. During the Eemian what is today Scandinavia, became an island. That's right, what is now Holland, Denmark, Northern Germany, probably parts of Poland, the Low Countries, were submerged. At that time most of the Greenland glacier melted."

"Of course the Earth then followed a cooling trend due to Milankovitch cycles, and the glaciers then rebuilt and the water receded. Obviously if this were to occur again human civilization would probably collapse." He paused for a moment and looked at everyone, "I have to ask you, looking at that graph and knowing that this time we have added an enormous new blanket of gas for trapping heat: what chance do we have to "not" see this happen?" People were very still, and they could be heard talking between themselves. "Humans are ingenious and may find ways to adapt to some of these challenges. But to have a chance we will need a wise strategy for change, not just a clever one, and soon."

Dave found a bottle of water and cooled his throat. "Before I leave this graph I want to point out one other very important event relative to human emergence. About here, at 74,000 years ago, humanity nearly went extinct. It's hard to imagine isn't it? Scientists think there were probably 10,000 or less individuals, when prior to that time there may have been one or two million normally. You can see it probably occurred at a very cold point in the cycles. The likely most important factor was the eruption of Mount Toba in what is now Indonesia. Something in us got us through then, maybe that quality will emerge again? We can only hope."

He noted a new place on the image, "Okay, then by about 20 to 25,000 years ago the coldest part of the last Ice Age was occurring. It would have forced what populations that had been living in much of Europe and Central Asia south as the continental glaciers grew. At that time there were distinct pockets where people were congregated, scattered along the southern borders of the continent-covering glaciers."

He moved to a new graph titled *Temperature Change Over the Past 20,000 years*. "You can see that through this period it was harsh, very cold, then at about 15,000 years ago it starts to warm up. There's a dip right here, I know why but won't go into that. Then by about 10,000 years ago we get to this interesting period where the temperature is quite stable. At 6,000 years ago it was at the warmest and Northern Europe had a thriving population of people living there."

"This little dip right here, when it got cold, about 3,200 years ago, most likely led to a great deal of migration out of Northern Europe. This little bump up right here correlates with the rise of Rome and bumper crops in Egypt, which is where the Romans got most of their food. The point I'm making here is the correlation between this temperature average and food production. With temperatures and carbon dioxide concentrations rising rapidly our food crops will be challenged considerably. Likely the first parts of our civilization to begin breaking down will be our food production system. Crop losses will equate to price rises. This can quickly escalate into violence. Many of the problems in the middle east can be traced to food shortages and price spikes."

He changed the image. "So let's look at the current temperatures. In the late 1800s and early 1900s the average temperature was around 13.73 degrees Celsius (56.71 F.). By 2012, we got to about 14.53 Celsius or so (58.15 F). This is a total increase of about .8 degrees Celsius or 1.44 degrees Fahrenheit. With that much, or little, increase we are seeing all the current effects: glaciers everywhere melting –and more rapidly than expected; deserts growing; storms increasing in number and intensity; crop losses; water shortages. Because of a lag effect between when carbon dioxide goes into the atmosphere and when the temperature actually rises we know that we will have "at least" another .6 degrees of temperature rise."

"Two degrees total Celsius rise is all that the scientific community has agreed was safe and we are assured of 1.4 rise. That leaves us with this very small window of .6 degrees to possibly stop within. Few now think that is possible with the momentum already in the system. If the rate of temperature rise, which is currently .2 degrees every 10 years (.02 per year) was to remain the same we would have about seventy years before crossing the 2 degree increase. Will that rate stay the same? That's an unknown. But what nearly all the scientists will tell you is that we have been consistently underestimating how fast the glaciers are melting and other effects occurring. We are into uncharted territory with our climate. We don't really know where the true limits are; where tipping points might occur."

"What keeps me awake at night is wondering if we've already passed the point where we inevitably trigger the release of the vast stores of methane that is sequestered all around the world. Some scientists now believe that is exactly what happened around 250 million years ago when the greatest extinction "till now" occurred. I'll leave it to you to study that more on your own. Let's hope we still have a chance to avoid tipping that edge."

"Since the advent of agriculture humans have been cutting down forests, turning the soils, and over grazing the land. This led to a legacy load of carbon dioxide in the atmosphere above pre agricultural times that would not have been there normally. So it is not in just the last 200 years we've been adding carbon dioxide to our air and water, but it is then that the rate vastly accelerated."

Dave pointed at another image. "Recently, the Potsdam Institute in Germany asked a really good question; how much more carbon dioxide could be added to the atmosphere without exceeding what they "think" would lead to the 2 degree rise. This is what they came up with ... about 565 billion more tons. By one estimate to date and since 1750 we've added about 329 billion tons. At current loading we're adding about 32 billion tons each year. Some part of that is absorbed; the net amount is perhaps half that or so. If you do the math, that gives us about 20 to 25 years before we cross that threshold ... or about the year 2035 or 2040."

"Currently there appears to be no slowing down on the adding of carbon dioxide, if anything the rate is increasing. The fossil fuels companies continue to expand their operations. You've probably heard about the plan to develop even more? The tar sands up in Alberta, Canada for instance. If we go another ten or twelve years at this rate do you think there would be any chance at all of changing directions? We need the energy in the carbon we can yet burn to build the new energy infrastructure. Instead we're squandering it on all types of senseless uses."

"And some recent studies say the atmosphere is even more sensitive to the heating than previously thought. So the estimate I just explained may be too optimistic. *It's a system we just don't truly understand. And if we get it wrong it could kill us. Why push our luck?"*

"It's important to keep separate the carbon dioxide that's being loaded in to the atmosphere from the combustion of fossil fuels with that which is coming from very poor management of the Earth's soils. Some scientists now believe that humans have been unwittingly, in addition from burning wood, releasing carbon from the soils for thousands of years, ever since we started plowing the land to grow our crops; basically since the advent of agriculture. One estimate is that something like 80 billion tons are circulating in the atmosphere from this activity alone. Of course in the twentieth century that process went into hyper drive and most of that 80 billion tons was created then."

"I'll give you just a hint here on what I end the second part of the lecture on: it's really new and could be the path out of this mess we're in. And it has everything to do with the soil and the life that makes it soil."

A picture showing a distressed landscape appeared on the screen. "All of these factors I've been talking about taken together have been referred to at various times as the green-house affect or climate change. I've been telling some of my friends recently that I think it really should be called biosphere destabilization, since the biosphere is the sum of all the intricate ecosystems around the world. Maybe it will catch on, who knows."

End Part 1 showed on the screen. "That's the end of my discussion of the existing conditions. Part Two is our answer to the question: what can we do? It's short, but I need a quick break. Give me five minutes and I'll come back and finish."

~~~~~~~

Stone got up so he could stretch his legs some. He walked out the door and over to a nearby window, it was getting close to twilight. He had just taken in a lot of information and his mind was sifting through it all trying to decide what he thought. Then, a familiar face appeared as a reflection in the glass. It was the same man with the pronounced nose he'd seen at the phosphate talk the week earlier. He was questioning himself. Was that the guy he'd seen on Black Jack's yacht? What was he up to? Was he following him, maybe Dave? He'd need to warn Dave somehow, but should he actually talk to him with this guy around? Where was the line with the family? When would he become their target? The man returned to his seat. Stone made note of where he sat and returned to his own. "What's this?" he thought. Sitting on the seat of his chair was an envelope, his name was hand written on it. He was curious and opened it right away. 'Please review your emails TONIGHT!' It was signed, Glinda.

Part Two, showed on the screen.

Dave clipped his microphone back on then looked at his computer screen; he forwarded the images to Part #2. It was titled: The Politics and the Solution.

"Okay, I'll get part 2 going." People settled and the room became quiet. "So Part 1 was about the problem and the science that explains it. In Part Two I will be explaining:

- Consciousness and awareness briefly.
- The steps leading thinkers say we need to take urgently to avoid the worst scenario of climate change and disaster for our civilization.

221

- The politics that have to date stopped us from dealing effectively with the problem, and what needs to occur to change that."

A picture of Albert Einstein appeared on the screen along with one of his famous quotes: "We can't solve problems by using the same kind of thinking we used when we created them."

Dave began speaking, "This guy was amazing for a lot of different reasons, but his observations about human shortcomings really give me a little laugh. What he's talking about there is raising our consciousness. When I first listened to *The Kingdom of Good* lecture, Dr. Sherman early on identify's what he feels the problem is: a lack of enough people operating at a high enough level of consciousness to grasp the enormity of the problem. Some may consider that snobbish to say like we're suggesting they have inferior levels of intelligence. We don't think it is directly intelligence because there are plenty of people who would score above average or even high on standard intelligence tests who are deniers. As well, there are many who would score just average on intelligence tests that are not deniers."

A new image appeared, "This is a diagram that shows varying levels of "consciousness" and explains a person's mental model of reality. This is what we think is the nexus of the problem. There is a marked difference between the two ends of the spectrum, as consciousness is in essence about your sense of your place in reality. The best way for me to explain that is to just start reading the definitions for these ascending levels. The colors are interesting to relate to this as well."

His graph showed seven levels, from instinctual up to transcendent. "There are six or more other similar representations of these levels of consciousness you may want to explore. This is the one Dr. Sherman selected and it makes a lot of sense to me and the KOG directors. As you read along with me, please note the approximate percentage of people around the world researchers think are at the varying levels."

"It starts out here at instinctual. Some consider this about equivalent to archaic, almost like that of an animal; chimps, gorillas, dogs. Of course we're talking about humans and we don't want to suggest these folks are simply animals as they certainly are not. We think they are stuck here for varying reasons. Often just the conditions they were born in to capture them here. These are people living nearly on pure survival instincts. They are reactionary and focused on obtaining just the basic necessities of life.

The next level is individualistic. These folks are focused on eliminating threats to their ego. Then conformists who are individuals focused on acceptance in a social group. They have a strong desire to belong to a tribe and live within the rules of that tribe and to hold a high social ranking. Supposedly, today, about 40% of the human population exists at this level. I would say from my observations, I think there are a lot of folks at this level that I know of. The fourth level up is the rational level of consciousness. These people focus on logic and reason as relevant to situations and relationships. They're looking for fairness, justice, and effectiveness."

Dave moved his pointer showing the graphic that was signifying that this was where significant movement of people from the lower levels up, was urgently needed. "Everything I've been talking about can be summed up right here at this jump from the fourth to the fifth level of consciousness. This is the nexus of the problem. Solve this and it will be like moving a stuck raft off of a rock. We can get things going."

A picture of a person with a look of an epiphany showing on their face began the next part. "At the fifth level - Pluralistic consciousness – an egalitarian social view emerges and predominates. People are valued simply because they are people and not because of some special skill or trait they have like mathematical reasoning or physical beauty. Love and empathy emerge as dominant behavioral motivators. It's here that a person truly begins to revere nature and grasp the special place and responsibility humans have within it. The true spiritual person begins to emerge. People of all social and economic classes are on either side of this line. A high level of intelligence or a stratospheric sized bank account is not required. No, it's all about what's in the "heart" of your mind."

Pictures of activists appeared, "There are millions of people all around the world right now who have made the jump to this level, though most of them don't even realize this connection. They are the vanguard trying to get others to understand the errors in the ethos of modern civilization."

A picture of a large city and sprawling miles of agricultural land appears, "Here is the world we have built in the last 150 or so years because of the cheap energy we were able to release in coal, oil, and natural gas. If these energy sources would not have emerged those images most likely would not have either. Had we gone solar, as some futurists attempted to convince us to do in the late 19th century - and it was possible - who knows? Check out the World's Fair in Paris in 1900 for more on that. Those images require a lot of energy everyday to maintain too. We've come to really enjoy the life we have because of the instant warmth of our water for bathing or cleaning, or the rooms we are in, or the lights that we use, the mobility we have, the entertainment we enjoy. The list is long. But we have not accounted for our effects on nature's current balance and that reality some think is now an imminent threat to our survival."

A series of new images appeared on the screen. "The following are examples of actions we must take."

Bending the Temperature Curve: "Currently the average surface temperature is rising at about .02 degrees Celsius (~.036 F) each year. This is the most important metric to contain. Just like when any of us are sick there are underlying factors causing that. Pollution of the atmosphere is causing the temperature to rise which leads to all the adverse consequences. Therefore, all the mitigating behaviors need to focus on controlling that temperature rise. *We must 'Bend the Curve'.*" Dave was pointing to a graphic that showed the temperature being contained below the 2 degree rise and not allowed to just run away.

"The really scary idea to remember from this image is the Mephistopheles Moment." He pointed to the little devil figure with question marks at points around it. "This is an unknown and unknowable threshold of heat gain where we lose all control of heating. Some people are calling it humanities Faustian Bargain." He looked at them all. "Will our greed and lethargy allow us to pass this point from which we cannot return to safety?"

TAX CARBON NOW: the next image on the screen read. "Like a nation preparing for an inevitable war, our entire civilization must aggressively move to a war-time mentality and activity. Since the ongoing release of carbon into the atmosphere where it forms into carbon dioxide is the most egregious factor, this must be stopped. We must use what small window of carbon loading there is still available to us to construct a new non atmospheric destabilizing energy infrastructure. To date, solar, wind, hydro and geothermal have been the leading candidate methods. Nuclear fission has proved too dangerous and expensive. There is growing speculation that fusion power may be nearing a point where it can be scaled into use, but we're still waiting to see that occur."

"Carbon should be taxed at its source and dividends sent directly to the people or by vouchers as it works out best. The cost of anything with carbon in it will go up. Entrepreneurs will answer with new low polluting replacements. The taxed money will then flow there."

THE CARBON AND NITROGEN CYCLES ARE OUT OF BALANCE: This was the next image. "The most basic way to explain what is causing the climate crisis is just to say that the carbon and nitrogen cycles are out of balance. **This is the 67 challenge.** Carbon is number six in the periodic table and nitrogen is number 7. Carbon is the second most abundant element in the biosphere behind oxygen. It's the most ubiquitous element in life. It's everywhere: in all of us, the animals and plants, in the forests and the prairies, the oceans, in rock, very importantly in the soils, and in the atmosphere. Where the problem lies is that there is just too much in the atmosphere and oceans to keep things stable in the climate and destroying the ocean life."

"Nitrogen is the most limiting element in growing things. We've taken the lid off that by discovering how to synthesize new nitrogen. This is leading to all sorts of problems. Plowing fields and spreading nitrogen starts the whole downward spiral of the vitality of our soils: erosion, pollution, inferior food, health issues, and very importantly the creation of nitrous oxide that floats into the atmosphere and creates even more greenhouse gas. In affect we are making the stuff that is over-heating the planet. If we hadn't gone down this road civilization would have had to remain organic agriculturalists. So many benefits from that would have followed. We've got to get back to that paradigm of agriculture. There is a lot of great information about all this on the KOG website. Please check it out."

"What we know now that we didn't really know just a few years ago is the importance of carbon in the soil. It's the food that drives the life of the microbes. When there's plenty of carbon in the ground available to the microbes you should have a terrifically fertile soil. Plants pass some of the carbon that goes through them to the ground where the microbes and certain fungi can store it as glomalin in humus. The humus is like the pantry in your house; it's stored food for the microbes. There is a vast and ready reservoir for us to start pulling all that excess carbon from the atmosphere and getting it safely stored in the ground."

"But because of the misguided management of the soils and the grasslands, which is farming and ranching, for the last hundred years or so, where carbon capture and sequestration wasn't understood or practiced to any good degree, we've instead released vast amounts of carbon to the atmosphere. Of course we're releasing it through all kinds of other ways too like burning the coal, oil, and natural gas. But we've compounded the problem because we didn't know how to manage them. It's hard to blame people when they just didn't know any better but that's changed. We do know now how we should be managing our effect on the carbon and nitrogen cycles and what we need to do with both of them to get to safe and sustainable levels. That's what I'm going to talk about next."

THE SOIL, OUR GREAT HOPE: That title appeared on the screen.

"People have been coming up with all sorts of high technology type ideas concerning what we can do to avoid disaster: space mirrors and shields to reduce the amount of incoming solar radiation, seeding the atmosphere with a blanket of sulfur to reflect the solar energy again, even massive 1,000' long by 300' tall vacuums to suck the carbon dioxide out of the air. Under scrutiny they all appear to have serious and potentially catastrophic downsides. But with what probably could be the lowest technology solution imaginable, scientists from New Mexico State University are now saying they can create compost with a highly balanced number of bacteria and fungi, that when properly incorporated in the ground can sequester a staggering 50 tons of atmospheric carbon per acre. **At that rate an area of 11 million acres with the soil biology operating at this level could theoretically sequester all of the annual carbon dioxide emissions created worldwide. They add that there is twice that amount of land that is fallow every year."**

"If this could be developed, the soil becomes this colossal vacuum cleaner pulling the carbon dioxide into the ground and storing it there. When that happens that soil in turn becomes this magnificent plant productive and water storing medium. This just might be the greatest technological breakthrough of our time; perhaps ever. The knowledge of this discovery is so new, we'll just have to wait and see how it actually emerges. This could have a staggering social impact also. Carrying for the land in this organic way would require millions in America, and tens or hundreds of millions of people moving back onto the land around the world. Millions have been forced from this land under the current paradigm. Just imagine how much more stable, fair, and healthy such a world would be."

"But I can tell you that the biotech and industrial agriculture structure won't like this if it turns out to be true. This would be a paradigm shift in thinking how we manage the soils and agriculture in general. Believe me, there will be massive push back, regardless of how sensible a solution it might be. The weight of the status quo will be a blizzard of a head wind in everything we'll need to do."

A picture of the world's oceans appeared on the screen. "As wondrous as that may be for the atmospheric problem, the issue of the oceans continuing to be ravaged by the excess carbon dioxide falling into them can't be forgotten. The carbon dioxide is altering the pH values which are leading to all sorts of issues for the small creatures that live there. And of course the larger creatures depend on the health and productivity of all the smaller creatures. This could lead to extensive disruption to the balance of life there and have catastrophic effects to humanity. So it's no time to stop focusing on green house gas production, reduction."

An interesting graphic of a person heading down a path to a cliff, and one farther back who avoided the cliff, showed on the screen. "Now if you're this guy and you realize that by continuing to follow this path you are going to inevitably come to that cliff. And the ground gets more slick as you get nearer to it, where at some point you know you will go over the cliff, wouldn't a reasoning person stop and say: 'Okay, it's a long way back to that trail up there that goes around the cliff. I'm going to have to leave some of my stuff in my pack here so I can get back there. It's going to take some effort, but when I get back there I can keep going and not die by going over the cliff.' "Isn't that the reasoning a sane person follows?" He stopped for a moment, "Well that's what I believe and like this guy we need a plan on how to get turned around and heading back to that other path."

POLITICS: the next image read. "A lot of people and families have grown extremely wealthy around the world during the past 150 years as the modern world emerged. They are exceedingly invested in the status quo; especially the fossil fuels energy and petrochemicals sectors of the economy. Think of the trillions of dollars of infrastructure in finding the raw material, extracting and transporting it, the processing plants, the pipelines to disperse it around the continents, the fueling stations to sell it through. And then of course on the receiving end all the buildings and transportation vehicles that use the energy. And then there is the investment in the future use of raw materials still in the ground that represent the wealth for retirement plans. To a varying degree nearly everyone is invested in this architecture of civilization we have built. It is an absolute Gordian knot and a conundrum."

"That's why we believe that only a "wise" government controlling and untying this *hell-knot* is the only hope for effective action." He paused, "Unfortunately the structure of our current economy will kill us if we continue to use it as we are."

GOVERNMENTAL CHANGE: was the next heading. "In 1992, 1,600 of the world's senior scientists specialists in Earth science including Nobel Laureates' warned the world we are heading for potential calamity:

"Warning to Humanity." 'Human beings and the natural world are on a collision course ... that may so alter the living world that it will be unable to sustain life in the manner that we know it.'"

"In 1988 the United Nations brought together the World Meteorological Organization and the United Nations Environment Program to create the Intergovernmental Panel on Climate Change (IPCC). There have been four assessments released to date: #1 in 1992, #2 in 1995, #3 in 2001, and #4 in 2007. A fifth is schedule for released later this year, 2014. Each of these assessments has made it more and more clear about the cliff we are speeding towards."

"The National Academy of Science for: Brazil, Canada, China, France, Germany, India, Italy, Japan, Russia, the United Kingdom, and the United States of America, and others signed a joint statement saying that climate change is real, caused by human activity, and if not dealt with effectively portends dire consequences."

"In the United States a partial list of professional organizations that also support this assessment include: The American Geophysical Union, American Society of Agronomy, The Soil Science Society of America, The American Meteorological Association, and The American Institute of Biological Science. These are just a partial list of scientific organizations that continue to warn us of the dangers we face by not responding effectively to this challenge."

"To date the governments of the world have been ineffective in reaching a unified plan to meet the challenge. This is due to the entrenched financial interests both in America and around the world. It is our opinion that only the United States of America can lead an effective response, being the largest and most powerful nation in the world. We are also responsible for the largest portion of the pollution to date and hugely in the future without change. This gives the United States a special responsibility."

Existing Conditions and Strategy for Change: At a minimum, the leadership of the United States government should provide a clear and concise assessment and explanation of the best science and current conditions relative to climate. Following that, the strategy to deal with the problems effectively should be clearly defined. Influence by powerful contrarian interests on what is described, should be confronted. Unfortunately it is very doubtful this will occur without nationwide grass-roots activation that actually removes from power the existing party system that is infested by money'd or the corporate interests that seek only to maintain the status quo."

"There was a lot of hope when President Obama was elected that his administration would lead a truly effective response to the problem. For reasons that are murky to us at best, his administration has allowed the fossil fuels industry to grow, especially with oil and natural gas development. We do know that his former Director of Energy, Steven Chu, was criticized by members of the administration for speaking his mind on climate."

"Since neither of the two leading political parties in the United States has shown a seemingly competent level of response to the crisis, we call for an entirely new party to rise and take hold of power. I'll explain that next."

ELECTIONS: was the next topic. "Midterm elections occur in 2014 and an organized movement with momentum doesn't exist right now calling for all candidates to answer specific questions about climate and how they will vote on major initiatives like the carbon tax. It's our view that most Republican candidates will continue the deny-and-stall tactics they've used for years. Democrats have not shown the will to make this a cornerstone of their agenda. We also think that politicians in both parties have ties to the fossil fuels industry that are basically bought so make them ineffectual."

"With all that, it's our opinion that only a third party can be trusted to truly carry this issue with the tenacity that is needed. The Green Party is organized in America and elsewhere around the world. It is a world party whose platform calls for responding to the climate crisis effectively. Because of that, *The Kingdom of Good* organization based in Cambridge, England endorses the Green Party of America and all those individuals running at all levels of government in upcoming elections. Where no Green Party candidate is running, those who are must be vetted for their stand on climate, and vote appropriately. A major strategy will be to bring as many of the 40% of eligible voters in the US who have not been voting to vote with us."

"In 2016, the United States will be electing a new President. Our group is calling for a march on Washington DC, similar to that of the Civil Rights Era, to demand that our position be heard. The date we have chosen is Earth Day, 2016. This should give the movement sufficient time to then organize the vetting of all politicians, especially the Presidential candidates for their position on climate."

OPPOSITION: then appeared. "We have not begun to respond to this crisis effectively. Of course, because of powerful people and corporations and those they manipulate for political strength, are fighting change primarily for financial reasons. There are ways, certainly, to structure this massive change in our relationship to nature where people retain a certain position of wealth. But yes, they will have to except a much different standard of living –reduction in excessive living – to that they are accustomed to. I think many will fight senselessly to protect the status quo, but I also believe there are those currently stuck in the level of consciousness that has created this problem, which will change. Hugely what we have to do is to appeal to their ancient human instinct for survival and reaching consensus on what the common good is and how to create it fairly."

Mothers and Grandmothers of the World: then appeared. There is an instinctual/basal male and female drive or energy throughout nature. The male tends to subdue and the female nurture. Even at conception the sperm is battling those around it for the nurturing egg. Perhaps this can be thought of as the female mystic? However it may be, I believe there is a place in this effort for the mothers and grandmothers of the world to hear the call to protect their babies. This is what the female energy has done through the eons. Would it be possible for such a baseline-grassroots movement to emerge?

Preserving a Habitable Planet: None of the other problems our societies face will matter if we lose in the effort to retain a habitable environment on this planet. If we manage to make the needed changes in our current dysfunctional behavior then so many of the other problems we face will fade away. This is the biggest goal of all and it has to be center in our strategy."

"*The Kingdom of Good* website has many ongoing ideas about all of this. I encourage you to visit the site where virtually everything I've talked about is explained, and more. I think I need to end with that."

~~~~~

It was in the question and answer part where Dave's mind got taxed some, trying to remember all the links. Every so often he'd take a question he just had to pass on, knowing to give an answer he wasn't totally sure about could come back to give him problems.

A woman stood up not far from him, he walked over and handed his microphone to her. "So you mention two degrees Celsius temperature increase from pre industrial times as the goal to avoid, I see this on your image. How did scientists come to that amount and with what you know do you think we'll be able to stop it there?" She handed back the microphone.

"That is a great question. It's a critical question and unfortunately I'm not entirely sure how to answer that. But, I think originally the hope was that they could figure out a temperature where the two big ice sheets one on Greenland and the other Antarctica, would remain stable indefinitely, and limit sea water level rise to a few feet. Well, like I was saying, the temperature has already risen about .85 C. of a degree, very close to one. And we're seeing melting happening far far more quickly than what was thought could occur, just ten years ago or so. The problem is we just don't know those critical numbers so we're like someone messing around with the wires on a bomb that could go off."

He pointed to the *Kingdom of Good* symbol representing the organization in England that controlled the website. "The climate scientists with the KOG are among the best in the world. I have to tell you that they are saying now that the two degree limit is too much to avoid the massive melting of the continental glaciers; the limit they say now is actually just around one degree Celsius rise. No matter what, we have a massive challenge on our hands."

Dave continued, "There's that lag time I mentioned, scientists now believe, built into the temperature rise; 35 to 40 years between when the carbon dioxide is added to when the effects occur. We know we'll get to at least one and three quarters Celsius increase by 2060 or 70 even if every last new molecule of carbon was stopped from going into the atmosphere today. By one estimate we are adding 90 million tons a day and don't seem

230

close to slowing down. Unfortunately, there's little chance we'll stop the temperature rise at two degrees. The hope has got to be to keep it as low as possible."

A man raised his hand and Dave handed him the microphone. "Some people have said that the increased carbon dioxide could be a good thing because plants would grow more. Do you know anything about that?"

"Yes, there's been some good research being done on all that. First, plants need more than just carbon dioxide for growth, they need water, minerals, and very important a conducive air temperature for photosynthesis. Consider water as we know that the changing energy dynamics in the atmosphere is causing the natural cycles of where rain has fallen historically to move. Compounding this problem is that we've been over using the water in our aquifers so it's getting more expensive to pump it to the surface. Areas where they depend on the melt waters of glaciers that are quickly melting away will soon not have that water. What happens then? Minerals, well their use by plants is quite complex. The loss of so much humus in our soils compounds the ability of plants to draw on them. But air temperature is probably most critical and we're already seeing the effects of temperature in excess of where photosynthesis works properly for our seed types. For example, in 2012 about 40% of the US corn crop was lost to higher temperatures that interfered with the plants ability to photosynthesize. Remember, plants and animals have evolved to match up with the current balance of temperatures. Change things too fast for evolution to keep up and species go extinct. That's what we're facing."

Dave took a drink before continuing, "Higher levels of carbon dioxide have been studied recently and what they are finding is that they tend to cause leaf wilt which change from a green to a yellow-green and are lower in overall nutritional value in plants. There's also research showing that certain plants we consider to be weeds actually are stimulated greatly by the additional carbon dioxide. So, these arguments that this can be seen as a good thing are just part of the denier handbook to try and continue to lull the public into not believing there is a real problem."

Another woman raised her hand. "I've heard that the range of mosquitoes and other insects are moving further north and can be carrying virus's that are dangerous. Could you comment on that?"

"Ah hah, yes. I was reading recently that there are two species of mosquitoes that are capable of transmitting the virus that causes Dengue Fever that have now expanded as far north New York and New Hampshire. These milder overall winters and hotter summers exacerbate this trend."

"To me, the most important take away is to understand and appreciate the fine balance in the natural world we inherited over the past 10,000 years or so. That balance will always be changing and that's just a fact. It's the rate and intensity of change that is most important. Remember the graph where I showed that we are at the end of the Holocene warm period right now and would just be dropping slowly into another colder period? Of course life would have to react to that. Evolution would work its ways and life would continue. But we're so vastly impacting the factors that work into that **balance** that human civilization and so many of the creatures living on Earth with us will likely not have the ability to evolve at a rate to meet the change we are creating."

No one seemed to have another question ready to go. Dave thought it a good time to end the evening. "Well, I tell you, my voice is getting pretty worn out so I'll just leave it at that. Thanks."

The people applauded.

Stone took a moment to stop by and mention to Dave he enjoyed the lecture and found it quite enlightening. He handed his business card to him and suggested they might get together for lunch.

"I'd like that." Dave said.

As Stone left he glanced at a few female faces he thought might be Glinda, but no one caught his eye. "What's that all about," he wondered?

Chapter Eighteen

(San Diego, late March, 2014)

'Who is Glinda?' Stone was thinking to himself, driving home. 'That name sounds familiar.'

Entering the kitchen, he saw that a bottle of wine had been opened and a glass left there for him. The lights near the hot tub were on.

Her body was beautiful, there, naked in the water. Stone moved carefully but, directly removing each of the elements of clothing he was wearing. Gezana's pulse quickened as he entered the water. They did not talk. Gezana's fingers soon dug into Stone. They were sufficiently far from any other home that her sounds of pleasure would not invade. Little noise ever emanated from Stone in their love making. But if you could see his eyes they would bear witness to his intensity.

He wrapped her body in the heavy white gown she had brought with her from the house and carried her to their bed. They were both spent. Gezana desired sleep the most.

Comforted by his own bathrobe, Stone perused the refrigerator for a little snack. He spotted some of Gezana's healthy cookies and some veggies. Moving to his office, he adjusted the mouse and his computer screen lit. As usual, there were the work emails to review and a few that his junk filter had not intercepted. And there was the one he most wanted to read. It was simply titled "Glinda".

"Stone:

I want to invite you and Gezana to visit me in Oregon. Gezana will know me as one of the girls from the bowling league, but she knows nothing more. Dave, Joan and the others have been told of the watch list they are on so you can do nothing there. I am with The Kingdom of Good organization and others. Everything will be explained when (if) you visit. I deeply hope you will. Gezana has the address, I'd hope you might visit next weekend. It sounded as if you might be free. I'll wait to hear.

Glinda"

He sat for a moment a bit confused. How had his girlfriend become a part of all this? A woman in her bowling group? He'd have to wait until morning to find out what was up.

Stone slipped into some shorts and tried to get into bed as lightly as possible. "Did you get an email?"

He smiled and rolled over so they could talk. "Uh hum. Want to clue me in?"

"I just found out this afternoon that this gal was not just a local friend of Jamie's. Turns out she lives in Oregon and runs a bed and breakfast. Her name's Tyler, but I know she calls herself Glinda when she emails you. I don't know what that's all about."

Stone was thinking, Glinda sounded familiar? 'The Wizard of Oz, Glinda?' He got up and went to his computer and Googled the two. Glinda was the Witch of the South, and a good witch. Her character was actually revealed in a second book that is not a part of the movie. In the movie Glinda is the Good Witch of the North.' "Enough on that for tonight," he thought.

"Did she give you a card?" Stone asked getting back in bed.

"Yes, and she said if we're free next weekend there was a festival going on and we should come up if possible. I told her I didn't know your schedule for sure, but I was free and we'd see. That's all I know."

"Well Glinda or Tyler or whoever she is, seems to have information she wants me to know about." He thought for a moment. "I think we need to go to Oregon next weekend."

(Damascus, Oregon; late March. 2014)

Stone knew he was looking for the Clackamas offramp and Highway 212. They went a short distance then a sign read: Damascus, Boring, Sandy. "This must be the right way," Gezana said.

Stone was smiling, "Boring, Oregon, is as catchy as Athol, Idaho."

"That's a town?" Gezana responded, pithy.

"That's what I've been told."

"Lots of green around here," Gezana then observed.

"They get a little more rain here than we do. Every place you live has its price, I guess." Stone smiled.

"There it is, right next to SE Red Dirt Road, just like her little map shows." Gezana had Tyler's business card out "Changing Hearts Bed and Breakfast" Tyler Contadino, Proprietor. A neon heart that glowed from grey to red was set as an icon next to the name. "That's cute!" Gezana said.

The place had a Kentucky Bluegrass charm to it somehow: an old feel, wooden with interesting trim, very tidy in appearance. The flower pots even had winter color in them.

Stone was stretching himself a little having just got out of the rented BMW. He shuffled his feet slightly in the loose gravel of the parking lot.

"Hi."

They both looked to the door that was just opening. A middle aged woman of a nice height and weight approached them. Her hair was pulled back behind both ears. She had a broad smile and quite feminine eyes. 'I never thought a witch could look like that,' Stone thought to himself.

Her aura was immediately warm. She reached out a hand to Gezana, they then hugged. "Hi, I'm so happy you've come."

"We are too," Gezana answered directly. She turned to Stone, "and here, of course, is Stone."

He'd taken off his sunglasses and extended his hand. "My pleasure, Stone." Tyler smiled and firmly shook his hand. "You'll have to tell me about your name sometime," she said, smiling and squinting her nose just a touch towards Gezana. Stone just raised his eyebrows with an 'okay, sometime look.'

"I have one of my nicest rooms for you. I hope you like it!" The walls were a light blue and Tyler had selected some linen with colors she thought Gezana would like.

It was so clean and fresh smelling was the first thing Gezana thought to herself. A large window offered a nice view out to a grove of spruce trees not far away.

"I'll let you get settled in then take you for a short walk so you can see the garden and a few of my friends that live with me." Tyler pulled the wooden door with 19th century trim closed as she left the room.

"Nice place. There must be an interesting story behind how she's come to own it." Stone said.

"She bought the house from her mother years ago and started fixing it up. At least that's the story I got when she was in San Diego."

"Well there's a little mystery going on here I'm anxious to understand. But I guess we'll need to get the tour of the place before we get to that."

Tyler met them in the lobby as she had just finished helping someone else with a room. "Have you been to the Portland area before?" Tyler questioned.

"Quite a bit on business," Stone said. "I'm usually staying downtown. I like it there and they've got some good restaurants in that part of town."

"I know, it's a nice city, especially in the summer. This place keeps me so busy I rarely get over there."

"Do you live here?" Gezana then asked.

"I used to, but then I found a little cabin just north of Sandy I really like. So I live there now and commute. I grew up in Kentucky so the green and the rainy weather suits me fine. As long as I have some reasonably unfettered nature around me, I'm happy. That's what I get at my cabin."

She pointed towards the door, "Let me show you around here a little, then we'll sit down and talk." She pointed towards the porch where there were several chairs. Tyler picked up a small basket to take with her to the garden. It was slightly overcast and the light rain that had come down earlier left things damp, but Tyler's attention to design detail, grading and drainage, those sorts of things, made the place not soggy, which can be a bane to many landscapes.

"Before we get to the garden, I want to introduce you to my two Billy Goats: Sam and Irene."

The two looked at Gezana and Stone with those all-too-human looking eyes that always seem to have a question for you. "They were six when I got them and they're about nine now, so they're old. They probably have a year or two left in them." They walked a short distance to a place that had been leveled with small rock retaining walls. Eight or ten levels extended above where they were standing. The leveled areas were about six feet wide and twenty or thirty feet long.

"I had no idea you could grow so much during the winter." Gezana observed.

"Well, temperatures are pretty mild here through the winter, but people have been experimenting for a long time and the list is getting pretty extensive of what you can grow. Let me show you a few here. I'm going to pick some too, so we can have a nice salad after a little while. This little guy here is called Bull's Blood and it's a beet. This one is called Komatsuna, also called mustard spinach." They moved to a new level, "And here I have a little Aichi Chinese Cabbage. Watch your step here, that rock's a little loose. I like to have a little bit of these radishes in the mix too. This is Shirahime Hatsuka, the daicon radish. What are really good are these little tiny sprout guys, just emerging. They're jammed full of all kinds of micronutrients, right at the height of their potency. Yummy too."

"It smells so good standing here?" Gezana noted.

"Oh, you noticed? not everyone does. Well the sequoias help some, but I think my soil is a factor too. This soil has gotten a lot of TLC for a number of years. In fact, before I started trying to grow much I invested in building my soil. There's a connection with that for Stone and I'll explain that soon."

Back inside the building, Tyler brought them both a glass of Pinot Noir to sip on while she was putting the salads together. She'd sat them down on some cushy chairs that faced a small fire a helper had got going for them.

She was very near so they could chat easily while she worked. "Are you going to go to the play tomorrow night in Hood River? I did hear someone say it was quite good. *The Scarlet Pimpernel*, right?"

"Yes, this wine is great by the way," Stone began, "We'll catch that tomorrow afternoon, then catch a flight back to San Diego on Sunday morning."

"We saw *A Christmas Carol*, you know Dickens," Tyler was nodding her head in agreement, "a few weeks ago. It was good. It's always spooky when the ghost comes." Gezana said.

"Here you go," Tyler said, setting the stylish bowls down next to each of them. The salad looked absolutely delectable and she'd even garnished it with flowers. "Everything there is edible; I save the flowers in my cooler. These are some marigolds and dianthus. I like the gold's and purples mixed together." She gave it a little body language of 'I hope you like it.' "I know," Tyler continued, "the ghost is scary, but I've seen shows where they are flying from place to place, I rather like that."

Tyler pulled a chair up close so they could converse easily.

"So, where to begin?" Tyler smiled.

"I'm going to leave that to you." Stone replied.

She straightened herself, "Many years ago I met Louis and Minori Krastle." The name immediately made a connection for both Stone and Gezana. "Yes, I know you know Louis, Kurt Krastle's brother. The connection to you is through Louis. You worked with him for several years on plant food labeling for the State of California. That was before you went to work for his brother."

Stone was nodding, "I got to know Louis pretty well. I liked him a lot. We just saw business differently."

"Well, I'm talking to you because he thinks you might be open to ideas we have. I'm assuming that because you are here, you are interested in why I contacted you?"

"Yes, I'd like to understand that."

"We need people to break rank with the status quo, the powers that are holding this country and the world hostage to their short-sighted greed. You have connections, that you aren't directly aware of, to a part of the Family we think is most egregious." Tyler explained.

There that association was again: the Family. "What do you mean by the Family?"

"Let me come back to that. I need to tell you more of how I came to know Louis and Minori."

"I was telling you about how I spent time building my soil. Well, I learned from Louis and Minori. They were offering classes in how to build great soil, so I journeyed down to their farm near Santa Rosa and started in their classes. In the process, we became very good friends. What could be more basic to life, you know, growing great food. Oh, I learned so much from them! I went one weekend and could hardly wait until I could go again. It was sort of like falling in love. Maybe, I'm not very good at that, anymore at least." Gezana knew she was single at the moment, at least that was her story in San Diego. She had told Stone that Tyler had recently broken off a long-term relationship and was just floating for the time being.

Tyler had a small book lying next to her. She set it on the small coffee table that was sitting in front of all of them. "Do you know about this?"

Stone picked it up and read the cover, *The Kingdom of Good.* Yes, I heard about it in Dave's lecture."

"Louis and Minori told me about it. Anything they suggest of course gets my attention. There's a website that goes along with it, but I'm tactile so I ordered the book."

Stone was leafing through it, seeing many different graphs and then what was titled as being a lecture. "W. W. Sherman, he's the author?"

"Yes, he's dead now. He passed away about 3 years ago, not long after he'd put this together and went on what ended up being a short lecture tour. But in that time he was able to connect with quite a few people that get what he's saying. I wish I could have seen the lecture, but I've read it extensively so I feel I understand quite well what he was trying to tell everyone."

"And what's that?" Gezana asked.

Tyler pulled both of her arms back on the arms of her chair, "That our generation most likely holds the key to the long term habitability of our planet for humans and other larger forms of life." She paused, raised her quite beautiful eyebrows and looked empathetically towards her guests.

They both looked at her a bit taken back but still engaged. "You strike me as a very smart and sensible woman. Do you truly believe that?" Stone questioned.

"I do and with every day that passes, I believe it more. It's, well, look, I don't like making statements like that, but I've come to the conclusion that if people don't start speaking their mind forcefully, we'll just dither until it's too late. I know you went to Dave Herrick's lecture. I was there but not dressed as I am now."

"Why didn't you approach me there?"

"We know there are people watching Dave. I'm a known activist so they could easily have seen me talking to you and your cover would be blown. Someone else put the note on your chair too."

"Do you know that people are watching me?" Stone continued.

"No, but why take the chance?"

"How did you connect in my bowling league and why?" Gezana then wanted to know.

That was arranged by members of the West Coast Family, I filled in for someone who got paid to go elsewhere, I think was the deal. Why? I got to know a little about your man's heart. We needed little clues."

"Who or what is the West Coast Family?" Stone wanted to know.

Tyler switched her crossed legs and looked more directly at Stone. "In the US, there are about 1,500 people whose wealth is extremely influential in running our country and world. They represent the pinnacle of the Family. But it's really about 20% of our population who make up the Family over all. And of course that represents about 60 million people. So of course they don't know each other or even have similar political leanings. But they are bound by an invisible hand of wealth to which they respond. Even among the pinnacle they don't all know or even like each other, and in most cases they don't know are even members of the Family. There is just a very small number that actually know and think of themselves as part of this elite group and very often they are the ones pulling the levers of power. And all the others just naturally follow like herd animals will do with the leaders. But known or not they have a spider's web that connects them and information. That's all I can tell you. But it's through them that I know this, Dave and Joan are targets."

There were details she couldn't tell them. There were just some things she couldn't share.

Stone turned the book to its back cover and was startled by how it read.

He was staring at the words; Tyler could see the puzzled look on his face. "You have a question?"

He looked towards Gezana and turned the page so she could read it. She looked back at him with astonishment as well. Stone wasn't sure how to respond.

He decided to explain his thoughts to Tyler. "Did you know I was in a diving incident a few months ago? You seem to have a lot of information about me."

"Yes, of course we know of Kurt's death and there was some incident with a squid, and you were part of the dive team, but nothing else." Tyler replied.

Gezana was shaking her head as she knew what he was about to say. "I was in the grips of the squid and it was trying to rip me apart. I was terrified and fighting for my life. Then like someone had changed the speed on the projector everything slowed down, way down. I could see how to grab my knife and cut myself loose, and just as I was doing that, a thought came to me, and it questioned me 'what do you believe?' It was as clear as anything I've ever seen or heard, just solid. Then like the projector was turned back to full speed everything was spinning and churning, I fought my way to the surface. It's just really odd, that's all." He shook his head, puzzled. He read the short question out loud that was posed on the back of the book, "What do you believe?"A few moments passed before they continued.

"That's very curious, isn't it?" Tyler then commented.

"Is there more you can tell us about the Family?" Stone continued.

She opened the *Kingdom of Good* book to the third page and pointed at several graphs. "This starts to explain the Family." It was titled 'Wealth Distribution in America.' "This is how the wealth of the American population is distributed. What it depicted was that 20% of Americans own about 87% of the country's wealth, so 80% share the remaining 13%. "It's probably an even greater split now because the numbers used to calculate this are from 2009. Every year, the trend is for the top 20% to have more and the bottom 80% to have less. The connection between them grows less each year. At some point there will be virtually no connection. They will be like two different worlds floating away from each other."

"At this rate, sometime in the near future there will be no middle class as this 80% has been flattened out to having virtually no real wealth. You may have a middle class among this 20%, but this 80% is gone. This is what tyranny begins to look like. The economy is structured so it flows within this 20%, the life blood; the 80% get less and less blood. What happens?" Tyler's eyes reflected the question she had just posed.

Tyler pointed to the other line on the graph: the one that 92% of the people say would be a fair distribution of the country's wealth. "This is what most people think a fair distribution of wealth would be. This is where democracy can flourish because all the people have enough resources. You have a strong middle class, money flows. But that's not what we now have, and it's only getting worse. And since we don't have a properly functioning democracy, we can't even deal with the horrible threat of climate change effectively."

Tyler pushed her finger on the top of the 1% distribution of wealth. "This line sticks up here so high that it's obnoxious and obscene. What would be so wrong if you could just …" Her finger moved down along the line, "Push down on this line some and fill up that bottom with more dollars? The country's wealth has been accumulating for over two hundred years, fifteen or sixteen generations. A lot of it was created by the hard work of countless and unknown people like the grandparents, great grandparents, on and on of that 80%. I think the 80% have a lot more claim to all that wealth. Just because you can do something doesn't mean it's right or that you should. And a lot of that wealth is there because they didn't pay the true cost of the energy and other hidden costs that they should have been required to do. On further thought, I think the 80% have a huge case against a lot of those people in that group. If you make your money at the expense of others, you don't deserve it."

She pointed to another image relating to the Family. "Of course like I said the vast majority of the 20% don't even know they're in the Family. They tend to implicitly recognize it though because they have a pretty stable life, money for vacations so they can play quite a bit. There's a status quo that's serving them well. The vast majority of them are not evil. In fact given the chance they'd want to do good things. It's a part of their true nature, if they don't block it with their ego. Mostly they just leave well enough alone because it's working for them."

"There are a lot of them, counting their kids and all, maybe 63 to 65 million. It's not a homogeneous Family; there are lots of different reasons why they are in it. One faction, we call them the Black Goats because they get their wealth from the dark rock, ooze, and mist they get from the ground. They are enriched by fossil fuels like coal, oil, and natural gas. They are some of the worst players in the Family. There are many tentacles that lead through them. Think of all the things made from petrochemical raw materials. There's not just gas for your car or to heat your house or office, or to run the power plants that provide us electricity. There's much more: irrigation pipe, bags and packaging, pesticides, herbicides, fertilizers, ballet tights, panty hose, golf balls, fishing line, cheap hamburgers, you start to get the idea. There's probably a list of 500 to a 1,000 of those types of products that they all depend on the cheap crude oil or gas. The pricing in our economy is pegged to the raw materials being inexpensive and abundant."

Tyler settled back in her chair gathering more to say. "We activists point towards the fossil fuels companies being the villains, and they partly are. But just like the Nazi leaders were evil and led the German people to the atrocities they did, enough of the people allowed it. There were some of course that wanted none of what the Nazi's were doing, but they weren't organized and got cut off. That's what's going on with the Family now. There are some, a lot actually in real numbers, that don't want the tyranny to grow, but they're not organized properly. They don't have all the information they need. That's how the evil players can thrive."

She stopped. "So why did you refer to yourself as Glinda?" Stone asked.

Tyler gathered her thoughts, "History repeats itself. The same struggles the people at the turn of the 20th century were having are happening again, just in different ways. In 1939 *The Wizard of Oz* was a metaphor for their struggles. Dorothy represented the resilient people who just wanted to make it on their own. The Wicked Witch of the West represented the robber barons and fickleness of nature. The Scarecrow was the impression many farmers had of themselves; as not so smart. The wizard was the President and other politicians in their many forms. The Emerald City was Washington DC. There are many other analogies."

"But the high point and I think the deep moral in the story is when Dorothy throws the water to put the fire on the scarecrows' arm out and hits the witch and she shrivels away." Tyler paused and leaned towards them both, "Dorothy represents the nobler and knowledgeable ones among us, wanting what is good and fair. The robber barons only succeed as long as the people remain intimidated. That's what the real power in her ruby slippers was I think: the courage to stand up to evil."

Stone was remembering this segment from the email he'd received.

Tyler continued, "But in the face of clear wrong doing Dorothy stands up to them and splatters them with the magic potion: water. Goodness! And the witch withers away as she's not truly strong enough to endure the water separating the weakness of her life force. Nothing left but her broom and her hat. Remember how the witch told Dorothy and her friends that she'd kill the scarecrow first and the others and Dorothy would be last? It's analogous to what's happening in our world now. They've started with the farmers, just look what's been happening in India, South America, Asia, and Africa, millions are being pushed off of their land so they can no longer grow their own food. They either starve or try to live in those horrible shanty towns. I have no idea how they manage to live there."

"Corporations, hedge funds, and dirty political leaders pull this off together. Farmers in India are committing suicide by the hundreds of thousands because they can't pay their bills because they changed to industrial agriculture which didn't work. Then they lose their land. What else can they do?"

"They start with the farmers; then the other workers, the Tin Man. Then the political class, the Lion; and then noble do-gooders: Dorothy and Wilbur Gale. That is *unless they fight back*!"

"But then remember that after the witch withers away the most remarkable thing happens: Dorothy thinks the witch's guards and the flying monkeys will go against her, but they don't. They are thankful for what she's done by ridding them of the tyrant."

"You see, Stone, we think you are unwittingly one of the witch's guards. There are millions of you. Actually, you and them, just need the illusion of being captive to the evil ones ways vanquished."

He slid slightly in his chair and looked at her with a large question on his face. He wasn't sure if he liked being thought of that way. He was no pawn, to his mind.

"Evil ones?" Stone then asked.

Tyler adjusted how she was sitting, "Well, what do you think, are there truly evil people in the world?"

"Oh yes," Gezana spoke quickly, "of course, horrible people." Stone was nodding his head that he agreed, while savoring the salad Tyler had just given him.

"When do you cross the line to evil?" he then asked.

"That line varies from person to person, I think." Tyler replied. "But I would just say that acts or behaviors that don't respect the health and happiness of others start to define it." Tyler stood up and retrieved the tea-pot refilling everyone's glass. "Denying that your industry is destroying the habitability of the earth gets you an extreme distance down that line," she said, sitting back down. "There are thousands of actors in that group. Some are just worse than others."

"So assuming for a moment that I agree with your premise, what do you think I can do about it?"

"We need some major defectors to show others that it's okay. People are born with an inner sense about goodness and fairness. To some, it becomes quite inconvenient to listen to that voice and they begin to shut it off. And just like a limb that never gets any blood, you shut the voice off long enough, eventually it goes away entirely. That's when true evil enters them and the world. There are truly evil people sitting in places of power right now, Stone. We have to crack their hold on the system. Dorothy had to hit them with some water."

Stone stared at her for a short while, "Who's the main Dorothy? And what is water?"

Tyler had to think for a moment herself, "The main Dorothy, I don't know he or she has yet to emerge; though I think someone is out there, I just feel it. She, I'll be biased because I'm a woman, will have goodness as her weapon. She will throw her righteous and indignant goodness out to save the most vulnerable, and in doing so save everyone else, including herself."

"What about you?" Gezana said, seeing the charismatic person in Tyler.

"Oh, well, thank you." She shook her head, "I don't hear the beat of the calling in my heart. My place is more like." She thought again, "I'm like an enzyme, I assist things to happen!" She smiled and a good laugh emerged.

"And the water, I'm still trying to figure out what the water is?" Stone questioned.

"We live in a democracy. The thing tyrant's fear most is losing the control over the munchkins, the people who don't really think for themselves, and the ability to manipulate them, like a border collie does sheep.

"If the munchkins and those that would lead them were to wake up and understand their true power in numbers, the tyrants would just dissolve like the Wicked Witch. The water, Stone, is *knowledgeable votes*. Forty percent of the people who are eligible to vote in America, let's say for president, *don't*. Why not and where are they? If even half, maybe less, of those people registered and then voted for candidates who believe we need an entirely different direction in this country, and for the world, things could change fast. Why do you think there is so much effort by Republicans to block voter access? That's the Achilles heel for tyrants in our system. And you watch, if they are able to fool the people and regain control of the Congress for even a short time, high on their to-do list will be to set road blocks for the masses to vote. That's when we'll really be fucked!"

Gezana and Stone's eyebrows lifted, hearing her.

"Well, I think I need to leave it at that for now. I have some chores I need to attend to." She pointed to a broom in the corner. Perhaps we can chat a bit more tonight before bed-time? I'm sure you'll have some questions that come to mind between now and then."

Chapter Nineteen

(a magical ride)

"Just a sec," Tyler said from the kitchen, "I know I have some here." Stone and Gezana could hear the sound of glass clinking together. "Ah, how about that." She entered where they were sitting. A small fire was going and the house was only dimly lit. It was raining outside some, but it could not be seen through the darkened windows.

"It's hazelnut Bailey's too, we're in luck. This is a pretty bold blend of coffee. I tried not to dilute its flavor too much for you." She handed them both the mugs, light brown with a large handle, moderately heavy. The logo of her business was engraved on the front and the heart was red.

"Do you have kids, or nieces and nephews you're concerned about their future for, Tyler?" Stone coughed slightly, "Bailey's always gets me a little that way. If I breathe a little too much it tickles my throat I guess." He took a smaller sip, "Sure tastes good though."

Tyler answered. "I have a daughter. She's in college at Portland State, and she lives with me out at my cabin on the river. Her father is around here someplace. He helped me some through the years." She shook her head, "And the two of you?"

"I'd need to be married," Gezana looked at Stone, giving him a look 'well?' "I guess I'm not too old for that yet, I don't know, we'll see."

Tyler then began, "The truth is I'm very concerned for my daughter and all the younger people. I fear we have a problem that is complex and far more potent for destruction than even the scientists have suggested or are willing to tell us about. Unfortunately, we just don't know exactly how things might unravel and how much time we have. With glaciers melting faster than ever thought possible just a few years ago and these storms we've been having already, prudence tells me that something bold needs to happen."

She took a small drink then continued. "There's a big picture to all this. Rather than having a virtuous cycle where the parts work together to an ever greater good, we've managed to create a non virtuous cycle that runs counter to nature and it's grinding more and more people into despair. Somehow we have to get back on the virtuous cycle."

"If you wouldn't mind, explain that cycle a little, as you understand it," Stone requested.

Tyler held her right finger up letting him know she needed a moment to gather her thoughts on that. "Every person on earth needs, at a minimum, food, water, shelter and protection from dangerous forces, like a bear that might want to eat you, to simply survive. Beyond that it's just extra. That was pretty much the state of things while our ancestors were hunter gatherers for millions of years. When we discovered agriculture 10,000 years ago or so that all changed. People began living in one place, their numbers grew, and all the extra stuff did too. Over time we extracted more and more from nature, but what the vast majority of us missed was the fact that there are limits to our intrusion into the natural cycle. And when we pass them we start destroying ourselves and everything else. A virtuous cycle understands those limits and lives within them. And where we find our joy and satisfaction in living comes from a deeper and balanced relationship with nature and not from unlimited material things."

She pointed to the veggie dish on the table, "Ground zero is how we grow our food. Before World War II everything was grown organically meaning no synthetic fertilizers, pesticides, gmo's, all that. That all comes along after World War II when the chemical companies are looking for peace time uses for the technologies invented for chemical warfare. Can you believe that? Our food supply created from chemicals originally invented for mass killing? We're plenty clever, the question is how wise are we?"

About then her phone rang. "Sorry, this is my daughter, I need to take it."

Hanging up she began again, "I do need to go. She needs a ride back to the house. Listen, a great source for all this information is the *Kingdom of Good* website. Just add a .com to that name and you'll get it. I'll catch you in the morning before you leave, okay?"

~~~~~

Again, after following his normal attention to his girlfriend, Stone left Gezana resting comfortably by making sure the blankets were pulled up around her before grabbing his iPod and heading out to the sitting area. There was still a warm glow from the solar powered heater next to the chairs they'd been sitting in earlier. '*The Kingdom of Good*,' he thought to himself. The website soon appeared and he began his review. The numerous graphs and charts created a story, some of which he was to a degree familiar with, and some not. He found the organization on timelines particularly intriguing and satisfying.

Over an hour passed as he studied all the information, sifting and sorting, comparing what was depicted against his own knowledge. He sat for a while just staring at the glow from the heater, orange and red, comforting against the dark recesses of the night-cast room. He slipped away into sleep without consciously recognizing the transition.

(Come ride my broom)

Like the sprinkling of fairy dust across the screen of a Disney introduction, Stone realizes someone or something has appeared in the room.
Some part of him looks towards the new arrival while the rest of his body
sleeps. It's Tyler and she's standing holding her broom, smiling at him.
"Did your reading go well?" she asked.

Stone looked at his iPod that was still sitting on the lap of his sleeping
body. "There was a lot there," he replied.

"It takes everyone time to fathom through it. What you believe when
your done is what I'm most interested in. Sometimes it helps to get a little
more one on one explanation going." She was smiling broadly now, her
pretty face a bit pixy, but deeply intelligent and portraying warmth. Her
eyes nodded towards the broom, "Care to take a ride?" she queried. Her
free hand gestured towards the broom.

There was some part of him that knew this was a dream, but it seemed
fun, and who could resist riding on a broom with such a beautiful woman?"

In a flash they were riding together, a moonlit and starry night sky all
around them. Beyond the horizon he could see that the sun was rising.

~~~~~

The perspective suddenly was from many miles in the sky his innate
fear of heights caused him to grab on the broom handle more tightly.
"Hah, hah," Tyler smiled and laughed lightly, "Don't worry, you can't
fall." He did feel secure, and warm, 'okay, play along, some part of him
thought.'

The sky around him suddenly transformed from being seemingly empty to that showing the many molecules that float about, mingling in the
atmosphere. Predominating were the nitrogen molecules, a little over 78%
of them; then there were the blue oxygen molecules almost 21%; then just
a little under 1% were the yellow argon molecules. These made up about
99.964% of them all. But there were a tiny few more: thirteen other molecules distinguished by color, but of course they were very very few and
scattered all about.

Tyler stopped them; they were next to a carbon dioxide molecule
which she made about the size of a basketball. "Let's start here," she began. "This pesky guy is ground zero for about everything. This is carbon
with its six neutrons and protons in the nucleus and two electrons in the
first shell, and four in the second. It's probably the most active and important element on Earth for its function in living things and in the atmos-

247

phere. See how it bonds with two oxygen atoms, sharing electrons in the outer shell? Look around, there's only about 1 of these carbon dioxide molecules for about every 4,000 of the other ones. Now look how the radiation interacts with it. See how it lights up like a little piece of coal. There are other ones that do this some too, but this guy is the most important. Before people started doing things like turning the soil for farming, or cutting down forests, which releases stored carbon from the ground and biomass, this was about what the quantity of these carbon dioxide molecules looked like. And this was all it took to keep us balanced: not too hot and not too cold." Tyler twitched her nose, "But this is what it looks like today, maybe 1 ½ times as many as there were before we started turning the soil, burning the wood, coal, oil, natural gas, cutting down forests and prairies. These were activities that released carbon to the atmosphere where it binds with oxygen and creates more and more of these little heaters."

Suddenly they were back in Tyler's kitchen. There was a pan on the stove with the lid rattling around on top of it. "See how the lid is trapping the steam energy and getting rattled around?" Stone nodded. "Now, if I just move the lid over a little it stops rattling and everything seems to be balanced. In a nut shell that's what's happening in the atmosphere. We're trapping more heat and there's more energy to get dispersed around the planet. That's what climate change is." Stone knew that, but since Tyler was the guide he just played along.

"So if about 1 in every 4,000 of these is just right to keep the goldilocks balance – not too hot or cold – just think what two, three, four, six, etc. would mean." Her face became very serious. "This balance is the keystone to our civilization, Stone. If we disturb it too much we will crumble just like an arch where the keystone collapses."

Her hand opened and on it Stone could see a great glacier, "The continental glaciers of Greenland and Antarctica are melting much faster than anyone thought possible just a few years ago. Glacier Park will soon be without glaciers. You know the story of the rising sea waters and the rivers of glacial melt waters that are vanishing which are the source of crop growing and drinking water for tens of millions of people. What will they do when they no longer have the water?"

They didn't seem to move but suddenly a large vessel with the number 350 written boldly across its front appeared. "Our most distinguished climate scientists have told us that 350 carbon dioxide molecules in a million is the maximum level for maintaining our balanced climate." She twitched her nose again and little balls started flowing from on top, but none would go into the vessel. It was already full, so the little balls flowed over the edge. Tyler lifted her shoulders and leaned in towards Stone, "The atmosphere is already full. Stone. There's no more safe room to add the carbon dioxide molecules and expect to maintain the comfortable balance." The pot image returned, "See how the lid is starting to rattle?" She looked at him with even more concern in her gaze. "What part of 'the atmosphere is full,' do people not get?"

Suddenly they were moving again. There were clouds all around, then they dropped through their bottom and a bucolic mountain and meadow scene appeared below. They came to rest on the edge of a low grassy covered hill where they could see the small wooden buildings of a farm. There were cows and chickens about, hay stacked in bundles loosely together in the field and nothing motorized could be seen. The air smelled clean even musky from the metabolism of the microbes in the life-promoting humus in the ground all around.

To Stone it looked like some vision he'd had of life in Germany many years ago. "These are some of your ancestors just 150 years ago, Stone. They raised all the food they needed without using any of the synthetic fertilizers and pesticides of industrial agriculture, just as their ancestors had done for thousands of years. The carbon dioxide loading was still minor, but that was about to change. There was much about it they did not know, things that could help them have even greater healthy abundance and fertility. But most importantly they weren't impacting the Goldilocks balance appreciably, not yet. I think many people of our times would prefer this life to the one they have now: living in cities where they have little involvement in the production of their food."

"Hang on, we need to go a little ways." This time as they lowered there were many old weather-beaten brick buildings with slate roofs about. They settled to rest just beyond a building where vast amounts of black and "uh, uh," Stone had to cough, sooty smoke was belching out. They could not be seen as they walked past the caldrons where the coal was burning. The heat from which was boiling water creating steam that powered multiple pistons, turning a large wheel whose motion was then used to animate other mechanical devices to make cloth. "This is the 1750s, Stone. People, very cleverly, have found ways to produce different things like this cotton in quantities never before possible with so few workers. But as you can see the carbon being released is not being considered. It's bonding with the nearby oxygen and the carbon dioxide molecules continued to accumulate and many released here are in our modern atmosphere today heating it up."

~~~~~~

They moved quickly into modern times where a jet airliner was cruising not far from where they were traveling. Soon they were standing on a mountain top looking out across a vast expanse of fields covered in mono-lithic crops, in the distance the towers of a large city could be seen. "Of course this is our modern world. Nearly everything you see was construct-ed since the end of World War II. That's when civilization really took the wrong road, Stone, trying to go around nature's ways. You see the endless miles of monolithic crops growing on soil that is basically dead. It's being killed by the toxic chemicals of industrial agriculture. It's dependent like a junky on synthetic fertilizers and pesticides to grow things now because the microbial life has been so diminished. Topsoil is being washed away because it has lost the connectivity that the microbes in healthy soil create. What soil there is can't hold the rain that falls because all the properties of an organic soil, that naturally holds water and nutrients, has been de-stroyed."

"When the war ended, the Earth's human population was only about two billion, which coincidentally is considered about our true carrying ca-pacity using only organic agriculture with no synthetic chemicals being used. You know the story about the chemical companies looking for a way to use their technology invented for wartime use? So by the late 1940s it began. Of course to begin with there were amazing gains in productivity. And all the energy to build and power tractors and combines, you name it, became available about over night for agriculture. Crop yields were astro-nomical. And of course, our population growth exploded right along. All across much of the world this became the scene, over and over; more and more."

"And now there are over seven billion of us, all needing enough food, water, and a safe and warm place to sleep. And we still have not figured out how, in any cost competitive way, to sequester the carbon we release to power this new monster world we've created. So the lid keeps rattling more and more."

They were suddenly in an old laboratory. "It's 1909, Stone, over there is Fritz Haber the German chemist, he has invented a new way to synthe-size nitrogen, taking it from the atmosphere. In my mind this is the most consequential invention of all time! Virtually the entire climate crisis can be traced back to this event. As you learn more, Stone, keep connecting the dots back to this. It is the true nexus of the climate crisis."

Now they got small, very small. Tyler flew them up close to the ex-posed edge of a stream bank and some exceedingly rich soil. "This is an example of Mother Nature's premier work in creating extraordinarily fer-tile and secure soils," Tyler explained. She showed him the thousands of species and billions of bacteria, fungi, protozoa, arthropods and nematodes in just a small handful of the soil, interacting in a virtuous cycle that con-nected intrinsically to organisms above the ground. The more diverse and bountiful the soil, so too were the organisms consuming its production. This was the true source for a healthy civilization and its people, she noted.

And there were the many worms moving through it, passing the soil through their gut where it was enriched even more, obtaining the deep layers of nature's magic. The same type of worms that E.O. Williamson had shown Louis and had so captured his imagination all those years ago.

"See here how the carbon is bound in this vast network of humus?" Tyler was holding some of the deep brown fluffy material in her hand. She enlarged the bonding of the carbon molecules so Stone could more easily understand. "Vast amounts of carbon were stored in the meadows, woodlands, and prairies before people began turning them into crop producing factories. What they did not understand, because they could not see it, was that when they turned the soil this carbon was being exposed to the atmosphere where there was plenty of oxygen atoms to which they could and did bind. This new carbon dioxide would then drift up into the atmosphere and ever-so-slowly back then –even thousands of years ago- begin to add to the warming effect. But there were not that many people then, so the effect was minimal and possibly to some degree even beneficial. Storing carbon in the soil, taking advantage of natures natural programming to do so, may be one of the most important and effective strategies for combating the climate crisis."

She whisked them on, this time to the modern delta lands where the Mississippi flows into the Gulf of Mexico. As they descended he could see great swaths of orangey-brown colors in the otherwise blue-green of the water. "This is just one of the many detrimental effects of industrial scale, non organic, agriculture," she said as they passed over head. "This is not normal. The spraying of synthetic nitrogen starts the process of soil degradation which ultimately leads to soil that washes away easily. And then the excess nitrogen and phosphorus sprayed on the thousands of square miles of America's heartland leaches and washes down the countless little streams into the Mississippi and ends up here. This then leads to massive algae blooms which deplete the water of oxygen which the larger organisms like the fish need, so they often die in large numbers. This would not happen if the agricultural system was organic, and ecologically sound. These materials would never be sprayed on the fields and they could never wash down into the ocean. This activity, by the way, through the manufacturing of the nitrogen and mining of the phosphorus, releases great amounts of carbon and therefore carbon dioxide into the atmosphere."

Tyler looked towards Stone with an expression an indignant person will have, "Do you see much wisdom in all of this, Stone?" He was speechless.

"Look how the topsoil just washes into the river and out into the gulf too. Those soils of the Heartland are so weakened by the chemical treatments that destroyed most of the life in the soils that gave them their ability to hold together against the pull of the water and gravity, they end up here. They wither away like sugar in water and end up in lakes and oceans where their minerals are of no use. It required millions of years of grinding of the rock by the glaciers and other physical agents to create the small fragments of stone minerals that life needs for growth. When it's all washed into the oceans, how do you grow your food? What happens to your nation?"

She stopped them next to a particularly large and binding looking weed. "There are at least 180 different types of pesticides available. Some if not all have been linked as endocrine system disrupters in human bodies; cancer, birth defects, and other developmental disorders like ADD are associated."

Straight away they were standing next to some horsetail looking plants that were six of seven feet tall, "Here is what's thriving in this mindless campaign against nature's ways: super weeds. There are at least 24 different species that have developed resistance to the major herbicides. Some of them are considered super weeds like pigweed, horseweed, and ragweed. 60 million acres are currently affected. The chemical industries answer is to go back to older pesticides like 2,4-d and dicamba that have been associated with non-Hodgkin's lymphoma and other deadly consequences. And, of course, eventually even these won't work as the weeds mutate and re-spread."

Glinda, as Stone now thought of Tyler on this ride, looked more directly at him. "The industry you currently serve is destroying the balance in the soil which is the foundation for the rest of civilization, Stone. What I have just shown you are the results. Stone, as much as 30% of the carbon dioxide footprint of the United States comes from its agricultural sector. Just imagine if a massive transition to organic practices was to occur where you can sequester carbon in the soil by growing cover crops like legumes to pull the carbon out of the atmosphere like a great giant vacuum cleaner. As much as 7,000 pounds per acre per year, that would be huge."

If this approach to food production is not changed it is likely only a matter of time before all is lost. Remember the first temptation of Jesus: 'turning stones into bread,' do you understand the connection?"

"Now I want to show you how it should be done, and I've got just the farm in mind." They were off again riding through the sky. As they settled down through the clouds, Stone thought he recognized the area and he did. There was the bay and San Francisco, and there was Santa Rosa. "I know you've never been to his farm, Stone, but you know Louis Krastle, one of our great agricultural ecologists."

They settled down on one of the fields that had been planted with a cover crop for the winter. "The plants you see growing right now aren't even a cash crop. They've been planted to increase the fertility of the soil for the cash crop. You see here, this is common oat, and this is brown mustard, and over here is little barley. They all have their slight different functions, but mostly they're pulling carbon from the atmosphere and getting it to the soil where the microbes process it into humus, which the cash crops then use for a nutritious food supply. You don't find any synthetic fertilizers or pesticides or GMO seeds, nothing that's a part of the industrial agriculture approach. These guys are organic to the end of the last hair on their head. Admittedly Louis' hair is getting a little short and grey."

None of the workers could see them as they walked through the greenhouse. "The organic approach has required trial and error. Nature doesn't send us a guidebook so we have to carefully observe and learn. And like anything you can get better and better at this. Devices capable of analyzing the nutrient densities in these foods can now quantify their superior content of polyphenols, flavonoids, and other phytonutrients that scientist think is the source of increased health by eating fruits and vegetables. And most people will tell you organic just tastes better. And you just seem to maintain an attractive and healthy weight when you eat this real food."

Next they were standing near the end of one of the greenhouses. "Every day workers harvest the veggies and fruits that are at their peak of nutrition possible and are distributed around town where people can walk and purchase them. Every lunch can be made from this peak food supply. The people who eat this highly nutritious food are much healthier. Weight problems, tiredness, tooth decay, high blood pressure, high cholesterol, heart disease, type- 2 diabetes, osteoporosis, some cancers, even depression are linked to poor nutrition. Just imagine a US or world population getting great nutrition every day and think of the health care cost savings alone. Is this making sense to you, Stone: healthy soils, healthy people, a balanced and healthy world?"

Their next stop, nearing the end, was to a lake in Siberia. "Feel how soft the ground is, Stone. It hasn't been this soft for several million years. This is tundra and it should be hard even now in the summer." She then pointed out into the water, "See those bubbles rising out there? That's methane that's coming up from under the lake. All around these northern lands there is enormous amounts of this frozen methane in huge blocks, like ice cubes. They're called hydrates. It's been stable that way for millennia, but that's changing. It's warming just enough that this methane is starting to leak out. If a tipping point is hit, Stone, and these hydrates release all this methane. The heating will cause catastrophic consequences which is our worst nightmare. Hopefully wisdom will rise more quickly than the methane."

Tyler had them flying through the air, "There's just a couple more places I want to show you Stone, and something else, then I'll get you back to Gezana." They seemed to fly for a longer time and they left the familiar blue skies and quickly headed into some drab clouds. They seemed to get darker as they went on. Soon lighting was flashing around them and the air began to smell like sulfur. They lowered down through the clouds this time to a landscape that seemed alien. He could not think of a place like this on the Earth. It sort of resembled what he'd once seen that Venus might look like. The sky was grey with a hint of lemon green. There was no vegetation only rocks that appeared to be covered with lichens and it was spooky.

"We could not actually be here except through the portal I have brought us," she explained. "You could not breathe this air or endure for long the temperature, they would kill us. This is the end result of the methane finally being released massively. The temperature of the Earth shot well past the six degrees of warming. The process was horrific. Nothing but bacteria made it through Stone."

"This is Earth 5,000 years from now should the efforts of sincere people who dream that the experiment of advanced life on Earth will continue, should fail. *The Mephistopheles Moment was passed.* Far from impossible, a few top scientists now think this is likely without drastic change.

What could lead to this? Well, it might unfold something like this. By 2020 the effort to dramatically change the government of the United States to the Green Party, or one based on similar stated values, fails to obtain sufficient political power and the status quo of corporate dominance strangles the movement. The corporate controlled status quo retains power long enough so that the critical threshold of carbon emissions is crossed, sometime shortly after 2025 perhaps 2035 at the latest; the point of no return. The mega storms grow in number and intensity. Heating of the atmosphere causes widespread crop failures as the monocrops hit their heat induced photosynthetic limits. Our cattle and other meat producing industries begin to have extensive losses due to species heat intolerance for reproduction; population collapse follows. Costs of food soar, rioting begins. Lack of employment casts millions into poverty and they rebel, civil wars begin. Nuclear exchanges occur. The seas rise by four feet by the end of the 21st century and hundreds of millions are forced to move inland leaving trillions of dollars of buildings, roads, bridges, pipelines and the infrastructure, behind."

"Horrible local warring follows. All glacial water is lost to the oceans and millions perish as they have no water to grow crops. Most of civilization is gone by this time, perhaps a few hundred years from now, or less. Then the cleanup crew begins; the flooded oceans that are now 300 feet higher against the land, inundating the majority of agricultural land now begin to burp toxic gases. The oceans no longer have the thermohaline current of water to move heat and nutrients around the planet. The oceans transfer from an aerobic oxygen producing equilibrium to an anaerobic hydrogen sulfide releasing equilibrium. This is poisonous to just about everything growing on the land, the seas are already dead. The oceans belch this toxic crud for centuries. Virtually all life is eliminated and the human experiment proving to be a total disaster." Tyler walked a few feet away then put her hands up gesturing to all that was around her. "Stone, our generation makes the decision whether or not this happens! It will be too late 20 years from now if the massive change required to avoid this is not well under way."

Tyler held out a large piece of paper. There was a graph on it she wanted to explain to him. "There is no reason this dreadful end should happen Stone, the natural patterns of the Earth driven by Milankovitch cycles would slowly be dropping into a cooler world. Humans could easily adapt over the thousands of years it would play out. But not so if what I just showed you doesn't change very quickly and we lose control."

"This problem, like nearly all of them, is of our own making. It's what's in certain people's hearts and minds! The lack of concern for the Earth that is killing the planet is similar to the lack of concern for all people by the few. So many people are asleep, like in a dream, unaware of the dire circumstances gathering around them."

~~~~~

*"Across the world we are not living by the central moral ethos Jesus directed us to: **Love Creation Entirely**. When we conveniently forget about our responsibility to all of creation, which includes all of us, we destroy ourselves and everything else.*

~~~~~

Tyler snapped her fingers and a colorful image appeared and floated in front of them. This has much to do with the many social problems and even the climate crisis. "Look at this graph, it shows the current distribution of wealth in the United States. Most people have had no idea how inequitably wealth has become spread very recently in the US. You can see

255

here, about 20% of the people own about 87 or 88% of the wealth. Conversely 80% of the people share the remaining 12 or 13% between them." Stone had the feeling he'd heard this material before, but it was being played again because of its importance.

The graph was astounding. It showed how 80% of the people barely registered along the bottom line of the graph, then a sharp spike, similar to the population growth curve, started up and the up was almost inconceivably up. The top 1% of families was shown owning more of the country's total wealth than the bottom 90% of families.

"This is what tyranny looks like. Year by year the 80% loses more and more to the 20% (the Family). The system has gotten rigged that way, not consciously by all of them, but by a few bad actors manipulating tax laws and high jacking government to work for the few rather than for everyone." For the time being it's a very convenient status quo for those in the 20%. This could only be happening because the 80% lost sight of what was happening and are asleep. They outnumber the 20% (or the 1%) enormously. They have a democracy where limits could be managed, but they don't effectively do so. They've lost control of their democracy and their government has been manipulated by those bad actors to allow for this inequity of wealth distribution to accrue."

She pointed to a second line that was superimposed against the other line. "If a part of being human is to seek a good and fair society, and I believe it is, this is what that curve would look like. In fact 5,000 people from all social and economic parts of American society were asked to describe what they thought the ideal wealth distribution line would look like and 92% said that's it. What the other 8% thought probably explains why it looks like it does now. But with this distribution which 92% of the people say is fair, no one is below the poverty line. Everybody gets covered at least to a minimum for reasonable survival; food, water, shelter. You can see how there is an entry level, then a middle class with plenty of wealth and disposable income to keep things moving well. A virtuous cycle. Then it moves up more to a higher level of wealth as it compensates those that have made some pretty great contributions to the common good. But everyone is sharing in the overall growth. And then again there is a place for some super stars … maybe even an actress," Tyler's body language suggesting possibly herself.

"Over time as the economy grew so would the overall height to this distribution. All ships would rise together as President Kennedy described. Of course you would have to work to remain in this virtuous cycle, but the ladder would always be there for you. This pinching off is not remotely natural for the true human talent and motivation distributed there. Not for 80% or maybe more of the population! It is only through deviant and treacherous manipulation of our system, and so many asleep, that this injustice exists."

She then pointed to the enormous spike at the far end, "but this is our current reality. And you're about right here, Stone, just sitting at the base of the super rich." She was pointing to those in the 90th percentile bracket. You know their life style intimately. You and many just like yourself see their life styles with their enormous yachts, multiple homes, jet setting around the world and you imagine it for yourself. But as I've shown you our civilization is not in balance and these life styles and the structure of our current society/civilization that support them, are not sustainable. In fact they are destroying the balance we so desperately need. The system will crumble and our stable biosphere will be destroyed and so will all of us."

Suddenly, they were lowering down through some trees and the sky was darkened like late afternoon on a very cloudy day. A castle appears, perched on the edge of a rocky bluff, a large gate is drawn closed. A moat surrounds the sides of the castle not perched at the rocky ledge. Thousands of feet appear to fall away beneath it. They are small and cannot be seen by the ensemble gathered in front of them. There is a young woman, bright and honest looking and she has a small black dog with her. Stone knows he has recently discussed this scene with Tyler or Glinda or whoever she is. It's obviously important to her. Fleeing with her are three companions and they are being chased by a dreadful looking woman with a green face, hawkish nose, and dressed in a black cape. Monkeys with long tails, and men who look like they would guard Buckingham Palace, are in pursuit as well. The girl, her dog, and three companions are cornered. The scarecrow attempts to stand up to the evil looking woman, but she pushes him back and lets them know they are done; 'the last to go will see the first three go before her. You're mangy little dog too,' she says, in a wicked tone. She then lights her broom on fire and proceeds to light the scarecrow's straw arm on fire.

Outraged by the act, the young girl grabs a nearby bucket filled with water and attempts to douse the flame; a portion of the water strikes the evil witch. She begins to melt, 'You cursed little brat, I'm melting. Who would have thought a good little girl like you could destroy my beautiful wickedness.' She thoroughly melts away into the floor. There was a short silence, and then one of the flying monkeys examines the melted cape and begins to clap. A guard observes that the witch is dead, that Dorothy had killed her. Dorothy tries to explain and then the most amazing thing happens. The same palace guard says 'hale to Dorothy, the wicked witch is dead.' They too were now free from her wickedness they did not truly admire. She requests her broom and they give it to her.

"You see," Tyler began, "The witch had been evil so long the blood of her shared humanity was virtually nonexistent. She could no longer feel the deep ties with the rest of life. Her emotional being was so porous the water of goodness dissolved what little bonds she had left in her body, and she quickly disintegrated. Stone, Dorothy represents the noble people in society: the school teacher, the doctor, the librarian who wish for the greater good to prevail. You remember the Munchkins?" He acknowledged that he did. "They are the everyday people; mayors, bakers, flower shop owners, the kids. They're not stupid but are just in the dark about the winds that seem to blow them around from time to time. The flying monkeys are the hard working doing often the dirty work in the world: garbage collection, digging in the ground. And the palace guards are the millions of workers that at times support forces who in truth they'd rather not."

They were now flying back towards the light. The sky was getting that clear-day color of blue. The sun was warm and he could feel that warmth now for some reason. "Stone, our world needs those with the spirit of Dorothy to awaken. To be indignant to the wicked ones first attack on those with little power. And through the ancient instinct to react to insults to what is good and fair, act and throw water on the wicked ones among us, releasing the goodness of their indignant and suddenly awakened souls. Because if a sense of fairness for those first in line fails to move them, then it will just be a matter of time before failure to do so will ultimately lead to their demise as well. If the Dorothy's of the world will just emerge and throw the water of their indignation on the evil ones, they too will melt. And they will find that the munchkins, the flying monkeys, and the palace guards were actually with them all along!"

They settled down onto a gravel road, on either side there were fields of soybeans. She was pointing at the fields. "These are DK Corporations genetically engineered soybean plants with seed designed to be resistant to their weed control product Cleanse. I know you are aware of that Stone, but did you know this? Some say that they've been able in some places, like here, to make it illegal for any of their soybean plants to be growing on a farm which they don't have a contract with? That means farmers with fields of soybeans grown by using their own seed can be held legally liable for soybean plants growing on their land whose seed simply drifts onto their fields. I can't even tell you if that's entirely true. But if it is it would be an abomination of logic. And supposedly some judges are finding in DK's favor in these cases. That would be tyranny."

Tyler stepped closer to him, "The foundation of any nation's stability is based on the health and integrity of the soils and water from which the food supply comes. Silently, Stone, America and many other nations around the world have been losing this foundation. This would not happen if the people understood what has been quietly being done to them. Change is desperately needed to install a government to power that grasps the destructiveness of the current industrial agriculture system and associated issues with fossil fuel burning. If done, perhaps civilization may still have a chance."

"Here is the key: the super wealthy could not exist without their lieutenants doing their bidding, propping them up and protecting them. Some of the ultra rich are the ultimate culprits in our dire planetary situation. But just like the guards, with their tall bushy hats, protecting the wicked witch of the west, their empires would crumble without their small army of protectors. They depend on the lieutenants desire to obtain their status, or nearly so, to live in their world of abundance."

Her face became indignant, "Their true grip on society though is as imaginary as that of the border collie over the sheep it herds. It's all what they perceive to be true. You, and millions like you, hold the key to the future on this planet. Not those kids in the video, they can protest until they have no voice left. The real power lies with people like you; you wear the true ruby slippers. It's what you decide is true and how you respond that will ultimately matter."

She stood there staring at him a little bit longer - a little bit longer - and then, at last, she asked ... "So tell me, Stone, what do you believe?"

She had one more visceral observation to make, "I guess we'll see if you live up to your moniker or not, Mr. Stone."

He heard the thud of his iPod hit the floor and he awoke. For a moment he was disoriented. He looked to the floor and muttered, "Oh shit, have I broken this thing?" It had a sturdy cover and the screen moved properly with a quick check. He got up and moved around a little feeling that he needed to stretch his legs. The light just outside seemed to keep moving from dark to red. He walked to the window so he could see more clearly. Above and to the right he could see the sign as it changed its colors. He said the words just barely detectable, "The Changing Hearts Bed and Breakfast." He needed to get some sleep.

(the next morning)

"Sleepy head," Gezana said it again getting her mouth a little closer to his ear, "sleepy head."

"Uhh, huh, whaat?" Stone squeezed his eyes, then rubbed them slightly. He looked up and could see Gezana looking at him. She was already mostly dressed. "What time is it?" he was looking for his phone.

259

"About a quarter to eight. I've already been up drinking coffee with Tyler. She's been here since six getting breakfast ready. We need to get a bite then on the road."

He quickly showered and dressed and was sitting ready to eat by shortly after eight. "Good morning, you must have gotten off to some really good dream land." Tyler said as he sat down to the plate of scrambled eggs, grilled veggies, whole wheat bread, and some drink that looked mostly like grapefruit juice.

Stone shook his head, "Yeah, I guess I fell asleep out here. I dropped my iPod on the floor when I woke up. I think I had been dreaming a lot. Pretty strange, I think I went for a ride on a broom," he looked at Tyler, he remembered she was a part of the dream. Maybe he should keep his mouth shut on this … letting Gezana know he'd been dreaming and Tyler was the big player in it probably wouldn't go over very well. "I don't remember what it was all about now." He didn't even want to speculate.

"Must not have been too important," Gezana observed.

"I guess not," Stone finished.

The car was loaded and they were ready to leave. Tyler handed a copy of *The Kingdom of Good* by W.W. Sherman to Stone, "Please take this with you. We can only hope you decide to join us!" Tyler's voice was earnest. Stone thanked her.

"Oh Stone, I'd really like to know, if you don't mind of course, just my curious side I guess, what name did you give up to be called Stone?"

Gezana looked at him wondering what he'd say; he'd rarely ever tell anyone.

He smiled, "Paul, my real name is Paul." Tyler nodded and thanked him for revealing it.

They turned out of the parking lot heading east and in a moment they past the sign denoting the city limit line of Damascus.

Chapter Twenty

(Dallas: Frank, Black Jack, Tex; early April. 2014)

The tall man looked out from the top floor of his fifty story office building. It was a bright-sunny morning. His still thick, but slightly graying collar-length hair was slicked back and behind his ears. His shirt bulged from the muscles he'd been born with and sculpted in his football playing years. A large ring on his left index finger, a national championship ring from his playing days at Oklahoma, was always there for all to see.

He'd just finished the commute from his home near White Rock Lake in his brand new black Weismann coupe from Germany. Tex had picked out every possible option available to him so it was muscled and tough and it said power in every way.

An email was sent to him several weeks earlier with the Moab Manifesto video clip attached. It had really irritated him and he'd made the decision quickly that the "little fucks" who did all the talking needed to be illuminated. He'd passed the word along to Frank Hicks who had a history of taking care of the dirty work for him. He needed several layers of insulation on such matters. Frank had contacted Black Jack and was to get a plan together. They were meeting with Tex this morning to go over the details.

"They're here," his personal secretary informed him.

"Okay, send them in." Tex responded.

The room was a testament to Tex's football and hunting passions: a picture with a legendary Dallas football coach was prominent in a cabinet full of such pictures. In one corner was the trophy water buffalo from South Africa he'd killed using a bow and arrow. It was a lengthy story, Frank and Black Jack had both heard it.

"Want a drink?" Tex asked, heading to make one for himself.

"Already had my Bloody Mary for the morning," Black Jack responded.

"How are the permits for the loads heading to Alberta coming?" Tex then asked.

"We've got 'em. Montana's a little slow. The first load will be heading out next Tuesday."

Tex shook his head that he understood. "We got all the blue cards and red cards played on that?"

"They've been in the pipeline for some time. We've sent some communiqués recently to make sure everyone stays on message."

"How about the media? We got our dogs lined up there to keep the sheep where we need 'em?"

"Yeah, JUDN has Lickedy interviewing Krautenschugel about every other hour for the next two weeks. That new campaign with Lickedy and Heller, Stellar Americans, that's rolling out real soon too. We'll keep 'em listening." Frank told him.

Tex nodded his head that he understood. He moved his lips a little bit and grabbed a remote control sitting nearby. "There's more of these fucking manifestos coming out. This one's from Sun Valley."

They took some time to watch it fast forwarding when Tex was too pissed off to watch anymore. Then Tex brought up the *Kingdom of Good* website. "Those bastards in England are at it some more. These manifestos direct people to this site. God damned Internet; how do you stop this shit?" Tex's face was getting red. "I guess we need to start scaring these little fucks. Get the message out, they'll stop."

Tex was leaned back in his heavy leather chair, "Give me some details."

Black Jack pushed a single paper across the table. On it was a chemical diagram. Tex studied it for a moment, then raised his eyes towards Black Jack, "How's it work?"

"Similar to glyphosate, we just tweeked it some. It'll freeze up their intercostal nerve system in about 30 seconds. We killed a large sheep in about 3 minutes. The molecules break down real fast. Make it look like food poisoning if they do toxicology on them. We'll add some staphylococcus aureus in the mix to throw the lab people off. They'll just assume that's what got 'em."

Black Jack didn't tell him that they'd been using this chemical on some of his Mexican land to kill the new generation of weeds that had been showing up. Super weeds they'd never seen before.

"Okay, get it done. Make sure you get the word to a few of these other fucks that they'll be next if they don't shut up and go away!"

Frank was nodding his head, "Okay, we all ready have some email addresses. They'll get our slippery little messages pronto once we know we got 'em dead."

"Good." Tex smiled. Then he wanted to show them the latest mount of some tigers he'd shot.

Chapter Twenty-one

(back in San Diego, early April, 2014) (Stone goes for his walk with Gezana)

"How about here?" Gezana said, motioning towards a bench near the ocean's edge. They'd walked for a half mile or so along the Coast Walk already.

"That looks good," Stone responded. To their left a rocky bluff met the ocean and the blue of the Pacific Ocean stretched to the horizon. On either side of the bench were shrubs three to four feet tall. It was a clear day and a small boat could just barely be seen several miles out to sea. There was a car parked nearby but the owner was nowhere to be seen.

Gezana handed Stone one of the chocolate and peanut energy bars he liked. "What a gorgeous day," Gezana fluffed her hair back and took a deep breath.

"82 degrees and fair, just like clockwork around here," Stone smiled.

They both spent some time just staring at the scenery. Several seagulls flew by and they seemed to be checking the two of them out.

Stone had been thinking, "Have you ever gone for a drive and suddenly realize you took a wrong turn a long way back and there's no easy way to cut across to the road you need to be on? Finally you decided you just have to go back the way you came to wherever you missed the junction." He was still looking out to the ocean.

She thought for a while, "Probably but I can't think of it right now though."

Stone stood up and walked down the short dirt path a ways still comfortably close to talk. He turned, "That's where I'm at. I've been working my way on a career path for a long time. I've had those thoughts at times where I questioned what I was doing, but I always thought the science was on my side. You know that I was actually doing the right thing." Gezana's hair was blowing slightly and she just looked at him coaxing him for more. He looked back towards the ocean, "But that's changed. What I do, in the end, is about creating a food supply, and now I think the way we've mostly been doing it for the last 65 years is wrong. Way wrong!"

"I could tell you were working things in your mind since we met Tyler." Gezana said to him.

He sat back down next to her, "Oh, in reality I've been questioning all this since I first heard about the organic approach. You know viscerally it just makes more sense, just working with nature. But when I was in school, and of course I went to a school that got a lot of money from the industrial agriculture sector. The statistics for growing things their way were overpowering, and that's where the good paying careers were. I bought into it."

"That book, and the website, *The Kingdom of Good*, Tyler showed us, pretty clearly lays things out, like a detective story connecting all the dots. I didn't tell you what happened the night we were at Tyler's, after I got up to do some reading. I spent quite a bit of time reviewing *The Kingdom of Good* book and website. At some point I fell asleep, somehow my iPod was just sitting on my lap. So, I had this dream," he shook his head, "most of the time I rarely remember much of anything I dream about, but for some reason this dream seems pretty vivid. I think because it is so closely tied to the information in the *Kingdom of Good*." He laughed thinking Gezana could now handle his revelation, "Guess who was in the dream and in fact who explained everything to me?"

She thought for a moment, "Oh, I don't know, maybe Tyler?"

Stone looked at her with his eyebrows raised, "Good. Yeah, that's right." He chuckled again, "And what's funny she was a witch with a broom."

Gezana looked at him with an 'are you serious' gaze.

"Yes, kinda like Samantha in Bewitched and wiggled her nose too. As I read back through the Kingdom data and graphs I get these little images that shoot through my head. Geez, there's even this part from The Wizard of Oz. I'm not sure how that got in there."

"So what's the big difference between the two ways of agriculture; organic or industrial?" Gezana had studied general business in college. She'd picked up a little on nutrition from her mother who was an avid reader. The notion that they should clean their produce carefully to remove pesticide residue was known to her. But much beyond that simply had never crossed her mind. The blending of physics, chemistry, biology, and ecology would only be slightly understood. The understanding of the vast web of life that worked symbiotically in the soil to support the growth of plants was even more remote for her as it was for many.

Stone moved his head from side to side thinking through an answer, "Well, with organic you don't try to change the natural process. You focus on building the life in your soil and try to make it as diverse and prolific as possible. When you do that, nature's army which is the bacteria, fungi, nematodes, worms, all kinds of little organisms, supply the nutrients needed to the plants and help suppress weed competition."

He was nodding his head even more, "I don't know why it took me so long to figure this out. With industrial agriculture the approach it to go around nature's way and the microbes, and super charge the soil with nitrogen, phosphorus, and potassium. You have to use chemicals to control weeds and pests because you suppressed the biology in the soil, and then all that happens over time is they both get harder and harder to control. And then you have to use more and more toxic chemicals to control them and that gets on the food people eat. And one day, we'll have no way to control them at all. I can just see it. We're heading up against a wall."

"We have to manufacture or mine those elements too and it takes energy to do that. And of course just in that process we're releasing massive amounts of carbon dioxide into the atmosphere and the atmosphere is already full of all the carbon dioxide is should have. With organic, you plant cover crops that draw nitrogen and carbon dioxide from the air. You probably have to add some phosphorus and potassium but with what they call humus they're held and made available to the plants better."

"And we're just trying to feed too many people." He looked at her and his eyes seemed penetrating, "If there were just way fewer people then we'd need way less food and everything else. Pollution of the atmosphere would be less and very likely we wouldn't be overheating the planet."

Gezana shuffled a little as this sort of talk had never come out of her guy before and it was obvious something major had changed in him. "Was it the squid, Stone?" She asked somewhat abruptly.

He stared at her for awhile then he looked out towards the ocean. "My body could have been drug a 1,000 feet below the surface. My bones could be laying down there right now. That voice, that something that was in," he thought about that more. "A part of my mind asking me what I believe, why did it do that, and then why did Tyler ask me that too? Yes, that has affected me. I think you could say I had an epiphany. I'm no longer the same person I was, I see the world differently. I see new ways to deal with problems."

Gezana smiled, thinking to herself; "Do I have a new man?"

Chapter Twenty-two

"Forty-five minutes and twenty-eight seconds," Dave told Joan right after hitting the stop button on his watch. "Pretty good. I think that's about two minutes faster than Wednesday."

Joan had leaned over holding her torso with her hands on her knees. "Just that little extra and I can really feel it in my lungs," she noted. It was late Saturday afternoon and the sun was getting low out above the horizon at the edge of the Pacific Ocean. There were a few high clouds, but for the most part it was a great day.

"I'm going to check the site and see if any more manifestos have been uploaded. What is it now seventy six, a new one will be seventy seven?" Dave queried.

"Ah hah, isn't that great!" Joan was removing her jogging shoes and was headed to the bathroom for a shower.

Looking at the log, Dave saw that there were actually 2 new manifestos, another had come in while they were on their run. The first one was from Glasgow, Scotland he knew of earlier and then a new one from Baghdad. 'What will that one be like?' he thought to himself. He opened the one from Glasgow first. Scenes reminiscent of "Braveheart" scrolled on the screen: highlands covered in heather, moss covered outcroppings, and deep forest-covered valleys; waterfalls, and ocean waves breaking against the rocky shore. Then the sound of a distant drum, and soon the bagpipes became loud. One by one, the fourteen came in and sat on a large boulder, a fire was going in the foreground. The camera passed and each of them in turn said their name: Alastair, Fiona, Barclay, Heather, Boyd, Kirsty, Duncan, Sheena, Padraig, Bonnie, Gavin, Rose, Tavish, and Mackenzie. The drummers and the pipe players fit in behind them.

At the center, one female and one male stepped forward and said their names again. The girls were all dressed in matching purple tartan shirts and navy blue skirts. The men all wore light green kilts and dark green tartan shirts. In a slight Scottish brogue the male said, "my name is Duncan Ferguson." The girl then said her name, "My name is Sheena McCrary."

The crackling of the fire could be heard and the green of the spruce trees seen behind them. Duncan began, "This is our home, Scotland, and our ancestors have lived here for thousands of years. It's a beautiful land and we'd hope it stay so green for thousands of years to come. But we know there is a big question now whether that will happen or not. We believe people are putting that future at risk by all manner of ways, but most

266

important is the polluting of the atmosphere that's causing the warming and changing the dynamics of the world's climate system. All of us here and thousands who've signed the manifesto along with us want the rest of the world to know were behind the movement to save the planet from ourselves. We endorse the Principles of Action for a good and fair future for the world as defined by *The Kingdom of Good*."

Sheena then spoke, "I speak for the mothers of Scotland and the rest of the world. Our babies have always been our most precious responsibility. It has always been our job, more than the men's, to nurture them. I have one daughter who is now three. I have to ask myself 'what sort of world have I brought her in to?' There is an enormous wave of climate instability caused disasters heading for us already, we know that. To date, there is no unified world-wide plan to deal with the root causes of the climate crisis. Because of that we have endorsed as Duncan said The Principles of Action defined by *The Kingdom of Good*. Please join the movement and create your own manifesto. We must act!" The pipes and the drums began again, more scenes of the Scottish landscape.

"Awesome," Dave said, just loud enough that Joan could hear him while finishing drying from her shower.

He felt a slight hunger twang and he could find something in the kitchen for that, he was thinking. The cookie jar was full with the carrot and zucchini cookies Joan had baked up just a few days earlier. He grabbed a couple, a large glass of water, and headed back to the computer. Joan joined him and they started watching the manifesto that had come from Bagdad. It was great and was produced in an Arabic style. Keeping them short and to the point, endorsing the principles of *The Kingdom of Good*, was always included.

Dave was feeling a little odd so he excused himself. "I'm going to get my shower now," he said, as he was removing his jogging shirt. "Take a peek at the one from Scotland. It has a really good look to it." He finished the second cookie and then downed the water, he was thirsty.

Joan could hear the shower running. She was watching the Glasgow Manifesto. All the young people had introduced themselves and the drums and pipes were done, the fire was crackling. Crash, thump, crash, crash. "What was that?" Joan said out loud and to herself. It came from the bathroom. She hurried there to see what had happened. She opened the door, water was spraying almost directly at her. Dave's naked body was sprawled out on the now slippery floor. He was convulsing, he vomited white mucus with hints of red and pink in it. In short order, he lost control of his bowels.

Joan's first impression was of disgust. She overcame it quickly and got the water from the shower turned off. She grabbed nearby towels and cleared the detritus that had ejected already from his body away from him and into a pile. She rolled him over and looked at his eyes and could just barely see the color of his light green iris. Something horrible had happened. She was not a doctor and her first thought was that he'd somehow had a stroke. He was so young for that, though. She leaned his head back and reached in to clear anything that might be blocking his ability to breath. She pulled another towel close, rolled it like a sleeping bag and fitted it under his neck. It would hopefully hold him while she got to the phone and called 911.

"What's his name?" the paramedic asked, getting down next to him.

"Dave," Joan told him.

"Okay, Dave can you hear me?" There was no detectable movement.

"Grip my hand if you can." He felt no response.

They checked his blood pressure it was reading in the hypertensive crisis level 185 over 115. They immediately got an IV going. "We need to get him to the hospital, fast." The paramedic said to his assistant.

Joan was standing just a few feet away; feelings of being scared were now beginning to creep in to her thoughts. "What had happened?"

She followed the ambulance to the hospital, of course not at the speed they traveled. They were heading to Scripps Mercy Hospital. She turned right off of Washington Street onto 5th Avenue; there was a parking lot on the right. Joan ran to follow as closely as possible as her love was being moved inside the building.

"Who are you?" a nurse asked.

"She was at the scene," the paramedic said.

"Is this your husband?" The nursed followed.

"No, he's my boyfriend. We live together."

"Okay, you're going to have to stay right here for now."

Doctors were already hovering over the top of him. They'd been alerted to what the paramedic's thought was a poisoning incident.

The nurse began asking a multitude of questions to Joan: his age, weight, existing medical conditions, any medications he might be on at the moment, any idea of what he might have ingested? She did have an answer for the last one. She remembered that he had a handful of her cookies and a glass of water when he left the room to shower. 'My cookies couldn't have done this?' she was thinking to herself. But she had to tell them of the cookies, because she could not see anything else he'd consumed since they returned from their run.

All they would tell her was that they'd reasonably stabilized him, were checking his blood to determine if they needed to pump his stomach and what sedatives they might give him.

She tried to reach his younger brother, but could only get his answering machine. His dad had passed away several years earlier. There was very little other family. She'd better call Matt.

Matt was spread out in his lounge chair. He'd picked up the HBO *John Adams* series and was about half way through, and he was finding it really well done. The sound of the church bells his phone was tuned to began to sound. It was the buzzing on the table his phone was sitting on that most caught his attention. He could see it was Joan calling. "Miss Labeau, how are you?"

"Matt, did I get you at a good time? Are you tied up?"

"Just watching how our country was founded. It's on pause, so I'm good. What's up?"

"Dave's," she hesitated, "Dave's in the hospital. It's serious, but I'm not sure what's going on."

She went about explaining the last several hours and brought him up to speed.

"They've told me he's critical, but stable. I don't know what that means." There was plenty of tension in her voice.

"His vital signs must be holding at some elevated level, not going up but not coming down either." Joan didn't really know so that was just a guess.

"Your best guess is that it was the cookies, huh?" Matt asked.

"He had those 2 in his hand as he headed to the shower. He was fine before that. I don't know what else it could be. He had that great big bottle of water he'd just filled up. I know he was drinking that too."

They pondered the situation for a few more minutes, but there was nothing more they could figure out. "I'll call or text you when I get anything more," Joan said.

"Okay, keep your head up, Joan." Matt ended with a very serious note to his voice.

(Toxicology lab, Scripps Medical Center; Sunday 1:30 in the morning)

An enlarged image of the material extracted from Dave's stomach and under the view of the electron microscope, was showing in the computer monitor. "Looks like staph to me," Erin said, looking at her lab partner.

Uva scooted over next to her and looked more closely at the screen. He studied it for a while. "Maybe we should look at one more sample, just to make sure." He would always have that faint German accent.

They both studied the new image. "What's this here?" Uva said, pointing at a small patch of puss. Erin redirected the electron microscope so it could get a closer and direct view of the material Uva noted. Visual examination could only tell them so much and even a close up could only tell them general properties. But their experience looking at these things led both of them to question whether this material seemed appropriate to be there. "Let's run a DNA on this." Uva instructed. He made the calls to advance something to that level.

45 minutes passed the results were back. They had to read a spectral graph which noted the various chemical compounds and it stood out to Uva right away. It was a compound that he'd never seen associated with a human specimen. "It's hexavalent chromium, I'm nearly sure. See how it's attached to the fiber. This should not be here. It looks like it was not completely broken down by his liver. We need to send this to CAL/OSHA and get a final on it."

A doctor finally emerged to explain to Joan what the situation was. "I'm Doctor McBray, you are with Mr. Herrick?"

"Yes, my name is Joan Lebeau. He's my boyfriend."

"Okay, good. Well he's stable for the moment. It appears he drank a lot of water about the same time he was eating those cookies and that's probably a very lucky thing. We're not out of the woods yet, but that probably saved him to right now."

Joan's eyes widened and she felt a deep pit in her stomach. The visceral knowledge that he could already be dead hit some deep level in her and froze her momentarily. "He could have died?" she finally asked.

The doctor's face and nodding answered her question."He's still unconscious, how that works through we just don't know. We're sending some toxicology information to the state for some more analysis and we won't have that information back for a few days. We're using the best protocol we have, so information from them is not critical to the care we provide now. But we need to know better what got into his system."

"You'll let me know when you have that?"

"Certainly." The doctor answered.

Joan took a left off of Richmond's onto Pennsylvania Avenue and parked in front of the little white house with green trim. A neighbor's palm indicated the place was kind of tropical. As she walked towards the front door, a woman in the apartment complex next door walked over. "Is everything alright?" She'd seen the ambulance the night before and had occasionally interacted with Joan.

"He's stable." She was moving her head with a look of despair and 'that's all I know.'

"He's sure a nice young man." The neighbor lady said with sincerity in her voice.

The police had put yellow tape around the house as it was a crime scene. The front door was open and Joan could see at least one person inside. "Hello," she called, not wanting to pass over the tape.

A person in a San Diego Police Department uniform met her at the door. "Can I help you?"

"Actually, this is my house. It is my boyfriend that got sick last night. When will I be able to come back and stay here? I need to get a shower."

"We're just about done. You need to talk to Detective Rogers though before you try to do anything here."

"Is he close?" Joan asked.

"I'll give him a call. I think he was intending to get here this morning."

Momentarily she learned that Detective Rogers would be there in a half hour or so.

Joan decided to just go over and sit in the shade of the palm tree. Sitting down, she realized just how exhausted she was. She'd been up all night, maybe she dozed off a little waiting for the doctor. 'God, what was she going to do?'

Sitting in a car just a few hundred feet away, a man with binoculars studied Joan. The programmed singing of Lady Gaga suddenly sounded in her purse as her mobile was being texted. She did not recognize the caller's identification. Maybe it was the hospital? There were just a few words on the front of her screen, she had to open the messages file to get the whole text. '*Joan Lebeau, you are fucking with the wrong people, end all of your eco activities immediately or you'll be next. Other tactics will not be so pleasant!!!*'

Joan shook her head, 'What had she just read?' She scanned back through it. 'God, who sent this?' she was thinking. She stood up and walked over to her car. As she was walking she heard a little beep from her phone and she looked at the cover. The message she'd just read was disintegrating and then it was gone. She opened the message file again and it was not there. 'How could...who, who did this?' she was saying just barely audible.

'I thought we were just on a watch list. They did this.' Joan was thinking to herself. It suddenly made sense; they knew they were on some list by people that didn't like what they were up to. But trying to kill them never was discussed. 'Jesus!'

A car pulled up, a lean man got out. He was casually dressed looking as though he might be headed to the golf course. He slipped a cap on, San Diego PD.

"Detective Rogers?" Joan asked, walking away from the shade of the palm tree.

271

"That's right," he answered, briskly.

"My name is Joan Lebeau. You are here on the Dave Herrick case, right?"

He opened the file under his arm. It noted a girlfriend named Joan. "Yes, I need to take a look around. You mind answering a few questions?"

She was of course receptive and helpful. "The jar of cookies went over to the lab earlier this morning and it looks like that's the source of the problem. There was a lot of staph in them."

"What's that?" Joan asked.

"Staphylococcus aureus. It's very common to food poisoning and it looks like something in the ingredients was old."

Joan was shaking her head. She was running everything she'd used through her mind: the sugar, flour, butter, maybe that was it. Huh, but she had another thought go through her mind quickly; the carrots and the zucchini squash were both fresh from the market. There was oil too, and then that old pan she cooked them on. She'd never had any problem with them before though.

Joan was trying to decide if she should say anything to him about the text message she'd just got. Of course, she decided. They had walked out near his car; he was digging for a card so she could call him if needed. "I have one other thing to tell you, I think."

"You think?" he coyly answered.

"Well, I received a strange text message just before you got here. I'd show it to you, but it just disintegrated on my screen."

The detective's eyebrows narrowed, "What was the message?"

"I wish I would have written it down, I'm not sure I know exactly the words, but it was something like "stop what you're–sorry–"fucking" doing, eco activities or you'll be next, and then like - other tactics will be worse, or something."

"Let's get that written down as best you can," he then said. "Have you seen anyone that was out of the ordinary around here, especially when that text came?"

Joan thought for a moment, and then shook her head 'no'. "I can't remember seeing anybody, except the lady next door. She's nice and wanted to know how Dave was."

The detective had seen this before. Usually someone was watching he'd learned, when the text was read, just to make sure it was the right person reading it.

"Do you have any idea why someone would send you that particular note about eco activities?"

She was nodding her head that she might, "Dave and I are environmental activists. We're on a video called the Moab Manifesto where we go

272

over a bunch of grievances we have about how the world is being ruined by bad management, particularly burning coal and oil and natural gas."

"I see." His mouth muscles were moving and his eyes looked about.

"I really don't know what that's about and I can't tell you what you can and can't do. I guess I'll just say be careful."

The ball was back in the Family's court. Would these kids stop their shit? Maybe if they are alive they'd be of more value passing on to the others what had happened.

(Several weeks later on a Skype call to Matt)

"Can you see Dave alright?" Joan asked.

Matt was trying to keep his composure, seeing his friend looking so listless, almost absent.

Dave attempted a wave. Joan had explained she was setting it up so they could do a Skype call with Matt.

"Yes, maybe move the computer a little to the right," she started, "No, it's the other way. I have it backwards in my mind. Yeah, there, that's good."

"Can you see Matt okay?" She then said to Dave. He nodded that he could.

"Hey man," Matt was waving.

"Hey…man," Dave's words were slow and breathy. "I'm here," these were more direct.

"The doctors say he's progressing well, he knows all the letters in the alphabet and the list of words he can make out has been growing every day."

Joan was putting a tough face on the long trajectory of recovery Dave faced. The poisoning had deeply affected his nervous system and the connection to his brain was short circuited. The speech pathologist was truly encouraged, though, with his ability to put words and concepts together. She'd seen others who never really recovered from such a severe compromise of their systems. Joan had been able to get a leave of absence from her job as a liaison to the Green Party. But at some point she'd need to resume those responsibilities.

"He made it back and forth through the walking exercises six times today." Joan told him.

"Regu…lar, spr…in…ter," Dave added, attempting a smile.

She smiled at him, her heart breaking her spirit compromised. "What do we do next?" Joan asked, looking at Matt. He knew of the warning she'd received.

"Well, whoever sent that hasn't been able to stop the Manifesto's from continuing to build on the net. Last I heard there were over two hundred and fifty of them. A Girl Scout troop made one which I saw yesterday. Geez is it cute!"

Right then Dave interjected, "don'...t sto...p." Both of his fists clenched together.

Matt felt a surge of emotion flow through him as his eyes filled with tears. He could feel the defiance of a warrior rising in him. "FUCK THEM!" he suddenly cried out. He then caught himself, hunkered his body down, looking towards the ceiling. "I hope they didn't hear that."

"Look, it's been over a month. What, five weeks, right? Has that detective got any more information on who might have done this?" Matt was tired of waiting.

"They don't know. Whoever did it covers their tracks really well. The lab people said the molecules in the small sample they were able to get had been synthesized by a pretty high tech group. There are evidently only ten or twelve labs around the world with that ability, but there's no way to track which one might have made it." Joan explained.

"I keep asking myself why did someone go after you and Dave? Look how many people have written books, lecture, or are on television talking about the climate crisis. What makes what we did stand out to them?" Matt questioned.

"Eff...ec...tive." Dave wanted to say.

Joan shook her head, "Yes, look how many Manifestos are now being uploaded. We've hit the right nerve. People are getting involved who hadn't known how to before. It's like a drum that keeps beating louder and louder at them."

"Okay, but Manifestos alone don't do anything. They need to be organized and to do that we have to go out with another video. Don't we?" Matt was leading to the plan they'd had for sometime if they could get enough momentum with the Manifestos; a march on all the state capitals and Washington, DC, on Earth Day, 2016.

Joan was looking at Dave. What would be in store for them if they made another video? They knew the threat had to be coming from the people with the entrenched financial positions based on the fossil fuels world. Which ones? They had no idea. But they had certainly touched a highly sensitive nerve with someone.

Dave stared at both of them and again he said, "don' t, sto...p!"

Chapter Twenty-three

(Tyler sends Stone information on Dave, mid May, 2014)

"I heard from Tyler today," Gezana said, sitting across from Stone at their patio dining table.

"What's up with her?" Stone was working a clam shell apart and seemed mostly occupied doing that.

"There's some guy who lives around here, I think she said his name is Dave, he's connected with the *Kingdom of Good* movement?" Her voice trailing as a question.

"Okay, she probably means Dave. What was it? Herron or something like that?"

"She's sending you an email about him. I guess he was poisoned a month ago or so."

Stone stopped what he was doing and looked more attentively towards her, "poisoned?" She nodded her head yes.

'What the hell could that be about?' he thought to himself. Then it dawned on him, 'the bastards must have actually done something. Evidently it was more than just a watch list they were on.'

Stone sat down to his computer, "Tyler, Tyler, okay, there you are." He scanned through her message. She was letting him know that she had learned through the KOG connections that Dave Herrick had been poisoned. He had lived through it, but was impaired. His long term prognosis was not known. They had been told that few people seem to come back very well from such destructive episodes. She also mentioned to him of the texted message threatening Joan to stop with her eco activities or there would be consequences. And, a final lab report by the State of California had been prepared and it had a lot of technical information in it on the chemical compounds from Dave's assay. There was one notation she had found particularly intriguing-interesting: the report noted that the chemical structures of what was considered the true culprits in Daves' severe and rapid response, were similar to those found in agricultural chemicals. She was hoping he'd take a look and see if he might have any idea from where they might have originated.

What Stone saw very quickly made him quite upset: the base chain of the molecule had amino acids connecting in ways only his team had succeeded in uniting. It'd taken three years of research and significant trial and error in the lab to get the enzyme structure just right to catalyze the reaction. Only his people knew about that. Even the most rudimentary parts of the protocol couldn't be found on the internet. There was only one person through which that information could have gotten out and he was pretty sure who that might be.

(At home with Gezana)

Gezana was particularly aroused by his touch this night. He wondered at times about her cycles and how that might affect her responding to love making. For the moment it didn't matter, but attending to her did. A half hour later, as usual, he left the bedroom to other matters.

He cleared his goggles, holding on slightly to the pool edge with his feet. A cascade of water fell just to his side. He wanted to make four more laps before calling it a night.

Having met his goal, he slipped from the pool and pulled a heavy towel around him. Stone's flip flops were nearby which was good as he wasn't keen on walking through the house barefooted. It had occurred to him that he might have a picture in his office from the trip to Socorro Island with the image of the same guy he saw at Dave's lecture and the one on glyphosate. He could remember the guy circling around when Black Jack was talking to him on the fishing boat. He'd snapped off a few pictures then and it just seemed like he'd seen that guy in one of the shots. "There it is, Socorro 2013." There were thirty or so images to pan through and on about the seventh one he stopped. That was the guy, such a distinctive nose, the Roman nose he'd heard it called.

Stone was running everything through his mind. Black Jack would be one of only three people he could think of who would have the knowledge of that chemical structure and the codes to get through the layers of security to where it was stored. Kurt was dead, that left just himself and Black Jack. Black Jack wouldn't know how to synthesize the molecule without help from lab technicians but with the information from that super secured file certain select chemists from around the world certainly could. He checked the login data to see if anyone might have left some cookies letting him know who it was and when they were in. But there was no listing. Stone knew it was possible though to slip into that file and cover your tracks going out. He was betting Black Jack knew about that. He could be extremely meticulous when necessary.

The next morning while shaving, Stone was continuing to process in his head why Black Jack would be involved in trying to poison Dave. It occurred to him that Kurt would mention conversations he would have with Black Jack about the Ecos and the need to keep them corralled. And there was that book he'd seen in Kurt's office at various times. The one that said American Prosperity; and it had the symbol with the human eye. Stone had a vague memory of seeing that logo too, when he'd been going over some data with Kurt while Kurt's Chrysalis file was open on his computer. He'd told Stone that one day the information in that book would be revealed to him, but at that time he wasn't ready.

Through the years, Stone had heard the rumor about a group of families that supposedly had intertwined wealth going back for hundreds of years, clear to about the 1400s, supposedly. People speculated that they actually control the deep levers of power in the American economy and elsewhere around the world, but particularly in the United States. But he knew of no credible proof of some master conspiracy. He didn't like conspiracy theories as they're almost always figments of people's imaginations, he felt. A little voice inside his head, though, was telling him to find out what was in that book as it might explain what Black Jack was up to.

(Two days later at Stones' office, late May, 2014)

"Krastle Enterprises," a young woman answered the phone. She was in charge of directing calls to the nine executives that ran the company.

"This is Stone Fischer at NGB labs. Could you put me through to Ted Rosser please?" She had a list of people she could pass through directly. Anyone not on the list required greater screening.

She saw Stone's name, "Sure, just one moment please."

Ted was selected by the Krastle Board to be the interim CEO until they could interview others and make a decision to stay with him or choose someone else. He'd been with Krastle for eighteen years and knew the operations extensively, including the Biotech startup that Stone directed.

"Stone?" Ted was direct and chose to use words very sparingly. There was no need for asking why he called as that was up to Stone to say.

Stone was aware of this style and was not taken back by it. He was prepared to answer directly. "I needed to get back to you on the technology transfer protocol the government is requiring on CC2. It's going to take a little while, maybe two months, their lab is backed up I'm told."

"How does that affect roll out?" Ted then asked.

"Well, we'll have field trials the rest of this year. If all goes well we should still be on for 2015 as we'd planned." There was more technical information the two worked through, several minutes passed.

"I need to access Kurt's Chrysalis file to get some data from the CC1 trials he had done with some comparisons with DK's work. I'll need the username." Stone explained very matter of factly. Kurt kept his own files on the work that Stone's group did. He organized things the way he liked it.

Ted knew of Chrysalis, but had done virtually no work on it since that had been Kurt's baby. He had no reason to question if Stone should have access.

"Hold on." He actually had to get the codes from Denise, the gal who originally answered the phone. She had been with Kurt a long time too and held certain responsibilities, like maintaining codes and usernames.

"Klondike," Ted said. He then spelled it so there would be no mistake.

Stone felt a little tingle; the first step in his detective work had gone off without a problem.

He had things to attend to during the day, and doing something that could be considered espionage within his own company didn't sit well. Things might be tracked back to this computer too so it was just better to do it elsewhere.

Gezana was off with her friends, so with a light drink in hand he headed to his computer to see if he could access Chrysalis. Stone had kept Kurt in on all the work that had gone on. All the files were kept separate from the rest of the Krastle Enterprise business.

Stone typed everything in and hit Enter. Very quickly he was able to get to the main page. He knew the routing protocol to get to the main file of information he was after. From there, he'd just have to enter the username, and he'd be in.

"Dike …" he muttered the letters as he typed the last four in. "Enter," up came a different and very Old World looking cover page.

The title, **American Prosperity**, was written boldly across the top. There was a brief introductory paragraph that explained the establishment of the Committee for Economic Development (CED) dating to 1942 and a few words about its mission. The American Farm Bureau and US Chamber of Commerce were also listed and noted as being affiliates. Stone wasn't quite sure what they represented. He was thinking he might need to look them up. The five sectors of the North American Economy: Agriculture, Manufacturing, Service, Investment and Banking and Tourism were listed below the title: a user could click on any of the sectors to get more information.

Stone chose agriculture and three pages of names appeared. He started going down through them; every seventh or eighth name was familiar. Some he actually could associate with agriculture, others he thought were a part of a different industry. "Hmm." He opened the other branches. It was more difficult to find names he knew and he just assumed they must be important in those sectors.

There were more buttons that broke the divisions down even further. In agriculture for example there was petroleum, seed, fertilizer, transportation, packaging, legal and many more. A diagram showed how these cross connected to the other sectors. Though the diagram was meant to be general, it still illustrated how interconnected in a web of activity all the sectors were. You could click on each of the subsector names and get more information about their current status. There was a link to Boards of Directors and he thought that might be interesting. There he found virtually all the big name corporations in America and the names of people who sat on the various boards. There were lines that connected these names back to other corporations that these individuals were associated with. The big picture of the flock was starting to take hold in Stone's mind. It occurred to him that it might be good to take some notes as getting back into this file more than once might be problematic.

He turned to another page where he found topic statements that discussed the dynamics of the world economy and trends. The third topic down was just "Climate." He opened it. His eyes widened. It looked quite a bit like the content on the *Kingdom of Good* page and he would learn eventually there was a good reason for that. "Why is this being presented this way?" he was wondering. The case was laid out well as it followed the science as he knew it. The introduction and growth of carbon dioxide in the atmosphere even the 350 ppm safe level was noted. Removal of forests, expansion of tilled farm land, rising average temperature explained with the carbon dioxide molecule and others, increased energy in the system spreading changing weather dynamics, ocean acidification, glaciers disappearing, oceans gathering heat which will provide more energy for even more severe storms, species extinctions…it went on and on. They went out of their way to note near the end that the ideal population of the Earth should be between one and two billion.

The nitrogen problem. 'Amazing,' Stone was thinking, 'they're even explaining this.' Just like he had learned from *The Kingdom of Good* website, the discovery of how to manufacture new nitrogen was discussed. All the mounting evidence about the downsides of its use was also explained. The need to change to a sustainable agriculture was briefly detailed. Topsoil degradation and human health impacts were noted. They even went to the length to say its discovery and use is at the very center of the climate crisis. But they also said there was time and engineering methods to employ to overcome this problem.

There were all sorts of graphs to help explain everything: Pictures of the methane hydrates beginning to breakdown all around the world with the potential to release vast amounts of the incredibly powerful methane molecule, was shown. A temperature rise threshold of 6 degrees Celsius above the IPCC baseline average was highlighted. It was noted for the need to stop the rise to between 3 and 4 degrees Celsius would be absolutely required, but doable. The two or three years directly on either side of

2060, in particular, were highlighted as having a high statistical chance for severe consequences to begin on a business as usual trajectory. 2040 was noted as the statistical date at which their scientists believe any conceivable chance for averting catastrophic climate related disasters could be averted on a business as usual trajectory. But that was without the massive geo-engineering intervention methods the Family was planning.

The problems with methane use in industrial agriculture was even explained. The explanation touched briefly on the pollution created in the manufacture of synthetic nitrogen, and the fact that natural gas extraction and use (also known as fracking) was not "less" but is at least equal to oil in the release of carbon dioxide and damage in the long term to the environment. It went on and expanded on how the synthetic nitrogen actually degrades the soil and leads to its blowing or washing away and creating problems further along such as the dead zones in the oceans around the world. They went on to note that new research was showing how the entire existing industrial agriculture system "will" need to be changed eventually to a biological-sustainable system. Not if, but when.

The planetary boundary concept was explained which were limits science was warning human activity had to work within. There were even the warnings dating to the early 90s from the world's top scientists that should things not change, we were heading towards a catastrophic future. He was amazed at how clearly a no-holds-barred way the information was presented. 'But why, what was all this for? Why would someone associated with Kurt and Blackjack be presenting this information this way?'

There was one last graph which when understood explained this person's intentions. It was showing the curve for carbon dioxide removal from the atmosphere. On the vertical line the carbon dioxide concentrations starting at the 1990 level which was about 355 ppm was the starting point and the numbers extended up from there, all the way to 600 ppm. The horizontal axis was shown in years with 1990 being the first year. There were two lines: one showed the desired quick transition back to the 350 range by the year 2050 and the other allowed the ppm to build to around 550 or 600 and then fall very rapidly back to the 350 range by around the year 2100 or a little before. The area in between was shaded so it stood out.

He turned to a new page where there were diagrams for three yet to be delivered technologies shown. The first was fusion nuclear power. In great detail it illustrated the design and workings of a fusion power plant from which the promise of producing liquid hydrogen fuel for the existing fleet of cars, trucks, construction equipment of all type, and aerospace was explained. It went on to detail how fusion power could use the spent nuclear material from the fission age or other sources to get the Deuterium/Tritium pellets needed for the reaction. They could produce the equivalent of 500,000 barrels of oil in the form of hydrogen, 15 gigawatts of electricity, and 2,000 acre feet of potable water in one day and still be carbon neutral. It would have an 'energy in to energy out ratio of 1 to 50', and could be on line by 2025. The plants would be so safe they could be located at the center of cities.

The second diagram was of an artificial photosynthesis machine. Its design would filter the atmosphere of carbon dioxide and sequester it. It was called a convection tower and it stood about a thousand feet tall and was about three hundred and fifty feet wide at the top where the air would be drawn into it. This tower would not only scrub the atmosphere of the un-wanted carbon dioxide. It would also generate vast amounts of electricity.

These two major technological breakthroughs, the statement noted, would generate the massive power needed later in the century by the next generations of people to return the Earth's carbon balance.

And the third seemed out of place because of its seemingly low tech approach. It was an eco approach, elegant and so full of common sense. It was simply titled The Soil. Quickly Stone realized this information was matching up with his new understanding of how soil actually works that he'd acquired from the *Kingdom of Good* material and from Tyler. It was all about how the plant life and soil microorganisms have a profound propensity for sequestering carbon from the atmosphere. It took him about five minutes to read through, but what he came away with was that cutting edge soil scientists, working with the biology in the soil, could sequester up to 25, and they projected 50 in a few years, tons of carbon dioxide per acre per year. They noted that if somewhere around 10 to 12 percent of the world's agricultural lands were biologically enhanced with the level of microorganisms in their test areas, then the current level of manmade emissions could be sequestered each year. Drawing down the legacy load of 80 billion tons of carbon dioxide already in the atmosphere would take a larger area.

A picture of herds of animals being moved about was also shown. The author noted how the herding of animals around the world, done correctly, would also be a strategy for sequestering carbon dioxide. It was a quick read and in a few minutes Stone understood this principle as well. It all seemed to be leading to something very positive and a way forward from this crisis Stone now believed was true.

But this is when the message turned a different color: dark? Stone likened it to watching someone you know get beat up, or worse, but you feel like you can do nothing or you will have the same fate. The person or persons responsible for putting together this information then noted the following:

'A world filled with nine or ten billion people is not desirable even if it is sustainable. A world of from one to two billion is much more desirable, there would be so much more room and comfort for each person. A strategy to attain this population level should be pursued.'

A list of the remarkable technological advancements especially in robotics was shown. It pictured a world in the near future where humans were truly "god-like" with just a few workers and then armadas of machines that took care of them. The question was how do you get from nine or ten billion down to the desired one or two billion?

Controlled climate chaos seemed to be the author's answer. The basic message was: don't respond too quickly but rather allow a certain amount of chaos to occur and populations would then naturally reduce. The author was quick to point out that the unknowns of how far the system could be pushed before the physics of tipping points might be passed was something to keep in mind.

The mystery visionary went on as he observed that there was no coordinated conspiracy leading the world down the road as it is. No not really. It was just human motivations to seek wealth and power that like some invisible hand was molding our country and our civilization worldwide in the current dysfunctional way. He noted that the original goals of the CED in the United States had been like the little ball that gets a bigger snowball going.

The top 1% and the following approximate 19% of the world's existing population, it explained, would soon control enough of the overall money supply and assets over the economy that the flow of money or wealth to the rest would just naturally slow to almost nothing. Then those people would quickly stop having families as they could not support them. Robots would soon take virtually all of the niches of work the working class has depended on and this would hasten their removal.

Hedge funds managing the money of many high net worth clients were busy buying up farmland in the United States and elsewhere around the world. In fifteen or twenty more years they'd own nearly all of it. The top 20% could then feed themselves as things became tight. Militias that already guarded the top 1% would need to be expanded. Fighting with the 'Eighters' (Stone assumed that to be the name for the 80% that is to be purged) would certainly occur and the elites just needed to be ready for that.

Control of many of the small countries and their governments was already happening systematically. The mystery author went on to reason that the militaries would fall in behind those that controlled the money as it would all just happen organically. Stone found that analogous word to be an odd selection, but he understood what the author meant. He concluded by just noting the process 'just needs fifteen or twenty more years to coalesce.' The architect of the Families ascent conceded that they were betting on how far they could push the ecological system, but to attain the ends they desired they needed to.

The article ended there. It left Stone bewildered and hanging. His mind began to race with questions. And then he noticed that there was a separate file with the name *Stones to Bread* on it. An attached note indicated that this was never to see the light of day with anyone anywhere. It noted that the author had been silenced. Stone turned to page one. There he found an itemization of steps the author, a Dr. W. W. Sherman, had listed that was leading to what he saw as the breakdown of our civilization. Stone knew of this Dr. Sherman of course, but couldn't remember any lecture titled as this one. Stone knew Dr. Sherman had suddenly died in 2010 and now he knew he'd been silenced.

Dr. Sherman had prepared a step-by-step outline of how our civilization had made the biggest blunder of all time which had many follow on effects that have rippled through the vast economy and was now threatening to destroy us. Seeing how long the list was and knowing he would not have another good chance to review it, Stone looked for some more paper so he could take even more notes. He began to read:

- The concept of the *Kingdom of Good* is simple: hold in the highest respect, esteem, and reverence all that is; all of nature which includes all other people, and all those yet to emerge. Direct your life's activities within this simple paradigm and you will exist within "the way" and a sustainable civilization can be attained. But as a civilization, worldwide, this is not occurring!
- Human activities for the last 10,000 years have been releasing more and more stored carbon from the soil and plant material into the atmosphere and the oceans. The amount of carbon on the planet has not significantly changed; it is where it's located that has changed: there are normally balanced relative amounts in the soil, air, or water; and that matters greatly. Because of the new imbalance the planets habitability is now in jeopardy.

- Human awareness of the true workings of, and our place in nature; our collective level of consciousness…is at the nexus of the problem. Too many in power consider the physics of our world as mechanistic; part by part like an automobile. They erroneously don't recognize the quantum reality we are embedded in. Our actions are often similar to throwing rocks into our most advanced computers thinking this can be done with positive effects.
- Almost unbelievably it is the erroneous and recent course change of our agricultural system based upon the fundamentally incorrect premise that our food supply can be produced sustainably using industrially synthesized nitrogen as currently practiced. This is a fundamental misunderstanding of nature; it leads to destroying the biological life in the soil that is the true foundation of our civilization. If we do not change this course we will perish.
- The historical most limiting factor for plant growth and thereby animals lost seasonally is nitrogen. Before the beginning of the 20th century humanity had not figured out how to manufacture new nitrogen; though some additional sequestration using certain legume plants had been discovered. Though it makes up about 78% of our atmosphere, nitrogen is very tightly molecularly bound and does not interact with other elements easily. Nature trickles this element into the environment through lightning and bacteria that sequester it where it becomes available to plants. By the late 19th century human population was maximizing the use of the naturally created nitrogen, this was seen as limiting the human enterprise. This led to the search and desire to find a way to create new nitrogen.
- This was achieved by Fritz Haber in 1909, scaled up by Carl Bosch in 1917 and began to be used by the Germans to produce more food in the 1920s. It actually assisted in feeding their populations during the two wars. It was also used to make bombs for the world wars. World War II slows its economic dispersal to other nations around the world. This changes quickly after the end of the Second World War.
- Directly following World War II the use of synthetic nitrogen from the Haber-Bosch process spreads quickly around the world, and in particular to the United States. The understandings of the biological processes of the soil are very poorly understood at this time. So the new process that has

dramatic initial success overwhelms the organic or biological process. With this new technology which can be implemented with less labor certain business people conspire to move millions of Americans, and others around the world, off the land and into the big cities for work in the expanding factories and where their extra numbers assist to keep wages low. This leads to great wealth for a few.

- Millions of acres of existing and new land are converted to the new process of spraying synthetic nitrogen on plowed land. Again, as currently practiced this is the single worst cultural activity humanity has ever developed; though certainly well disguised for a number of years in what seemed to be a great success. Science was ill prepared for this avalanche of new technology, which on the surface seemed such a wonder. We did not broadly understand that the "biology" in the soil; the bacteria, fungi, nematodes, micro arthropods, and protozoa actually were the engines of fertility. Or that the outright killing or repression of their natural activities would degrade the environment and our civilization eventually. Spraying the soil with the synthetic nitrogen over stimulates certain species of bacteria that grow rapidly in number then go about consuming the stored soil carbon that is the food source for all the other micro organisms which ultimately leads to the soils destruction. The easily obtained synthetic nitrogen also causes the plants that usually work to provide exudates (carbon molecules, food) to the soil biology, to slow in this process leading to the soil biology's reduction in function. The soils destruction has many consequences including loss of fertility and ability to hold water and resistance to erosion. Excessive synthetic nitrogen flows into water ways and ground water and pollutes and kills. Some of the excess nitrogen creates polluting smog and worst of all it binds with oxygen forming nitrous oxides that drift into the atmosphere becoming green house gases that are 20 to 300 times more potent than carbon dioxide. This obviously can only go on a short time before disaster is caused.

- In 2010, when I am writing this, over half of the people alive would not exist if it were not for this process. Please stop and consider that intently; an industrial process that is destroying the habitability of the planet is also the source for providing the food supply for about half of our population! This, of course, is not sustainable. We are dependent upon something that if we continue to use it will eventually destroy our climate and us.

- Over time as the soils ecosystems through degradation lose their ability to control weeds; mutant super weeds evolve and have come along. This led the biotech industry to invent herbicides to combat the weeds. The most well-known herbicide is *Cleanse,* with its active ingredient glyphosate.

- When it was developed in the 1980s we were told it had no effect on human beings. It is known now that is not true. It kills or damages much of the good bacteria we have in our bodies systems, this leads to sickness and disease in people.

- Eventually more and more of the herbicides, insecticides, pesticides, etc., must be used to control the weeds. This causes problems of potentially killing the cash crop (corn, wheat, soy, etc.).

- The original true great wealth of the United States was the vast and fertile soils. Some say over half of these soils have now washed into the oceans. Toxic loads of nitrogen and other chemicals create dead-zones where our great rivers meet the oceans.

- As mentioned briefly, much of the synthesized nitrogen is "not" incorporated in plant material and becomes chemically bound to oxygen, creating nitrous oxide, a greenhouse gas, which enters the atmosphere and contributes greatly to warming.

- This is when genetic engineering enters the process. The primary use of this gene insertion technology is to provide the cash crops with the ability to withstand the heavy dosages of herbicides (primarily Cleanse). This gene insertion technology which creates the genetically modified seeds, was speedily rushed through the United States governments FDA approval process against the will of many of the government scientists. Five administrations, including the new Obama administration, have given a quick green light to these GM crops being widely grown in the US. Europe has for the most part rejected the introduction of GM food. It is again sold to the public as safe; serious scientists say it is not safe.

- Stocking the supposed inexpensive food stuffs of the tens of thousands of chain grocery stores around the United States (and elsewhere in the world) is part of the Committee for Economic Developments original business model.

- Conventional (synthetic chemical industrial agriculture) makes up about 99% of the US food production system. The Organic system (where synthetic nitrogen use is not allowed) makes up about 1%.

- Growing plants to be used for synthetic fuels for automobiles is a massive contributing factor to the problems with synthetic nitrogen use. More land is cleared, loading the atmosphere with carbon. Indigenous people all around the world are being forced off their land to make room for this new use of the land. Without land to feed themselves from they often starve to death. Some move to the slums of the cities and eke out a miserable existence; forced there by those living outside The *Kingdom of Good.*

- The Pharmaceutical and Insurance industries profit from a population that is not as healthy as possible. Moving to a agricultural system that creates truly healthy food would create healthy people that would not need the current level of health care and the associated costs. The status quo will resist this logic.

- A proven way exists to withdraw the dangerous levels of carbon dioxide out of the atmosphere and store it in the soil as soil carbon; it is called regenerative carbon farming and ranching. Cover crops and crop rotation works by farmers planting specific plant species that work the best for drawing carbon out of the atmosphere. The plants then secrete exudates of sugars to the soil that the soil biology feed on. They in turn grow in numbers and do as their programming tells them to do; build healthy soil. The same goes for ranching where herds of animals are properly used to graze the land to the correct levels, in the process their droppings and urine enrich the soil with food for the soil biology which in turn continue to build the soil. This healthy soil then works to store more and more carbon, thereby removing it from the atmosphere where it is causing the heating of the planet.

- Of course for this to be done millions of people will need to move back to the farms from the cities. This all goes against the current status quo's business model and the wealth that is a part and anticipated from it.

- There is a large constituency of corporations and people that profit from the status quo to remain. Including the fossil fuels industry that actually produces the initial input of natural gas (methane) that is the fuel source for the Haber-Bosch process.
- We wildly misunderstood the basis of our civilization; our soils. They must be managed ecologically and not chemically. This is the root cause of the climate crisis. If we had remained as organic agriculturalists following ecological wisdom our population would have grown much slower. Perhaps only about three billion would exist today rather than 7.3 billion. And most importantly the consciousness of our civilization would have been required to emerge through a paradigm of ecological wisdom. A return to an organic versus chemical paradigm of agriculture is the single most important cultural change needed by humanity! This will be resisted greatly.
- A massive movement (like that which occurred in the United States when World War II began) must emerge very soon to move millions of people back onto the lands of the United States and around the world so that ecologically sound biological farming can take control of food production. This will create a vastly more secure foundation for our society and a true safety net for millions of people.
- This is the ultimate "Stones to Bread" mistake humanity has made. Our cleverness outpaced our wisdom. Just because you can do something doesn't mean you should. Unfortunately this is where humanity finds itself. There is no other true answer to the climate crisis and the larger picture of the ills of our worldwide civilization. To effectively challenge and defeat the status quo, that will ultimately destroy the planet if it is not removed, will require a revolution of consciousness to a level that values a healthy-verdant world over money. And remember, you cannot eat money. A spark must ignite the movement somewhere, someplace, and very, very soon.
- I will finish by reiterating how I started: The fundamental idea of the *Kingdom of Good* is for an individual to move from the "I" ego-captured consciousness of our evolutionary ascent. To the "we" ego-aware consciousness that allows your spiritual being to emerge. This is where holistic (Holy) thinking dwells. Look to the concepts of the Akashic

Paradigm and Noetic Consciousness. I believe they are pointing towards the same source. This enlightened or awakened version of yourself will then naturally be empathetic to Creation and behave in ways that sustain life on Earth. I believe this was in essence the message delivered by Jesus. This is my 21st Century interpretation of that message.

Dr. W. W. Sherman

Stone clicked to the last page. Nothing was there, but then as he was still staring at the screen suddenly all the images and text were gone. It evidently had been programmed to self destruct once the intended viewer had reached the last page. But Kurt had died shortly after it was emailed out. Black Jack was responsible for its distribution to Kurt's computer and in the turmoil of the events at Socorro Island, Stone imagined, it must have simply slipped his mind to make sure the email was eliminated.

His hand holding the mouse dropped to his knee, Stone sat back in his chair. 'That was a lot to take in,' was his first thought. His arm was tired from taking notes. It was a good thing he'd been doing that, now that he understood it would be destroyed once he was done. The reading and writing had tired him out and he slipped back into bed next to Gezana.

~~~~~

Stone slept hard and at four he woke up. Gezana was still sleeping soundly, so he quietly moved out of the bedroom. An ice cube dropped into a whiskey glass and he poured a particularly stiff one. Sitting near the spa, he stared into the small fire in the raised hearth powered by natural gas. The connection did occur to him. Thoughts were rolling through his head: if what he'd just read was real and considering the way he learned of it, how could it be otherwise? There was a conspiracy of "*do nothing*" at least by a few but very powerful people. Do nothing now. They wanted more time to let the pot boil.

Thinking to himself he imagined that even without a plan to do nothing, we were anyway. Our civilization is just stumble bumbling along. We're asleep. Pretty much like a drunk heading towards a home he can't place the location of.

Then a very disturbing thought occurred to him: **'What if they are wrong in the time frames for reaction?** What if we pass the Mephistopheles Moment Dr. Sherman has warned us of and all the strategies they employ do no good, and run away heating has started? What then?'

Stone suddenly realized that a bet or a wager was being made and literally billions of people's lives would be on the line along with the habitability of the earth. Even the lives of the Platinum Family would be in jeopardy if the worst scenarios play out.

They didn't say it was a wager or bet, but that was it. As he thought it through it seemed it was something like betting on when a balloon that's being inflated, and which a person has no deep understanding of its properties, will pop. He'd seen the graph that the Green Party suggested was the safe glide path back to carbon dioxide levels under the 1990 level at about 350 ppm by 2050. He also remembered the list of unknowns *The Kingdom of Good* site listed: such as when the methane releases might pass a tipping point and spew out uncontrollably. The glaciers were melting much faster than the scientists had thought possible just a decade ago with less than one degree of warming. Could the two degree goal actually be too high? If the do nothing approach this (he decided to give them a name) Platinum Family suggests occurs, then they'd theoretically massively draw carbon dioxide out of the atmosphere later in the century. In the process let our population "naturally" fall. 'Would their strategy fail because of unknowns that may emerge coincidentally with allowing the carbon dioxide level and related temperature increases to happen?'

Stone reflected on the notion that at the very core of the climate crisis was the invention in 1909 of how to create manmade nitrogen to grow things. 'Of course, it's so obvious, billions more people that would not otherwise exist require more and more from the earth. That is the ultimate driver. It's all a part of **The 67 Challenge** *The Kingdom of Good* website explains. We don't just have carbon to deal with; there is nitrogen too. He understood now how they both must be confronted.

He stood up and walked over near to the pool and looked into the lightly swirling water illuminated by the blue light. 'How powerful was this individual or small group? Could their will actually over-ride the will of the rest of those that want an aggressive response *now*? They've decided to use the crisis as a way to "naturally" purge or prune our population.' His mind was working this new information.

Stone knew the concern that many in the status quo had to cover the costs of their earlier investments; every conceivable device or mechanism to use a liquid energy source. How long would that take? All on the one planet we all depend on for survival. "That was their bet." Stone clarified it in his own mind how it all appeared to him, now.

"Who was this Platinum Family? This pinnacle of the 1% group. Names passed through his head. Were they American only or did they have ties back to Europe?"

He laughed, 'If someone came to me with this scenario I'd tell them they're full of shit, these conspiracy theories are for the screw-brained who see everything that way.' He puffed some air through his nose, but then he reflected, 'But I've seen otherwise.'

Gezana appeared in the door leading to their deck. "You're up awfully early. I didn't hear you at all, I guess I was pretty out. When did you get up, or come to bed for that matter?"

"About four is when I got up. I came to bed a little after midnight."

"Why were you up at that time?" She now had a long blouse pulled over her previously nearly naked body.

"Let me get some coffee and I'll tell you."

Gezana had started the prep on breakfast when Stone came in.

He went on to tell her about the email from Tyler concerning Dave and his suspicions that led him to the file. Gezana had been spreading hummus on a bagel when she learned of the plan from the group Stone was calling the Platinum Family. She stopped and raised her eyes at him. "Come on," the words were emphasized, "are you kidding me?" Her hand was still on the counter top and still holding the knife. Her head fell with one of those, I'm not very sure about this looks.

She moved over to the bar and sat next to him. "So, you think this note came from some very shadowy person or group that has tentacles on our government and the economy? Her voice took to a higher pitch and was a bit nasal. "They're going to let things go so that some chaos, as they call it, actually does happen and then hundreds of millions of people die "naturally"?" She took several bites of the oatmeal she'd prepared, "It's just insane enough that it might be true. I'm not saying I believe it, but."

"Well, there's hundreds of millions of people who died by violence in the twentieth century that some time or other didn't believe others could think of "them" that way. I've lived long enough to know there are some really bad people in this world and some of them masquerade pretty well as being good. I don't know what I really believe yet, but I need to do something with this information."

"Tyler?" Gezana said, then took a drink of juice.

"Uh huh," he was biting his lip. "Probably call."

He had some research to do also as he wanted to know more about the Committee for Economic Development. What were they really all about?

"Changing Hearts Bed and Breakfast," the voice wasn't familiar; it was younger than Tyler's.

"Tyler Contadino, please."

"Sure, just a sec," there was a pause and then he could hear the young girl say, "Mom, there's some guy on the phone asking for you."

"Okay," he could hear Tyler's voice faintly reply. She made it to the phone in about ten seconds; she'd been cleaning cupboards in the kitchen. "Hello, this is Tyler."

"Tyler, this is Stone Fischer. How are you doing?"

"Oh, hi, Stone. Let me get to the phone in my office, hold on," a few moments passed. "Okay, I'm here. What can I do for you?"

Tyler had told him while they were in Damascus that if he called in the future and didn't want anyone to monitor their conversation he should just mention something about "vegetables" and she'd find a secure way to get back to him.

"I have some information on broccoli preparation I'd like to share with you. Do you have time for that? Tyler immediately understood the code word. "I'm a little tied up right now; can I get back to you a little later like after seven?"

"Sure," Stone knew she'd made the connection.

The whole Edward Snowden, NSA revelations were a current affairs topic. Conversations could be monitored and certain algorithms might catch the conversation and who knows where that might lead?

Dave assumed he'd hear from her in a day or two.

~~~~~~

The next afternoon, he and Gezana went for a short run on her request. Arrangements had happened fast as she let Stone know they'd be meeting Tyler and Joan but for precaution they had a plan to lose anyone who might be tracking Joan. She was obviously a target for whomever it was that had poisoned Dave and only through serendipity didn't poison her too. She didn't like it at all, but she was living her life scared these days. They would meet at Stone's house and Gezana had a plan to meet Joan and Tyler and lead them to the house by a route no one else could follow. Stone would just return to the house.

They didn't actually walk together. Joan and Tyler just watched as Gezana led them through a few buildings and into tree covered areas and finally to the back entry to Stone's house.

"All for the "them" we don't even know are out there," Tyler said, seeing Stone sitting at the lounge chairs under the pergola.

"Good to see you," he said, giving her a hug. "If someone's followed you here through all that I guess were doomed anyway." Stone went on, considering their security precautions.

Tyler turned and Joan was standing near to her. "I know introductions are needed. This is Joan Lebeau." Stone and Gezana then both said their names to her. They then both gave Joan a hug. Both of them were quite aware of the stress she was under and would have little knowledge of when it might change.

"Let's sit over here," Stone gestured to the lounge chair area.

"I'll get us something to sip and nibble on," Gezana said, heading towards the kitchen.

"What a beautiful place," Joan began.

"Thanks. It's a good place to come home to. I'm sorry about Dave," Stone offered straight up.

Joan was shaking her head in appreciation. She had to look away for a moment feeling the surge of emotion for not only Dave but the apprehension she now felt day to day by potentially being a target.

"It's hard to know who you can trust," she looked more closely at Stone, direct to his eyes. "Can I trust you?" her voice had a sense of yearning.

Stone took a moment and looked at her intently, "I understand why you might ask. I am your friend." His voice was direct. Joan sat back as her intuition felt good.

"Here we go," Gezana had their snacks. There was a bit of small talk before Tyler moved them to the reason they had met.

"I told Joan the little you told me," she was smiling slightly, "We didn't discuss anything on the phone and just a little when I met her at the mall. We've traveled here separately so who knows."

Stone was shaking his head. He knew it was time he explained what he had discovered. He briefly explained his position at NGB Lab and his association with Krastle Enterprises and then the trip to Socorro Island and the horrific diving event with a Colossal Squid. Joan was spell bound, as was Tyler since she didn't know the details of all that either. He told them that the moment where something asked him 'what he believes' became a turning point: it started him on the road to his epiphany. It was what turned his heart and headed him to where he was sitting right then.

"I remembered that name from a page I'd seen in a very secret file only Kurt and I used, American Prosperity. You had to have a special username, which Kurt had and I didn't ask for. But, I got lucky, his secretary had it, and it got me in. That's where I found the edict from what I'm calling the Platinum Family."

"Platinum Family?" Tyler asked.

"I had to come up with something and I thought it fit." Stone was smiling. "All I can say is that it appears there is one main group that coordinates things with others they consider part of their group. I kept thinking I'd see some name for whomever it was saying this stuff, but I just didn't see one."

"There's that rumor that's been around as long as I can remember that there is some Family of families that go back to the Middle Ages that have deep connections." Joan offered. "My uncle was exceedingly rich, but I never had any knowledge that he was a part of anything like that."

Stone was rolling his head slightly, his expression suggested a question inside himself, "Old money ... old, probably going all the way back to the 1600s maybe earlier; the kind that's been accumulating for generations. Maybe that's who this person was part of but I don't know and I'm not sure it matters.

"The Family?" Tyler then began talking. "That's the name for the whole thing. Everybody that's connected. Those top 1,500 people I told you about have others connected to them. In one way or the other, the top 20% of people, relative to their wealth in our country, can be thought of as being in the Family. The truth is though, most of them have absolutely no understanding of that. The 1,500 are their lead birds. They just do as the lead birds do. You know like birds in a great big flock each bird follows the bird in front and in the end they're all just following the lead bird."

"I think I was about to become a part of all that. Kurt told me there was something he wanted to tell me about. Maybe a special place, I don't know." Stone told them.

"That's pretty ironic," Gezana observed.

"These are pretty much the richest people in the world and they're all entangled in this web that makes up the economy." Stone thought for a moment, "The base of that entire web is energy, and what produces it: coal, oil, and natural gas. The black devils, as I now believe." He finished a drink. "I've been asking myself for some time why the richest people in the world haven't been toning in on the climate stuff. They and their families have to live on this planet too. Maybe I found the answer?"

Tyler and Joan looked at him more intently wondering what was coming next. "They've made a bet." Stone began," They're betting more time is available to us to change course on fossil fuels and they think there's an engineering solution to removing the carbon dioxide from the atmosphere."

"How so?" Joan asked.

"Fusion power and artificial photosynthesis mainly; and some other ways." Their eyes widened as Stone continued. "Plants draw carbon dioxide out of the air. They have a plan for doing it on an enormous scale and that takes lots of energy. That's where fusion power comes in. They believe the technical issues have been figured out and these new plants can be ready in ten years."

Joan seemed puzzled, "So wouldn't that be incredible! They have all this ready in ten years and the scientists think we have at least that much time."

Stone was shaking his head, *"but that's not the plan!"*

"What!" Both Joan and Tyler reacted.

"They don't intend to start that process until at least after mid century. They plan to burn all the fossil fuels they can."

"But why would they wait and take a chance?" Tyler virtually blurted out as a sense of deep concern was moving through her.

"It's a part of their plan to allow the climate to destabilize to the point hundreds of millions, probably billions, die. With the planet in total turmoil, the ones who aren't killed by the droughts, storms, plaques, or wars, will be easy prey. They would just be forced out of the cycle in the economy that does exist. You can't last long without a secure source of food, water, and shelter. Cutting the population down would be conceivable. They want to make living room for the top ten to maybe twenty percent to re spread around the planet. The new Noah's Arc strategy. That's the end game and that's what the wager is all about!"

Everyone was stone quiet and the sound of the water falling into the pool filled the background. "That is genocide on a scale…" Joan's voice tapered off, not knowing how to really finish. Her heart had raced from thinking there was a solution just around the corner to realizing the depth of inhumanity that exists.

Stone continued, "And the really incredible thing is that way over 99% of that 800 million or a billion people or so they think will survive the purge, have no idea this plan is in the works for them. Their conscience can be clear as the vast majority of them being clueless as to their complicity with this crime against humanity. They just keep their heads down and follow the bird in front of them. They can be just like the Nazis. There was always someone up the ladder of command that they had to follow orders from. Think about it: even the Platinum Family can say they were just taking orders from this silent majority. And in the end it's like a firing squad standing in a circle!"

"There aren't just animals in that 1%, some of them are extremely good people," Joan then observed.

"I know," Stone then said, "It's the flood and Noah is the Platinum Family, the deviants in the 1%." Deep cynicism was in his voice.

"What can we do?" Joan asked.

"Somehow the word needs to get out that this is the end game," Stone then responded.

"Look what those black devils did already trying to poison Dave and Joan … what will they do if we go to the internet with this information?" Tyler said.

They were quiet for a short time. "Why do any of you have to release the statement?" Gezana began. "There are all kinds of manifestos out there now. Couldn't one of those groups do it? Wasn't there one from Scotland, that would put the message out on the other side of the world, a long ways from all of us?"

"We could contact *The Kingdom of Good* in England; they could probably work with the people in Scotland." Joan said.

Stone rubbed his hands together, "Yes, well they'll be taking a leap of faith to believe what we're telling them. Hopefully they will and actually do something."

"They know me and Dave and Matt quite well. If we're telling the people in Cambridge this information they will believe it." Joan observed.

"I'll contact them for you," Tyler said, "they might be able to tap your emails. They did get into your apartment and could possibly have checked your computer for that information."

"That's true," Joan acknowledged.

Chapter Twenty Four

(Tyler contacting The Kingdom of Good; Cambridge, England early June, 2014)

Tyler had interacted some with Simon Towbridge when she first became acquainted with the *Kingdom of Good* group movement. He had emailed her the package of information they had updated from the original material Dr. Sherman had created and spent some time helping her to understand it all. She was looking forward to hearing his slightly high-browed English accent; he laughed a lot so it didn't come off as too stuffy.

"Simon, this is Tyler Contadino, from Oregon. Do you remember me?"

"Oh, without question. "There was a smile in his voice, "You live in Damascus, just a short distance from Boring."

"Oh yes, I remember. You found that quite humorous." Tyler was laughing.

"There's always a funny name somewhere. So, is there something I can help you with?"

"Yes," she paused, "is this a super secure line?"

Simon slightly adjusted in demeanor. "Hmm, well I think so. I suppose I don't know that to a great extent. Can you give me a hint as to why that might be important?"

Tyler thought for a moment as to how to answer, "I have information that, well, I think explains a lot of why were having so much trouble getting the change in our energy sector, and others, here to respond to the climate crisis. And I'll just say when you understand what I think is the overall strategy…it will sicken you." She purposely only said "I" so a connection elsewhere would not be implied in case someone was already listening.

"How certain are you that your information is true?" Simon then asked.

"About as close to 100% as I can imagine."

Simon was rolling a pencil through his fingers, thinking of what he should do. "Give me just a few minutes. I need to speak with someone here, then I'll call you back. Okay?" Tyler agreed.

The phone rang five minutes later. "Tyler, Simon."

"Hi, what did you find out?"

"No one really can be sure about that, if the Chancellor of Germany's phone can be hacked, what does that tell the rest of us? So, on a scale of one to ten, how important is it that we get this information?"

"The way I see it: ten."

"Okay, I'll check with management and see what they want to do."

"Thanks," Tyler responded, and hung up assuming they'd call again soon.

A few hours later an older woman walked in the door to the Bed and Breakfast. She was dressed plainly and had parked an older car in the drive that said Jan's Upholstery on it.

"Hello," Tyler said greeting the lady. She could see the car beyond with the advertising on it. Tyler couldn't remember calling for such a service. "Can I help you?"

"Are you Tyler," the lady asked, the redness of her lipstick stood out to Tyler.

"Yes, I'm Tyler Contadino."

"Good, my name is Margaret Nix. A young man by the name of Simon Towbridge called and asked that I contact you for information. He said that would be all I'd need to tell you."

Tyler waited a moment to see if the woman had anything else to add. "So Simon called you and asked that you get with me?"

"That's right, he remembered a friend of his who is a friend of mine and thought this would be a good way to get him the information. I said I'd help." She laughed the way an older lady who likes flowers would.

Tyler, for reasons only she knew, had to think quickly and invent a convincing story. She had to move the people and locations far from San Diego and any mention of the American Prosperity group could not slip out.

It was a fictitious person in northern Washington state, she told her, who had come across the plan to use chemical seeding of the atmosphere to reduce the impact of solar radiation. So, the need to reduce carbon emissions would not be needed. It was quite taxing, trying to make it sound like such a revelation; something that was already widely being talked about could be the "big" news she was wanting to provide to Simon. Margaret took the information though, thinking she was doing her job interviewing this dim wit.

She was pretty mentally exhausted when Margaret finally left, "God, unless there was a mix up, they knew who she was and had tapped the call to Simon," she thought to herself.

A few more people checked in for the evening with each of them Tyler wondered if a contact from Simon would arrive. "How did he intend to get back to her?" she wondered.

It was now evening and it had turned dark and rainy outside. Tyler was intent studying the register when she saw another person coming towards the door. It was an older man wearing a tweed coat and hat, very northern

Brit looking. He smiled warmly as he entered. "Little damp out there to-night. Nice weather I guess if you're a duck."

She smiled, "Are you looking for a room?"

"No, actually I'm looking for the proprietor, Tyler Cantadino."

She extended her hand, "That would be me."

"Logan Spencer," he said as they shook hands. "Very pleased to meet you."

She was studying him more intently and her intuition was telling her the coast was clear. "Are you here on behalf of my friend Simon?" Tyler asked.

"Yes I am. Perhaps there is a place we can sit and talk?"

She pointed across the small lobby to the sitting room she had met Stone and Gezana in, "Let's go there, where it's quiet."

She had just brewed some coffee, so she quickly got them both a cup. He was good with his being straight.

Joan had warned Tyler of the possibility that her phone conversation to England could be monitored and that *The Kingdom of Good* group had let her know that face to face contacts with people you'd never met would have a simple code of talking about the weather and how some bird species would fit into it. When Margaret failed to say anything, Tyler didn't know if she was just not aware about the code or if she was a spy. Now she knew. But was she safe now? How about this guy? Would they be looking for him?

"Before we start, I need to tell you that someone was here earlier, a woman, and she was looking for this information."

Logan's eyes grew wider contemplating that knowledge. "What did you tell her?"

"When she didn't say the code, I just started making up a story. Good thing I'd read about the chemtrails whole deal a few days ago, so that popped into my head as the big story I had to provide. They should leave me alone now on the grounds that I'm a nut." She smiled.

"Oh yes, the seeding of the sky with aluminum salts, as I've heard. Not very sure there is much to that."

"Well, if you're not one for believing any conspiracy theories the one I have will probably really perplex you."

"Well, let's give it a go. Good coffee by the way."

"Thank you."

She went on to explain the connection with Joan and Dave, Stone and Gezana. Tyler continued with how Dave was poisoned and Joan was nearly so and how Stone following a hunch found his way into a file that was meant to be very secure. She explained what she could about the American Prosperity letter.

"Stone had to just remember all this because the letter self destructed before he could have the chance to copy it. So what's next is his best description of what it said. I wrote down what Stone told me," she reached into her shirt pocket and retrieved a piece of paper. "I have these bullet points, so let me see here," she slipped on some reading glasses, "Okay,

- Number one: need for immediate curtailing of fossil fuel burning and a need to recover the cost of existing infrastructure.
- Number Two: because of technological advancement there is an engineering solution to the problem. Fusion power and artificial photosynthesis, and others.
- Number Three: this is where the evil really starts showing; let climate instability reduce human population, a necessary correction.
- Number Four: loss of 70 to 90% of human population and other species is acceptable as the "purge" will allow room for those left to re-spread around the planet.
- Number Five: Using natural systems, like soils to draw the carbon dioxide out of the atmosphere.

I'll give you this copy of everything Stone wrote down. It's pretty complete I think."

"I can understand why you didn't want to say all this over the phone. If there is real gravity here, you may have just uncovered a secret cabal."

"Stone thinks there's just a very few people who are a part of this group he discovered. He says the success of this group is probably more a factor that they aren't a big group with meetings and minutes and a set agenda. It's more like when a herd of animals or a flock of birds take off. It can be just one animal that's leading them, and the rest just fall in behind that leader. Things just happen organically then."

"A real lizard's stew." Logan said with British sarcasm in his voice.

She went on. "Well, you always assume there are those back door deals going on and lots of money being spread around to sway votes. But until now I never really took it serious that there could be an organized network or family like this dictating the biggest decisions. And it's so insidious, no real leaders, nobody directly calling the shots, just these tentacles that spread all over." Tyler had that awful bottomless feeling in her stomach.

"Well, more than just a few people have been trying to understand Obama and how his administration's original rhetoric to deal with the climate crisis and what actually is being done don't match up. He evidently

300

doesn't think it's the urgent problem you and I believe it is. Did somebody get to him?" Logan answered.

"He seems so trust-worthy. That's my women's intuition. I don't know, I don't get it. It seems like there's a veil over him on the subject. Like something's holding him back."

"Well maybe we've found at least a part of that something? I seriously doubt he's aware of the most insidious of this."

"Oh, of course not. But the engineering solutions/adaptations part makes some sense to me." Tyler responded.

Logan put his hat on, "I'll get this to Simon and see how they want to use it."

"Oh, tell him we're hoping that the group in Scotland that recently posted a manifesto on the Internet reveals it. That gets the point source a long ways away from Joan and Stone.

He jotted that down too, "I'll pass it all along."

"Do you think anyone could be watching," she nodded towards the front door. "Possibly, but I really doubt it. Whoever was curious about this had no notion of what it was all about. That could have been CIA here earlier, for all we know, and had nothing to do with this American Prosperity group. If the guys in Cambridge decide to release this, it will take a month or more to go out. There's virtually no way it can get traced back to our discussion. You can feel safe, I'm sure. But just to add a little drama, I will slip out your back door, if you don't mind. I parked several blocks away, so I should give the slip to anyone that might be watching." He was grinning. Logan left through the front door as he had come in.

(Late June, 2014; the Scottish updated manifesto is released)
"Stone, look" Gezana said, pointing to the computer. She'd heard that another manifesto from Scotland was up on the net and had been anxious to see it when she got home.

Stone set the several bags of groceries he'd picked up on the counter and joined her. She clicked on the arrow. As with the last video the pipes and drums can be heard in the distance, getting louder and louder. Then the group of young Scots start to appear, one by one taking their place around the fire. The pipes and drums stop and again they state their names. The brogue adds to the drama. As they finish an older man dressed in his tartans joins them. His hair is long and grey and he is clean shaven, dignified looking and has a long walking stick. He moves in front of them all and the crack of the fire can be heard.

He begins and his brogue is particularly pronounced:

"My name is Alistair Ramsey. I am 92 years old and two of the young people you see standing behind me are my grand children. When I was a young man, I fought in World War II. I sat in the belly of a bomber and protected her from the Luftwaffe's Messerschmitts and their fighter planes. I somehow survived 47 missions. My generation saved the world from the tyranny of the Nazis and the rest of the Axis Powers. Over fifty million people died in that war. What did we learn?"

*"My grandchildren and the rest of their generation now confront a threat greater than the one my generation faced and like my generation, they must hear the call. Our world is crumbling because we are not wise! Our climate is staggering and our leaders are paralyzed to react. Why? We are clever beyond the wildest of imaginations of only a few hundred years ago. **But we are not wise.**"*

"I will tell you why. There are those in the shadows with long tentacles of power who have profited obscenely in the past 65 years and their greed blinds them to reality. It is their opinion that no change in our polluting of the atmosphere, or population growth caused by a bubble agricultural system based on water and nutrient flows that are not sustainable and is now poised to burst and kill billions, is acceptable. In fact, to them it is desirable as it will provide living room – lebensraum – for those that survive the purging of the planet. They believe a technological or engineering solution will deal with fixing the problem sometime late in this century, but after the purging."

"When I was young, I questioned that there really were people capable of wanting to kill me and my countrymen to take our land. I learned from the most vicious of ways that there were. Young people of the world, I tell you, there are those who care nothing for you. They can seem perfectly ordinary, and still carry a dagger."

"You have little time and there is only one hope for the world. The rest of the civilized world knows that to have any chance to deal with this problem in time the federal government of the United States must be won by the Green Party, which is a world party, before this decade is over. This is how little time you have. They are the only ones with the true wisdom of vision to lead effectively. You have the power to do it. You have a democracy, your votes count. In two election cycles you could purge the leaders who are controlled by the tentacles of the black devils: the fossil fuels and petro chemicals industries and all those who close their hearts and minds to the truth and side with them."

"Hear me now. It is only the young who are not soured and captured by evil or ignorance. You will either rise up in a massive and righteous force and lead the planet away from catastrophe, or the purge the evil ones imagine, will begin."

302

The old man looked solemnly at the camera for several long moments, then turned with his cane and led the young ones out behind him. The drums and the pipes following along as they faded into the verdant Scottish highlands.

Stone looked towards Gezana, "I guess the word is out."

"So what do you believe now Stone?" Gezana felt that something maybe a transformation was in the works.

He thought for a moment. "When I was a kid, I was maybe twelve or thirteen, there was this one Saturday when the mood in the house hadn't been that good. Mom was always struggling with money and I think she was lonely too. At any rate it wasn't a particularly good day, so I decided to go for a long walk. I got to the end of the asphalt on this one road near our apartment and it turned to gravel, but the sun was still high so I just kept walking. After a little while, I came to this canyon. I remember this huge tree was right at the top. I could see there was some spot down at the bottom that looked like there was a bunch of trees and shrubs growing, so something told me to just head there. I probably was on someone's property but it seemed pretty remote. When I got there it just seemed pretty cool, so I found this big rock and sat down. When you're by yourself and only the wind, your mind can sort of settle. I'm sure I didn't really think of it that way then; but looking back I know that's what was happening. I seemed to get really still. Then, it was just funny, it was like the trees and the grasses, the shrubs were tickling me. I wanted to laugh and I remember it felt really good. Have you ever looked really close at the colors and the textures in everything that's growing out there?" Gezana was nodding her head that she had. "All at once it just struck me as beautiful. I'd never known that before; it was just sort of out of the blue. That made me happier than I'd been at the house. Somehow it made the day good."

"You had an epiphany," Gezana noted.

Stone was nodding his head in agreement. "I'd go there every so often when I kind of needed that punch." He was quiet, Gezana waited. "Money, wealth and power have a certain gravity that can turn your mind, make you see just what you want to see, just the things that are convenient to see." He was thinking again and looked towards Gezana, "I want to go back to seeing the world the way I saw it on my trips all those years ago. I've got to change!"

"I'm going to quit NGB. I've already looked into it. UC Davis has a program in agro ecology. I should be able to test into the advanced classes. In maybe two years I'd make the turnaround. There are venture capitalists already buying land and spending the money needed to transform the soils to make the land ready for some young farmers to come in and start growing cash crops. I want to work for them and maybe become one. That's where I'm going. That's what I'm going to do."

"Am I invited?" Gezana had a serious look to her face.

"With bonbons!" Stone returned.

Part Four Joining the Revolution

Chapter Twenty-five

(Matt talking to Joan late June 2014)

"I know, I've watched it about ten times. Where'd they get that guy? He was like Sean Connery and some sorcerer all mixed together. That brogue is incredible." Matt said, as they briefly discussed the latest video from Scotland.

Joan had something more immediate on her mind. "Matt, I've got to find some way to take care of Dave. He's plateau'd and still needs help. The doctors just don't know when or even if he's going to make it to the next level where I don't need to be around so much. My two months of partial leave are just about up. I'm going to have to get back on the road. I can only do so much from this apartment. I could put him in an assisted living if I have to, I guess. His brother really isn't set up to help either. I'm not sure what to do."

A plan had actually already been cooking in Matt's head. He'd told his uncle Dan about Dave and without flinching he told Matt to 'get his butt up here' and he could live in his house. They had all kinds of room. "Joan, I want you to bring him here, to Boise. I already talked to my Uncle Dan. He's got a heart about the size of Montana and says he wants him here."

Matt went on, "You can base your travels out of Boise, can't you? You could stay at Dan's too until things got settled and maybe get an apartment later, I don't know."

"Oh, I haven't told you yet? Maria is moving here. She got Norse Aquatic to make her the manager of the salmon farm on the Columbia River up in British Columbia. Great deal, huh?"

"Really?" Joan's mind was turning. "That would get all four of us together. It might help you know, with the whole movement."

"I'll talk it over with Dave and get back to you, but you know, it sounds like the right thing to do."

(Matt and Maria's apartment, a month later, mid July 2014)

"Matt, pull the shades. Ahh." Maria draped a robe around her naked body and tippy toed across the cold concrete floor to the bathroom. They'd been up late hanging with Eric and Aubrey the night before watching all the Friday night late shows. Before that they'd been to the Bouquet listening to the acoustic act of Two Girls from Kentucky; that was the name of their combo, and described them perfectly. Matt had secretly set some chocolate out on the counter-top as they left and of course they conveniently found it upon return. Of course chocolate had long been their personal and silly code for … well. Maria had been feeling the effects of the wine a bit much when they got home. She'd promised a different act when they woke up.

Maria dropped the gown revealing her sleek body, tastefully curving, but not over stated. She was just lucky that way. It never took Matt long to respond to her. He was just very, very, very lucky he had found her. She was the archetype of his dreams. Very few of us are so fortunate, and so young, and now if he could keep from blowing it.

For Maria it was different; Matt was cute enough, certainly talented, their values were very similar, but probably more than anything she intuitively understood how much he loved her. There was enormous security in that. And deep in most women's laundry list was the need for security.

Very few ever end up with the person of their dreams, but instead adapt to their reality. But those who are patient with someone they like and allow the indecision part to work its way through, sometimes love may emerge. But feelings of love can be fleeting. Being good friends is not so bad, and often enough. People who have been together a long time and split apart will sometimes tell of the entangled roots they feel in their heart for the other person, they didn't really know were there before they split. It makes the process of separation so much more difficult, even when both believe it best.

"Uh…uh…uh," Matt pulled the blankets over the heads of them both; he didn't particularly want the owners up above to hear. But what did they expect anyway.

Matt rolled to the side of the bed; Maria pulled the sheets up over herself. "Oh God, do I love doing that. She rolled herself over next to where Matt was lying.

"How much of that was love for me and how much was just animal?" Maria could ask direct and often unusual questions.

Matt rolled onto his side, "You think I can answer that?"

"You can try."

He used his fingers to play with some of her hair hanging down across her forehead. "80-20. What do you think?"

She massaged the area that was spent. "I like that." Her voice was full of affection. She was silent for a short while, "sometime, sometime I want you to be 10–90…like a mad dog." She pulled the sheets up over her face as she was laughing so much.

Matt was laughing too and then had something he wanted to tell her, "A little more of what you were just doing and the Norwegian Wolf hound in me will show up."

"Ummmmm … Show me big man!"

~~~~~

Maria had her long white fuzzy gown on, with nothing underneath, as they sat and shared the little breakfast Matt had prepared them after their morning of intimacy: scrambled eggs over muffins, a slice of really good ham, some orange juice and that little bowl of fruit with yogurt on top.

"You'll be amazed at how well Dave's doing. I think getting him to Uncle Dan's was incredible for his spirit." Matt told Maria. Maria had been gone for several weeks up in Canada and had just returned the day before.

Matt continued. "Joan's been in and out of town. I think she said she was going back to DC on this trip. Those Greens really have her hopping around."

"I haven't talked to her very much since the video from Scotland went viral. Do you know how that's been impacting the party, new membership, all that?" Maria questioned.

"I don't know. I've been gone too. That new Organic Blessings in Aspen has had me down there a lot. We've just been passing. We texted now and then just to touch bases. I know she's excited with how far Dave's come. Dan and Leslie are fantastic. They've always got cool music going and he hangs out with Dan in his shop watching him build the cabinets. You just wonder when the right strike of the drum might get him over whatever hump it is that's holding him back."

"Funny how the mind works. Which reminds me; Dan's got his band coming over tonight and they get together out in his shop. You've never heard them, right?" Maria shook her head in agreement. "Danny's played some by himself a few times. I'd heard about the band, but no, I've never seen them."

"Rosewood Harmony," he smiled. "Acoustic Greatness might be another good name."

~~~~~

Matt had a few other excursions he wanted to take Maria on that day. Since she'd been to Boise last, his firm had moved to their new office location on Front Street and he was eager to show her the new place.

They had ridden their bikes across town and had already stopped at a coffee shop for some good Joe. It was a warm late June morning, around 10:30 and they were both dressed for coolness and for being on their bikes. Matt pulled a key from a zip pocket, "We can leave our bikes here." There

307

was a room designated and designed specifically for that. A lot of the staff lived within a few miles of the office and could follow the spine of the Greenbelt that runs through Boise for most of the trek, then branch over a few hundred yards to the office. It was a Saturday morning and the place was basically empty. There were two people though, sitting at their desks. One was on the other side of the large studio and the other was in a cubicle close to where Matt worked.

"Hey Scott," Matt said as they walked near to him, "you got a deadline?"

"Not really, just needing to get caught up for a meeting Monday morning. I didn't want to have to get in here at 5:00 or something then, to get ready. But yeah, kind of a deadline."

"Scott, this is my girlfriend Maria Ladacci. This is Scott Hansen." They shook hands. "Scott's one of the civil engineers so he does the site civil design on a lot of the projects I work on."

"Nice place you have to work in." Maria then observed, "Very open, lots of light and very energetic I'd think."

Scott's head nodded in agreement, "It takes a little getting used to for some people I think. I had no problem with it. We're all like little busy bees, buzzing everywhere."

"I'm going to show her around a little bit." Matt said.

"Nice to meet you," Maria offered. Scott answered similarly. He didn't say anything but he noticed how cute she was and liked her faint Spanish accent.

"This is my cubicle." Maria straight away saw the three pictures he had of her and him tucked back near his computer console. He had two large monitors where he did his AutoCAD work and other related things. There was table space just to his left where he could lay out drawings that had been printed out. Drawings for the Organic Blessings building he was working on currently were there. "This is the project I flew to Aspen on last week. We're adding some delivery area and I had to walk through the program with the store director and talk to the city planning staff to make sure we're getting it all just right."

He pointed around his desk. "Everybody in these ten cubicles is in the overall group I'm a part of. This is where my main boss sits. He doesn't draft but it's his job to keep us all lined out."

They wandered towards the front, "There are the main bathrooms, and two more are in the back. This is where material samples are kept." Maria was studying the walls seeing the racks of catalogs, tile and carpet samples, and wood, concrete block, large brick, some metal contraption which she had no idea of how it might be used in architecture. But it all looked interesting.

They moved from there past the front desk. She really liked the color of turquoise that partitioned the entry area from the large studio behind it. Matt waved briefly at someone sitting in one of the large glassed in offices. It looked like a pretty important location to Maria. "Just a sec," Matt said to the woman. She nodded.

They passed through an amazingly large door into a big room with multiple chairs and a podium area. Obviously, it was a place for large meetings. "This is our large conference room where we have meetings with the entire staff once a month." Matt noted.

"Morning," Matt said stepping into the woman's office. Matt had worked with Nancy quite a bit before she finally bought the stock and moved up into top management. She now had the responsibility to watch over the entire place, not only here in Boise, but at their offices around the western United States as well.

"Hi, I got in from Dallas last night and need to get caught up on what's been going on around here. But I'm getting out to the mountains this afternoon, headin' to the cabin." Matt had been there so he knew where she meant.

"I know you haven't met Maria, seems like you've been gone when she's been here before. Anyway, this is Maria Ladacci and this is Nancy Lindstrom." Matt said.

"That sounds Swedish, kind of like Lundquist," Maria observed.

"Oh, I married a Swede, I'm actually pretty much Irish, a little Welsh and English in there, some German just to be aggressive I guess."

"What's the most important thing about Swede's I need to know?" Maria asked playfully.

"Well, I don't know if it's a Swedish thing or not, but mine can be exceedingly stubborn at times." She made a bubbly sound, "but I suppose they all can." Nancy laughed.

"What are you two up to?" Nancy then asked.

"We've got our bikes and I just thought we'd ride the greenbelt out to the Barber Park area, and then back to Veterans. Maybe take a spin through Boise State. It's looking like such a beautiful day; we just want to be out. We should get going too to let you get your stuff done. Say "hi" to Gunnar."

Matt had them back track just slightly so they could catch the bridge at Julia Davis Park and then make a circle around the Boise State campus. His Uncle Dan had told him how much it had changed since he'd taken some classes there back in the 70s.

Having a large university at the center of town is a very good thing. Universities are places of new and dynamic thinking and professors tend to be cutting edge; often times progressives. They challenge students not only analytically, but emotionally as well. Students who are paying attention should shed a few skins along the way and then grow new ones as they work through their majors.

They were riding next to each other, "Of course this is Bronco Stadium and that's the new practice building." They rode around to the north end and got on the Greenbelt. "This is the new Varsity center, it's where the coaches offices are, meeting rooms, the weight rooms, lockers, showers, all that stuff. Pretty nice don't you think?"

Maria was nodding her head in agreement. "They must be doing well."

"Yup!" Matt answered.

They crossed a bridge further down that took them over to the north side of the Boise River and to where they could ride through Warm Springs Golf Course. The warming air was working to release many of the Earthy chemicals of the ground and plants. There was something very invigorating about it: alive and refreshing.

"Some Hollywood types live back there I've heard," Matt said as they went by a few houses just barely seen through the cottonwoods and undergrowth. An old sandstone wall held the grade along the left side of the path. The sandstone is an iconic material of Boise, the quarry where it had been gathered from for well over a hundred years lay only a few miles away up in the foothills.

The path scene widened, they were entering a new little valley. "This is the Barber area. I guess a long time ago there were actually a little town and a lumber mill here, but they were gone long before I ever was born." They rode down to the far end of the park and found a nice bench to stop and rest next to. Maria had water for them both. She sat for awhile studying first the river and ponds around her and the vast manicured grass. Further up she could see the amber foothills that led to the more verdant forests higher up. It was all contrast against a Boise State blue sky. It was in the mid 80s with a nice morning breeze, the kind of mornings she longed for.

"This is nice. It's a little like Spain, and maybe southern France but no ocean." She raised her eyebrows.

"It's home." Matt began, "I thought I might want to leave after college, maybe head to the Southwest or Portland. Maybe find someplace where the politics matched up with mine better. But really, where is that? You get to small towns around Idaho, except in the Wood River Valley I suppose, and people get very conservative very fast. There's probably token Democrats or Progressives around, but they are the definite minority. I've found my friends around here who think like me. I avoid talking politics much at work as its not good. If you're on the same page, it comes out around a few glasses of beer. It's great to have Eric, somebody who I don't work with, so we don't get caught up in the 'shop talk' shit. You gotta be careful with that."

"That's true in any organization." Maria began, "I don't have people around me anything like you do on a daily basis. But there's times some of my colleagues and I go for a drink and topics about work often get discussed. I know, I don't like the personal stuff, but whenever you have people working together it's just going to be there."

Her attention was suddenly moved. "Look at that kite." Maria said seeing the kite a young boy had launched; it was multi-colored and had a long tail. "So you can fly a kite in Boise too." Maria joked.

They rode back across town. People were already surfing at the new Water Park near one of the old Boise Cascade Ponds. "I think these ponds were built for when Boise Cascade would bring logs down here for milling. But it's great we have these really huge ponds that are fed by the river, so the water stays clean because it's just flowing through. During the summer the top two or three feet gets a nice temperature, so I swim here a lot."

They walked out to the edge of the viewing platform where people were lined up to jump into the wake created by a concrete structure that had been built in the river. "This just got finished a couple of years ago. So we have all the great white water rafting and kayaking up on the Payette. You can learn the basics of kayaking here."

"Remember the river next to the road as we went up to McCall?" Maria nodded remembering it. "That's the Payette. So the Boise River doesn't have the white water that the Payette does, but the kayakers can come here and play around on this wave. People just starting out learn the basics here. It's kind of cool."

"It's way cool," Maria then said, "These kinds of natural ponds, the Greenbelt, the River. I wonder if people who live here really appreciate what they have?"

"It depends on where they came from I guess. But what I hear is that most people really do appreciate it all."

Matt had one more place he wanted to show her. They had to cross the bridge that was very near the White Water Park. They rode past a few larger single family houses and then came to some high rise buildings that looked quite contemporary in design. They parked their bikes and went up some steps to the front door of one that was noted as being an "open house." Maria was wondering what this was all about.

The sales lady gave them the basic information, including the price... Maria had to gulp, and told them to look around as they wanted to. Matt only commented on how nice the views out were. Some of the finish work was not exactly what he'd like, 'but some of that could be changed,' he thought to himself.

"So why did we do that?" Maria asked.

"I don't want to live in that basement a whole lot longer. I've been saving, I have enough for a pretty good down payment on a place. This is just one idea I've been thinking about. There are old places around you can get pretty cheap, but they need a lot of fix up to make them very livable. And of course you'd never have the big expansive views you have with a place like that. But these are a lot more money. I don't know. There are all these different factors to consider."

"What happens if you lose your job, like a really hard recession hits again?" Maria was aware how the '08-'09 recession had hit so hard everywhere, including Boise. Tens of thousands, even in just this area had their lives turned upside down.

"I know there's always that possibility. If things go to total shit a few years from now, this could be a bad deal. Do you ever know?"

"No, you don't ever know." There was a very wise place in Maria.

It was early afternoon and getting hot. They decided to head back to Matt's apartment and just lay low for a while. They'd head to Uncle Dan's around 5:30. Matt knew he would have a bunch of ribs on his home-made barbecue going and a bunch of other really good things to eat. He let Maria know she should go light on snacking because there would be plenty later.

(Uncle Dan's, early evening, late July 2014)

Leslie waved from inside at the kitchen bar. She had the corn-on-the-cob ready to go out to the barby just in front of her. "Danny's out on the patio and Dave's there too," she said, leading them outside.

"Hey puckerbutt," Danny said, seeing his young nephew coming.

Matt looked to Maria, "He's called me that ever since I was about five. I guess my swimming suit was way up the crack of my ass and he thought it was funny." Maria was giggling.

"How about a hug?" he said first to Maria.

"Hugs are good," she replied, smiling. "Boy, things smell good."

"Yeah, I wonder what sort of cologne barbecue fragrance would make for a guy?" he chuckled.

Matt had popped his uncle on the shoulder and had already walked over so he could be next to Dave. To work his mind and relieve the boredom of the rehabilitation period, Dave had taken to sketching. He'd found some black and white photographs Dan had of old timers, the weathered type people who had worked hard in the elements for years. It could be seen in their faces and often their hands. He'd come up with this style he liked of pencil sketching. It gave the people a slightly different quality and was more abstracted and interesting. And like anything Dave put his mind to, he would find a way to excel and challenge himself more than anything.

Matt seemed to be spending extra time studying the one of the Chinese man that had worked the gardens of Garden City, the sister city to Boise, in the early 1900s. They had come to the valley in the 1860s and found a way to make a living growing the produce to feed the miners in Idaho City and for some of the earliest settlers of Boise and for the soldiers at Fort Boise. This man might have been second generation as the photo had been taken in the 1890s, but maybe not. "If...you want...it, keep ... it." Dave struggled to say–though the hesitation between the words seemed to be getting shorter.

"Only if you'll sign and date it for me." Matt smiled at his friend. Dave's writing seemed to be almost normal although maybe not quite as spontaneous as before.

Before he could sign it, he had to give Maria a hug. They'd seen each other briefly Friday just after she'd flown in, that was the first time since the poisoning. Maria understood, to some degree, the burden Dave and Joan now had, having been the target by someone to be murdered. She asked herself how she would handle that? Her face and name were on the Moab Manifesto like theirs. Would she and Matt and the others be targets too?

"How about a little of my rot gut?" Uncle Dan asked, approaching Maria with a drink in his hand. "My home brew cider."

She took the glass, "Interesting print on your shirt," Maria observed.

Dan looked down at it. He had this curious desire to remove the sleeves of pretty nice shirts to the point so one could see the top of his arms...and his arm pit as well. "Goofy lookin' isn't it?" He responded while giving her a quick hug.

Leslie stepped into the conversation, "I hear you made a nice swing around town on your bikes today. Did you like the parks?"

"I loved it and them, especially out on the east end of town. That area has an especially nice feel to it." Maria responded.

"I used to hunt pheasants out there when I was a kid." Dan injected. "There were just a few old farms then. Probably weren't supposed to be there, but my little 4/10 didn't pop very loud, so nobody ever knew we were there I don't think."

"You were always pushing the limits on something weren't you, Danny?" Leslie said, giving him a small hug.

"Pushed the limits chasing you, didn't I?" He was referring to the fact Leslie was nearly a full-blooded Shoshone Indian. One of her grandfathers was actually English, which seemed to come through in her appearance.

The blending was quite attractive. And being exotic like that Danny had been very attracted to her a few years earlier when they met in a bar. Marriage had not worked well for Danny, having failed at two before meeting Leslie. She'd played hard to get for a while, not sure about this guy in his late 50s. She was fifteen years his junior, but she loved his voice and came to find his cantankerous temperament endearing. They'd only been a couple for a little over three years. They talked about jumping over a stick or something someday; maybe, someday.

Leslie could see through the foliage around the patio that Denny Blackcloud and his wife Denise had arrived. "I need to get the door." Denny was an architect and Matt had briefly talked with him about employment, but decided the big firm was probably the better place for him to start out. Maybe one day moving to a smaller firm might make sense.

Denise made sure everyone was introduced. Most everyone had met the summer before last up at the Silver Creek camp area where all the guys in Rosewood Harmony had been going to since they'd first got together as a band in the early 70s. Different people had come and gone but the core of the group was Danny, Denny, Evan and their buddy from Germany, Juergen. Juergen was typically a wild card if he would show for their reunion gigs. Even tonight, they didn't know if he'd appear. They knew he was in the States, probably down in Utah or maybe Montana. He'd shown up when they last tried to get everyone together with a girlfriend named Gisela.

Matt's mom Micky and her husband Jack Harris arrived. Micky had her "always requested" three layer tort desert tray with her. She hadn't seen Maria for over a year so was eager to give her a hug.

"You look so nice," Micky began, "it's been so long since we've seen you."

"I know, I was back in Spain for eight months. We'll I should say Europe, because I spent most of my time in Norway learning about salmon."

"I know, we heard about that. And now you have this job working on the salmon farm in British Columbia?" Micky said parenthetically.

"Yes. I was so excited when I learned there might be an opening with my company there. Not only because it got me closer to Matt, but they really are raising high quality salmon. They're fed only real food like sprats, red krill, and juvenile hoki."

"I have no idea what those are, but if the salmon are eating what they typically would in the ocean I'd think that was better than what I've heard some farm raised salmon are fed: corn and soy. I mean, really."

Maria shrugged her shoulders, "If they can get a fish to grow on cheap food and people will buy them, they'll do it. Norse Aquatic will never do that. If they did I'd quit."

Danny moved a large group of the barbecued ribs to the counter where everyone could dish up for themselves. "Oh, those smell so good," Maria said, "Matt told me to not nibble earlier so I've got quite an appetite going."

Matt and Maria got in line behind Dave. He was doing just fine with most of his motor skills. Golf certainly wasn't in the bag yet, but filling his own plate was very doable. "Have you talked to Joan in the last few days?" Maria asked.

"We talk…almost every…day. She makes…me tell her…about what …I'm read…ing. She's got more…pat…ience than I do."

"Where is she now?" Maria continued.

"Last night…she was in…Seattle. She had to go to…Portland today, then back…to San Diego. It looks like she…might come hear later next… month."

They found a table and everyone was pretty quiet for awhile as they nourished themselves. The plan was to eat then after a while head to Danny's shop where they could get their instruments out and do some acoustical magic. They avoided any amplification. Danny had learned how to finish a part of the shop out to get some pretty good acoustics. Small and intimate was what Rosewood Harmony was all about these days.

Maria was in the kitchen with Leslie finishing up washing and drying the last of the dishes. It was getting pretty dark when the lights of a car showed up in the drive. Leslie smiled, "Looks like somebody's here." She put her towel down and headed out the door, "Why don't you come along," she said looking at Maria.

'Who's this?' Maria thought. Very quickly Maria understood why Leslie was smiling. Leslie looked at Maria and put one finger over her lips, "shhh." She gave the blond haired woman a hug just after she got out of her rented car.

Maria smiled, "Joan!" She said lightly. They hugged as well.

"I have a few things saved for you in the frig, if you're hungry." Leslie told her.

"That sounds good. Probably should say "hi" to Dave first, though."

Dave was sitting near the piano watching as Danny was working a few chords. He had a new tune he'd heard; something from the folk era of the early 60s he wanted them to work on a little, if they'd go for it. Danny had stopped for a moment, "What's that … one called?" Dave questioned.

Danny turned, about then he could see Joan moving towards them. They all had their finger up to their mouth, he moved his concentration back to Dave, "Uh, that one's called 'A Hard Rains A-Gonna Fall.'"

Dave could see something was happening behind him from Danny's expression. He turned and saw Joan, followed by Maria and Denise. His eyes widened and his heart jumped. Joan moved up and embraced him. It had been over a month since they'd been physically together and the embrace felt exceptionally good.

"So you we're…teasing…about going … to Portland."

"No, I did have plans to go there, but Leslie called and told me about this rendezvous going on tonight and I just decided to change my plans."

Maria and Joan had to catch up and everyone mulled around. The guys were tuning their instruments: Denny had a stand up bass and sometimes played the piano. Evan was the percussionist, some tall bongos were his primary instruments, along with things he could rub, rattle, and shake. He'd also picked up an old steel guitar and found places where he'd stick a few licks with it into their mix. Danny covered the rhythm and instrumental parts on his guitars, as he had three he would choose from, depending on the song. He had a violin as well and could make it wine with his Scotts-Irish moodiness. Juergen, when he was around, moved between the guitar and the piano.

For nearly an hour, they just played instrumental pieces with no singing. There was a tranquilizing effect with that and the mind could just ride along on a melody and find whatever pleasure it might.

"Oh, I love the melody to this one," Denise expressed to Maria. "The Last Cheater's Waltz, do you know it?"

Maria listened a bit more, "No, I don't remember hearing it."

"Well, it's old to begin with and mostly a country kind of tune probably didn't get much air time in Spain." Denise then said.

Maria had a comment, "My uncle Sebby, that's short for Sebastian, loves all kinds of music. So when I'd visit him he'd sometimes have music from America for my sister and I to listen to. Sometimes it was you're country music. He really liked Johnny Cash. I like his daughter Roseanne's music."

Denise then made an observation. "I loved Johnny Cash, very soulful guy, a walking talking contradiction partly truth and partly fiction, they say of him though."

Maria looked at her with a quizzical look, "What did you just say?"

"Oh, it's just some lines from a song Kris Kristofferson wrote about Johnny Cash…funny and catchy I suppose."

"Oh my God, look who is here," Denise said, looking at Maria. "This is the vagabond of the group, Juergen Kestle. Good grief, I don't see a girl with him, maybe he's shown up by himself. Come on I'll introduce you."

Juergen had a large black and brown scarf wrapped around his neck that stuck out a little from the tweed jacket he was wearing. His hair was now graying substantially and he wore it a bit long.

316

Leslie was the first to meet him with a generous hug. She offered to get him some food that was in the refrigerator. He agreed that sounded good.

Denise was next; and Maria and Joan were standing near. "World traveler, are you by yourself? Is Gisela with you?"

"I'm by myself. She's in Germany. I've been in Utah and the water skiing is really pretty good."

Denise continued, "I can see you've been getting sun. You have a little extra color in your cheeks."

"I've poured the sun screen on too. I don't like getting burned."

"Let me introduce you to some young ladies I know you've not met yet."

She turned first to Maria, "This is the young woman from Spain who Matt's been seeing for a few years, Maria." She tried to say the last name but had to stop.

"Ladacci," Maria finished for her.

"That's a pretty name for an equally pretty lady," Juergen enjoyed flirting with the younger gals. Maria thanked him. "Is that a Spanish last name? It sounds Italian to me."

"My grandparents on my father's side immigrated to Spain to the Basque country from Italy. My mother is Basque."

Juergen could understand why Matt might have fallen for her. She was pretty and had that rare willowy quality: gracious and dignified.

Denise continued with introductions. "This is Joan Labeau. She's Matt's good friend and Dave's girlfriend."

Matt joined them and introduced Dave to Juergen. Juergen had the names of the three new people in the group down right away.

The evening moved on. Juergen had eaten and the Jagermeister had been passed around. He and Danny talked skiing and hunting for a short time before deciding to continue playing.

For a while, it was a jazzy messing around with different chord progressions either Danny or Juergen had come up with while the other two would just fill in. After finishing one rather long free for all they got a request: the one Danny could hardly ever get through an evening without being asked to play. "When You're Only Lonely, Danny Bonner," Denise said loudly with a request in her voice. She actually preferred Danny's rendition better than John David Souther's, regardless of how great his work with the song had been.

Danny heard her but didn't respond directly. He was chatting with Juergen while they both played with a few chords. Juergen was at the piano. Years ago, when Rosewood Harmony was such a big act playing across Southern Idaho and over to Jackson, Wyoming, this had become the

317

most requested song for them to do. Juergen and Danny had worked out a distinctive chord progression that sent a tingle down the spine of those who had come to love the song, when they first heard it begin.

There it was: "When the world is ready to fall on your little shoulders … .

Maria and Joan were spell bound at the sound. They were up so close and it all felt so personal and just cool.

When they were done, Danny had an idea, "Matt, grab this guitar," he pointed towards his Tacoma used mainly for rhythm work. "Has Maria ever heard you do 'Take It Easy'?" It's the anthem of about every Baby Boomer Guy, Gen X and some Millenials like it too. "I like the way Matty does it. You good?"

"Have you ever heard him do it, Maria?" Danny asked.

"I'm not sure. Have you ever played it for me?" She asked looking at Matt.

"I don't think so. We're always in my basement apartment and I can't be very loud, so I just pluck around at some quiet stuff."

"Here we go," Danny said. The rhythm guitars began their steady introduction which felt right, like in an open-topped pickup with a cooler of beer, sunshine, some good buddy's, a long gravel road and a free and easy spirit. "Take it Easy, take it easy…"

When he was done, Matt came back and joined Maria and she gave him a kiss, "That was great, I mean I loved it." She scrunched her nose the way she would do before saying something a little risky, "I like it chocolate good!" Matt felt a little adrenaline rush.

"Where did you get that shirt? I love the little profile view of Thomas Jefferson, and what's that say?" Joan was noting, looking at a shirt Micky, Matt's mom was wearing. 'No occupation is so delightful to me as the culture of the Earth, and no culture comparable to that of a garden.' "Oh, that is just wonderful. He said that?"

"I guess so. I spotted it in a book I was reading a while back and thought how great that would be to have on a shirt. Since I have my big organic garden going every year now, I feel really good about wearing it."

"I'd love so much to have a place where I could grow a big garden, fiddle around in it, watch things grow." Joan pined.

"A picture nearly all of us dream of." Maria added.

"I think an awful lot of people think just like Thomas Jefferson. Food is so central of course to our living. We're so displaced anymore from the process of creating it. You just go to the store and there it all is." Micky said.

Natalie, Evan's wife, joined them. "I think people lose so much about living when they are so detached from the actual growing of the food they eat."

"We need more neighborhood gardens, fresh stuff." Micky continued.

"Speaking of food," Joan began, "I don't think it's widely understood how many people around the world are starving or nearly so; a billion of us, about." Joan was also a liaison to the United Nations FAO, the Food and Agriculture Organization. "Industrial agriculture, right now, could feed twelve billion, but it's all smoke and mirrors. That system is destroying the fertility of the land, the pesticides and herbicides and all the other "cides" weaken if not kill the soil. Much of the soil material ends up just washing away because the microbes that build the structure to hold it together are killed."

Joan went on, "And we're using water sources that are going away or getting undependable. Aquifers are drying up, glacier melt is just passing into the oceans and not available when it's needed. So we've created a people bubble and a huge number of those people don't have anything to trade for that food, so it never gets to them. There are people around the world who speculate financially on food and their maneuvers can cause millions to starve."

Joan stopped, her eyes seemed to focus, "In my mind it's murder. They pull the safety net out under these people and let them fall to their deaths. Starving to death is a horrible way to die too. Most of us have no idea how excruciating it is. You can read about it. It's horrible and so many are the children. Did you know that every five seconds somewhere in the world a child under ten starves to death? And that is totally preventable if enough people just thought differently."

Still holding their interest, Maria stepped in and shared one more example. "Biofuels," she began, "there's one that on the surface sounds like a great option to burning gasoline. But like so many things, when you dig into the details you can come to a very different conclusion. First off, you divert land that food crops can be grown on. So you drive up the cost of food in a world where you already have about a billion people either starving or nearly so, to death."

"Then, when people around the world rush to grow the raw material - corn, sugar cane, soy…you often force indigenous peoples off their home land. Industry then disturbs soils and forests and releases far more carbon than we would save in any reasonable time frame using it as a fuel for automobiles. You exacerbated the climate problem. Like in Brazil, where they keep moving farther and farther into the rain forests, which are the lungs of the biosphere, which then affects rainfall patterns and all kinds of things."

319

"Why is the world going so wrong?" Leslie asked.

Joan held up one hand as she was thinking. "We don't get the big picture. We haven't clearly strategized a long-term, sustainable, peaceful and fair way for humanity to exist on the planet. Ecology is the basis of life on this planet. Everything we do should be based on being in harmony with the Earth's balance and the well being of all life. There are just far too many people that don't understand this to any competent level; that's the biggest problem."

"Moneyed interests have far too much control of our government too. I believe there are a few of the very wealthy that are truly driven by the desire to promote the common good, but they are a minority. Far too many people in positions of power are only interested in maximizing their wealth at the expense of people and the balance in the biosphere we need. *Our values have been skewed*. The elite moneyed interests of all kinds, are at best vastly confused about what they do, and at worst horrifically evil!"

The conversation continued for some time as Joan and Maria had a group of empathetic listeners. Joan went on. "The dismal truth about fracking, or hydraulic fracturing, is exposed for the snare and delusion it is as well, its use becomes senseless. It does not stop the release of carbon dioxide and other bad gasses. The atmosphere is full; right now it is full of these gases." She continued explaining a few more of the details."

"What can be done?" Micky asked after a long time listening to Joan and Maria explain the predicament.

"I'm not entirely sure," Joan said, "but if you're in a bus heading towards some sharp curves and cliffs you know are there, and the bus driver is acting like there is no problem, in fact he or she is accelerating, I'm thinking you need to get that driver out of the seat and get someone there that grasps the situation."

"Pretty good idea it sounds like to me," Micky acknowledged.

320

Chapter Twenty-six

They'd gotten home late; Maria seemed to be very content deep in sleep. Matt had gotten up and got the coffee going, he'd even wandered outside to get the paper and a little early morning fresh air. It was Sunday morning; he liked to watch the Science channel with all the interesting information about the universe from the tiniest of stuff to the most mind blowing limits. He had his earphones on so Maria wouldn't be bothered; the program he was watching was showing animals from around the world and their behavior relevant to how they make a living. The show's host was explaining the flight of birds that flew in large waves, amazing patterns where they seemed to move around in such an indiscriminate way, but yet thousands of birds followed along in perfect harmony. As the host explained their behavior it was noted that all one bird had to do was follow the lead of the bird directly in front of them. It required split second responses, but they didn't have to have some grand design for the flight path in their head. One bird would jump up in response to something and the others would simply follow.

He kept watching the birds fly. Then someplace in his mind it occurred to him how similar that behavior could be thought of to what humans do. In our work-a-day lives most people have someone they follow, even if you are the CEO of a company, you still have a board of directors and share holders to be responsible to (at least theoretically). The status quo is the easiest line to follow too. Most people have homes and mortgages, car loans, or rent and have all the costs of living associated with it. Keeping your head down and focused on pleasing the next person up the line is the path most of us simply, and for the most part, reasonably follow. Matt could see a similarity to that and what the birds were doing. Birds, just a little ways away from the very front, virtually had no idea of what the factors the first bird was responding to…why it chose the path that it did.

So he thought some more. People are different than birds, far more complex, but geez, didn't that to some degree explain how we seem to be operating now? Aren't we pretty much blindly following the actions of some unknown leader that's choosing a path through life for us to follow? We're all caught in this flight being selected for us.

It continued to be perplexing to Matt and the others, why it was so many celebrities, so many of those we think of as the "elite" aren't weighing in on the climate crisis. Were they too, just like one of those birds caught in that huge dance being orchestrated by one bird at the front?

Maria stirred, she looked towards Matt, and strands of her hair fell across her face. "Have you been up long?"

"An hour and a half, maybe … long enough to drink two or three cups of Joe."

She walked past him, roughing up his hair on her way to the bathroom. He heard the toilet flush, she was gorgeous and also human. He had a cup of coffee waiting for her. She liked just a little bit of cream in the cup. Matt set his iPad so it was playing music they both had selected the last time she was in Boise. Nora Jones was first up.

"That was so much fun last night, how many people get to sit around four really good musician's right up close and listen to them without any amplification?" She took a sip, "Your uncle is way talented, it just makes you wonder how he didn't get to the really big time." She drank some coffee, "Oh, I liked 'Take It Easy', by the way." She paused, "I don't think you played that for me before."

"I don't think so either. You know that song is some sort of anthem for young guys everywhere. Like who hasn't had a girl that just wanted to be your friend…and a lot of them do want to own you…or at least change you to their liking."

"Me?" Suggesting she was trying in some way to change him.

"No, nothing I've really noticed."

"Changing the subject, have you heard about these "megaloads" of machinery heading to Canada?" Matt asked.

"I think so, so what's the deal?" Maria had settled back onto the bed with her coffee.

"Well, I was just reading that one of the loads is sitting down at Marsing right now."

"Where's that?"

"South of here, down on the Snake River, maybe an hour's drive at the most."

"Drive?"

"I'd like to see it directly. It's a pretty big deal really…really!"

Maria knew that was true, "Okay, I'd like to see it too."

They took the freeway exit at Nampa, a major town south of Boise. From there it was out Karcher Road.

"Chicken Dinner Road," Maria was laughing, "That's pretty classy, I'm hungry."

They rounded the corner which then dropped you into the Marsing Valley. This was the fruit and wine country of Southwestern Idaho, massive orchards of apples, cherries, plums and probably others covered the incline of the valley down to the river. "We'll stop there when we come back," he pointed to the diner; it was homey with the vines growing on the outside of the building.

On the far side of Marsing, they could see what so many people had been talking about. Matt parked his little pickup and the two of them got out. He pulled the spec's he'd printed out from his rear pant pocket. "So, this things 23' wide, 18'-11" tall, and geezes it's 349 feet long. That's longer than a football field. And it weighs 800,000 lbs." Matt stood looking gazed-eyed at the monster.

"Where does it end up?" Maria asked.

He looked at the print out again, "looks like some place near Fort McMurray, in Alberta."

They both knew what they were looking at was part of what many of the leading climate scientist in the world believe will be the death knell for our planet: burning of the vast amounts of tar sands in Canada being dug up and shipped around the world. This machinery would be used in that process. Probably, without this machinery, the ability to pump the black ooze to where it could be shipped around the world, or refined in America, would be stymied.

"They'll be using this stuff to build our own gallows." Maria observed.

Matt was quiet for a while, he'd been studying the workers that were looking after the contraption. He smiled and looked at his girlfriend, "Or maybe, it's like Jesus carrying his own cross through Jerusalem to Golgotha. Are we going to nail ourselves to our own cross?" Matt had a faraway look as he asked that.

Maria wasn't sure how to respond, was it really like that?

He looked back towards her, "he was crucified because of human senselessness…if there was ever senselessness these days…we're looking at it."

Maria nodded in agreement.

"Can we go back to that little diner and just talk about sunshine, flowers and things growing? I need some feeling that the world isn't falling all to pieces." Maria was feeling saddened.

"This is what we're fighting Maria, I want sunshine and things growing too." He stopped. "I think there are lots of other people out there that feel just like we do…lots of them. And some of them don't know they feel the way we do. They've got to be shown the way. But that's the good news, we can help show them the way, how to organize. Our manifesto is going great. We just need the next step."

"What's that, what do we do next?" Maria asked.

"I've got to really pick it up and start making the same presentation Dave's been giving. And we need to be heading towards some bigger goal. I think a march on the State Capitol Building would make sense. Start someplace and end up at the Capitol steps, then people talk. I see other groups gathered down there every once in a while. We could try to get some press coverage."

Maria's imagination was going now. "I think there's an even bigger march to make."

Matt studied her face, "what?"

"Washington DC." Her eyes narrowed with concentration, "I've seen the film clips of the Civil Rights March, the one that Martin Luther King spoke at. Let Freedom Ring. Didn't things change?"

"For a while; the Great Society stuff started then. We still have lots of troubles."

"Did they have realistic expectations?" Maria responded.

"Or did they have a realistic vision." Matt replied. "The stakes are so much greater in this struggle. Maria, if the world somehow got turned the right way with the climate crisis most all those other issues would follow I think. Just before you woke up this morning, I was watching this program where they were showing flocks of birds that make those wild ass massive movements, you know they look like a blanket that's getting shook." They were back in the car and moving. Maria nodded she was following. "They don't all have to know this big acrobatic movement, all they're doing really is just following the bird in front of them, on up the line to the front bird. So it's the whims of the front bird that's leading the whole thing. We've got the wrong front bird. Well, probably in our case it's plural. There's not just one, but there aren't that many. The key to this whole thing is a strategy to get the right front bird in place."

"Who's the front bird?" Maria then asked.

Matt hesitated only a moment, "The President of the United States. That's who the top bird needs to be. I think to a great degree Obama's hands have been tied. The next President needs to have theirs free."

~~~~~

Maria got her wish. They stopped at the diner and had pie and ice cream and talked about sunshine and growing things.

Chapter Twenty-seven

(October, 2014)

Six months had passed since the poisoning incident and Dave's mental faculties were basically back. His speech may be impaired to some degree and the therapists said it would just be a wait and see deal. The lab he worked for had agreed for him to return as he could fit in on a team they were putting together. It meant moving back to San Diego. Dave had been working with Matt on *The Kingdom of Good* presentation and Matt was more determined than ever to now take his part in the struggle. Neither he nor Maria, or any of the others on the Moab Manifesto had, anything happen. They'd all talked at length about not living their lives in fear.

Matt and Maria had decided to get a bigger apartment once she was living with him on a regular basis. They'd found a nice one just off the Connector across from the new JUMP (Jack's Urban Meeting Place) development. They liked the young energy created by the new growth downtown and it was an even closer bike ride for Matt getting to work.

Every other Tuesday night, Matt was giving the short course *Kingdom of Good* lecture. He'd particularly targeted the young people going to BSU. Like him, they were pretty much in the cross hairs of the climate crisis when world conditions were thought to potentially start to crumble on a business-as-usual path, by 2030 or 35.

It had been in a sit around, at their new apartment just before Joan left, where the four of them were brain storming, that they realized a set action plan was needed. Joan had been reflecting on something she felt was appropriate to tell her friends now.

She told them about the analogy with the Wizard of Oz and how all the characters and the story represented the struggle between people in the economy. She got to the part about, "...righteous indignation is boiling over. Its goodness, and it hits the witch and she melts. Don't you see? It's that goodness, righteous indignation that we need now more than ever. The Dorothy in us needs to awaken all around the world!"

The other three were silent for some time hashing around in their own mind how they felt about that analogy. One-by-one they came to agree: it was Dorothy that needed to awaken!

But what does Dorothy awaken and do? What would be the specific actions? To that, Dave began by explaining and promoting again the Plan B that the Earth Policy Institute, headed by Lester Brown, had been advocating: basically to reduce income taxes, putting more money in people's hands to renovate homes, businesses, automobiles and anything else that would lower carbon emissions. At the same time taxing carbon which gets paid to the government to offset the tax reductions. The cost of fossil fuels would go up, thereby making all the clean and green energy sources cheaper and therefore attract the investment money needed to scale them all up. It was a market based solution.

"I've heard there's even a more direct way to do that," Joan said, "You just tax the carbon right where it's being produced and send the money directly to people all around the country. Everybody gets a check in the mail. Everything that has carbon in it starts going up in price, like Dave just said. People have this extra money then entrepreneurs start providing everything we need to get off of fossil fuels, and they buy those products."

"Some of it will obviously get used for other things, but there would be such a strong economic interest to switch to electric cars, or to put solar panels on your house, that the majority would go where it's needed. Especially if our culture could switch fast enough to put social pressure on everybody to do what's right."

Joan went on to explain, that was the plan in action part. The political change needed to allow that to happen required an even more transcendent agenda to emerge. The modern Republican Party, of course, is the enemy; they are hopelessly confused and are simply the protectorate of the status quo, including in, particular, the fossil fuels industry and all the others that are wrapped with in its tentacles. The Democrats had, for sometime, talked of being the leaders to a green future. But they, too, seemed to have been infiltrated by the moneyed interests holding to the status quo as well. They have been impotent to act at an intensity that is truly needed.

The only alternative, they all agreed, was to go to an entirely new political leadership, and that they decided is the Green Party. Their platform represents wisdom based in the realities of how our planet works that science had revealed. Their social agenda was consistent with their values as well. Part of the end game strategy would be that by 2016 and every two years after that, their central effort would be to get Green Party politicians elected in greater and greater numbers to the Congress.

"I read the other day that someone's come up with the name 'The Great Transition'. That's what we'd call this massive societal revamping of the economy from fossil energy to renewable energy." Maria said.

Joan had a question. "Do you think we can ever get our country or the UK, France or Germany to accept the debt we all have to the smaller countries around the world that haven't contributed to the vast majority of for the carbon pollution? 'Our factories have been spewing more of that stuff into the atmosphere by far, compared to the small and poorer countries around the world, like the Philippines? They're getting hit hard already by outrageous weather and they didn't do much to cause it."

Maria continued, "I don't know, but what really scares me is all this talk about geo engineering, spraying sulfur or aluminum in the atmosphere to block the sun's rays. It's the techno fix for if the all else fails will rush to our defense. A planetary experiment that no one really knows how it would work or what the unknown consequences might be. Why would we ever put ourselves in such a position as to need to try some Hail Mary nonsense like that to begin with?"

Dave had an insight he wanted to share. His speech was a little slow but steady. "I was thinking the other day that if we were living in a way that was sustainable, like growing our food without voodoo chemical agriculture and go to ecologically based agriculture, such a change would require that millions and millions of people would move back onto the land where a family farm was 30 acres and not 3,000. And then the millions of acres that are left tilled every year, that are just releasing carbon and not storing it the way cover crops would do, get covered and start storing carbon. Society would just naturally be much more balanced, and we'd be storing vast amounts of carbon to boot."

"Wouldn't that be really good?" There was agreement. Dave continued, "And if we generated our energy with the free sources like solar, wind, waves, all those then just a small portion of people wouldn't have this enormous control over the rest of us. The world would be so much more fair too, it just would be."

"The 1% is so rich because they control the base of the economy, our food and our energy. If the land gets distributed back to sustainable ways the inequality goes away too." He stopped for a moment, "Geez, it's like a fair world and a sustainable world are coded into the DNA of life. When you grow your food the way it's meant to be a much more stable and fair society simply emerges."

They talked things over for several more hours. In the end, they decided the goal they'd push for in addition to getting Green Party candidates elected, would be the march on the State Capitals of all the fifty states by Earth Day 2015. They'd try to unite all the other environmental organizations around the country for this. And then the big march would be the next year, 2016. That's when Washington DC and the other national capitols around the world, would be the goal.

They'd meet just as the Civil Rights Marchers had in 1963. The question started to emerge, who would be the Martin Luther King of this fight: Al Gore, Bill McKibben, Lester Brown? Or would there be someone else? Was there someone yet to rise rapidly and emerge with some transcendent charisma?

(February 2015, Boise; preparing for the march on the State Capitol building)

"I like it. The red really grabs your eye." Joan, from her office in Washington DC, was commenting on the poster Matt had developed to be distributed around Southern Idaho in the effort to have a march on the State Capitol on Earth Day, April 22nd.

"I've already got permission to put it up on all the colleges across the state. I've got to ship some up north to my friend Ron and he'll put them at Lewis and Clark in Lewiston, the U of I in Moscow, and The College of Northern Idaho in Coeur d' Alene. I've got Pocatello, Idaho Falls, Twin Falls, and the Boise Valley." Matt explained.

"Any idea yet how many people might show?" Joan followed.

"We're hoping three to five thousand. There's a place on the website where people can let us know if they plan to attend. All of the environmental activist groups have been invited. Once I get these posters up and do the other media blitz, then we'll know better. By mid March, we should have a pretty good idea."

"What day of the week is it?" Joan asked.

"It's a Wednesday. I wish it was a Saturday, but you know getting people to make the sacrifice from a work schedule might be good."

The hard work of organizing continued. Being the point person, Matt was already getting a buzz about his politics around town. Not everyone found what he and his associates were planning to be a good idea. In fact, some absolutely hated the notion.

"I'll take a quarter pound of the smokejumpers," Matt told the young girl standing behind the counter at the peanut shop, downtown.

"You really should try the 'holly hot nuts' some time," she suggested, enjoying the play on words and watching how the guys react.

Matt smiled at her, "Ah, trust me, I have, the nuts too."

He bumped into the owner as he was going out the door, "There's a bunch of us going to see Josh Ritter this weekend and you're invited to come along if you want?" The owner was a good friend of Uncle Dan's.

"Maybe, I'll drop you an email and let you know, but I think that works." Matt said.

~~~~~

Matt had to cross Main Street right across from the site where the new JUMP complex was being built. A poster had recently been going up around town with the picture of two well known rightwing talk show hosts on it. There was a caption that said "Great Patriots" and Matt had to laugh to himself. All he saw was a couple of border collies.

Chapter Twenty-eight

March on the Capitol

(Saturday April 18th, 2015; Boise Airport, Maria arriving)

"Missed you," Maria said, after a quick kiss from Matt where he was picking her up at the airport.

"I'm exhausted." She was on the last leg of flights that had taken her home to Spain, then to Norway for several days to meet with her boss at Norse Aquatic, then a week in British Colombia at the fish farm.

"Well, there's nothing we need to do today but sleep. Tomorrow Mom wants us to come over and Uncle Dan and Leslie will be there too. Joan gets here Monday night."

"I know. We've been texting a little."

Matt got on the freeway and then took the connector back downtown.

"There's some salad stuff in the frig and some juice there too," Matt said, after they'd settled into his new apartment. He had a book of specifications he'd brought home with him from the office. He was doing the redlining that would then be given to the office staff for word processing.

"Um, I like the light you have here so much better than that basement place." Maria had a small bowl of greens and nuts with her.

There was something he'd wanted to tell her about, "My boss pulled me into his office Tuesday. He wanted to talk to me about my activism, as he called it."

"You mean Mike?"

"Yeah, I guess some client of ours has seen my name on the posters around town and isn't thrilled he's paying for my services." Matt's voice carried the sense of indignation he was feeling.

"My mom told me that sooner or later if you take a stand on things you're going to get cross ways with someone and probably more than one."

"Did he tell you who or what they might do?"

"No, he just told me that the word was getting around and a few people we do business with don't approve."

"Can it affect your job?"

"He told me I'd probably figure out where it was coming from by the jobs I don't get put on anymore and he thought it would just be better to leave it at that. I guess they didn't require that they fire me."

"Littleness," Maria observed.

"I have a whole bunch of students from Boise State who are going to be in the march; maybe 35 or 40 of them. They are mostly people in the science departments. I think there are two that are studying accounting."

"They're probably planted by the Nazis around here." Maria was teasing but there was reason to be cynical.

"The weather is supposed to be good on Wednesday," Matt began. "I'm not totally sure this will happen, but one of the television stations said they would be out to where we start, up at the train station, giving us coverage that morning. I'm pretty sure we'll get at least two of the local stations at the Capitol when everyone starts giving their speech." Representatives from several of the local environmental groups had agreed to give short speeches. Since Matt and the others were the local *Kingdom of Good* representatives and had started the idea of the march, the others agreed that someone representing the KOG should give the keynote.

Joan had become something of a celebrity due to the Moab Manifesto. Between the four of them they'd decided that it was Joan that should continue to be the voice of the KOG here.

"Have you seen a draft of what Joan is going to say?" Maria asked Matt.

"No. Maybe she's just going to surprise us." Matt answered.

Joan had written several articles that had made it to print in several national magazines which gave her a little growing star power nationally too. Her affiliations around the country with various activist groups and her position as the liaison to the Green Party, were also good reasons for her to be the main act. Matt was fine in just a support role, for now. Maria too, for the time being, was fine just being one of the bodies.

(Tuesday evening April 21st, 2015; at Uncle Dan's)

"Pass me some of the cranberries, please." Matt was directing the request in the direction of his Uncle Dan. They were all gathered at his place for a nice meal before the big march that would occur the next day, Earth Day.

"I've always liked that tart taste you get from cranberries. They're such a contrast to what everything else seems to taste like." Matt was dishing several scoops onto his plate.

"They're so colorful too." Micky noted.

"I've got those ribs marinating up real good. I'll have the smoker going by 5:30 in the morning down there at the park across from the Capitol and they should be real tasty by 1:30." Uncle Dan told them. Several hundred people had sent money so they could share some food after the march and the speeches had been given. Most people would probably just disap-

330

pear to the various restaurants scattered around the central business district in downtown Boise, where the Capitol building is located. That was encouraged by the planning letter sent to everyone that returned their notice that they'd be a part of the march.

Matt was up early as there was just extra juice in his tank this morning. This event they'd been imagining and planning for the past year was now about to happen. How many people would really show? He knew from his life's experience how people could talk about doing something, then when it came to actually following through; well, that could often be a different story. They had signed letters back from only about 350 people. Far short of the ten times that they were hoping might show. They just didn't know.

At least the 350 or so who had committed would have shirts with messages on them that they wanted to get people seeing and thinking about. Several hundred people had selected the yellow shirts with the black letters that read 'TAX CARBON NOW!' on the front and the back. The other shirts were in black and had yellow type that read 'STOP KEYSTONE XL.' That is the pipeline that industry wants to build to ship the tar sludge from Alberta, Canada to the Gulf of Mexico, and then ship around the world. The same project the megaloads carrying the processing equipment Matt and Maria had driven down to see were heading to.

And there was one more T shirt they'd come up with. The other two told them what they were "against;" this one would tell others what they were "for." On a white shirt in light green lettering it said, 'GREEN PARTY USA and WORLD.' Their logo was also on the shirts. In a nutshell those T shirts said what the march was about.

"Looks like we've got media," Matt noted to Maria as he parked his small pickup near the train station.

"Several, there's one over there too," she observed.

"I really didn't expect that station to be here," Matt added.

"Well, I guess in the next half hour we'll find out how concerned Idaho is about saving the world." Matt continued after they walked over near the front entry to the train station.

One volunteer had already set up a small table where people could write down their name, phone number, and email address so that they could get a larger network. A mailer had gone out through Friends of the Snake River who had about the largest mailing list of people involved in activism in Southern Idaho. But gatherings like this offered the chance to get even more people located.

331

Matt felt a tap on his shoulder, it was a young woman dressed for business, a face he recognized. "Are you Matthew Lundquist?" she asked. Matt could see the camera and lights heading towards them.

"Yes." He nodded his head acknowledging that fact.

"I'm Cynthia VanPappegan with KTOP. You are one of the organizers of the march I was told, would you be willing to make a few comments for us?"

Matt felt that little pang in his stomach; that thing he'd always felt since he was a kid when he knew he'd be the center of attention. "Okay, sure I'll do that."

A few moments went by; Cynthia heard the cut from the studio. "Thank you Leah, yes I'm at the train station this morning with one of the organizers of this march today. It's Earth Day for any of you that might not know that. I have with me Matthew Lundquist and he's agreed to share with us a few of the reasons for the march today. So, Mr. Lundquist, can you explain what the people gathering here right now will be wanting the rest of us to know?"

She extended the microphone so he could be heard. He had told himself just talk to her, not everyone else all around, stay focused there. "We've got a huge problem on our planet right now. Us, all of us, are not living in a way that is sustainable."

"You mean like with climate change?" The young reporter prompted him for more.

"Yes, climate change is just one aspect. We're causing the extinction of tens of thousands of species of other life forms every year when only ten or twelve would be average. Millions of people are starving to death around the world, a huge number of them just children and that is totally avoidable. And we're loading the atmosphere and the oceans with so much pollution that they're about to give out in any way that can support us. So a lot of "us," he emphasized, "think it's time to take a stand to change all that, if we still have time. This is how were starting. Millions of people around the world have already started."

He was young, about her age, and so passionate. She was being drawn in, "What will you be doing? You start with a march to the Capitol building, is that correct?"

"Yes, in about fifteen or twenty minutes we'll start the march. It will take about an hour to get everybody down there and set up to listen to our three speakers. We have two speakers from groups around Idaho, and then Joan Lebeau. She's our keynote speaker and she's had several articles published recently in major magazines on all this."

"Thank you for that." The reporter turned and noted where she was and turned the program back to Leah in the studio. With the camera off, she thanked Matt one more time, and wished them good luck.

"Good job." Maria told Matt.

While he was talking he hadn't noticed the large group of people who were walking up the street towards them. "Matt look!" Maria said, pointing towards them all.

Matt turned so he could see, his heart jumped, "Holy shit!" It was the college kids. It looked like an assembly had just ended and everyone was headed out.

He looked at Maria, "There must be a thousand people, maybe more, walking this way."

Joan and Dave were now standing next to them, "Maybe some of them are listening after all." Maria said.

Uncle Dan and some of the guys and their wives from the band, they were there too. There was a special feeling of something great happening right then. The flags and banners were stationed at the front. The banner that would lead the entire march and about eighteen feet wide read, 'SAVE OUR PLANET.' That pretty much set the tone.

Matt had a bull horn; he thanked them all for coming and then said, "Let's roll!"

~~~~~

Along the way, like a magnet moving past grains of lead, the group grew larger and larger. It was more than just students, as a few middle-aged people with coats and ties joined them.

But not everyone was impressed. On the far side of the Boise River Bridge a group had gathered intent on heckling the marchers. They had their own sign which read, 'GOD IS ON OUR SIDE!'

As they passed, a few words were said, but the hecklers had not expected such a large crowd. They anticipated a much smaller group that they intended to intimidate. But they were not ready for such a showing of support. The chant of the marchers, 'save our planet' by far dwarfed that of the hecklers.

But for one, the image of these traitors fueled his already jaded mind. These were the ones the "Bold Americans" told him were destroying the fabric of his country. This was all their way to pervert the land he just knew would be made a cesspool if they had the chance to come and take power. That's what they told him so it must be true. His camera was busy photographing.

"Again, I just want to tell you all how excited I am to see this size turn out," Matt was talking to the crowd that had gathered at the Capitol steps. They stretched across the road and into the parks on either side of the drives. Anticipating that if a large crowd did show they'd never be able to hear the speakers well, Matt had written copies of the speeches ready to hand out. That turned out to be a great idea.

The two lead-up speakers did their part to set the tone for Joan and now it was her time.

Matt waved at everyone he knew were out beyond where they could hear easily. "Pass it along to follow Joan's outline," Matt said. In turn, people passed the message on down.

Joan took the lectern. She knew her comments needed to be brief and very to the point. She had the three points she wanted everyone to take away with them.

There was applause as she took the lectern.

"Number One," she held one finger up and it was quickly passed along.

"Thank you, thanks, thanks. I've offered three parts to my comments. Of course I'll start with number one. 'Something's Wrong.' A lot of us know that, we know that the weather is a lot different from when we were kids. Depending on where you live, you see and feel it more. On the coasts they've seen the unprecedented hurricanes. The heartland experiences the tornadoes that grow in number and intensity, just ask the people of Moore, Oklahoma or Joplin, Missouri. The Mountain States see the forests turning brown because of infestations of bark beetles that no longer die out over the winter, and then the drought and the fires that follow. The farmers have seen their crops wither in the heat waves where 40% of America's corn was lost in 2012. We see the lightning far more than we used to. Around the world, tens of thousands of species of plants and animals are going extinct each year when normally only ten or twelve would. The mountain glaciers are melting and will soon no longer provide water for millions that have grown to depend on them for their livelihood. The continental ice sheets on Greenland and Antarctica are melting at unprecedented rates. The oceans are becoming toxic to the life that lives in them because our polluting of the atmosphere with excessive gases. The oceans are rising and forcing people already to migrate. There is enormous inequity in wealth. There is mass starvation with nearly a billion of us vastly under nourished. Indigenous farmers are forced from their ancestral lands by the millions by rich country speculators. Regional wars and mass migrations are becoming endemic. This is not a picture of a civilization that can last much longer!"

She held up two fingers. "Humanity is to blame! The other creatures we share this planet with are not causing this to happen but *we are*!!! It is our over reach. There are now more than seven billion of us where only two billion at most could live reasonably. And it is not just our numbers it is the way we live, massively burning fossil fuels to create the energy we only want and not need. There are limits we must live within on our little planet drifting through the immensity of the cosmos. The gases we release are creating a blanket that traps heat that must be dispersed in the biosphere. This disrupts the historical weather patterns and temperatures our civilization emerged from. We are reeking havoc with our home and there is only a small amount of time left, if we are lucky, to act in ways to preserve a habitable planet for our descendents and the other life that shares the planet with us. Leading scientists are warning us, we are nearing limits or tipping points from which we might lose all control of our climate and begin a stupefying descent into hell."

This time she held up three fingers. "What can we do? Each of us alone is as helpless as a fly stopping an ocean liner. But together, like a cloud swarming on an enemy, we can stop the advance of the out-of-control engine of industry that is poisoning our world. I'm not the first one to suggest this. Millions of people have been trying for decades to get the silent majority of the people to awaken. They do a bit here and there, but mostly they are still asleep. But the knocking of the planets failing systems is hopefully awakening them."

On December 1st, 1862 our great President Abraham Lincoln, in what was his second address to Congress, said this as they contemplated the civil war that was already raging due largely to the moral issue of slavery: 'we shall nobly save, or meanly lose, the last best hope of Earth.' President Lincoln probably meant our American Democracy, but I think there is more: I submit that the last best hope of Earth he was also referring to is the goodness we "can" feel in our hearts, but so often ignore to satisfy our greed or desire for power. It is exactly that sense for goodness and fairness we need now most to emerge. We have to acknowledge our connection to the future and our responsibility to it and them: the people and all the other life forms."

Suddenly one, then three, then fifteen, then nearly all of them listening began to clap, to cheer…she touched that deeply human part of them. A minute passed and then she continued. "But it is not just with our hearts that we can change our path. The federal government of the United States of America, used properly, is the one and only organization on Earth that can now lead us from this precipice. No other country or government is so influential or capable. If the United States does not lead, then we are doomed." She paused for a moment; everyone was intent on her next words. "We have a democracy; we have the capacity, at least in theory, to remove those who are leading us towards Armageddon. Nearly 40% of those eligible to vote in the United States, don't. We must awaken this sleeping giant. There is only one political party now with the moral and intellectual integrity we need to lead us: The Green Party of America. Please, go to the website '*The Kingdom of Good.com*' everything you need to understand is there."

She had just a little more to say. "Please join us. It is our great hope that next year, 2016, on this day, Earth Day, we will march on Washington, DC and make our voices heard there." She lifted her hand with the peace symbol, "On to Washington!" She again paused before finishing, "May goodness be with us! Thank you."

Those directly around her began to clap with great enthusiasm, further out those seeing that she'd finished the words they were reading, began to clap as well. They knew, intuitively, that something remarkable had just happened. Perhaps a star had been born.

Maria was the first to greet her. "You were wonderful." she had tears in her eyes. They hugged. Matt was next, then Uncle Dan and others near her. Dave let the crowd subside before taking his turn.

"You really touched them," his voice did not break, "they needed that, they needed you!" He grabbed hold of her giving a place in himself to her we rarely find.

Part Five: Unforeseen Consequences

Chapter Twenty-nine

(Silver Creek, the mountains north of Boise; mid July 2015; camping)

Maria rolled down her window just a little more. It was hot and she wanted to let her hand ride on the wind just outside the pickup. "I see why they call it Horseshoe Bend," she said as they made their way down Highway 55 above the town.

"Yeah, the river heads into this corner where Harris Creek connects with it, then turns and heads on down towards Emmett. My mom told me it used to be real easy to get a speeding ticket here. Knowing how she drives though it probably had more to do with her lead foot."

"Like the little old lady from Pasadena?" Maria was smirking.

Matt looked over his sunglasses at her, "That's pretty good. I wouldn't have thought you know that song."

"My mom loved the Beach Boys, oh and; Surfer Girl, Fun Fun Fun, Wouldn't it Be Nice. There was a beach near our farm," Maria began to explain. Matt was trying to remember the landscape around her home from the time he'd visited there four years earlier, "Mom would take me and Ladwina and these big colorful beach balls and we'd head there for the day. Um, what fun."

"We'd come up here," Matt then explained, "We'll be going by the beach we'd come to, it's just up here four or five miles. The rafters were always going by. We had a big squirt gun and would try to hit them. I remember one time this one raft of people we got wet decided to come back and get us. They paddled over to where Donny and I were standing. They acted like they just wanted to talk, then when they got close this one woman jumps out. She has this enormous squirt gun and it was powered by a pump. She just lays us out. They'd done some hand signals to my mom I found out later and she'd told them to go ahead." He thought for a moment, "Oh, we heard them call her GI somebody, there was a movie out about then called GI Jane, I think. She got us good."

(Boise, the same day)

There was one channel Larry listened to constantly because every red-blooded American listened to it. For months now, the hosts had been showing short segments of manifestos on the Internet from groups all around the world. The normal spin was to show a small part then an "ex-

337

pert" in climate research would be interviewed who would cast serious doubt on the entire premise that the manifestos were aimed at: the climate crisis and biosphere destruction. There was always a backdrop imaging of a serene landscape, with plenty of sunshine, waterfalls and flowers. Where's the problem, was the implicit message.

Scattered on the small table in front of him were the magazines he subscribed to: guns, military, mechanics and electronics were the themes of their content. Earlier that morning, Larry had watched the clip he'd saved from the news cast of the march on the Capitol, last April. The "bitch" as he had named her in his own mind, became more and more a target of his inner hatred. He didn't like women in general, any more; especially uppity ones who just wanted the liberal agenda to ruin his country.

For as long as he could remember, he had a difficult time relating to the opposite sex. Not that at times he didn't want to, but they always seemed to want something that he didn't have. Of course the girls who might have shown him attention were never of interest to him. And there was that time in high school when three of them seemed to be making fun of him. They were acting out something about the way he walked. That had really left a sour note.

Like nearly all the boys, he'd had some dream of being good at sports. But with each successive grade, as the athletes tended to aggregate together on the teams, Larry got left behind. There was no shame in that; it's just life. Everybody has to find the niche they have some aptitude for. His family had farmed down near Homedale, so he'd gotten a good understanding for mechanics helping his dad with the machinery repair. In his sophomore year, he discovered the Electronics Club and found a group there he could relate to. When their club successfully put that first radio together, with just transistors, diodes and wires, following the basic crystal set design that first emerged in the 1920s, and picked up a local radio station, he was hooked. That was his thing.

Following high school, it had been his plan to become an electrical engineer, as that was what people did that were interested in electronics. But after the first year struggling with the math and physics he needed to master, his dreams of that dwindled. Larry didn't want to farm as he'd seen how his family struggled with that.

The military was advertising a lot back in the early 80s and the draft no longer existed. It looked exciting, and so he applied and was accepted. Once in, he discovered a track where you could apply for computer simulation design. It required a knack for programming which it turned out he had. In the end, it lead him to a career designing tank battle simulator programs or extremely cutting edge video games, as he would describe it later to those who asked what he did.

The military had given him a great platform to become acquainted with weaponry, and particularly hand held guns. After basic training, he was one who continued and competed with others in marksmanship. It became a passion and Larry came to love guns and wanted to own as many as he could. There was power there.

He was married once, a long time ago, it didn't work as there was so much compromise. Over time, he really came to not like woman very much so it was just easier to live by himself. He had so much freedom. He could play his video games whenever he wanted, go to his gun shows and what he loved the most: the competitions. He'd advanced to using small rapid fire arms, and did quite well.

It had not happened all at once, but since 9/11 he'd come to rely more and more for his news content from that one source. The main stream media or the lame stream media, as he'd been taught, were never telling him the truth. In particular, this whole concoction over climate change was just the tweedy jacket type looking for money from the government for their research. What a bunch of crap that was. They needed to do real work like he did with tanks and guns; that's how America would stay strong. As far as he was concerned now, all these eco types wanted was to subvert the American way. And uppity women connected to this eco stuff were really bugging him.

Larry had done his part when the march on the Capitol had taken place. His group had set up just north of the Boise River Bridge and let the marchers know there were others who didn't agree with their leftist views.

(Saturday morning July 26th, 2015; at Silver Creek)

"Did you sleep well?" Joan asked as Maria joined them next to the camp fire. Matt had been the first one up, he'd got the fire going. Dave, and Matt's younger brother Donny, and his girlfriend Sam, had followed soon thereafter. Uncle Dan and Leslie were supposed to get there sometime around noon as Leslie had a golf match that kept them in town the night before.

It was after eight which was late for getting up when camping. The sun had already cleared the top of some nearby evergreen trees, so the coolness of the morning would be giving way soon. Maria's hiking boots weren't even laced up and she had one of Matt's big jackets wrapped around her as she approached.

"Coffee's still hot if you want some," Matt told her. "I'll get it for you if you want?"

"Sure." Maria answered and rubbed her forehead some.

"Damned smoke," Matt said, waving at the air to get it to go away.

"So you have to go to Dallas?" Maria asked, looking at Joan.

"Yes, there's a lot of effort going into trying to elect Wendy Davis governor down there. I'm working with some local groups helping with organization. It's going to be close as the Republicans of course have deep roots there. But the state looks to be going purple. We'll see."

"Do they know you're called Joan of Arc in Idaho?" Donny asked.

She laughed, "I hope not. I haven't done anything down there to attract attention."

"That whole Joan of Arc thing got its play in Boise and Sun Valley, then settled away pretty fast." Matt added.

Dave's ability to speak had nearly returned to normal, "You think you know someone then they turn out to have lived six hundred years ago, she does have that thing about fire too, you know."

"What?" Matt then questioned.

Dave looked at Joan, "Do you want me to tell them?" She just shrugged her shoulders; it was something that actually bothered her. "She's had this fear of flames since she was little. It's like PTSD connection to emotions."

"Seriously?" Matt uttered.

"Really?" Maria then asked.

"Don't make more out of it than that. But yes, some people have some innate fear of heights or snakes but flames seem to trip some circuit for me."

"Anything else, like riding in front of French soldiers on a big horse with flags waving all around?"

"Matt, don't tease," Maria scolded a bit.

"Oh, I know it's weird and then there's my name. I don't understand, I don't know what to make of it." Another thought traced through her mind. "Have any of you ever had a premonition of something or someone?"

"What do you mean?" Maria requested.

"Like a feeling or a presence passes near you, so close you could touch but just not quite?" Joan explained.

Maria was thinking, "Yes, but you first."

"Well you all know about the boyfriend, Harry, I had who died in the 9/11 attack?" It was still difficult even to say his name; a shadow Dave knew would always be there. The others acknowledged that they did. "A few years ago, just after the first part of the memorial grounds were opened, I went there by myself, I wanted to see where his name had been etched in the stone." She stopped briefly, controlling a bit of emotion, "It's beautiful, the fountain and the water falling like it does, into a bottom you can never see." A little more time, "I was standing there, touching the

340

carved letters of his name, and then I felt something, I thought it was wind my hair did move, but everything in me says it was something else."

"What something else?" Donny needed to ask.

"I don't know. Something was there, as close as my breath. I guess I'll never know."

"Okay, I'll tell you mine," Maria then began, "Matt was with me. We were at the Vatican in Rome, and Poppy, the girl I told you about who we met over there, the black girl; she was in the hospital on life support following the accident she and my sister were in." She looked at Matt, "We were just out on those front steps, right?" He nodded his head agreeing, "I remember the bright colors of the Vatican guard who was at attention just a few feet away. Then something felt like it flew right through me, like two galaxies passing through each other. And I just knew," she paused, "I knew Poppy had died."

"She just started running," Matt then continued with the story, "She's pretty quick too. I had the cameras and had to get them tucked away. But I was able to stay close. I don't know, but we were probably a mile from the hospital. We went running in and the look on the nurse's face told the story. It was awful."

"The Akashic Field, that's what Dr. Sherman would say." Dave then said.

Donny was the only one not familiar with that concept. Matt quickly explained that it was a cutting edge physics theory of a field or matrix that connects all space and time, and that in reality all things are connected by it, including us, and that everything being separate was an illusion. And the name was derived from the ancient Hindu concepts of Prana and Akasha, which held a similar notion to the new physics.

Matt saw Uncle Dan's car go by on the road above where they were camped, "Looks like they're here," he noted.

They talked for a few hours after they arrived. The plan was for them all to hike into the hot springs that were about a mile or so from a trailhead several hundred yards from their camp. Matt and Uncle Dan had their packs filled with the goodies they'd eat once up at the hot springs. Uncle Dan had some brew and some weed for a little extra enjoyment. The 70s never ended for him and Leslie.

~~~~~

The hike in was easy, just a little up and down and some places where the grass nearly covered the trail. Matt took the lead and used his walking stick to poke around in the weeds in those shadowy places a little voice says 'watch for snakes' which are mostly never there. One group of people passed them as they headed in. They reported that the hot springs were full of water and no one seemed to have trashed them. At times that would happen, people leaving their wrappers, toilet paper, sometimes worse.

After about 45 minutes, they made it to the fork in the trail where you go up a little draw to the hot springs. The steam from the various pools could be seen right away.

"Looks like we're here," Leslie said.

Those they had talked to were right as the pools were full and clean. People had stacked the rocks to make the pools, so sometimes they got knocked down by people or just the winter weathering could get them falling apart some.

The water coming out of the ground was way too hot to sit or even stand in. It had to be mixed with the stream water that was flowing past. There were rocks at the point where the hot spring water flowed into the main stream and the pools. The rocks could be adjusted to get the temperature just to their liking or as close as possible.

"Love your brown polka dots, "Joan said, commenting on Maria's bikini."

"My sister bought this for me and she gave it to me the last time I was in Spain."

"It's cute and it looks great on you." Joan added. Matt liked it a lot too.

Donny and Sam moved to one end of the pool where from time to time you'd catch them kissing.

Conversations varied as they mostly just sat and soaked, then got out and took in the sunshine. After about an hour, Uncle Dan told them that he and Leslie were going to head back to the camp, maybe catch a little shut eye before firing up the grill for some more of his ribs. The others wanted to hang a little longer; maybe wander up the trail a ways and see the big waterfall. They'd be an hour or two behind.

Danny and Leslie reached the trailhead and started down the road that led back to the camp area. There was a camp site nearby. No one had been there when they'd walked by a few hours earlier. Dan could tell from a distance that there was a vehicle there now, but pretty well hidden in the woods. It seemed like they wanted to be out of site as best possible. As they got close, Dan thought he could recognize the truck. He stopped at the fork that lead down to where the pickup was parked. "Looks familiar," Leslie said.

"Yes, it does." Dan responded, an edge of concern in his voice. He glanced towards Leslie, "let's take a look."

Dan looked all around to see if he spotted the person he was thinking connected with this vehicle. He could see no one. As they walked closer the jacked-up and dark-grey pickup with the flashy chrome wheels looked more and more like the one they'd seen earlier that morning. They looked in the windows, just as before the interior looked like a fortified military command center. But what was different were the guns that had been easily seen earlier that morning, were gone. So too were any license plates.

Just before they arrived at the camp, Dan and Leslie had stopped into the little store there at The Plunge and picked up a few supplies they'd forgotten that morning. A man walked in shortly after they'd entered. He seemed to not recognize them, but Danny recognized him. For whatever reason Dan was good at remembering faces and this guy stood out. Where had he seen him? He worked it around in his mind as they got their stuff. Leslie needed to use the bathroom so this guy made his purchase and was out the door ahead of them. When she returned, they ended up walking right past where the guy had parked. He was in the back end doing something, the door to is pickup was open and they could see the military looking arsenal he had inside: several handguns and a large assault rifle. The entire cab looked to be black, grey, and chrome.

Dan got one more look at him as he was getting out of the back end when they acknowledged each other. Once back to his car, Dan remembered where he'd seen the man: he was the one standing closest to the street with the group trying to heckle the Earth Day march. 'Okay, that was where I saw that guy,' he had thought to himself. Dan mentioned that fact briefly to Leslie as they had left.

"I don't have a good feel about this," Danny said, concern growing on his face. "Why would that guy have parked here and headed out with all of those guns. It wasn't hunting season and nobody comes all the way up here to target practice. He knew of the threatening letters Matt and Joan had received too. This didn't smell right.

"Come on." Leslie knew better than to try and stop him. She knew he was headed to get his .45.

"Get down to The Plunge, tell them what's going on and get some people with guns back here as fast as you can to block this road!" She agreed.

Dan got his gun then strapped it around his waist as he headed back, running towards the trail head. Before every blind corner along the trail, he pulled the .45 so he would be as fast as possible if needed. A quarter mile in he had to stop and catch his breath. He could see up the trail several hundred yards and he listened intently. He thought he heard some cracking on the hillside a good distance ahead and above him. Dan grabbed his binoculars and scanned the area intently for over a minute, but could not see anything. Then, just briefly, quite some distance ahead he thought he saw some movement, but when he found the area with his binoculars he again could see nothing. The only thing he could think to do was to continue in. He didn't want to holler as he had no idea where the guy was or what he might do if he heard someone yelling. Be quiet and get to the hot springs he decided was what he had to do.

(At the hot springs; 2:38 PM)
Larry had been watching them from a distance the night before and he'd counted just the six of them, the same number that was there the next morning before he'd left to get a few supplies. He'd taken the high ridge in behind them. His military camouflage outfit did help to blend him into the pine and spruce covered rocky hills. From his perch, he had been able to watch as Dan and Leslie left. He never did actually see them all together though so he wasn't sure if they knew each other. The six he'd counted that morning however were all still there. There was his little tribe to mess with.

He had no real intent to kill anyone, but his desire was to scare the Holy shit out of them and get some real adrenaline kicks for himself. He had live ammo in the magazine, but he didn't expect to use any. From where he was at, he could see the trail for over a mile each way. He'd been watching for some time and felt that no one was in the little pockets he couldn't directly see. It was time to act.

They were all still sitting in the hot springs when Larry suddenly was upon them. His head was disguised by some black head gear that covered his entire head and face. His large automatic rifle was pointing directly at them. He'd found a device on the internet that disguised his voice and it made him sound a bit like Darth Vader. He said nothing for a few moments as everyone was just frozen in terror. Matt and Dave had moved the short distance closer and in front of their girlfriends. Donny and Sam just froze.

"If you want to live, keep your mouths shut and do what I say." The voice added to their fear. "Wrap these around your waist." He threw them short pieces of chain link. "Wrap them around your waist like the one is around mine," he pointed to it. "Make sure they're really tight." He watched to make sure they were. "Now run this cable through the two middle links, blond woman at the end." Joan hesitated then moved slightly so she was next to Dave, but at the end of the six of them.

His intent was to leave five of them bound together and then to a tree. He'd take Joan some distance away, bind and gag her and fire a shot so they thought she'd been killed. Before doing so he'd explain to her the need to stop any and all activism and to pass that around. He would tell her

344

where a key could be found several miles or so up stream to release her friends. He would be long gone before they could ever get free. That was his plan.

From his place hidden in the tall willows that lined the stream above them, Danny watched what was going on. He had no idea what the man's intent was; if he acted hastily he might lose any advantage he currently had with the man not knowing he was there. If it looked like the man was about to start shooting, he'd have no option but to rush him and hope to cause enough confusion so that some of them would get away.

When the cable passed through Matt's two links, Larry told Joan to hand the end to him. No one knew what was going on. He had them all walk over next to a big tree. "Sit down there," he said, then pointing at Joan he said, "pull that chain out and sit over here." She was confused but did as he said.

Looking at Joan Larry said, "You and I are gonna go have a little chat!"

He locked the chain so the five were held.

"Joan!" Dave yelled.

Larry looked at him through his mask, "Keep quiet or she'll die. I just want to have a chat with her."

"Blondie, come with me." He started to walk.

"No!" What was he going to do?

He looked towards her, raised his rifle and fired. The silencer made the "puff" sound. The bullet struck the ground beyond. "Don't make me narrow my aim, Blondie."

He could have killed her right then, if that was his intent; maybe he did just intend to scare her.

She looked towards Dave and the others. She was terrified, but trying to maintain her composure.

"If you hurt her I'll find you, you bastard!" Dave blurted out.

Larry turned, slowly. "Not one more word or I start destroying knees. Understand pencil head?" Dave said nothing.

The two disappeared around the corner. The five of them sat dazed for a moment.

"Psss't," the sound came from the nearest brush. Danny had moved quickly from his hiding place in the trees. He had one finger over his mouth as they turned to see him.

"Clear?" he said, just high enough they could barely hear him. They looked, and then nodded quickly.

"He said he was taking Joan to have a chat. We don't know," Dave whispered.

Danny handed his Handyman knife set to Matt, "If you can get it open, follow as you can." He left them and headed after Joan.

He had to move with stealth. They may have gone only a short distance and he didn't want to lose the advantage of surprise.

The grass at the bend was long, maybe four feet tall, and there was wild dogwood and a small stand of alder as well. Dan was on his hands and knees as he worked around the corner. He parted the grass so he could see up the trail. There they were, 60 or 70 yards on. She was sitting down and he was standing above her. He could just barely hear the sound of the lunatic's muffled voice as it was inaudible. He moved on through the brush as far as he dare lest he be seen. Her hands were bound behind her and her feet were bound as well. He was adjusting a gag around her mouth.

"Now you Blondie bitch, realize that I could leave you here with a hole right through your head, but you're more valuable telling the rest of your ilk how they need to forget their plan to ruin this great country." Oh, what a rush he was having! That was the biggest thing he wanted, that rush of adrenaline you can only get in really tight situations. He'd got the word to her and the other miserable bastards as well. He'd be back in town hearing about this whole thing on the news. How fucking cool was that?

Larry had one last thing to do: just to put that final scare into her, and them. He began to pull the Baretta M9 he had in his holster out with the intent to just scare her with it.

Dan had been holding his gun on a stick as steady as possible waiting to see what he had to do. He only had three bullets and knew he'd have to use them carefully. But seeing the man starting to pull the gun from its holster he decided he had no choice but to fire.

"Thwaaack," he hit him, Larry tumbled forward, Joan threw herself to the ground and rolled up tight as she could. He'd been hit in the side, the bullet protecting armor had taken much of the impact, but he was hurt bad. Larry struggled to pull his weapon up and find whoever it was that had shot him. He didn't see anyone. He picked up the rifle and shuffled bullets into the magazine. Who'd shot him? Those little bastards had a gun? He had a bigger gun. She wasn't going anywhere with those chains on her legs. He wacked her face with the butt of his gun. He'd finish her after he got them. The pain was making him even crazier than he already was.

Larry moved up the slope away from the direction the shot had come from. Dan was hoping he'd just leave and they'd catch him below when they had help. But that's not what Larry intended.

Dan moved back and could see that the five were now free; that Handyman evidently did the job. Having heard the shot they had begun moving towards him.

"Bam, Bam, Bam" Matt, Donny and Sam were hit and went down, Maria and Dave ran for the cover of the nearby trees. Larry assumed that one of them had the gun and started down the slope towards where the three were lying in excruciating pain. Dan knew it was now or never. If that crazy bastard got close to either of his nephews and Sam, he'd finish them for sure.

At the top of his lungs he screamed, "MOTHER FUCKER, I HAVE THE GUN!" Larry spun to see where he was. He saw Dan for just a moment before he disappeared behind the slope. Larry was confused, where had this other person come from? He'd expose himself to an open shot if he went any closer to the three down. No, he had to kill this son of a bitch first and then get the others. He had to be on the other side of the ridge he'd just come up over. Jeezuz his side hurt. He was sweating hard.

Dan knew he had to keep the man on the run. He couldn't let him have time to stop and take aim on his nephews and Sam. He had to show himself and keep him moving. What the man did not know and Dan did, was that he only had two more bullets, the last time he was out target shooting he'd used the others up. He knew going in he only had the three shots; they had to be good.

"Hey," Dan yelled at him before dashing into the long grass. Larry was bent down, his ability to concentrate was getting severely strained. He didn't hear as his Berreta fell out of the holster he had not buttoned down. "I gotta kill that bastard," was all he could think of. He headed down towards the grass and he could see the trail of bent foliage Danny had left. He bobbed up and down trying to get a view of the mystery man.

Suddenly, there was motion to his right. It was Danny who hadn't gone the way Larry was hoping, Larry shot and missed. Danny had the cover of a large pine so he decided to take it and shoot. He missed. Get to higher ground was all he could think of. He scrambled through the rock, slipping, trying to hold the gun so he could save for the last shot.

Another shot rang out. This one hit Danny in the leg, and he went down hard. He had the gun in his hand, but he wasn't sure if he could even shoot it. Danny was lying in the rocks when Larry mistakenly moved to where he could see him. There was one little corridor he could fire through and Larry filled it. "Thwaaack." Larry tumbled down the slope. He'd been hit in the armor again. But he rose quickly and was moving rapidly towards a place to get a shot off at Danny.

"THWAAACK" the Berrata's armor-piercing bullet punctured the vest and ripped through his stomach. He lost consciousness in only a moment.

Dave moved carefully towards him with the Berreta firmly in his grip should he need to fire again. Larry's rifle was a good five feet from his hands and he couldn't pull on him fast if he still had the life to try. Still holding the gun directly at him, Dave grabbed a long stick and stuck it up under the black mask he was wearing. He didn't seem to react.

He grabbed the rifle and rushed to Dan's side. He was bleeding hard from the leg. Dave pulled his belt off and wrapped it as tightly around as he could. The flow of blood seemed to slow.

He needed to get to Joan. Dave was horrified as to what he might find. He ran down the slope to the trail, he looked 40 or 50 yards distant and there she was sitting up. He rushed to Joan and pulled the cloth that had been gagging her. She coughed and spat, and sucked for breath that her swollen nostrils had been compromised to allow, following the blow Larry had given her. But she was breathing so he could leave her for the moment. "I'll be right back."

He ran to where Maria was trying to comfort Matt, Donny and Sam who lay a few feet away. Tears were streaming down her face. "Donny," her voice trailed off caught in the grip of horrendous anxiety and pointed towards him. Dave felt for a pulse at Donny's throat, it was slight but it was there. Dave then moved a few yards to where Sam was laying motionless. He checked for her pulse but he knew he would not find one as the wound to her abdomen was wicked. He checked Matt who was unconscious, but there was still a pulse. Maria had already used her belt to stem the bleeding from Matt's leg.

The shot Donny had taken hit his left shoulder, luckily missing a large artery. But like them all, except Sam and the crazy one, bleeding to death now was the enemy.

"I've got to go for help." Dave said. "Keep the tourniquets tight on them all, Danny too; he's in those rocks up there. Get them all water. If they regain any consciousness make them drink it."

Maria had her faculties about her so she would do everything possible to keep them all alive.

Dave had not run far when he met a group of men Leslie had been able to gather from down at the Plunge. A Forest Service Patrol Officer happened to be in the valley. He'd been told by his supervisor in Boise to not go up the trail knowing there were people with guns. They'd been waiting at the trail head, hoping Danny would bring them out, but when they heard the shooting Leslie told them she was going in with or without them. What does a guy do in that case?

(Saint Lukes Medical Center, Boise; 11:30 Saturday night)

The three sat stone-faced in the waiting room knowing that Micky and Jack would soon join them. Another group they did not know sat across the room, caught in their own concerns. Dave had his hand on Joan's leg softly rubbing it. Maria had her cell phone in one hand expecting a call from her parents. She'd left a voicemail asking them to give her a call when they got up, which could be anytime because they were early risers.

Leslie was sitting across the aisle from them with Denise and Denny. Evan and Natalie were on the coast and it wasn't possible to contact them. A voicemail had been left for Juergen. Denise had her arm around Leslie's shoulder understanding the deep anxiety she was feeling just now.

They'd watched the evening newscast an hour earlier where the shoot out in the Silver Creek valley had been reported. The reporter had noted that two deaths had occurred and three people were in critical condition from gunshot wounds, and were currently in surgery at Saint Lukes. The names of the dead would not be released until notification of the next of kin was confirmed.

Like anyone suddenly finding themselves in a nightmare of real life, each of them was involved with an inner reconciliation of what had and was happening. There were still great unknowns they would have to grapple with.

Two people entered the room. Maria was first to meet them. They hugged without talking. Micky and Jack found chairs next to where the three were sitting. Micky's mascara was washed down beneath her eyes, some as far as her cheek. Both eyes were quite puffy and red as she'd obviously been crying a great deal. Jack was somber and he looked like he'd been punched hard, multiple times. All you do at these times is hold on.

"Do you know when the doctors might come to talk to us?" Micky asked, her voice strained and weakened.

"The nurse that just went off shift thought that by midnight someone would come." Maria answered.

Micky just swayed her head. "How are you dear?" She was looking at Maria.

She answered first with the body language of confusion, fear, anger, helplessness, survival. "I can deal," she at last answered.

Micky reached over and touched Joan and Dave as well, letting them know they were all together in this.

Jack brought her a glass of water and a Tylenol as she'd complained of a slight headache.

"We've been to see Sam's body," she stopped. "What can we say to her parents?" Sam's folks were in California and it would be the next day before they could get home. She was biting her lip trying to hold back the intense emotion she was feeling. Jack had his arm around her, giving what comfort he could.

There was some activity in the hall. A nurse was standing there and was looking back down the hall evidently waiting for someone to follow. She seemed to not have much emotion on her face. The nurse turned and walked in, still very stony. A tall man in a light blue shirt and matching head cover then followed. The nurse led him to where Micky and the others were sitting. She took a moment and pointed out to him who the mother and wife and girlfriend were of the three in surgery. The doctor grabbed a chair and pulled it towards the group.

"I'm Dr. Lantz," he began. He looked towards Leslie, an extra sense of emptiness shot through her. "Okay, there's no easy way to say this; we lost Mr. Bonner."

Before he could say anything more, both Micky and Leslie released a sound of emotion you never experience until such moments of emptiness and despair. Jack grabbed hold of Micky tightly. Denny jumped up and added an arm of compassion for Leslie.

The doctor continued, "We have Matthew and Donny Lundquist stabilized." They have both lost a very large amount of blood but fortunately they both seem to be responding to the transfusions we've been giving them. They could still turn for the worse but we'll be watching them very closely."

There, he'd given them the hardest of the information. He thought there might be questions, but none came. There was so much sensory overload going on, it would be awhile before reasoned questions would formulate.

Processing the loss of someone only begins when you are first told, in truth you spend the rest of your life holding it in context, and it changes places over time.

Leslie could not contain her tears. She'd dropped her head into her lap to hold herself. The others were just stunned.

Micky seemed to withdraw even further into some shell she'd already created. There was a scaffolding of strength she'd need now, not only for herself, but for Leslie as well.

A call came from Juergen to Denny, Denny moved into the hallway to talk.

"Where are you?" Denny asked.

"Um, at my house, sitting at my bar." Juergen answered. Denny wanted him to be someplace comfortable.

"I have some really bad news." Juergen steadied himself, "We've lost Danny."

Juergen turned in his chair, feeling the shot of adrenaline. "What?" He moved to a larger chair he could spread in. "What happened?"

"It's unbelievable and we're still trying to get the details. Some son of bitch followed Danny, Matt, his friends, and Donny you remember, Danny's other nephew?"

"Yes! Fuck!" Juergen expressed, explosively.

"They've been involved in the environmental activism; there was that big march in Boise last April."

"I remember Danny telling me about that."

"So this guy decides he's going to teach them a lesson. He was mostly after Joan, probably because she'd done so much talking after the march. She thinks he intended to just scare them. But Danny got a hunch of what he was up to. I'll explain all that to you later. Anyway, they were up at Silver Creek where they'd hiked into those hot springs we've gone to a lot. That's where this all happened. There was a big shoot out. The guy who tracked them is dead. Danny killed him. Matt's friend Dave shot him too. But Danny took a shot to the leg and bled too much before they got him to the hospital. They did operate."

"Shizen." Juergen's mind was actually processing his feelings in German now; bits and pieces of words were coming out that Denny had no understanding of.

"Juergen, I need to get back with everybody. I'll call you again in a day or so with more of the details."

~~~~~

Everyone finally left except for Dave, Joan, and Maria. Micky and Jack went to get something to eat and planned to be back shortly. They agreed to call everyone just as soon as they got word on Matt and Donny in the morning.

By 2:30 a.m. Sunday, Dave had laid down on the floor. The nurse had given him a pillow and blanket and he had closed his eyes and somehow managed to fall asleep. Few understood the added anxiety he was feeling, being the one who had shot the final bullets that killed Larry. His body was still compromised from the poisoning as well.

Maria had been looking out the window. "Joan, let's go for a walk, it's much cooler out there now so let's get some fresh air."

"If Dave asks, tell him we've just gone for a walk outside," they told the young candy striper at the nearby information desk.

The night sky was clear and the city lights dampened the contrast they would have seen higher up in the nearby foothills. A few cars were going by, but for the most part the city was asleep.

Maria noticed that the convenience store across the street was open. They'd had a little food in the commissary at the hospital, but that was five or six hours earlier.

They wandered to the candy section; both had desire for some chocolate. They got some coffee and chips as well.

The two again crossed Warm Springs Avenue and found a seat in Noble Park. There were several street lights giving the space a safe level of lighting.

"It's amazing how much change can happen in one day," Joan began, "Just last night we were all staring at those same stars, enjoying life and a campfire. Those smores were good." Maria gave a small laugh of agreement.

"Now we both have men crippled, some, by their convictions and ours." Maria observed.

"Did you think anything like this could happen, Maria, when we made the Moab Manifesto?"

"No, no nothing like what's happened. I really had no idea. I guess I was just going to follow along with what Matt was doing, support him, you and Dave and the others. I feel passion for all this," she stopped, her mind worked some more. "I never thought our lives would be so in periled." Her eyebrows folded in slightly as she looked back at Joan. "I have no idea how this is going to impact Matt, the brother he loves so dearly, if he lives, is hurt horribly and the uncle he adored is dead. And Donny's girlfriend, she was so innocent; God! He'll blame himself for them even being there. Danny would never have probably gotten involved with all of this if it wasn't for Matt."

Joan suddenly stood up and walked out to the middle of the plaza and looked up to the heavens. "YES, I DO EXPECT YOUR HELP!" Her voice echoed off of the buildings around, someone in the parking lot at the convenience store looked in her direction.

She sat back down next to Maria. "It's fitting isn't it," Maria stared at Joan, "That bastard was killed with his own gun; that little twist of fate I'm sure he never expected. There are many unforeseen consequences in this life, in this world."

Joan continued, "We're going to have a big decision to make, maybe a few months from now." Maria looked at her even more intently. "Are we going to continue to lead in this thing? Put our necks out there for every crazy to take a shot at? Are we going to confront this conspiracy *to do nothing* and let climate chaos eliminate billions of us?" Are we going to lead this revolution of consciousness?" Her voice was filled with deep angst; it was a sound coming from the most basal part of her being.

She went on, "Joan of Arc, they call me. They killed her you know, tied her up and burned her alive. Do you think as the pain of her skin melting and her blood boiling she thought it was all worth it?" Joan looked off into the sky.

Maria's mind rushed back through the years: She remembered the first time she'd seen Matt in Rome and wandering off to have pizza with him and Dave and her friends. Poppy's dying and how it brought them so close so fast. Looking out across the vast Pacific with Matt from her homeland dreaming of what life might bring them. And those nights together in the log cabin in the north woods. Chocolate. The image of hedge fund managers profiting from the death of innocents all around the world. And of the world lost because it was just too inconvenient to change our ways. She studied the sky for a few moments and then she looked at Joan, "We don't know what's going to happen the next few hours. We could still lose Matt or Donny, and that will be horrible. If I lose Matt I don't know what I'll do." Alone as they were, Maria's voice was now quivering with fear and anxiety.

Joan waited before answering, "Recovering from loss seems to be one of life's experiences we all pretty much have to deal with to different degrees." Her mind wandered briefly to a memory and a bottomless waterfall where a tall building once stood. "Every experience that works to break us can, with time, make us stronger or at least better equipped to deal with the future."

Joan got up and stretched briefly then looked towards Maria, "If we give up now, what will we think in five or ten or twenty years? How do we know that it won't be something that we do, some little thing like when a humming bird beats its wings in Spain and causes a tornado in Kansas? We're both Dorothy's you know; and there are millions of others just like us that can be awakened," Joan looked intently at Maria. "We both have connections to wealth; we both have our silver spoons," Maria leaned her head to one side and acknowledged that she understood what Joan was saying. "Dorothy had a dream about a world or a home where her heart would be settled and happy over the rainbow ... pretty much like most of us have. But she had an obstacle she had to rise above to get there. And she only started her way home when she responded to the threat to her friend the Scarecrow. She wouldn't have ever gotten home otherwise. If we don't throw our bucket of water, Maria, I don't think we will ever get home either!"

Maria dropped her forehead and moved her hands so she could rub her tired eyes, "What's it going to take Joan?"

"What do you mean?" she answered.

"What's it going to take to get the big mass of people, the ones like the munchkins, to wake up? If they did we'd have so many votes it would be like nothing to elect a government that would lead. Lead us away from this Armageddon we're heading towards passing the Mephistopheles Moment. And if we don't do anything, and too many are like us, what kind of world will we, or if by some miracle I have some kids or everybody else's kids, inherit? Jesus Joan, do we have a choice, really? "

"I don't know, so many millions just caught up in their own lives and have almost no idea of what's going on." Joan's voice was weary.

Maria rubbed her nose, "It's going to take something horrible or horrific, that's what I think; like some stupendous outrageous storm. Something we never saw coming; … an unforeseen consequence."

"Yeah, but will it happen in time to matter, we only have a few years, you know they are saying this is decade zero, we're on the countdown to the year 2020?" Joan looked to the heavens again.

She moved back over and sat down next to Maria, "We can wait for others to do what we know has to be done; let all this destroy our courage and our will. But we both know that the scarecrows arm is already on fire. Certain really bad actors in the reductionist industries, the Family, are already seeing to that. Somewhere, somehow, someone has to react with indignation and throw that water on them and hit the witch. Somehow the Dorothys of the world have to emerge and endure."

Coming: Book Two - Endurance of Consciousness

About the author

Paul Wesley Norberg is a long-time resident of Boise, Idaho. He is dedicated to environmental activism. He can be reached at paul@harvestdesign.tv.

www.ingramcontent.com/pod-product-compliance
Lightning Source LLC
Chambersburg PA
CBHW050434290526
45786CB00006B/2023